18.95

BETTER HEALTH CARE
for Less

BETTER HEALTH CARE
for Less

Neil Shulman, M.D.
& Letitia Sweitzer

HIPPOCRENE BOOKS
New York

For information, address:
HIPPOCRENE BOOKS, INC.
171 Madison Avenue
New York, NY 10016

Library of Congress Cataloging-in-Publication Data
 Shulman, Neil.
 Better health care for less / Neil Shulman & Letitia Sweitzer.
 p.cm.
 ISBN 0-7818-0122-2 (pbk.) :
 1. Medical care—United States—Cost control. 2. Consumer
 education. I. Sweitzer, Letitia. II. Title.
 RA410.53.S58 1993
 362.1'0973—dc2093-10821
 CIP

Printed in the United States of America

To Emory University, Emory University School of Medicine, Grady Memorial Hospital, and Morehouse School of Medicine—all institutions with a lot of heart—and to all my wonderful friends there.
—Neil Shulman

To Ron and Machin Sarros
—Letitia Sweitzer

CONTENTS

CAUTION TO READERS

The health status of every individual is different and must be evaluated individually. No one general piece of advice applies to everyone. The tips in this book are suggestions for readers to consider and should never replace the advice from an individual's doctor.

Government definitions, regulations, requirements, and provisions are complicated, detailed, and subject to change. Information in this book about laws or agencies is not complete and it may not be current by the time you read this book. Such information is offered only as a suggestion of possible resources for the reader to investigate further.

While most organizations, agencies and services mentioned are government sponsored or nonprofit, in a few cases, services or information lines are sponsored by for-profit organizations (usually noted as such). Be aware that for-profit organizations may steer inquirers in the direction of their products or services. Some products mentioned are sold for profit, also. Organizations mentioned in this book have been recommended to us; we have made appropriate inquiries but we cannot be responsible for the quality of advice, information, or services.

Costs of services and products vary widely and change frequently and are mentioned in this book only to indicate what a reader might look for or compare with. Guided by the suggestions in this book, the reader must check specific details before applying them to individual cases.

*   *   *

BETTER HEALTH CARE FOR LESS NEWSLETTER

If you have a tip for saving money on health care or if you know of a resource which would help the consumer get better health care, please tell us. The best tips along with new developments from many sources will be published in a bimonthly update, the *Better Health Care for Less Newsletter* available for $24 a year.

Mail tips and/or subscription orders along with a check to Better Health Care for Less, P.O. Box 15369, Atlanta, GA 30333-0369, or call 404-816-6548.

ACKNOWLEDGMENTS

We would like to thank all the many people who gave us health tips or help in the preparation of this manuscript including Hugh Barndollar, Jack Birge, Lisa Bodemann, Kathy Carl, Andrea Chastain, Kaye H. Coker, Ora G. Douglass, Linda Emerson, Charles Foreman, Robert J. Fulkerson, Shirley Green, Muriel Griffen, Sally Harris, Josephine Jamison, John Jones, Ron Karp, Joyce Lewis, Dan Mackey, Denise McCarty, Mary Helen Mele, Darryl Mull, Ivor Royston, Lysa Sampson, Machin Sarros, Charlene Shucker, Israel Shulman, Larry Shulman, Mary Shulman, Roberta Shulman, Stan Shulman, Dan Sweitzer, Denise Sweitzer, Kenneth Taratus, Russ Toal, Beverley Waters. We also thank many, many other people who helped us whose names we do not know.

Especially we give heart-felt thanks to our research assistant, Lynn Aaron, for her cheerful, energetic, and resourceful efforts.

PREFACE

WHAT IS *BETTER HEALTH CARE FOR LESS*?

Better Health Care for Less is an easy-to-use guide with specific tips for saving money and obtaining easy access to free information and other resources.

WHO CAN BENEFIT FROM *BETTER HEALTH CARE FOR LESS*?

This book is written for everyone: those who have a good income and good insurance, those who have moderate incomes and insufficient insurance to weather serious or prolonged health problems, and those who have neither the income nor the insurance coverage to meet even basic health needs. Also, we hope the book will be a resource for health care professionals who wish to help patients cut costs and gain access to valuable complementary resources.

Medical costs have increased to such a degree that even the very well off must be good consumers not only to withstand a bout of bad health but to keep insurance costs reasonable. Those who cannot afford basic health care or insurance are not just the illiterate and imprudent. They are often intelligent people doing good, honest, low paying work, people working without benefits, people doing the right thing. They may be the newly poor—divorced women raising children alone, laid-off workers, people between jobs who are caught without insurance, the elderly whose well-planned incomes are not worth much anymore, college graduates off their parents' insurance but not yet onto a steady payroll. Other cost-conscious readers simply want to avoid high-cost medicines and procedures because they know overuse of medical services drives up insurance rates for all of us.

No matter what reason you have for wanting to save money on health care, one tip from this book can save hundreds or even thousands of dollars, or, at least, the price of the book.

HOW *BETTER HEALTH CARE FOR LESS* WAS WRITTEN

We have gathered tips from interviews with cost-conscious doctors, nurses, and health care technicians, from clerks in billing departments of hospitals and clinics, from government and non-profit agencies and insurance companies, and especially from savvy patients who have questioned and learned from experience.

We have alphabetized and cross-referenced the tips in this book according to subject and disease. A longer explanation of the tip and the related situation appears below, and, where appropriate, we have mentioned how using this tip might affect the quality of care.

In writing this book, we have acknowledged several principles:

(1) that the more you know about your health or your disease, the better choices you can make;

(2) that the most expensive medical option is not always the best;

(3) that good consumer skills are necessary for seeking health care;

(4) that health insurance is not the least expensive way to pay routine medical bills but an important way to protect against catastrophic medical bills;

(5) that resources for those with low incomes exist in varied forms although they are often hard to locate, understand, and qualify for.

THE MORE YOU KNOW, THE BETTER CHOICES YOU CAN MAKE

We all can become health-literate so we don't just present our bodies to doctors, and say, "Do your thing." Many patients become such experts in their specific illnesses that they become actively involved in the decision making process. You too can become a partner with your doctors. Becoming health literate helps you decide when to seek the attention of a doctor, what diagnostic tests to expect and what therapies are available.

Educational resources are as close as your nearest library and as complete and detailed as the thousands of volumes and computer entries at The National Library of Medicine. The world's largest medical library can be accessed in various ways from reprints to computer hook-ups. The National Health Information Center will give you information on disease-related topics. The Centers for Disease Control and Prevention (CDC) provides detailed recorded information on many diseases.

In addition, information on one thousand rare and not-so-rare diseases is available from NORD, the National Organization of Rare Disorders. Advisers at the National Insurance Consumer Helpline will explain many aspects of insurance that may enable you to choose the best insurance for your situation. The Food and Drug Administration (FDA) can send you a host of consumer information about drugs, foods, medical devices, and specific health conditions and treatment through its Office of Consumer Inquiries. The FDA will also answer specific questions if you call the Public Affairs specialist at your regional FDA office. These are just some of the general sources of information where you can begin your education about a particular disease or health care subject. Look under GENERAL INFORMATION in this book for the numbers of these general information sources and much more.

Organizations devoted to specific diseases are also a source of information. Government and non-profit organizations distribute well-written brochures for patients. They also have access to networks of health care professionals whose expertise can be tapped by the general public. They publish newsletters and bulletins about the latest developments in their particular health fields. Cost-cutting tips and resources for those in financial need are often included. Such organizations offer referrals to support groups and people all over the country who know from experience the problems and options for those who have a particular disease.

Support and self-help groups can be a rich source of information, comfort, and sometimes financial and other assistance. Many organizations have hotlines or toll-free 800 numbers to call for printed or recorded information or in many cases an actual counselor who can discuss the caller's situation. We have included in this book dozens of numbers to put you in touch with specialized information and service.

Another way to get information about topics that may influence your health care is to regularly read health articles or the health section of your local newspapers. News of health fairs or free and low cost screenings, new developments in treatment, experimental treatment studies seeking patients in your area, and tips for prevention of disease often appear regularly in newspapers and magazines.

THE MOST EXPENSIVE OPTION
IS NOT ALWAYS THE BEST

The old adage—you get what you pay for—is sometimes applicable but in an amazing number of health related situations the money you pay is tied to the cost of the procedure but not to the benefits you receive. Out-patient surgery, for example, is almost always cheaper than in-patient surgery and the psychological and physical benefits of recuperating in your own home may be greater.

Lower cost procedures are by no means necessarily less effective or less "good." In fact, some cutting edge tests and procedures result in far less total cost—both medical and incidental such as lost work time—because they are less invasive. Examples are laparoscopic (microscopic) surgery for removal of the gall bladder, gall stones, or even the uterus; and new digital ultrasound (sound waves) technology that in some cases can be used instead of more expensive imaging methods. And a pregnant woman may receive thorough and free or inexpensive check-ups by nurse specialists or physician's assistants at the local health department.

This book will make you aware of less expensive options that should not compromise quality in health care and should help you find care when you can afford none. This book in no way suggests that the patient not follow the advice of his physician. Rather the patient should use this book to help ask questions about health care options.

USE CONSUMER SKILLS
WHEN SHOPPING FOR HEALTH CARE

A friend of ours was told he needed a hernia operation. In that discussion with his doctor, he asked how much the doctor's fee would be. The doctor's reply: Why?

That one-syllable response says a lot about some patients' and doctors' attitudes about medical costs. It seemed strange to the doctor that a patient would inquire about fees, and apparently few had asked.

When our friend explained that he wanted to be able to make a ball park estimate of the total cost of the operation, the incredulous doctor inquired, "Don't you have insurance?" Our friend said, "Yes, but we pay for insurance." Apparently that point did not go without saying.

Patients often come out of a doctor's office, just having been told they need this or that treatment or test, and say confidentially to the bookkeeper or receptionist, "Dr. T. told me I need this or that and I can't afford it." But did the patient voice the same concern to Dr. T.? Certainly not. He's the doctor.

Although many doctors are sensitive to health cost issues, because of the taboo against talking about money, doctors are generally shielded from the financial needs of their patients. They are also shielded from the costs. Our friend who was facing the hernia operation finally got a fee quotation from his doctor and then asked if the doctor could give him an estimate of the hospital costs for the procedure. The doctor confessed he had no idea.

"You do this operation maybe three times a week and you have no idea what it costs!" our friend exclaimed.

The doctor shrugged.

Americans are generally not good health care consumers. They don't use a good decision-making process for choosing health care.

In the not too distant past we had no strong stake in health care coverage. As long as we had coverage for our medical needs through our insurance policies, we didn't care what health care cost. More-over, once upon a time health care was not so expensive. Now, however, some of us have to make choices just as we do with other products and services. For example, we may choose to go to an inconvenient location to a less expensive health provider. Or we may choose not to have a $1000 CAT scan that would have certain benefits but choose instead a $200 test that is almost as effective. Or we may choose not to have optional surgery that "might help" and might not.

It is time to ask your doctors to be cost conscious on your behalf. Shop around, compare prices, check bills and reimbursements, insist on fair treatment, pick and choose services, and, when appropriate, negotiate fees.

HEALTH INSURANCE IS NOT A BARGAIN FOR ROUTINE CARE; SAVE IT FOR THE BIG STUFF

Insurance is to protect against the unknown, not the known.

Health insurance is not the cheapest way to pay for routine and expected medical bills like your child's ear infection or your office visit and prescription for bronchitis or even a typical broken arm. A very large portion of your insurance premiums goes for medical bills under $5000 and your cost for covering these with insurance may well exceed the total amount of those relatively small bills.

The portion of your premium that goes for protection against catastrophic illness, however, is surprisingly low. This is the better buy and actually a necessity for most people.

Disability insurance is also important for the wage earner; it protects against an unexpected and very serious catastrophe. Keep this in mind when you make an overall plan for your health care.

RESOURCES ARE AVAILABLE FOR MANY WHO CANNOT PAY FOR HEALTH CARE

One person you can seek out who can help when you need health care and cannot afford it is the social worker at a local hospital. The hospital social worker can help you get Medicaid if you qualify and knows many local resources that others may not know about. Every state has its own programs that you cannot find through national directories. Local churches and non-profit clinics offer an amazing array of specific one-of-a-kind programs as do local branches of national organizations with health care programs. Local support groups for people suffering from particular diseases have researched the community's resources and can tell you where to go for help. The local United Way has listings of many charitable centers that offer medical help to those who cannot pay.

Some other important resources you should not overlook are the Veterans Administration and local health departments run by states. Community health centers receiving federal grants provide primary health care in over 550 communities regardless of the patient's financial or insurance status. A list of these centers, supplied by the National Association of Community Health Centers, Inc., is located under COMMUNITY HEALTH CENTERS in this book.

HOW TO USE *BETTER HEALTH CARE FOR LESS*

The preceding remarks have been an overview to suggest to you what kinds of information you will find in this book. For specific information, look up a topic as you would in a dictionary or encyclopedia. For each subject, look up all related topics. For example, if you are considering going to the hospital to have a bunion removed, look for BUNION under **B**, HOSPITALIZATION under **H**, FOOT CARE under **F**, PODIATRY under **P**, SURGERY under **S**, and so forth. Also, browse a little and see what you can find.

BETTER HEALTH CARE
for Less

AARSKOG SYNDROME (See RARE DISEASES.)

AASE-SMITH SYNDROME (See RARE DISEASES.)

ABORTION (See PREGNANCY, UNWANTED.)

ACHONDROPLASIA (See RARE DISEASES.)

ACNE (See also DERMATOLOGY and MEDICATIONS.)

Tip # 1: For acne, consider alternatives to expensive over-the counter products sold as cosmetics.

How it works: Cosmetics advertised to be good for acne are generally reported by dermatologists to have a low level of effectiveness but can add up to a great deal of money over time. These include pore cleansers, facials, masks, and reduced-oil cosmetics. It may be more cost effective to pay to see a dermatologist and get an effective prescription than to spend money on ineffective remedies. Some prescription medications are much less expensive than cosmetics advertised to prevent acne.

Quality check: Ultimately, you are the judge of whether any preparation is effective for you.

Tip # 2: Of the over-the-counter acne remedies consider choosing benzoyl peroxide products.

How it works: Benzoyl peroxide is usually the most effective over the-counter agent for the prevention of acne, but try a 5% product instead of a 10% product because the stronger preparation may be irritating and cause more outbreak than it cures.

ACNE ROSACEA (See RARE DISEASES.)

ACOUSTIC NEUROMA (See RARE DISEASES.)

ACQUIRED AGRANULOCYTOSIS (See RARE DISEASES.)

ACROMEGALY (See also RARE DISEASES.)

Tip # 1: Consider reading a book about growth hormone and acromegaly, a condition of too much growth hormone. In the book *UNDERSTANDING GROWTH HORMONE* by Neil Shulman and Letitia Sweitzer (Hippocrene Books, 1993), you can find a description of the disease and its treatment as well as case histories.

ADDISON'S DISEASE

Tip #1 : Contact the Addison's Disease Association at 516-487-4992.

How it works: The Addison's Disease Association provides information and makes referrals to support groups and medical resources.

ADRENAL HYPERPLASIA (See RARE DISEASES.)

ADRENOLEUKODYSTROPHY (See RARE DISEASES.)

ADULT DAY CARE (See also AGING, ALZHEIMERS, HOME CARE SERVICES, LONG TERM CARE.)

Tip # 1: Consider adult day care for adults who need supervision and stimulation.

How it works: Adult day care gives supervision and therapeutic programs outside the home to those adults who need them. Such services give much needed respite to caregivers. Call local offices of United Way, state Departments of Aging, or Alzheimers Association (1-800-272-3900) for referrals to adult care in your community.

Quality check: Here are some questions to ask when considering the quality of adult day care programs:
- Where is the program located?
- What are the hours of operation?
- Is transportation for the participants available?
- What are the criteria for acceptance into the program?
- What is the daily routine?
- What activities are offered?
- Will people of varied backgrounds find enjoyment in the program?
- Are trial visits allowed? How are they handled?
- How does the program prevent participants from wandering outside? Are the doors locked?
- How does the site handle difficult situations, such as medical emergencies, fires, disruptive behavior?
- Is an outside area available?
- Can medical needs such as medicines and special diets be handled by program personnel?

• What is the ratio of staff to participants?

The preceding suggestions were excerpted from "Respite Report" published by the Dementia Care and Respite Services Program, a pilot project of 19 adult care projects in 14 states, supported by the National Council on Aging, Alzheimers Association, and Robert Wood Johnson Foundation.

For more information, write Dementia Care and Respite Services Program, Department of Psychiatry and Behavioral Medicine, Bowman Gray School of Medicine, 300 S. Hawthorne Rd., Winston-Salem, NC 27103.

AGAMMAGLOBULINEMIA (See RARE DISEASES.)

AGENESIS of CORPUS CALLOSUM (See RARE DISEASES.)

AGING

Tip # 1: Consider keeping an aged person living independently.

How it works: Small arrangements can sometimes make it possible for an older person to live independently in the community and save the enormous expenditures of institutional care. These include "meals on wheels" arrangements, adult day care, volunteer caregiving, home care services, special emergency provisions, buddy systems. See also ADULT DAY CARE, EMERGENCIES (Tips # 10-14), HOME CARE SERVICES, LONG TERM CARE.

Quality check: Coordinating extensive services at home such as hiring, managing, and scheduling can be very difficult. (See next tip)

Tip # 2: Consider contacting Aging Network Services (ANS) to help coordinate services to keep an elderly person independent.

How it works: ANS has a nationwide network of social workers who specialize in geriatric services. For a fee, ANS will locate a local social worker who will coordinate assistance from local and other government agencies, volunteer organizations, health care organizations, and even neighbors to support independent living for an aging person. ANS also provides counseling, support groups, and workshops for family members to help optimize resources. Call 301-657-4329 for more information.

Tip # 3: Participate in or start a "buddy system" to promote safety among elderly people living alone.

How it works: Churches and other groups sometimes form buddy groups of elderly participants. Each participant is assigned a buddy; buddies agree to call each other briefly once or several times a day to check on possible needs or problems. If a buddy doesn't answer the phone, it is the other buddy's responsibility to check on the reason and to contact a family member or emergency facility as necessary.

Quality check: Buddies sometimes refuse to keep calls short and become pests. Irresponsible buddies sometimes forget to call or forget to tell their buddy when they plan to be gone.

Tip # 4: Contact the National Council on the Aging at 1-800-424-9046.

How it works: The National Council on the Aging works through professionals and volunteers to improve the quality of life for older Americans. Intergenerational programming has been a major focus. It is a national resource for information, training, technical assistance, advocacy, and research on every aspect of aging. Ask for information and publications on subjects such as family caregivers, senior employment, and long-term care. Write 409 Third Street SW, Washington, D.C. 20024.

Tip # 5: Consider becoming a member or enrolling an adult aged 50 or more in AARP by calling 1-800-441-AARP.

How it works: AARP (American Association of Retired Persons) is an organization devoted to the well-being of those over 50. Its monthly magazine *Modern Maturity* is an upbeat, informative publication with the latest health news and consumer information as well as useful or entertaining general articles. Tips on saving money on health care are a staple of the magazine. The AARP offers members group insurance, a mail order drug service, and a hot line for help with Medicare claims. Membership in AARP is only $8.

Tip # 6: Contact the Well Spouse Foundation.

How it works: When one spouse takes care of another who is ill, disabled, or more fragile, the healthy spouse may feel enormous strain. The Well Spouse Foundation offers information and support for the caregiving spouse. For more information, call 619-673-9043.

Tip # 7: Contact Children of Aging Parents (CAPS).

How it works: CAPS is a support group for children facing the challenge of aging parents. For more information, send a stamped, self-addressed envelope to CAPS, Suite 302A, 1609 Woodbourne Rd., Levittown, PA 19057.

Tip # 8: Read this book: *We've Got to Do Something About Mother.*

How it works: *We've Got to Do Something About Mother: Eleven Accounts of How Individuals Found Solutions to the Problems of Caring for Aging Parents* by Marilyn Richardson is an honest, open account that may help readers find personal answers. To order, ask for publication # MR9232 and send $8.95 plus $2 postage to Vintage '45 Press, P.O. Box 266, Orinda, CA 94563.

Tip # 9: For the low income elderly, consider applying for Supplemental Security Income (SSI).

How it works: SSI is a federal program that makes monthly payments to the aged, blind or disabled who have low income and few resources. For details see Supplemental Security Income.

AHUMADA-DEL CASTILLO SYNDROME (See RARE DISEASES.)

AICARDI SYNDROME (See RARE DISEASES.)

AIDS (See also HIV Positive.)

Tip # 1: Call the Centers for Disease Control and Prevention (CDC) for up-to-date recorded information on AIDS and HIV at 404-332-4555.

How it works: The CDC provides very detailed and up-to-date information on transmission, testing, and treatment of AIDS and HIV, along with statistics and a wide range of current topics.

Tip # 2: If you do not have insurance that covers AIDS, consider going NOW to your nearest public hospital where care is billed on a sliding scale.

How it works: AIDS patients without insurance will most likely end up with more bills than they can afford, because bills will be high and income will probably be severely reduced at some point because of disability. Many AIDS patients without good insurance pay for their medical care out of their earnings and savings as long as they can. They sell their houses and possessions and go into debt. Then, when all of their resources are depleted, they go to a public hospital and/or go on Medicaid.

If you feel your resources may soon be depleted, consider going to the public hospital *now* while you still have some possessions and money to live on and are not deeply in debt. You can pay for treatment there on a sliding scale, an obligation that will decline as your income declines. Eventually, the cost may be nothing even though you still have your basic possessions and limited assets. Even if you choose occasionally to go to a private facility for some of your treatment, you will be in the sliding scale system, signed up for the time when you need it.

Quality check: The public hospital may offer excellent care; it may even have the advantage of being a teaching hospital of a local medical school. Paperwork and red tape may be greater than at some other hospitals and waiting in line may be quite difficult. Always seeing the same doctor may not be a possibility. Sometimes you may have to wait in public hospitals longer than in some private or community hospitals.

Tip # 3: If you do have insurance but cannot afford the payments, contact your state AIDS program or Ryan White program.

How it works: Federal funding, for example, the Ryan White Grants to Counties and Cities, and, in some states, additional state funding gives financial aid to help pay insurance premiums for people with AIDS who have insurance but cannot pay premiums themselves. Look up AIDS under your state agencies in the phone book or call the general information number for your state (See GENERAL INFORMATION, Tip # 1.) and ask for the AIDS program or the Ryan White program.

Tip # 4: Contact an AIDS resource organization near your community for help.

How it works: Almost every community has some free resources for a person with AIDS. A nearby city probably has several such organizations. Many large cities have dozens of organizations that provide services for persons with AIDS. These services vary from advocacy to meals and from financial aid to arrangements for pets to keep the patient company. Other resources range from church and synagogue outreach programs to support groups to organizations for the general public, which are especially applicable to the AIDS situation. Call your local health department and ask for an organization concerned with AIDS. Once you have made contact with one, you will undoubtedly be told of others.

If you don't find an AIDS group listed in your phone book under AIDS, call the National AIDS Hotline at 1-800-342-2437 (1-800-342-AIDS), which operates 24 hours a day. Staff at this number will give you basic AIDS information as well as tell you about AIDS support groups, clinics, and other services across the country.

If a person needs to talk in Spanish, call the SIDA National AIDS Hotline at 1-800-344-7432 (1-800-344-SIDA). Access for English and Spanish-speaking deaf is TTY/TDD number 1-800-243-7889 (1-800-AIDS-TTY). Native Americans can get general information and talk to a representative of the National Native American AIDS Prevention Center's Indian Hot Line at 1-800-283-AIDS 8:30 a.m. to noon and 1 p.m.-5 p.m. Pacific time.

Tip # 5: Contact the National Association of People With AIDS (NAPWA) at 202-898-0414.

How it works: The NAPWA is a national organization that offers supportive services to people with AIDS (PWA). The national staff will put you in touch with a local chapter.

Tip # 6: Consider buying medicine from a buyer's club especially for persons with AIDS.

How it works: The PWA (persons with AIDS) Health Group is dedicated to providing access to promising or experimental treatments for persons with AIDS/HIV. The group serves as a buyers' agent for buying medicine not readily available. Some of these drugs are for opportunistic infections associated with AIDS. Most of the drugs are imported from other countries where they are approved for sale or cheaper than U.S. equivalents. The FDA currently allows an individual to import up to a 3-month supply of medicine not approved in the U.S. for personal use while under a physician's care. Other restrictions may apply.

Contact this organization in New York at (212) 255-0520 from 10 a.m. to 6 p.m. They will send anyone their price list, bi-monthly "Notes from the Underground," and information on drug treatments free of charge or for a $35 annual donation.

Quality check: PWA Health Group has the best interests of PWAs in mind and is not making a profit on sales. It has hired a quality assurance, research and development person to help with quality and has the volunteer assistance of some American researchers, but it does not have the resources that drug companies or the FDA has. So, in some areas, buyers from PWA Health Group may be relying on the quality and effectiveness standards of foreign countries.

Tip # 7: Contact Pharmacy Management Services, Inc., as a confidential for-profit source of Retrovir (R) (AZT) and other AIDS drugs at wholesale prices.

How it works: The Retrovir Prescription Program for AIDS patients at Pharmacy Management Services supplies Retrovir and other AIDS drugs by mail at wholesale prices. Dept. 5-R, as the program is called, guarantees complete confidentiality in billing and mailing and a 24-hour turn around on orders. A counselor also answers questions and gives valuable confidential counseling on the phone as needed. Call 1-800-237-7676, ext. 6617.

Tip # 8: If you cannot pay for AZT or other drugs for AIDS seek out federally and state funded programs that supply these drugs such as the Ryan White Grants to Counties and Cities.

How it works: Federal funding enables states to provide AZT to indigent AIDS patients. Many states add further funding. In New York, for example, state and federal funds pays for 57 drugs to treat AIDS; Alabama provides seven drugs; Georgia provides AZT only. Look up AIDS under the list of state agencies in the phone book or call the general information number for your state (See GENERAL INFORMATION, Tip # 1.) and ask for the state AIDS program or the Ryan White program.

Quality check: Federal funding runs out early and almost half the states will sharply reduce or stop their programs part way through the year.

Tip # 9: Veterans Affairs hospitals will also provide AZT for eligible patients.

How it works: Veterans whose incomes are sufficiently low may be eligible for treatment with drugs for a small co-payment. Contact the local Veterans Affairs under U.S. government in the phone book.

Tip # 10: Contact a drug manufacturer's patient assistance program for HIV-related medication you cannot afford.

How it works: Some manufacturers of drugs used to treat AIDS and HIV-related disorders will help people who cannot afford the drugs. Here are contact numbers for some of these programs.

Epoetin Alpha (EPO, Procrit)
Manufacturer: Ortho Biotechnology
Program: Cost Sharing Program
Ortho Biotech—1-800-441-1366
Ortho Financial Assistance Program—1-800-447-3437
Procrit Line—1-800-553-3851

Filagrastim (GCSF, Neupogen)
Manufacturer: Amgen, Inc.
Amgen Safety Net Program—1-800-272-9376

Fluconazole (Diflucan)
Manufacturer: Pfizer Pharmaceuticals, Roerig Div.
Diflucan Reimbursement Hotline—1-800-869-9979

Ganciclovir (Cytovene)
Manufacturer: Syntex Laboratories
Provisional Assistance Program—1-800-444-4200

Interferon Alpha 2A (Roferon)
Manufacturer: Roche Laboratories
Roferon-A Cost Assistance Program—1-800-227-7448
ONCOLINE—1-800-443-6676

Interferon Alpha 2B (Intron A)
Manufacturer: Schering-Plough Corp.
Interactive Reimbursement Information Services—

1-800-521-7157
ICON Information Network—1-800-446-8766

Pentamidine (Pentam)
Manufacturer: Fujisawa Pharmaceutical Co.
Contact: Rick White—708-317-8638

Sargramostim (GMCSF Leukine)
Manufacturer: Immunex
Immunex Reimbursement Service—1-800-321-4669
Leukine Product Information & Professional Service Hotline—
1-800-33-GMCSF

Sargramostim (GMCSF Prokine)
Manufacturer: Hoechst-Roussel Pharmaceuticals
1-800-PROKINE

Zidovudine (Retrovir)
Manufacturer: Burroughs Wellcome
Patient Assistance Program
1-800-722-9294

Tip # 10: Consider enrolling in one of the many AIDS experimental treatment research projects. See also STUDIES.

How it works: Researchers testing different treatment variations for AIDS need subjects who are usually treated free. Your patient profile must fit the particular research needs to qualify. A person at the National Institute of Allergy and Infectious Diseases (NIAID) AIDS Clinical Trials Information Service will take down information on your condition by phone and do a data base search to find a protocol likely to be accepting a case such as yours. This is one of the quicker ways to get on a trial. Contact the Information Service at 1-800-874-2572 (1-800-TRIALS-A). TDD access for the deaf is at 1-800-243-7012. The international line is 1-301-217-0023.

NIAID will also send you a free brochure on AIDS clinical trials called "Talking It Over." This booklet discusses the availability, benefits and risks, ethical issues, and common terminology of AIDS trials. To order this booklet, call the CDC National AIDS Clearinghouse at 1-800-458-5231.

Other sources of information on AIDS research trials include:
• AIDS Treatment News (San Francisco) (offers a bimonthly news-

letter on experimental and alternative treatments) 1-800-TREAT-12

- PI Perspective (San Francisco) (quarterly information on treatment options and access from Project Inform) 1-800-822-7422
- Project Inform (information on experimental drugs for AIDS) 1-800- 822-7422; 1-800-334-7422 (inside California)
- Treatment Issues (New York) (Free monthly newsletter on experimental and alternative AIDS therapies from Gay Men's Health Crisis, 212-807-6655

Quality check: Experimental studies are unproven treatments with more potential for unknown side effects than proven treatments.

Tip # 11: Seek disability benefits when your ability to work is limited. See tips listed under DISABILITY.

Tip # 12: If your child has AIDS, contact The Foundation for Children with AIDS at 617-442-7442.

How it works: This is a national organization especially concerned with children with AIDS.

ALBINISM (See RARE DISEASES.)

ALCAPTONURIA (See RARE DISEASES.)

ALCOHOL ABUSE

Tip # 1: Look up Alcoholics Anonymous (AA) in the white pages of any phone book and ask for referral to a chapter in the community of your choice.

How it works: Alcoholics Anonymous has helped hundreds of thousands of people recover from alcohol abuse. The organization's method has been proven to work for those who are committed to recovery and there is no cost involved. Every chapter listed in the white pages of most phone books can give you a referral to an AA group near you or to a group in other communities in the country. If you do not feel comfortable in one group, try another. Every group has its own personality.

Tip # 2: If you prefer a non-spiritual or non-religious support group for self-help with alcohol abuse, contact groups that state their orientation as non-religious.

How it works: At least two self-help groups focus on rational, non-spiritual self-help. You can get information and referral through their national information lines:

Rational Recovery System
916-621-4374

Secular Organization for Sobriety
716-834-2921

Tip # 3: If you are a woman, consider contacting Women For Sobriety at 1-800-333-1606.

How it works: Women For Sobriety, a non-profit organization, will give you an outline of their New Life Program and principles and will put you in contact with local support groups.

Tip # 4: For help and information for families of alcoholics, contact the Al-Anon Family Group at 1-800-356-9996.

How it works: Al-Anon helps families of alcoholics help themselves. The health and strength of family members ultimately may provide a climate in which the alcoholic will want to commit to recovery.

Tip # 5: For families concerned about the alcoholism of a family member, especially a child, call Families Anonymous.

How it works: Founded for family members of someone abusing drugs including alcohol, especially children, Families Anonymous' program is based on the 12 steps of Alcoholics Anonymous. Its concern has expanded from substance abuse to include other related behavior such as truancy, hostility, and running away.

Contact Families Anonymous at P.O. Box 528, Van Nuys, CA 91408 or call 818-989-7841.

Tip # 6: Information on alcoholism is available from the National Council on Alcoholism and Drug Dependence at 1-800-NCA-CALL.

How it works: This toll-free helpline gives a recorded message and, if you use a touch-tone phone, the number of the affiliate office nearest you. You can also order free information on helping a teenager with an alcohol or drug problem.

Tip # 7: Consider contacting an alcoholism recovery organization for members of your profession.

How it works: Alcoholics from the same profession have banded together to form several support organizations for recovery. The groups listed below are not affiliated with any professional organization.

Dentists Concerned for Dentists
450 North Syndicate St., Suite 117
St. Paul, MN 55104
Phone: 612-641-0730

International Doctors in Alcoholics Anonymous
7250 France Avenue South, Suite 400 C
Minneapolis, MN 55435
Phone: 612-835-4421
(includes dentists, psychologists, physicians, medical scientists, and veterinarians)

International Lawyers in Alcoholics Anonymous
1092 Elm Street, Suite 201
Rocky Hill, CT, 06067
Phone: 203-529-7474

Lawyers Concerned for Lawyers
450 North Syndicate Street, Suite 117
St. Paul, MN 55104
Phone: 612-646-5590

International Nurses Anonymous
1020 Sunset Drive
Lawrence, KS 66044
Phone: 913-842-3893

Psychologists Helping Psychologists
23439 Michigan Avenue
Dearborn, MI 48124
Phone: 313-278-1314

Social Workers Helping Social Workers
c/o Dr. John Fitzgerald
Route 63
Goshen, CT 06756

Phone: 203-489-3808

Codependency Anonymous for Helping Professionals
P.O. Box 18191
Mesa, AZ 85212
or
P.O. Box 2174
Wheaton, MD 20902

Tip # 5: Consider contacting an organization that gives referrals to alcohol treatment centers, but note the difference between for-profit and non-profit organizations.

How it works: Several hot lines and referral services are listed in phone books in many cities offering personal counseling by phone 24-hours a day and referral to appropriate programs. Some of these numbers belong to programs of companies that operate alcoholism treatment centers and the toll-free numbers are in effect marketing tools for the companies' treatment centers. If such a company can treat you for your problem in one of its centers, the counselor reached by phone will probably recommend the company's own centers. Some of these companies may also recommend other programs and non-profit agencies; some may have sliding scale programs themselves.

Counseling over the phone by a counselor who works for the hotline of a profit-making organization may be a very valuable service, but be aware that referrals may favor the sponsoring company's own centers. Ask specifically what organization sponsors the helpline and if it is a non-profit organization.

Two hotlines affiliated with profit-making companies are:

Assessment Center, 1-800-888-9383. A counselor will give you personal counseling and may recommend a treatment center run by the sponsoring company. A counselor will also evaluate your financial situation personally and help you find a program you can afford such as an out-patient program, a treatment center with fees on a sliding scale, or a hospital that will accept your insurance and waive the rest.

National Counseling Center of the Humanistic Foundation at 1-800-333-4444. A counselor will respond personally to your inquiry about a problem involving alcohol or drug abuse and depression. Referrals may be made to the Foundation's own holistic treatment centers. Some financial help is available at the Foundation's centers. Referrals are also made to non-foundation treatment centers.

Here's a hotline sponsored by a non-profit organization:

Recovering Network, 1-800-527-5344. This service of the American Council on Alcoholism offers treatment referrals, counseling, and advice for recovering alcoholics.

Tip # 6: For referrals to programs for the elderly, call Alcohol Rehabilitation for the Elderly at 1-800-354-7089 or (in Illinois only) 1-800-344-0824.

Tip # 7: Consider trying to get into an experimental treatment study. See also STUDIES.

How it works: Some experimental treatment studies offer free care. In particular, the Clinical Center of the National Institutes of Health has ongoing studies on organic brain syndromes of alcoholism; biological, genetic, and social factors that contribute to alcoholism; pharmacological reduction of alcohol consumption; treatment of alcoholic withdrawal; and the neuropharmacology of alcohol. For more information on how to get into a study of experimental treatment at this and other institutions, see STUDIES.

Tip # 8: If you have a problem with alcohol dependency or abuse, consider buying disability insurance.

How it works: Sometimes an abuser of alcohol cannot control the problem through self-help and support groups and needs in-patient care in a center for alcohol dependence. Few patients, however, can afford the time off from work required even if the costs of treatment are covered by insurance. If you have an untreated alcohol problem or if you are a recovering alcoholic, disability insurance could enable you to get the treatment you may need at some time in the future. (See also INSURANCE, DISABILITY.)

Tip # 9: Victims of drunk drivers can get assistance through the MADD Victim Hotline at 1-800-438-6233.

How it works: Mothers Against Drunk Drivers (MADD) have a hotline to give emotional support and legal information to victims and families of victims of drunk drivers. Staff usually direct members to one of over 430 local chapters.

ALEXANDER'S DISEASE (See RARE DISEASES.)

ALLERGIES

Tip # 1: Contact an association concerned with allergies for information and referral.

How it works: The following organizations can provide information and referrals. Each has its own emphasis and publications.

The American Academy of Allergy and Immunology
24-hour hotline at 1-800-822-2762.

The American Lung Association at 1-212-315-8700.
(The ALA has Spanish speaking representatives.)

The Asthma and Allergy Foundation of America
1-800-727-8462.

National Allergy and Asthma Network
1-703-385-4403

Tip # 2: Consider participating in an experimental study of allergy treatment. See also STUDIES.

How it works: Experimental studies often treat subjects free. In particular, the Clinical Center of the National Institutes of Health has ongoing studies on allergic rhinitis, bronchial asthma, chediak-higashi syndrome, food additive reactions, and gluten sensitivity. For more information on getting into an experimental treatment study at this and other institutions, see STUDIES.

ALPHA-1-ANTITRYPSIN DEFICIENCY (See RARE DISEASES.)

ALZHEIMER'S DISEASE (See also AGING, DISABILITY, HOME HEALTH CARE, and LONG TERM CARE.)

Tip # 1: Contact Alzheimer's Disease and Related Disorder Association (ADRDA).

How it works: ADRDA, also called the Alzheimer's Association, is a national organization with 170 local chapters and 1200 support groups. To find the local group nearest you, contact ADRDA's national office at 919 North Michigan Avenue, Suite 1000, Chicago, IL 60611; 1-800 272-3900, in Illinois only (800) 572-6037

Tip # 2: Ask a local Alzheimer's support organization for resources to help keep an Alzheimer's patient at home.

How it works: Nursing home or long term care facilities are simply unaffordable for many families who may not qualify for Medicaid either. A less expensive but always difficult alternative is to keep patients at home. Visiting nurse agencies supplemented by a program of respite care for the caregiver can help make it possible. Also, check for day care centers for Alzheimer's patients. Some of these are for-profit centers and some are non-profit with sliding scale fees. Don't forget churches and synagogues for programs.

AMENORRHEA, PRIMARY (See RARE DISEASES.)

AMPUTATION (See also PROSTHESES.)

Tip # 1: Contact the National Amputation Association at 718-767-8400.

How it works: The National Amputation Association provides general information about prostheses, braces, and other devices and answers individual questions.

AMYLOIDOSIS (See RARE DISEASES.)

AMYOTROPHIC LATERAL SCLEROSIS (ALS or Lou Gehrig's Disease)

Tip # 1: Contact the Amyotrophic Lateral Sclerosis Association at 1-800-782-4747.

How it works: The Association provides information on the disease and will help you locate a local chapter. Some local chapters have equipment pools which loan medical equipment to patients.

Tip # 2: Consider participating in a research study of new drugs.

How it works: Research on ALS is being conducted in several research centers. For example, four research centers are currently recruiting patients for studies of a new drug called ciliary neurotrophic factor. The drug has shown promise with animals and is in the early stages of human trials. To participate in these trials, patients must be ambulatory and have no complicating diseases. The centers studying the new drug are Cleveland Clinic, University of Colorado Health Science Center at Denver, University of Wisconsin Clinical Research Center at Madison, and Washington University Medical School in St. Louis. For more information on these and other studies, contact the Amyotrophic Lateral Sclerosis Association. (See Tip #1.)

ANDERSEN DISEASE (See RARE DISEASES.)

ANEMIA, APLASTIC

Tip # 1: Consider participating in an experimental study of aplastic anemia treatment. Also see STUDIES.

How it works: Experimental treatment studies often offer free treatment to patients who qualify as subjects. In particular, the Clinical Center of the National Institutes of Health has ongoing studies of aplastic anemia. For more information on getting into a study of experimental treatment at this and other institutions, see STUDIES.

ANEMIA, COOLEY'S (Thalassemia)

Tip # 1: Call Cooley's Anemia Foundation at 1-800-221-3571.

How it works: Cooley's Anemia Foundation (CAF) provides information on this inherited genetic blood disease. The organization also provides infusion pumps, the drug Desferal®, batteries, and other supplies needed to treat the disease when the patient's insurance falls short. CAF also sponsors the Thalassemia Action Group, a volunteer support group for young adult patients which can be reached at 201-935-3366.

ANEMIA, FANCONI'S (See RARE DISEASES.)

ANEMIA, PERNICIOUS

Tip # 1: Have local health department nurses administer B-12 shots or learn to do it yourself.

How it works: In pernicious anemia, a defect in the gastro-intestinal (GI) tract of some people causes their inability to absorb vitamin B-12 from foods such as leafy green vegetables. The result is a shortage of red blood cells. Treatment often consists of shots of B-12 which by-pass the GI tract and get the vitamin directly into the blood stream. You can buy the B-12 medication and many health departments will administer the shots for you free or for a nominal charge, typically about $3. Having the shots administered by a nurse at a doctor's office might cost $10 to $20. You can also learn to give yourself the shots. Ask the nurse at your doctor's office or health department to show you how.

Quality check: There may be a longer wait at the health department than at a private doctor's.

ANEMIA, SICKLE CELL (See SICKLE CELL DISEASE)

ANEMIA, SIDERBLASTIC (See RARE DISEASES.)

ANGIOEDEMA, HEREDITARY (See RARE DISEASES.)

ANKYLOSING SPONDYLITIS (See RARE DISEASES.)

ANOREXIA NERVOSA (See EATING DISORDERS.)

ANTITHROMBIN III DEFICIENCY, CONGENITAL (See RARE DISEASES.)

APNEA, SLEEP (See RARE DISEASES.)

ARGINASE DEFICIENCY (See RARE DISEASES.)

ARTHRITIS

Tip # 1: Compare costs of drug treatment for arthritis.

How it works: It's easy to compare the cost of different drugs used to treat arthritis. But that's not the only cost your doctor should consider in choosing a drug. The costs of monitoring patients for toxic effects and treating them for the toxic effect are actually greater than the cost of the drugs themselves. The relative costs of administering drugs is another factor to be considered.

In a 1992 study by rheumatologist Mark Prashker at Boston University Arthritis Center, the total costs of treatment with six commonly prescribed drugs were compared. The chart below shows six drugs used to treat arthritis and the total cost of treatment including administration, drug cost, monitoring, and treating toxicity, for six months. Note that the least expensive drug to buy, D-penicillamine, is not the least expensive when total costs are considered. Dr. Prashker also noted that injectable gold and methotrexate have been shown to be comparable in effectiveness but because of the cost of the gold and its injection you could save about $1005 in six months by taking methotrexate instead.

Combined Costs for Six Months

Hydroxychloroquine.......$ 922
Oral gold.........................$ 1076
D-penicillamine..............$ 1261
Methotrexate...................$ 1484
Azathioprine....................$ 1515
Injectable gold.................$ 2489

Tip # 2: Contact the Arthritis Foundation at 1-800-283-7800.

How it works: The Arthritis Foundation provides free brochures and tips on coping with the disease, and information on drugs used for arthritis treatment. The national Foundation can direct you to local chapters which can make referrals to physicians and special services such as free workshops, videos, and self-help courses. Some chapters will loan a puppet show, "Kids on the Block," for working with children with arthritis. Farmers, ask for the pamphlet "Arthritis and Farmers, A Guide to Daily Living."

Tip # 3: Consider participating in an experimental study of arthritis treatment. See also STUDIES.

How it works: Experimental treatment studies often offer free treatment to patients who qualify as subjects. In particular, the Clinical Center of the National Institutes of Health in Bethesda, Maryland, has ongoing studies of rheumatoid arthritis and systemic lupus erythematosus. For more information on getting into studies of experimental treatment at this and other institutions, see STUDIES.

ARTHROSCOPIC SURGERY (See also SURGERY.)

Tip # 1: Consider having arthroscopic surgery on an out-patient basis.

How it works: Arthroscopic surgery on several joints is a less invasive procedure than traditional surgery. It may actually involve a larger surgeon's fee than traditional methods because the surgeon has special skills but it can usually be performed on an outpatient basis and recovery times are shorter so that total costs may be less than for traditional surgery.

Quality check: Before agreeing to surgery, ask the surgeon how much experience he/she has had on the particular joint. Ask about special training in arthroscopic procedures and board certification with the American Academy of Orthopedic Surgeons. Also, contact the American College of Surgery at 1-312-664-4050 for a booklet on arthroscopic surgery and certification information.

ASBESTOS

Tip # 1: Contact the Asbestos Hotline at 1-800-334-8571.

How it works: When concerned about asbestos exposure, for example, before renovating a house with asbestos materials, call the Asbestos Hotline for information. The organization has a list of laboratories that test homes for asbestos in the air.

ATAXIA (See RARE DISEASES.)

ASTHMA

Tip # 1: Ask for a free patient booklet and professional publications from the National Asthma Education Program of the National Institutes of Health (NIH).

How it works: A patient booklet called "Your Asthma Can Be Controlled: Expect Nothing Less" is a summary of care and a place to write notes, schedules, and important phone numbers. (NIH Publication No. 91-2664) "Guidelines for the Diagnosis and Management of Asthma" is a comprehensive guide for the medical professional which can also be of help to the patient who wants to know more. These two publications are available free of charge through the National Asthma Education Program (301-951-3260) or through most of the organizations listed below.

Tip # 2: Contact the National Asthma Center or the National Jewish Hospital and Research Center LUNGLINE in Colorado, both at 1-800-222-5864.

How it works: Your can order literature on asthma from the Center and a LungLine nurse can answer individual questions.

Tip # 3: Contact an association concerned with asthma and allergies for information and referral.

How it works: The following organizations can provide information and referrals. Each has its own emphasis and publications.

American Academy of Allergy and Immunology
1-800-822-2762.

American Lung Association at 1-212-315-8700.
(The ALA has Spanish speaking representatives.)

Asthma and Allergy Foundation of America
1-800-727-8462.

National Allergy and Asthma Network/Mothers of Asthmatics
1-800-878-4403

Tip # 4: Take your medicine as prescribed to avoid trips to the emergency room.

How it works: Often people who seek emergency treatment for asthma have not been taking their medication as prescribed. It's easy to neglect when you are feeling good but costly in the long run.

Tip # 5: Consider trying to get into an experimental study of asthma treatment. See STUDIES.

How it works: Experimental treatment studies often offer free treatment to patients who qualify as subjects. In particular, the Clinical Center of the National Institutes of Health has ongoing studies of bronchial asthma and aspirin-sensitivity intrinsic to asthmatics. For information on how to get into a study of experimental treatment at this and other institutions, see STUDIES.

AUTISM

Tip # 1: Contact the Autism Society of America at 1-301-565-0433.

How it works: The Autism Society of America (ASA) provides literature, newsletters, and referrals. Write the ASA at 8601 Georgia Ave., Suite 503, Silver Spring, MD 20910.

Audio tapes of the 1990 and 1991 ASA conferences are available through Educational Audio Recording Services. Contact Skip Fritz, P.O. Box 720135, Houston, TX 77272.

Tip # 2: Contact the Autism Research Institute.

How it works: The Institute has the largest database on autism in the world and will help professionals and parents locate information on request.

> **Autism Research Institute**
> 4182 Adams Avenue
> San Diego, CA 92116

Tip # 3: Contact the Indiana Resource Center for Autism.

How it works: The Center emphasizes research, conducts training, and provides materials on the subject of autism upon request.

> **Indiana Resource Center for Autism**
> Institute for the Study of Developmental Disabilities
> 2853 East Tenth St.
> Bloomington IN 47405

Tip # 3: Consider subscribing to a periodical on the subject of autism.

How it works: Current information is valuable for those concerned with autism. One publication available is *Family Forum on Autism* published by Robert Fromberg, 925 W. Huron Street #512, Chicago, IL 60622. An excellent publication for professionals is *Focus on Autistic Behavior* available through PRO-ED Journals, 8700 Shoal creek Blvd., Austin, TX 78758-6897.

BABESIOSIS (See RARE DISEASES.)

BACK PAIN

Tip # 1: Consider buying or borrowing *The Back Pain Book* developed through the Rehabilitation Institute of Chicago.

How it works: *The Back Pain Book* (Peachtree Publishers, Atlanta, 1992) is used for patient education about neck and back pain in the Pain Program of the Rehabilitation Institute of Chicago. It offers tips on quick pain relief, long term prevention, detailed exercise instruction, moves and positions to avoid, and stress reduction tips. Following the instructions in this book could save hundreds of dollars in therapy costs and is well worth the $12.95 price.

Tip # 2: To prevent back pain, learn and do regular exercises designed for the relief of back pain.

How it works: Many YMCA branches or fitness organizations hold classes in exercises specifically to prevent back pain. There are also books and videos to illustrate back exercises available at bookstores or your library. (See Tip # 1.) If you go to a doctor and are referred to a physical therapist, pay close attention to instructions; take home the directions most therapists will give you and do the exercises regularly. Many failures of the exercise approach have been because people became irregular or stopped doing the exercises.

Tip # 3 : Consider sleeping on a firmer bed or putting a board under your mattress.

How it works: Firm, straight mattresses often help prevent recurring back discomfort. Try a firmer mattress or a bed board for a few nights.

Tip # 4: Try an orthopedically correct chair, improving your sitting posture, and taking breaks from the sitting position.

How it works: Lower back discomfort is often caused by sitting with poor posture and sitting too long, for example, at a desk or computer or driving a car. Ask your doctor or physical therapist to critique your usual sitting posture. Consider switching to a chair design recommended by your doctor or physical therapist, and taking frequent exercise or walking breaks while working or driving. (See also Tip # 1, for a reference on positions and activities that are related to back and neck pain.)

Tip # 5: For relief of chronic back muscle pain, consider massage therapy.

How it works: The cause of back pain should be diagnosed by a physician; the problem could be a slipped disc, a fracture, a kidney infection, or other serious disorder which may need medical treatment. If your recurring problem has been diagnosed as a tendency to muscular strain or spasm, consider massage therapy. Massage is soothing and often improves back pain by relaxing muscles. It is one of the least expensive options. An hour of massage therapy may cost about $40 or as little as $20 from supervised students at a school of massage therapy.

Quality check: There may be something more serious wrong than muscle soreness. If you choose massage, you may wish to determine if the clinician is certified as a massage therapist.

BALANCE DISORDERS

Tip # 1: For information about balance disorders involving the inner ear, contact the Vestibular Disorders Association or the Ear Foundation.

How it works: Some chronic problems with balance are disorders of the inner ear. Information, referrals and support can be obtained from these two organizations:

Vestibular Disorders Association
P.O. Box 4467
Portland, OR 97209-4467
503-229-7703

Ear Foundation
2000 Church St., Box 111
Nashville, TN 37236
615-329-7807
615-329-7809 TDD
1-800-545-HEAR

Quality check: Sometimes problems relating to medications or blood supply leading to the brain are confused with vestibular balance disorders. It may be wise to have your doctor diagnose the cause of balance disorders.

Tip # 2: Veterans, contact Veterans Affairs office.

How it works: Eligible veterans can receive treatment for speech, language, swallowing, hearing, and balance problems at local VA clinics. Contact the Department of Veterans Affairs in Washington at 202-745-8270 or call your local VA office.

BALANTIDIASIS (See RARE DISEASES.)

BALO DISEASE (See RARE DISEASES.)

BARRETT SYNDROME (See RARE DISEASES.)

BECKWITH-WIEDEMANN SYNDROME (See RARE DISEASES.)

BEDWETTING (See also BLADDER PROBLEMS.)

Tip # 1: For printed information on children and bedwetting (enuresis), contact the Simon Foundation at 1-800-237-4666 or the Bladder Health Council of the American Foundation of Urologic Disease at 1-800-242-2383.

Tip # 2: Consider getting a book for children with enuresis (bedwetting) entitled *How You Can Be Boss of the Bladder.*

How it works: The 57-page softcover book written for children with bedwetting problems by psychologist Dr. Janet Hall is distributed by the Simon Foundation. Order the book for $9.95 by writing to P.O. Box 835, Wilmette, IL 60091.

Tip # 3: If urologic disease has been ruled out for children with prolonged bedwetting, consider contacting a specialist in sleep disorders.

How it works: Bedwetting is often a matter of not waking appropriately or insufficient awareness during very deep sleep. A child needs to know bedwetting is not "being bad." Telling a child, "This is a sleep disorder," gives the child a much needed explanation.

BEHCET'S SYNDROME (See RARE DISEASES.)

BELL'S PALSY (See RARE DISEASES.)

BILARY ATRESIA (See RARE DISEASES.)

BIRTH CONTROL

Tip # 1: Consider getting a gynecological exam, birth control evaluation, and birth control device or pills at your local health department.

How it works: Many local health departments offer some degree of free or low cost birth control. One county health department provides a complete gynecological exam, a PAP test for cervical cancer, a test for gonorrhea, birth control counseling, plus a supply of either diaphragms, condoms, birth control sponges or pills for $40 to $50 at most or for a fee based on a sliding scale for those with a limited income. The equivalent service from a private doctor's office would likely be over $100 plus the cost of the birth control pills or a device.

Quality check: Coordinate birth control services with your other medical treatment. Tell any doctor or health professional you may visit all the medications you are taking, including birth control.

Tip # 2: If you qualify for Medicaid, birth control costs are paid for in every state.

Tip # 3: Contact Planned Parenthood.

How it works: Look up Planned Parenthood in the white pages of your phone book for a local chapter or contact the national office for information and referral to a chapter near you. Write Planned Parenthood of America, 810 Seventh Avenue, New York, NY 10019 or call 212-541-7800.

Tip # 4: Contact the Association of Voluntary Sterilization.

How it works: For information on sterilization write the Association of Voluntary Sterilization at 122 E. 42nd. St., New York, NY 10168 or call 212-541-7800.

Tip # 5: Order free FDA publications on birth control.

How it works: The Food and Drug Administration (FDA) provides free current information in a booklet on a wide range of subjects. For information on birth control, order "Norplant Birth Control at Arm's Reach," Publication # FDA92-3194 and/or "Comparing Contraceptives," Publication # FDA91—1123. Write FDA, 5600 Fisher's Lane, Mail Code HFE-88, Room 1663, Rockville MD 20857 or call 301-443-3170.

BIRTH DEFECTS (See also HANDICAPPED CHILDREN, DISABILITY, and individual disease names.)

Tip # 1: Contact the National Clearinghouse for Infants with Disabilities & Life-Threatening Conditions at 1-800-922-9234.

How it works: This national clearinghouse has over 113,000 services on its data base. Staff counselors do case management by phone.

They give referrals for treatment and financial assistance for infants and toddlers with disabilities and life-threatening conditions and for Vietnam veterans' children of any age.

Tip # 2: Contact the March of Dimes.

How it works: The March of Dimes has educational literature and a vast resource bank with referral information. Call the local chapter (listed in the phone book) for information on particular diseases and local resources or call the national office at 914-997-4415. Their staff has Spanish speakers.

BLADDER PROBLEMS (See also BEDWETTING, CYSTITIS, URINARY TRACT INFECTIONS)

Tip # 1: Contact Help for Incontinent People (HIP) at 1-800-252-3337.

How it works: Help for Incontinent People (HIP) for a $15 one year membership will send you a resource book which includes coupons worth far more than the membership fee in savings on products designed for incontinent people. You also get quarterly newsletters which keep you up with the latest news in this health area. Send a self-addressed, stamped envelope to P.O. Box 544, Union, SC 29379.

Tip # 2: For information and a free product sample, contact the Simon Foundation for Continence at 1-800-237-4666 (1-800-23-SIMON).

How it works: The Simon Foundation for Continence will send you free information on bladder incontinence. The organization's newsletter, "The Informer," alerts members to new treatment developments and provides enormous support through its personal letters and pen pal connections. Also, Procter and Gamble, Inc., which gives a grant to the Simon Foundation, will send you a free sample of Attends, the company's diaper product for incontinent adults. Contact the Simon Foundation for Continence by sending stamped, self-addressed envelope (SASE) to P.O. Box 835, Wilmette, IL 60091.

Tip # 3: For free information about urinary incontinence and its treatment, contact the Bladder Health Council at 1-800-242-2383.

How it works: The Bladder Health Council of the American

Foundation for Urologic Disease will send you written information if you send a stamped, self-addressed envelope to 1120 N. Charles St., Baltimore, MD 21201. Or call toll-free 1-800-242-2383 and request mailed information.

Tip # 4: Get a "Urinary Incontinence Patient Guide" by calling 1-800-358-9295.

How it works: The Agency for Health Care Policy and Research Publications Clearinghouse will send a "Urinary Incontinence Patient Guide" if you call the toll-free number above or write P.O. Box 8547, Silver Spring, MD 20907.

Tip # 5: Try an exercise and bladder training program to improve continence without drugs or surgery.

How it works: Exercises of pelvic muscles can help reduce or eliminate incontinence in many women. Ask your doctor or nurse to teach you the procedure. Also, in a six-week bladder training program with a doctor or nurse, patients, men and women, learn to keep a strict schedule for using the bathroom. If such a training program is not available near you, write the Alliance for Aging Research, 2021 K St., NW, Suite 305, Washington DC 20006 for information on how to start one with the help of a doctor or health center. The telephone number is 202-293-2856.

Tip # 6: If you are a man with bladder problems caused by an enlarged prostate, ask your doctor to look into drug therapy before considering surgery.

How it works: Some incontinence in men is caused by benign prostatic hyperplasia (BPH) or nonmalignant enlargement of the prostate. Over 75% of all men over age 50 have some degree of BPH which may cause frequent or urgent urination, the constant sensation of needing to urinate, and/or leaking. Surgery has been one remedy, but newer treatment with drugs has in many cases proven useful in alleviating symptoms and even shrinking the prostate without surgery.

Quality check: Not all men with BPH are helped by drugs, and when they are, it often takes several months for treatment to be effective.

You MUST RULE OUT prostate cancer before starting drug treatment and have a PSA or test for prostate cancer regularly.

BLASTOMYCOSIS (See RARE DISEASES.)

BLINDNESS (See also EYE CARE and DISABILITY.)

Tip # 1: Social Security has special provisions to provide financial assistance to the blind.

How it works: Social Security pays disability benefits to the blind and other disabled persons under two programs: the Social Security disability insurance program and the Supplemental Security Income program. Social Security disability insurance provides payments for those disabled or blind people who qualify because of their record of paying into Social Security while they worked. Payments begin five months after the person is declared disabled or blind. Supplemental Security Income (SSI) is based on financial need. It does not require a work record and cash payments begin immediately after qualifying. (For more details, see DISABILITY.) Special rules for qualifying for Social Security disability insurance apply to blind people. You are considered blind under Social Security rules if your vision cannot be corrected to better than 20/200 in your better eye or if your visual field is 20 degrees or less, even with a corrective lens. You may apply for Social Security disability either as blind or as disabled. For example, if you cannot work because of your defective vision but do not qualify as blind by the Social Security definition, you may apply as disabled.

If you do qualify as blind, the rules are different concerning work earnings. You may generally earn more money than other workers and still qualify. Also, while Social Security payments are based on your average earnings over your working life, in the case of blindness, the payments will not be reduced because of lower income during the time that you have been blind. So apply for Social Security now, if you are blind, even though you may still be earning wages. Special rules for the blind apply to the SSI program also.

If you are under 65 and blind, you may enroll in Medicare (medical insurance) two years from your first Social Security payment. (See also MEDICARE.) If you qualify for SSI because of limited income and assets, you may be eligible to receive Medicaid (medical insurance) in your state. In some states, people on SSI automatically receive Medicaid; in others, they have to apply for Medicaid. (See also MEDICAID.)

For more information about your disability benefits and qualifications, call 1-800-772-1213.

Tip # 2: Contact these organizations for the blind for information and support:

American Foundation for the Blind at 1-800-232-5463 offers free information and referrals and a catalog of adaptive products for the blind. American Council of the Blind at 1-800-424-8666 gives information on an individual basis toll-free between 3 p.m. and 5:30 p.m. Eastern time on weekdays. A staff member may be reached immediately weekdays at 202-467-5081. Blind Children's Center at 1-800-222-3566 or 1-800-222-3567 in California offers information on early assessment, education, and stimulation for blind children. Guide Dog Foundation for the Blind at 1-800-548-4337 provides guide dogs and training.

National Alliance of Blind Students at 1-800-424-8666 offers college scholarships for the visually impaired along with monthly magazines in braille and a yearly convention.

National Library Services for the Blind and Physically Handicapped, Library of Congress, provides free library service to anyone unable to read or use standard printed materials because of visual or physical impairment. The Library delivers materials by postage-free mail and includes postage for the return. Materials include books and magazines in braille and on audio-cassettes. Special phonograph and cassette players are also loaned. Call 1-800-424-8567, M-F 8 am.- 4:30 p.m. EST

Recording for the Blind at 1-800-221-4792.

BLOOD DISEASES

Tip # 1: Consider participating in an experimental study of blood disease treatment. See also STUDIES.

How it works: Experimental treatment studies often offer free treatment to patients who qualify as subjects. In particular, the Clinical Center of the National Institutes of Health in Bethesda,

MD, has ongoing studies of immune thrombocytopenia, hemostatic disorders, drug-induced thrombocytopenia, idiopathic thrombocytopenia, congenital and acquired platelet abnormalities, bleeding abnormalities and Bernard-Soulier Syndrome. Testing and treatment is free if you qualify. For information on getting into studies of experimental treatment at this and other institutions, see STUDIES.

BLOOD TRANSFUSIONS

Tip # 1: Before planned surgery, consider setting aside some of your own blood in case you need a blood transfusion.

How it works: Putting your own blood in reserve to be used in case you need a blood transfusion during a planned surgery eliminates the risk of contracting a disease from someone else's blood or of having a bad reaction to imperfectly matched blood transfusion. A transfusion with your own blood is called an autologous blood transfusion. Arrangements for autologous transfusions must be made through your doctor who will determine if you are healthy enough to give blood and how often. Blood drawing under doctor's orders may usually begin 42 days prior to need and may be repeated as often as once a week. Drawing may be done at a local Red Cross unit and transported to the hospital or at another facility of the doctor's choosing. A donor's blood may also be frozen for future use. Using your own blood, because of the special handling costs, is usually more expensive than using general supply blood. For example, the Red Cross charge for one unit of general supply blood in one city is $66.75; the cost of one unit of autologous blood through the Red Cross is $137. Hospital fees for administering the blood may also apply.

For general information on autologous transfusion, call your local Red Cross chapter listed in the phone book and ask for Special Donor Services.

Quality control: Sometimes autologous transfusion is impractical because the need for one or two units is usually not critical, and yet, when the need for blood transfusions is critical, often more blood is needed than most patients would have been able to give earlier. In that case blood donated by others is still needed.

Tip # 2: Asking friends or relatives to donate blood when you need blood products does not save money.

How it works: When you need blood or blood products, you can ask friends or relatives to donate blood specifically for you. This is called "directed donation." The use of such blood requires your doctor's order and your written permission. Your friends' and relatives' blood donations will be tested for suitability the same as any other donation. Because of the special handling, the cost of using directed donation of blood is usually more than the cost of blood from the general supply. For example, the Red Cross's charge for one unit of blood in one city is $66.75; the charge for one unit of blood from directed donors is $119.

If you do prefer directed donor blood, ask your friends and relatives to be completely accurate answering health questions at drawing; all donor information is completely confidential.

Quality check: According to the American Red Cross, the safety of using directed donor blood is no greater than the safety of using blood from the Red Cross general supply and is sometimes worse. Friends and relatives, eager to contribute, may give blood even when they should not.

BLOOM SYNDROME (See RARE DISEASES.)

BOTULISM (See RARE DISEASES and FOOD POISONING.)

BRAIN DAMAGE

Tip # 1: Contact Family Survival Project for Brain-Damaged Adults.

How it works: Get information and support from the Family Survival Project by writing 425 Bush St., Suite 500, San Francisco, CA 94108. Or call 415-434-3388.

BRAIN TUMORS (See also CANCER.)

Tip # 1: Consider participating in an experimental study of brain tumor treatment. See also STUDIES.

How it works: Experimental treatment studies often offer free treatment to patients who qualify as subjects. In particular, the Clinical Center of the National Institutes of Health has ongoing studies of brain tumor treatment. For information on getting into studies of experimental treatment at this and other institutions, see STUDIES.

BREAST CANCER (See also BREAST IMPLANT and CANCER.)

Tip # 1: Contact Y-Me Breast Cancer Support Program for counseling at 1-800-221-2141.

How it works: Volunteer counselors who themselves have had breast cancer talk with callers to counsel them and offer information and resources.

Tip # 2: Contact the Cancer Information Service (CIS) of the National Cancer Institute at 1-800-4-CANCER.

How it works: Call the CIS for answers to your questions. In particular, ask for PDQ (Patient Data Query), a source of detailed information on treatments available for every stage of breast cancer and of contacts with researchers doing clinical trials in breast cancer. (See CANCER and STUDIES.)

Tip # 3: Order the FDA publication, "Progress Against Breast Cancer."

How it works: The Food and Drug Administration (FDA) provides current information in booklet form on a wide range of subjects. For free information on breast cancer order Publication # FDA91-1176. Write FDA, 5600 Fisher's Lane, Mail Code HFE-88, Room 1663, Rockville MD 20857 or call 301-443-3170.

Tip # 4: Contact the American Cancer Society at 1-800-227-2345 for information, programs, and patient services.

How it works: ACS Patient Services includes the following programs that relate to breast cancer:

1) Look Good...Feel Good, a program to help cancer patients improve their appearance.

2) Reach to Recovery, a patient-visitor program for support of women with breast cancer.

3) I Can Surmount, a short-term visitor program for hospital and home by a person who has experienced the same kind of cancer.

4) Patient and Family Education Programs.

5) I Can Cope, a program that provides information on treat-

ment, nutrition, resources, and other issues of concern to patients and families.

BREAST FEEDING (See also PREGNANCY, PRENATAL CARE.)

Tip # 1: Consider breast feeding your baby for the first year.

How it works: Not only is mother's milk designed especially to meet the needs of human babies, it is free. It requires only that the mother has the good nutrition she needs and plenty of liquids. Feeding the mother well is less expensive than feeding a mother and buying formula for an infant.

For information on breast feeding, contact La Leche League International, 9616 Minneapolis Ave., Franklin Park, IL 60131 or call 708-455-7730.

Quality check: Mothers taking certain medicines or with certain diseases such as AIDS should not breast-feed babies. Ask your doctor about medication you are taking or disorders you may have.

BREAST IMPLANTS

Tip # 1: Order the FDA bulletin on breast implants.

How it works: The Food and Drug Administration (FDA) provides current information for health professionals on controversial food and drug subjects. For a bulletin on breast implants, write FDA, 5600 Fisher's Lane, Mail Code HFI-42, Room 1663, Rockville MD 20857 or call 301-443-3170.

Tip # 2: Consider both sides of the controversy over silicone implants.

How it works: Many plastic surgeons say the FDA ruling that discontinued silicone breast implantation except in extenuating circumstances was unwise and unnecessarily scared women who have such implants. They point out that with every injection for diabetes, the syringes are generally sterilized with a silicone substance that results in as much or more silicone exposure as women with implants receive, and there has been no problem from the silicone among diabetics. On the other side, "victims advocates" disseminate information, some of which contradicts the plastic surgeon's view.

Tip # 4: Consider alternatives to breast implants following mastectomy.

How it works: Bras with prostheses are satisfactory for some women who have experienced mastectomy. A growing number of women who have lost a breast are also choosing to learn to have a healthy body image without breast reconstruction or a prosthesis.

For information about fitting prostheses, call the American Cancer Society (ACS) at 1-800-ACS-2345 and ask for contact with support groups of "veterans" of breast prostheses who can help you fit and use a prosthesis comfortably. For more information about body image following mastectomy, ask the ACS about workshops by psychotherapist Ronnie Kaye, who won the American Cancer Society's "Quality of Life" award for her work.

Tip # 4: Be cautious about groups that seek you out to offer breast implant removal.

How it works: The business of breast implant removal has been given a boost by the recent FDA ruling against the use of implants. Many women are seeking the operation. Some unscrupulous financial groups are seeking out women who want this operation but cannot pay for it and offering them loans at very high interest rates to cover the operation. It is wise to seek unbiased medical advice about your implant and use reputable financial institutions only.

BROWN SYNDROME (See RARE DISEASES.)

BULIMIA (See EATING DISORDERS.)

BULLOUS PEMPHIGOID (See RARE DISEASES.)

BUNIONS (See also PODIATRY and SURGERY.)

Tip # 1: Consider postponing or declining surgery to correct bunions.

How it works: A podiatrist or orthopedic surgeon can easily identify bunions and may suggest their surgical removal. Cutting is their business. But a bunion may not have to be removed if it is not causing serious discomfort. Many surgeons and podiatrists say, "Let me remove those bunions because some day they *will* cause you pain." But some bunions, even large ones, never become painful and some do not worsen. When bunions do become painful, often a change of shoes will relieve the discomfort. Increased shoe width across the bunion may be all that's necessary to relieve pressure and wearing a low or flat heel will help keep the bunion from worsening. Other devices such as toe wedges can help. Bunion surgery is very painful in the days after surgery and the results are not always worth the discomfort and expense. Ask your podiatrist or surgeon for the pros and cons of surgery in your case.

Tip # 2: For the surgical correction of bunions, consider both a podiatrist and an orthopedic surgeon who has done a lot of work on feet.

How it works: A podiatrist is not an M.D. and has a less broad background in medicine but may have more specific training in treating the foot than an M.D. A podiatrist's fee may be less expensive than a surgeon's and may be done in a less expensive setting. But compare estimates, because a podiatrist does not have to be less expensive. Whether you choose a surgeon or a podiatrist ask other patients who have had that operation about their experience and results.

Quality check: If you have other health problems such as a heart condition, you may want to seek foot care from an M.D. because of possible medical complications.

Tip # 3: Compare operating fees of surgeons and podiatrists with physicians' national averages.

How it works: For comparison, the mid-range physician's fee nationwide in 1992 for a simple bunion correction (Silver type procedure) was $750 while the most expensive doctors charged about $1300. Fees for a more complex bunion correction were more, for example, one including a resection of a joint with an implant averaged about $1400 with highest fees about $2000. Remember these are just surgeons' fees and not total costs which include anesthesia fees, supplies, use of the operating room, etc. If the doctor's quoted fee is considerably higher than the national average, consider asking the doctor to lower the fee.

BURNS

Tip # 1: Call Shriners' Hospital Referral Line at 1-800-237-5055.

How it works: The Shriners can give a listing of hospitals where burn care is available to children without cost.

Tip # 2: Call the Phoenix Society at 1-800-888-BURN.

How it works: The Phoenix Society puts out a newsletter for burn patients and provides a listing of support groups.

BYPASS SURGERY (See CORONARY ARTERY BYPASS SURGERY.)

CAESARIAN SECTION (See also PREGNANCY.)

Tip # 1: Consider a setting for childbirth where caesarian sections (C-sections) are less likely to occur or choose a doctor who tries to avoid caesarian delivery.

How it works: Total costs for a caesarian including hospitalization may run $3000 more than for a vaginal birth, not only because of the more complicated procedure but because hospitalization is often several days longer following a caesarian delivery than following a vaginal delivery. The doctor's fee alone for the caesarian averages about $700 more than for a vaginal birth. A caesarian section is less likely to occur when the mother is giving birth in birthing centers, at home, and centers where Lamaze training is common. Delivery nurses, midwives, and some physicians have a philosophy of calling for a caesarian section only when necessary. Talk to your doctor about his/her philosophy at the beginning of your pregnancy.

Quality check: Remember there are certainly legitimate reasons for delivering a baby by caesarian section and sometimes the procedure can save a baby (and even the mother) from injury or death. If you have discussed your feelings about caesarian delivery and you feel that your doctor has considered the matter thoroughly, be guided by his/her judgment.

Tip # 2: Note that a caesarian section is not always necessary for a mother who has already had one caesarian section.

How it works: For several decades it was commonly believed by patients and doctors that once a mother had delivered a child by caesarian section, any future deliveries had to be by caesarian also. This opinion added considerable cost and discomfort to later deliveries. Some doctors and patients still hold this opinion but increasingly the prevailing opinion is that vaginal birth is usually as good a possibility as caesarian for those who have already had one caesarian.

Quality check: Of course, a mother who has a permanent or chronic condition demanding a caesarian may need a caesarian each delivery. Ask a doctor to justify a request for caesarian.

CANCER

Tip # 1: Get routine cancer screening tests to detect cancer early.

How it works: Many cancers, if found at an early stage, can be successfully treated, even 100% cured, without extensive surgery and therapy. Cancer found later may require very expensive surgery, hospitalization, and therapy and may not be successful. Pap tests, mammography, prostate cancer screens, digital rectal exams, skin exams, for example, are all relatively simple tests to detect cancer early.

Tip # 2: Follow a diet that is thought to reduce the risk of cancer.

How it works: Call the Cancer Information Center (CIS) of the National Cancer Institute at 1-800-4-CANCER and ask for their free publication on diet for cancer prevention and treatment.

Tip # 3: If you have been diagnosed with cancer, order the *Cancer Research Institute HelpBook, What to Do If Cancer Strikes.*

How it works: This short but comprehensive guide offers cancer patients eight important steps to getting the best care. It includes a resource directory of organizations from research centers to groups that offer free lodging to patients being treated away from home. It also lists specific groups doing clinical trials and all the National Cancer Institute-designated cancer centers. For this publication, send $2 to cover postage and your order to the Cancer Research Institute, 133 East 58th Street, New York, NY 10022.

Tip # 4: For free information on cancer treatments, call the Cancer Information Service (CIS) of the National Cancer Institute at

1-800-4-CANCER and 1-800-524-1234 in Hawaii, 1-800-638-6070 in Alaska.

How it works: CIS is a comprehensive information center that can put cancer patients in touch with all the other local, regional, and national resources. CIS staff answer individual questions about cancer, provide free literature, and direct you to other sources of assistance and English and Spanish-speaking staff. The phone is answered from 9 a.m. to 5 p.m. Eastern time, Monday through Friday, except federal holidays.

Tip # 5: For free information on current cancer treatment options and clinical trials call Physician's Data Query (PDQ) through the Cancer Information Service (CIS) of the National Cancer Institute at 1-800-4-CANCER.

How it works: The PDQ system is a national computer network offering both doctors and patients up-to-date information about more than a 1000 cancer treatments for every type and stage of cancer, descriptions of ongoing clinical research trials in the U.S., locations where such trials are being conducted and by whom. Call CIS toll-free and they will search their database and send you a print-out without charge if you provide the diagnosis, the location of the primary cancer, and the stage of the disease. As a patient, you should take the print-out to your doctor who can contact appropriate researchers about your case. The telephone is answered from 9 a.m. to 5 p.m. Monday through Friday except federal holidays.

Also, for a FAX printout of information 24 hours a day, use CancerFax, designed to give physicians and others who do not use computers quick access to part of the PDQ database. There are usually two versions of CancerFax information, one for the physician, which averages ten pages, and one for the patient and family which averages six pages. For CancerFax data 24 hours a day, seven days a week, call PDQ at 301-402-5874 from the telephone on a FAX machine. A voice will tell you how to get the Diagnosis List. When you have found the correct diagnosis on this list, call CancerFax again and follow directions for receiving the information you need. The service is free; you pay only for the long distance call.

Tip # 6: Contact the Cancer Research Institute at 1-800-99CANCER for information and referral to a study of cancer and immunology.

How it works: The Cancer Research Institute answers individual questions on cancer and provides literature. The Institute will also give you a referral to research protocols studying an immunological approach to cancer. Tell the Institute staff member your exact diagnosis and stage of cancer.

Tip # 7: To get a multi-disciplinary second opinion on your cancer treatment, call Cancer Information Service at 1-800-4-CANCER, in Hawaii 1-800-524-1234, in Alaska 1-800-638-6070.

How it works: Multi-disciplinary CIS will give you information on Multi-disciplinary Second Opinion Panels. A volunteer panel of cancer experts can suggest the best treatment for you after reviewing your medical files. Some panels are free, some are not.

Tip # 8: Contact the AMC Cancer Research Center Information and Counseling Line at 1-800-525-3777 or 303-233-6501 in Colorado.

How it works: This information line provides answers to individual questions about cancer, counsels, and makes referrals from 8:30 to 5 p.m. Mountain time.

Tip # 9: Contact the American Cancer Society at 1-800-227-2345 for information, programs, and patient services.

How it works: ACS Direct Aid Assistance offers financial assistance through local divisions. Aid is limited to two years per diagnosis of cancer. Help can be given for prostheses, ostomy supplies, artificial larynges, housing, prescription medication, and edema sleeves. Available free of charge for patients that meet financial requirements are items used for home health care and dressings such as gauze, bandages, and incontinence pads. There is a special fund with additional financial resources for children with cancer. ACS Patient Services includes the following programs:

1) Look Good...Feel Better, a program to help cancer patients improve their appearance.

2) Reach to Recovery, a patient-visitor program for support of women with breast cancer.

3) I Can Surmount, a short-term visitor program for hospital and home by a person who has experienced the same kind of cancer.

4) Laryngectomy Rehab, a program of pre- and post-operative support for patients who have their larynx removed.

5) Ostomy Rehab, a program of one-on-one support by trained volunteers who have experienced the same operation.

6) Patient and Family Education Programs

7) I Can Cope, a program that provides information on treatment, nutrition, resources, and other issues of concern to patients and families.

Tip # 10: Keep or get insurance or enroll in a health plan. Even a very expensive insurance or health plan is usually better than none for the cancer patient. (See also INSURANCE and HMOs.)

How it works: If you have comprehensive insurance, keep it; don't jeopardize your coverage, for example, by changing jobs. If you must leave your job, look at the conversion clause in your present policy; you may be able to continue the same coverage as an individual, although at a higher premium, under the same insurance policy. Make your decision quickly because many plans require application for an individual policy to be made within 30 days of the end of employment. See also COBRA. If you don't have comprehensive coverage, look for a "guaranteed issue" plan, that is, one for which applicants are eligible regardless of health history. Consider, for example, seeking employment with a large company which offers employees guaranteed issue policies. Look also at HMOs which sometimes accept applicants during an "open" period each year regardless of health history. Explore Medicaid or Medicare eligibility. When comparing insurance policies, examine differences in coverage. Ask about choice of physicians, protection against cancellations and increases in premiums. Determine what the plan really covers, especially in the event of catastrophic illness. What are the deductibles? (Sometimes higher deductibles go with better comprehensive coverage.)

For more information or assistance, contact your State Insurance Commission.

Tip # 11: Ask your state health department if any cancer relief program exists in your state.

How it works: Some states have funded a special program to help cancer patients financially. Some states can only help a few hundred patients and funds run out. Ask when is the best time to apply so you can make application for funds when they are newly available.

Tip # 12: For information on childhood cancer, contact Candlelighters Childhood Cancer Foundation at 1-800-366-2223.

How it works: Candlelighters is a national organization which provides referrals for second opinions and information on medical help and financial assistance.

Tip # 13: Network. Get involved. Keep your hopes up.

How it works: Your attitude affects your immune system's ability to fight. Good spirits can win out over cancer (and other disease). But keeping up your spirits is difficult when the prognosis may be uncertain or poor and the treatment is uncomfortable. Some people get help from inspirational books, some get their spirits lifted by expressions of caring by friends, many find laughter is the best medicine. Books that can lead you toward healing are Norman Cousins' bestsellers *Anatomy of an Illness* and *Head First: The Biology of Hope.* Another invaluable book of encouragement is *Where the Buffaloes Roam: Building a Team for Life Challenges* by Bob Stone and Jenny Stone Humphries, a story of a man who beat "terminal" cancer, including letters of encouragement from friends that you may find helpful. This book is available in book stores and by ordering directly from Addison-/Wesley Publishing at 1-800-447-2226.

CANDIDIASIS (See RARE DISEASES.)

CARNOSINEMIA (See RARE DISEASES.)

CARPAL TUNNEL SYNDROME

Tip # 1: Correct carpal tunnel syndrome by using correct positions for typing and other keyboard activities.

How it works: Carpal tunnel syndrome, a disorder in which the wrist hurts, is usually the result of over-use of the hands and wrists especially in certain positions. The syndrome is on the rise as more and more people use computer keyboards for long periods of time. Carpal tunnel syndrome is often treated with surgery. However, you can prevent the disorder or correct a case identified early by using a hand position that does not strain the wrist when typing, playing the piano or other repetitive activity. Keep your wrists straight without allowing them to sag or bow. If you need a reminder (besides the pain) you can wear a wrist brace, available at the drug store, to keep your wrist straight.

Quality check: There are other causes of wrist pain and other, rarer causes of carpal tunnel syndrome, so consider consulting a doctor.

CATARACTS

Tip # 1: Not all cataracts cause a problem. Consider getting a second opinion about surgery if your vision is not significantly impaired.

How it works: Cataract removal has become the number one surgery in this country because of improved methods, a high success rate and advertising of the service. But not all cataracts that could be surgically removed actually cause a vision problem. Some doctors advise removal of cataracts because they are there, even though the patient does not report a visual need. Consider getting a second opinion if you question the need for surgery.

Tip # 2: Consider not having your cataracts removed until they are "ripe."

How it works: Cataracts can be removed at various stages of growth, in the early stages and when the cataract is "ripe." A cataract removal done too early usually does not provide as good results as a cataract removed later. Ask your eye doctor to take this into consideration and perhaps seek a second opinion on "ripeness."

Tip # 3: Order the FDA publication "Lifting the Clouds on Cataracts."

How it works: The Food and Drug Administration (FDA) provides current information in booklet form on a wide range of subjects. For information on cataracts, order Publication # FDA92-1183.

Write FDA, 5600 Fisher's Lane, Mail Code HFe-88, Room 1663, Rockville, MD 20857 or call 301-443-3170.

CEREBRAL PALSY

Tip # 1: Contact the United Cerebral Palsy Association at 1-800-872-5827

How it works: Through state affiliates the United Cerebral Palsy Association may provide equipment for eligible children and trained caretakers for children with cerebral palsy to give parents a break. Information and referrals and state affiliate numbers are available through the national number above.

Tip # 2: Contact Easter Seals at 1-312-726-6200.

How it works: Easter Seals offers speech therapy and some medical services on a sliding scale, a lending library and parent support groups. The organization has Spanish speaking staff.

Tip # 3: Contact the American Academy for Cerebral Palsy and Developmental Medicine at 804-282-0036.

How it works: The Academy will refer families to physicians with expertise in treating cerebral palsy and offer other information on the disease and its treatment.

CHECK-UPS, ROUTINE

Tip # 1: When a person has no specific complaints, routine screening tests at health fairs may help keep tabs on potential health problems between physical examinations.

How it works: Many people put off routine physicals because they have no medical complaints and because routine check-ups are not reimbursed by many medical insurance plans. A battery of inexpensive screening tests offered by health fairs are an inexpensive option. For example, several suburban hospitals in one city offered a blood pressure check, blood analysis, pap smear for women, and a prostate cancer blood test for men for a total of $50. The prostate test alone was worth $50. At another health event, a group of dermatologists offered to check any suspicious skin growth or give an all-over dermatological exam at no cost. You can save money by taking advantage of such low-cost screening. Bring

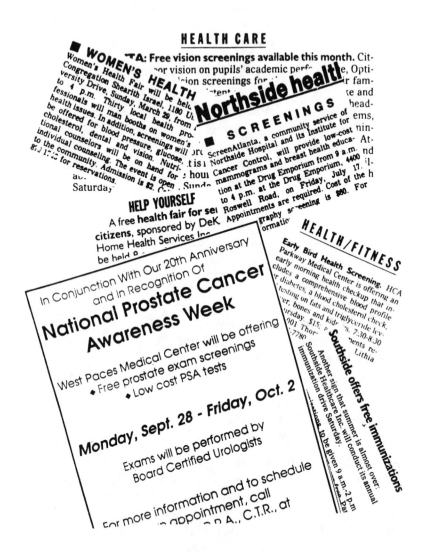

the test reports with normal findings on your next visit to your doctor along with documentation showing what professional or group performed the tests. Contact your doctor about abnormal findings right away.

Quality check: Abnormal results from screening tests often need to be verified by your doctor or other health professional. Screening tests, whether at a health fair or in your doctor's office, are sometimes falsely negative or positive. Health fairs will include only certain screening tests and are not usually as comprehensive as a complete physical exam by your doctor. Keep all your findings in one medical file and bring them to the attention of your primary care doctor.

CHILD ABUSE

Tip # 1: To get help for a child or if you are a child, call the Hotline of Child Help USA at 1-800-422-4453.

Tip # 2: To get help for an adult who may be abusive or at risk of being abusive, call Parents Anonymous at 1-800-421-0353.

Tip # 3: For referrals and information about child abuse and elder abuse as well as individual counseling, call the National Council on Child Abuse at 1-800-222-2000.

CHARCOT-MARIE-TOOTH DISEASE (See RARE DISEASES.)

CHILDREN'S HEALTH CARE (See HANDICAPPED CHILD, PEDIAT-RICS, and specific disorders.)

CHLAMYDIA (See RARE DISEASES.)

CHOLESTEROL

Tip # 1: Do not monitor high cholesterol by total cholesterol tests alone. Measurements of the ratio between HDL ("good" cholesterol) and LDL ("bad" cholesterol) ratio are far more meaningful and may save you worry and costs of further testing and treatment. Ask for a blood lipid profile.

How it works: Cholesterol tests are often useless. Measuring *total* cholesterol levels fails to test the more important factor: the ratio of HDL ("good" cholesterol) to LDL ("bad" cholesterol). The ideal ratio of HDL to LDL is 2:1. According to William Castelli, long-time director of the Framingham Heart Study, quoted in the *Harvard Health Letter*, "as many heart attacks occur among people with a total cholesterol level below 200 mg/dl [milligrams per deciliter] as among those with a measurement above 300 mg/dl." Some people have a high reading only because their "good" cholesterol is high. If routine screening measured HDL along with total cholesterol, these people "could be spared unnecessary worry, physician visits, and additional testing."

Tip # 2: Bring your cholesterol down by diet and exercise.

How it works: Exercise can increase HDL (good cholesterol) and to a slight degree lower total cholesterol. Change in diet is the most important way to decrease cholesterol. Animal fat and certain other fats containing cholesterol (coconut oil, for example) in the diet contribute to high LDL cholesterol, so eliminating most of these will help. High fiber found in fruits, grains and vegetables also tend to lower "bad" cholesterol. Oat bran has been found to be particularly helpful. Oils with a high number of polyunsaturates such as olive oil tend to increase "good" cholesterol. (See FITNESS and NUTRITION.)

Tip # 3: With your doctor's approval, consider taking psyllium along with an improved diet instead of cholesterol-lowering drugs for mildly elevated cholesterol.

How it works: Psyllium, from the seed of a common weed, works like some cholesterol-lowering drugs. You do not have to become a weed-eater; psyllium is available in common preparations like Metamucil (R) and Citrucel (R). In one study (Archives of Internal Medicine, Feb. 1988, pp. 292-296) one teaspoonful of Metamucil three times a day lowered the average cholesterol by 35 milligrams/deciliter and improved the ratio of HDL (good cholesterol) to LDL (bad cholesterol). The psyllium formula may be the first substance of choice in lowering cholesterol between 220 and 260 mg/dl, but drugs still may be necessary. Compare the costs of different psyllium preparations.

Quality check: Psyllium preparations seem to have fewer side effects than drugs commonly used for high cholesterol, but it is less effective than some prescription drugs. Drugs may be necessary for higher levels of cholesterol that require more extreme reduction. Consult your doctor about these options.

CHRONIC FATIGUE SYNDROME (See also EPSTEIN-BARR DISEASE.)

Tip # 1: For information on chronic fatigue syndrome (CFS), call the Centers for Disease Control and Prevention (CDC) at 404-332-4555.

How it works: The CDC is actively engaged in investigating CFS. Recorded information gives a general description of CFS and information on causes, diagnosis, treatments, support groups, and latest information on the disease. Reprints of the recorded information are also available. Call the 24-hour line evenings and weekends for cheapest rates.

Tip # 2: Contact an organization devoted to chronic fatigue syndrome.

How it works: These two non-profit organizations will answer questions, distribute literature, and make referrals.

National CFS Association
3521 Broadway, suite 222
Kansas City, Missouri 64111
Phone: 816-931-4777

CFIDS Association
Community Health Services
P.O. Box 220398
Charlotte, NC
28222-0398
Phone: 704-362-2343

Tip # 3: Try avoiding milk and grains to see if chronic fatigue syndrome improves.

How it works: Researchers at Georgetown School of Medicine have found that food allergies often trigger chronic fatigue syndrome (CFS). Some subjects who avoided these foods experienced a remarkable recovery. Food allergies may account for 50 per cent of CFS, concluded chief investigator Talal Nsouli. The main triggering foods in the study were, in order of frequency, wheat, milk, and corn. The allergies were confirmed by immunological tests and also by noting the CFS returned when the patient began to eat the foods again. An inexpensive and harmless way to test your own allergic reaction would be to try avoiding wheat, milk, and corn for a period of time and observe the results. If your condition improves, add the ingredients back to your diet one at a time to determine which one or more you are allergic to. If this does not change your condition, you could try eliminating other foods you might suspect.

CLEFT PALATE

Tip # 1: Contact the Cleft Palate Foundation at 1-800-242-5338 and the American Cleft Lip/Cleft Palate Association at 1-800-24-CLEFT,

How it works: These organizations can send you information on cleft palate treatment and resources and will make referrals to support groups.

Tip # 2: For psychological support for facial deformities contact Let's Face It at 508-371-3186.

How it works: One problem faced by patients with a cleft lip is the psychological difficulty of living with facial deformity. Let's Face It provides a newsletter, referrals, and psychological and medical support.

CLUB FOOT   (See RARE DISEASES.)

COBRA   (See also INSURANCE.)

Tip # 1: If you lose your job, it may be very important to take advantage of COBRA regulations as soon as possible.

How it works: If you have left or lost your job, you may be eligible for COBRA protection under a federal law called the Comprehensive Omnibus Budget Reconciliation Act (COBRA) of 1985. All companies with more than 20 employees must comply with COBRA regulations which require them to extend group coverage to employees who leave voluntarily or have been let go. COBRA says you must be allowed to continue for 18 months (and your dependents for 36 months) under the group insurance plan you had through your employer when you were working. However, you must pay the entire premium yourself and sometimes an additional small administrative charge. One important advantage of COBRA is that many other insurance plans you might consider buying after leaving your employment have a waiting period for pre-existing conditions. You may need the coverage extended under COBRA regulations to cover you for these conditions during that waiting period. Employers are obligated by the COBRA law to notify you of your rights within 44 days of your employment change and you have 60 days from notification to inform your employer that you want to continue benefits.

For details or assistance, contact the U.S. Department of Labor, Division of Technical Assistance and Inquiries, 200 Constitution Ave. NW, Room N 56658, Washington, DC 20210. You may not be able to pay for the premiums for your health plan without your previous income. Talk to a social worker in any hospital about programs in your state that may exist to help laid off workers keep coverage under COBRA.

COCAINE ABUSE (See also DRUG ABUSE.)

Tip # 1: Contact Cocaine Anonymous.

How it works: Cocaine Anonymous is a fellowship of men and women who help each other recover from their addiction to cocaine and other mind-altering substances. For referral to the group meeting nearest you, call 213-559-5833 or write:

Cocaine Anonymous
World Services
Box 1367
Culver City, CA 90232

COLDS (See also COUGH.)

Tip # 1: Eat chicken soup and gargle with salt water.

How it works: A cold is still not curable. You can spend a lot of money on cold medicine without speeding improvement. Here are some hints for treating colds without unnecessary expense. Hot steam makes a cold-sufferer more comfortable, but studies show that drinking chicken soup actually does make a cold pass faster than sniffling over plain hot water. An antihistamine may make you more comfortable by drying you up, but alone it does not make the cold pass. A decongestant, however, will help. Take analgesics such as aspirin, acetaminophen, and ibuprofen products only for headache or fever because analgesics not only do not improve a cold, they may suppress your immune response. Gargling with salt water for a sore throat is not only the cheapest but the most effective treatment. For a cough, consider products that contain dextromethorphan. Vitamin C taken in advance during the cold season may lessen the severity of colds.

COLITIS, ULCERATIVE (See and COLITIS AND ILEITIS and RARE DIS-EASES.)

COLITIS AND ILEITIS (See also CROHN'S DISEASE.)

Tip # 1: Contact the National Foundation for Ileitis and Colitis.

How it works: You can get brochures and other information from the National Foundation for Ileitis and Colitis by calling 1-800-343-3637 and referrals to support groups by calling 1-800-932-2423.

Tip # 2: For those who have had or are considering a colostomy or ileostomy, call the United Ostomy Association at 1-800-826-0826.

How it works: For those who have had a colostomy or are considering one, learning from the experience of others may be invaluable. The Association will send information and will put you in touch with support groups.

Tip # 2: Consider participating in an experimental study of colitis or ileitis treatment. See STUDIES.

How it works: Experimental treatment studies often offer free treatment to patients who qualify as subjects. In particular, the Clinical Center of the National Institutes of Health in Bethesda, Maryland, has ongoing studies of ulcerative colitis. For information on getting into a study of experimental treatment at this and other institutions, see STUDIES.

COMMUNITY HEALTH CENTERS

Tip # 1: Community Health Centers that serve as primary health care providers to underserved locations and populations are funded by the federal government and other sources. Migrant Health Centers and Homeless Health Projects are also federally and privately funded health centers which target migrant and homeless populations. Patients who can afford to pay for services are expected to pay. Medicare and Medicaid and privately insured patients are always welcome. Services are available to all patients regardless of their ability to pay. The following is a list of Community and Migrant Health Centers and Homeless Health Projects or resource offices listed alphabetically by state and city.

ALABAMA

Birmingham Health Care for Homeless, Birmingham, 205-323-5311

West Alabama Health Services, Eutaw, 205-372-4770

Conecuh Medical Center, Evergreen, 205-578-1163

Lowndes County Health Services Assoc., Hayneville, 205-548-2416

Mostellar Medical Center, Irvington, 205-824-2174

Franklin Memorial Primary Health, Mobile, 205-432-4117

Family Oriented Primary Health Care, Mobile, 205-690-8133

Health Services, Montgomery, 205-263-2301

Southern Rural Health Care, Russellville, 205-332-1631

Rural Health Medical Program, Selma, 205-874-7428

Southeast AL Rural Health Assoc., Troy, 205-566-7600

Health Development Corp., Tuscaloosa, 205-349-3250

Maude L. Whatley Health Center, Tuscaloosa, 205-349-3250

Alabama Comprehensive Health, Tuskegee Institute, 205-727-7050

ALASKA

Anchorage Neighborhood Health Clinic, Anchorage, 907-258-7888

ARIZONA

West Pinal Family Health Center, Casa Grande, 601-836-3446

Tidwell Family Care Center, El Mirage, 602-933-9671

United Community Health Center, Green Valley, 602-881-0535

Marana Community Clinic, Marana, 602-882-8504

Mariposa Community Health Center, Nogales, 602-281-1550

Lake Powell Medical Center, Page, 602-645-8123

Memorial Family Health Center, Phoenix, 602-243-1746

Maricopa County Department of Health, Phoenix, 602-258-6381

Valley Health Center, Somerton, 602-627-2051

El Rio Santa Cruz Neighborhood Health Center, Tucson, 602-670-3706

ARKANSAS

White River Rural Health Center, Augusta, 501-347-2534
Mid-Delta Rural Health Clinic, Clarendon, 501-747-3381
CABUN Rural Health Services, Hampton, 501-798-4064
Mid-Delta Community Services, Helena, 501-747-3381
Lee County Cooperative Clinic, Marianna, 501-295-5225
Mainline Health Care Center, Portland, 501-737-2221
East Arkansas Family Health Center, West Memphis, 501-735-3846

CALIFORNIA

Family Health Foundation of Alviso, Alviso, 408-262-7944
Inland Empire Community Health Center, Bloomington, 714-877-1818
Clinicas de Salud del Pueblo, Brawley, 619-344-6471
Intermountain CH Services, Brownsville, 916-675-2733
Buttonwillow Health Center, Buttonwillow, 805-764-6318
Clinicas del Camino Real, Camarillo, 805-388-5795
El Progreso des Desierto, Coachella, 619-398-7277
Drew Health Foundation, East Palo Alto, 415-328-5060
Sequoia Community Health Foundation, Fresno, 209-233-5747
Clinica Sierra Vista, Lamont, 805-845-3731
Long Valley Health Center, Laytonville, 916-984-6131
Alta Med Health Services, Los Angeles, 213-728-0156
Asian/Pacific Health Care Venture, Los Angeles, 213-484-6222
Community Health Foundation, Los Angeles, 213-266-4690
WATTS Health Foundation, Los Angeles, 213-564-4331
Madera Family Health Center, Madera, 209-673-7063
Merced Family Health Center, Merced, 209-383-1848
Nipomo Community Medical Center, Nipomo, 805-929-3211
Asian Health Services, Oakland, 510-763-4411
La Clinica de la Raza/Fruitvale, Oakland, 415-534-0078
West Oakland Health Center, Oakland, 415-835-9610
Northern Sacramento Valley Rural, Olivehurst, 916-743-6638
Northeast Valley Health Corp., Pacoima, 818-896-0531
United Health Centers/San Joquin Valley, Parlier, 209-646-3561

Porterville Family Health Center, Porterville, 209-781-7242
West Contra Costa Community Health Care, Richmond, 510-233-3851
Sacramento County Dept. of Health, Sacramento, 916-366-2171
Clinica de Salud del Valle de Salinas, Salinas, 408-757-6237
Logan Heights Family Health Center, San Diego, 619-234-8171
Curtis Jones-Robert Ross Community Health Centers, San Francisco, 415-821-8530
North East Medical Services, San Francisco, 415-391-9686
San Francisco Community Clinic Consortium, San Francisco, 415-252-7291
South of Market Health Center, San Francisco, 415-626-2951
Mission Neighborhood Health Center, San Francisco, 415-552-3870
North County Health Services, San Marcos, 619-471-2100
San Ysidro Health Center, San Ysidro, 619-425-7810
Community Health Center of Orange County, Santa Ana, 714-634-6206
Agricultural Workers Health Centers, Stockton, 209-948-5410
Northeastern Rural Health Clinic, Susanville, 916-257-5563
Tiburcio Vasquez Health Center, Union City, 415-471-5907

COLORADO

Metropolitan Denver Provider Network, Aurora, 303-343-6130
Columbine Family Health Center, Black Hawk, Colorado
Community Health Centers, Colorado Springs, 719-632-5700
Colorado Coalition for the Homeless, Denver, 303-293-2220
Dolores County Health Assoc., Dove Creek, 303-677-2291
Plan de Salud del Valle, Fort Lupton, 303-892-0004
Sunrise Community Health Center, Greeley, 303-665-9310
La Clinica Campesina, Lafayette, 303-665-9310
Uncompahgre Combined Clinics, Norwood, 303-327-4233
Pueblo Community Health Center, Pueblo, 719-543-8718
La Clinica del Valle/Migrant Health Project, Rockyford, 719-254-7623

CONNECTICUT

Bridgeport Community Health Center, Bridgeport, 203-333-6864

Southwest Community HC, Bridgeport, 203-576-8368

Charter Oak Ter/Rice Heights Health Center, Hartford, 203-236-0857

Community Health Services, Hartford, 203-249-9625

Community Health Center, Middletown, 203-347-6971

Fair Haven Community Health Clinic, New Haven, 203-777-7411

Hill Health Center, New Haven, 203-776-9594

DELAWARE

Westside Health Services, Wilmington, 302-655-5822

Henrietta Johnson Medical Center, Wilmington, 302-655-6187

DISTRICT OF COLUMBIA

Community Health Care, Washington, 202-582-7700

FLORIDA

Community Health Centers, Apopka, 305-889-8427

Florida Rural Health Services, Avon Park, 813-452-1870

C.L. Brumback Health, Belle Glade, 305-820-3110

Coconut Grove Family Clinic, Coconut Grove, 305-447-4950

Family Medical Practice, Cross City, 904-498-5626

East Pasco Health Center, Dade City, 904-567-0111

Family Health Centers of SW Florida, Fort Myers, 813-278-3600

Broward County Primary Health Care, Ft. Lauderdale, 305-357-6372

Tri-County Family Health Care, Greenville, 904-948-3225

Collier Health Services, Immokalee, 813-657-3663

Family Health Center of Columbia, Lake City, 904-755-5685

Lafayette/Suwanee Rural Health, Mayo, 904-294-1226

Camillus Health Concern, Miami, 305-577-4840

Stanley C. Myers Community Health Center, Miami Beach, 305-538-0423

Borinquen Health Care Center, Miami, 305-751-5322

Community Health of South Dade, Miami, 305-253-5100

Economic Opportunity Family Health Center, Miami, 305-637-6400

Family Medical and Dental Centers, Palatka, 904-328-0108

Manatee County Rural Health Services, Parrish, 813-776-1232

Sunshine Health Center, Pompano Beach, 305-972-6450

Gadsen County Primary Care Center, Quincy, 904-875-9500
Ruskin Migrant and Community HC, Ruskin, 813-645-3253
Central Florida Community Clinic, Sanford, 305-322-8645
Johnnie Ruth Clark Health Center, St. Petersburg, 813-821-6701
Pinellas County Dept. of Social Services, St. Petersburg, 813-892-7577
Project Health, Sumterville, 904-793-6855
Tampa Community Health Center, Tampa, 813-248-6263
The Medical Center, Trenton, 904-463-2374
Palm Beach County Health Dept., West Palm Beach, 407-684-0600
North Florida Medical Centers, Wewahitchka, 904-639-5986

GEORGIA

Albany Area Primary Health Care, Albany, 912-888-6559
Healthsouth, Atlanta, 404-688-1350
Mercy Mobile Health Program, Atlanta, 404-522-5659
West End Medical Center, Atlanta, 404-752-1400
NE Georgia Family Medical Centers, Colbert, 706-788-3234
Georgia Highlands Medical Services, Cumming, 404-887-1668
Oakhurst Community Health Center, Decatur, 404-3776448
Pineland Migrant Health Program, Metter, 912-685-5765
Palmetto Medical Center, Palmetto, 404-463-4644
Steward-Webster Rural Health, Richland, 912-887-3324
Westside Urban Health Centers, Savannah, 912-964-7811
Hancock County PHC Center, Sparta, 706-444-5241
Georgia Mountains Health Services, Suches, 706-747-3751
Primary Health Care Center of Dade, Trenton, 706-657-7575
Tri-County Family Medical Centers, Warrenton, 706-465-3253
Pike County Primary Health Care, Zebulon, 706-5676-3323

HAWAII

Kokua Kalihi Valley Comp. FHS, Honolulu, 808-848-0976
Waianae Coast Comprehensive Health Center, Waianae, 808-696-7081

IDAHO

Glenns Ferry Area Rural Health, Glenns Ferry, 208-366-7416
Terry Reilly Health Services, Nampa, 208-467-4431
Mountain Health Clinics, Nampa, 208-467-4431

Valley Family Health Care, Payette, 208-642-9376

Health West, Pocatello, 208-232-7862

Family Health Services, Twin Falls, 208-734-3312

ILLINOIS

Rural Health, Anna, 618-833-3233

Community Health Services, Cairo, 618-734-4200

Southern Illinois Healthcare Foundation, Centreville, 618-337-8153

American Indian Health Services, Chicago, 312-833-9100

Claretian Medical Center, Chicago, 312-768-1327

Erie Family Health Center, Chicago, 312-666-3488

Illinois Migrant Council, Chicago, 312-663-1522

Mid-Southside Services Health Plan, Chicago, 312-268-8113

Near North Health Service, Chicago, 312-337-1073

New City Health Center, Chicago, 312-737-5400

Travelers and Immigration Aid, Chicago, 312-281-4288

Christopher Rural Health, Christopher, 618-724-2436

Community Health Improvement Center, Decatur, 217-422-9797

Shawnee Health Service and Development Corp., Murphysboro, 618-684-5844

Henderson County Rural Health Center, Oquawka, 309-867-2202

The Health Center, Oquawka, 309-867-2202

Crusaders Central Clinic Assoc., Rockford, 815-968-0286

Frances Nelson Health Center, Urbana, 217-359-0134

INDIANA

Peoples Health Center, Indianapolis, 317-633-7360

Marion County Health Department, Indianapolis, 317-633-9638

Indiana Health Centers at Bluffton, Indianapolis, 317-632-1231

Indiana Health Center at Kokomo, Kokomo, 317-459-0662

Indiana Health Center at Marion, Marion, 317-632-1231

Open Door Community Services, Muncie, 317-289-5928

South Bend Community Health Center, South Bend, 219-234-9033

IOWA

Community Health Care, Davenport, 319-322-7899

Proteus Employment Opportunities, Des Moines, 515-282-2200

Polk County Health Services, Des Moines, 515-282-2599

Peoples Community Health Clinic, Waterloo, 319-236-1332

KANSAS

Kansas City Wyandotte County Health Dept., Kansas City, 913-321-4803

Kansas Dept. of Health and Environment, Topeka, 913-862-9360

Hunter Health Clinic, Wichita, 316-262-3611

KENTUCKY

Northern Kentucky FHC, Covington, 606-491-7616

Lexington-Fayette Co. Health Dept., Lexington, 606-288-2423

Seven Counties Services/FHC, Louisville, 502-589-8926

Park Du Valle Community Health Center, Louisville, 502-778-1422

Louisville-Jefferson County Board of Health, Louisville, 502-774-8631

Family Health Centers, Louisville, 502-778-4201

Health Help, McKee, 606-287-7104

Big Sandy Health Care, Prestonburg, 606-886-8546

Lewis County Primary Care Center, Vanceburg, 606-796-6221

Mountain Comprehensive Health Corp., Whitesburg, 606-633-4823

LOUISIANA

Teche Action Board, Franklin, 318-828-2550

Bayou Comprehensive Health Center, Lake Charles, 318-439-9983

Natchitoches Out-Patient Med Center, Natchitoches, 318-352-9299

New Orleans Health Care for the Homeless, New Orleans, 504-528-3751

Catahoula Parish Hospital, Sicily Island, 318-389-5727

MAINE

Arootook Valley Health Center, Ashland, 207-435-6611

Northern Oxford Health and Service, Bethel, 207-824-2193

Bucksport Regional Health Center, Bucksport, 207-469-7371

Fish RIver Rural Health System, Eagle Lake, 207-444-5973

Eastport Health Care, Eastport, 207-853-6001

Harrington Family Health Center, Harrington, 207-483-4502

Sacope Valley Health Center, Kezar Falls, 207-625-8126

Regional Medical Center at Lubec, Lubec, 207-733-5541

Rural Community Health Centers of Maine, Manchester, 207-622-9252

City of Portland/Dept. of Health, Portland, 207-874-8300

Kennebec Valley Regional Health, Waterville, 207-873-1127

MARYLAND

South Maryland Family Health Center, Baltimore, 301-354-2000

Total Health Care, Baltimore, 301-683-8300

Associated Program for Primary Care, Baltimore, 301-284-0030

Park West Medical Center, Baltimore, 301-542-7800

Baltimore Medical System, Baltimore, 301-732-8800

Caroline Health Services, Denton, 301-479-2650

Tri-State Community Health Center, Hancock, 301-678-7256

MASSACHUSETTS

Joseph M. Smith Community Health Center, Allston, 617-783-0500

Boston Health Care for the Homeless, Boston, 617-424-5090

North End Community Health Center, Boston, 617-742-9570

South Cove Community Health Center, Boston, 617-482-7555

Neponset Health Center, Dorchester, 617-282-3200

Geiger-Gibson Community Health Center, Dorchester, 617-288-1140

East Boston Neighborhood Health Center, East Boston, 617-569-5800

Holyoke Health Center, Holyoke, 413-536-8761

Hull Medical Center, Hull, 617-925-4550

Greater Lawrence Family Health Center, Lawrence, 617-685-1770

Lowell Community Health Center, Lowell, 508-937-6045

Lynn Community Health, Lynn, 617-581-3900

Mattapan Community Health Center, Mattapan, 617, 296-0061

Greater New Bedford Community HC, New Bedford, 508-992-6553

Center for Human Services, New Bedford, 508-990-8887

North Shore Community Health Center, Peabody, 508-532-4903

Outer Cape Health Services, Provincetown, 508-487-9395

Manet Community Health Center, 617-471-8683

Roxbury Comprehensive Community Health Center, Roxbury, 617-442-7400

Springfield Health Service/Homeless, Springfield, 413-787-6713

Worcester Area Community Mental Health Center, Worcester, 508-756-4354

Family Health and Social Service Center, Worcester, 617-756-3528

Great Brook Valley Health Center, Worcester, 617-852-1805

Worthington Health Assoc., Worthington, 413-238-5511

MICHIGAN

Downriver Community Services, Algonac, 313-794-4982

Baldwin Family Health Care, Baldwin, 616-745-2743

Bangor Community Health Center, Bangor, 616-427-7937

Nursing Clinic of Battle Creek, Battle Creek, 616-962-6565

Mercy Family Medical Center, Benton Harbor, 616-927-5400

Monway Family Health Center, Carleton, 313-654-2169

Detroit Health Center for the Homeless, Detroit, 313-393-4800

Detroit Community Health Connection, Detroit, 313-832-3102

Detroit Primary Care Network, Detroit, 313-876-4658

East Jordan Family Health Center, East Jordan, 616-536-2206

Solis Memorial Health Center, Eau Claire, 616-427-7937

Hamilton Family Health Center, Flint, 313-789-9141

Community Health Center, Grand Rapids, 616-235-7272

St. Mary's Health Services, Grand Rapids, 616-774-6162

Thunder Bay Community Health Services, Hillman, 517-742-4583

Holland Migrant Clinic, Holland, 616-399-0200

Northern Michigan Health Services, Houghton Lake, 517-422-5148

Family Health Center, Kalamazoo, 616-349-2641

Ingham County Health Department, Lansing, 517-887-6980

Alcona Health Center, Lincoln, 517-736-8157

Upper Peninsula Assoc./Rural Health, Marquette, 906-228-3613

Pullman Health Systems, Pullman, 616-236-5021

Health Delivery, Saginaw, 517-792-8751

Sparta Health Center, Sparta, 616-887-8831

Sterling Area Health Center, Sterling, 517-654-2491

Citizen's Health Council, Temperance, 313-847-3802

NW Michigan Health Services/Migrant Health Program, Traverse City, 616-947-0351

MINNESOTA

Cook Area Health Services, Cook, 218-387-2330

Cook County Community Clinic, Grand Marais, 218-387-2330

Indian Health Board of Minneapolis, Minneapolis, 612-721-7425

West Side Community Health Center, St. Paul, 612-222-1816

Model Cities Health Center, St. Paul, 612-222-6029

MISSISSIPPI

North Benton County Health Care, Ashland, 601-224-8951

Coastal Family Health Center, Biloxi, 601-374-4991

Rankin County Health Care Center, Brandon, 601-825-4090

Northeast Mississippi Health Care, Byhalia, 601-838-2098

Madison-Yazoo-Leake Family Health, Canton, 601-859-5213

Aaron E. Henry Community Health Services, Clarksdale, 601-624-2504

Jefferson Comprehensive Health, Fayette, 601-786-3475

Jackson-Hinds Comprehensive Health, Jackson, 601-364-5116

Family Health Center, Laurel, 601-425-3631

Greene Area Medical Extenders, Leakesville, 601-394-2381

Amite County Medical Services, Liberty, 601-657-4346

Greater Meridian Health Clinic, Meridian, 601-693-0151

Delta Health Center, Mound Bayou, 601-741-2151

Claiborne County Community Health, Port Gibson, 601-437-3052

East Central Mississippi Health, Sebastapol, 601-625-7140

Southeast Mississippi RHI, Seminary, 601-722-4269

Outreach Health Services, Shubuta, 601-687-1557

Three Rivers Area Health Services, Smithville, 601-651-4685

SW Health Agency for RH People, Tylertown, 601-876-4926

Vicksburg-Warren Community Health Center, 601-636-2023

MISSOURI

Big Springs Medical Assoc., Ellington, 314-663-2313

Caldwell County Medical Aid, Hamilton, 816-583-2713

Samuel U. Rodgers Community Health Center, Kansas City, 816-474-4920

Swope Parkway Comprehensive and Mental Health Center, Kansas City, 816-923-5800

Northeast Missouri Health Council, Kirksville, 816-626-2798

Northwest Health Services, Mound City, 816-442-5419

New Madrid County Group Practice, New Madrid, 314-748-2592

Central Ozarks Medical Center, Richland, 314-765-5131

Grace Hill Neighborhood Health Center, St. Louis, 314-241-2200

St. Louis Comprehensive Health Center, St. Louis, 314-367-5820

Family Care Center of Carondelet, St. Louis, 314-353-5190

People's Clinic, St. Louis, 314-367-7848

Metro Community Health and Mental Health Center, St. Louis, 314-361-8800

MONTANA

Montana Migrant Council, Billings, 406-248-3149

Deering Community Health Center, Billings, 406-256-6821

Butte-Silverbow Primary Health Care, Butte, 406-723-4075

NEBRASKA

NE Dept. of Health/Migrant Health Project, Lincoln, 402-471-2101

Charles Drew Health Center, Omaha, 402-453-1433

NEVADA

Central Nevada Rural Health Consortium, Hawthorne, 702-945-3381

Community Health Centers of Southern Nevada, Las Vegas, 702-647-9994

NEW HAMPSHIRE

Manchester Public Health Dept., Manchester, 603-624-6466

Lamprey Health Care, Newmarket, 603-659-2494

NEW JERSEY

Bridgeton Area Health Services, Bridgeton, 609-451-4700

CAMcare Health Corp., Camden, 609-541-3249

East Orange General Hospital/FHC, East Orange, 201-674-3500

Sa-Lantic Health Services, Hammonton, 609-567-0200

Jersey City Family Health Center, Jersey City, 201-915-2528
Newark Homeless Health Care, Newark, 201-733-5705
Newark Community Health Centers, Newark, 201-483-1300
Paterson Community Health Center, Patterson, 201-790-6996
Plainfield Neighborhood Health Services, Plainfield, 201-753-6486
Henry J. Austin Health Center, Trenton, 609-989-3599

NEW MEXICO

Albuquerque Health Care for the Homeless, Albuquerque, 505-247-3361
Albuquerque Family Health Center, Albuquerque, 505-768-5400
Centro Rural De Salud/Loving FHC, Carlsdad, 505-745-3690
Health Centers of North New Mexico, Espanola, 505-753-7218
Gallup-Thoreau-Grants Health Care, Gallup, 505-863-3663
Ben Archer Health Center, Hatch, 505-267-3088
La Casa de Buena Salud, Portales, 505-356-6695
La Clinica de la Familia, San Miguel, 505-233-4270
Presbyterian Medical Services, Santa Fe, 505-982-5565
La Familia Medical Center, Santa Fe, 505-982-4425
Shiprock Community Health Center, Shiprock, 505-368-5181

NEW YORK

Whitney M. Young Jr. Health Center, Albany, 518-465-4771
Joseph P. Addabbo Health Center, Arverne, 718-945-7150
Oak Orchard Community Health Center, Brockport, 716-637-5319
Montefiore Family Health Center, Bronx, 212-597-8500
Soundview Health Center, Bronx, 212-589-8324
Montefiore Comprehensive Health Care Center, Bronx, 212-992-9265
Ronald Fraser Health Center, Bronx, 212-994-2200
Morris Heights Health Center, Bronx, 212-716-4400
Comprehensive Family Care Center, Bronx, 212-597-8500
Bronx Ambulatory Care Network, Bronx, 212-294-4410
Brooklyn Plaza Medical Center, Brooklyn, 718-596-9800
L.B.J. Health Complex, Brooklyn, 718-636-2257
ODA Primary Care Health Center, Brooklyn, 718-852-0716

St. Mary's Hospital-Brooklyn FHCN, Brooklyn, 718-455-5400
Sunset Park FHC, Brooklyn, 718-630-7216
Geneva B. Scruggs Community Health Center, Buffalo, 718-894-3556
Northwest Buffalo Community Health Care Center, Buffalo, 716-875-2904
Suffolk County Health Services, Hauppauge, 516-348-2917
North Jefferson Health Systems, La Fargeville, 315-686-5757
Mt. Vernon Neighborhood Health Center, Mt. Vernon, 914-699-7200
Chinatown Action for Progress, New York, 212-233-5059
Community Health Project, New York, 212-675-3559
Covenant House Under 21, New York, 212-330-0505
East Harlem Council for Human Services, New York, 212-289-6650
NENA Comprehensive Health Care Service Center, New York, 212-477-8500
New York Children's Health Project, New York, 212-535-9779
New York City Health Care Homeless/UHF, New York, 212-645-2500
Settlement Health and Medical Services, New York, 212-860-0401
St. Vincent's Hospital, New York, 212-790-8025
William Ryan Community Health Center, New York, 212-316-7917
FHC Orange and Ulster Counties, Newburgh, 914-565-3138
Ossining Open Door Health Center, Ossining, 914-941-1849
Peekskill Area Health Center, Peekskill, 914-739-8105
Northern Oswego County Health Services, Pulaski, 315-298-6564
Anthony L. Jordan Health Corp., Rochester, 716-423-2801
Rochester Primary Care Network, Rochester, 716-325-2280
Westside Health Services, Rochester, 716-436-3040
Carver Community Health Center, Schenectady, 518-374-8464
Sodus Health Center, Sodus, 315-483-9133
Syracuse Community Health Center, Syracuse, 315-476-7921
Westchester Health Network, White Plains, 914-949-1800

Hudson Headwaters Health Network, Warrensburg, 518-623-2844

Greenburgh Neighborhood Health Center, White Plains, 914-682-7556

NORTH CAROLINA

Tri-County Health Services, Aurora, 919-322-7181

Orange-Chatham Comprehensive Health Services, Carrboro, 919-942-8741

Metrolina Comprehensive Health Center, Charlotte, 704-393-7720

Lincoln Community Health Center, Durham, 919-683-1316

Goshen Medical Center, Faison, 919-267-0421

Blue Ridge Community Health, Hendersonville, 704-692-4289

Twin County Rural Health Center, Hollister, 919-586-5151

Western Medical Group, Mamers, 919-893-3063

Morven Area Medical Center, Morven, 704-851-9331

Tri-County Community Health Center, Newton Grove, 919-567-6194

Robeson Health Care Corp., Pembroke, 919-521-9355

Wake Health Services, Raleigh, 919-733-7081

NC Migrant Health Program, Raleigh, 919-733-7081

Person Family Medical Center, Roxboro, 919-599-9271

Greene County Health Care, Snow Hill, 919-456-2181

Vance-Warren Comprehensive Health, Soul City, 919-456-2181

Stedman-Wade Health Services, Wade, ...

Bertie County Rural Health Assoc., Windsor, 919-794-3042

Caswell Family Medical Center, Yanceyville, 919-694-9331

NORTH DAKOTA

Mercer-Oliver Health Services, Center, 701-241-1360

City of Fargo/Fargo Community Health Center, Fargo, 701-241-1360

OHIO

Barnesville Health Services, Barnesville, 614-425-5165

PRAV Health Services, Chillicothe, 614-773-4366

Mt. Auburn Health Center, Cincinnati, 513-241-4949

Cincinnati Health Network, Cincinnati, 513-961-0600

Southern Ohio Health Services, Cincinnati, 513-752-3300

Cleveland Neighborhood Health Services, Cleveland, 216-231-0369

ECCO Family Health Center, Columbus, 614-253-0861

The Open Shelter, Columbus, 616-461-0407

Community Health Services, Fremont, 419-334-8943

Family Health Services of Darke County, Greenville, 513-548-3806

Ironton-Lawrence County CAO-FMC, Ironton, 614-532-3534

Townhall II/P.O. Box 781, Kent, 216-678-3006

CAC Family Health Center, Piketon, 614-289-2371

Toledo Family Health Center, Toledo, 419-241-7240

Cordelia Martin Health Center, Toledo, 419-255-7883

Youngstown Community Health Center, Youngstown, 216-747-9551

OKLAHOMA

Konawa Community Health Center, Konawa, 405-925-3266

Southeast Area Health Center, Oklahoma City, 405-632-6688

Community Health Centers, Oklahoma City, 405-769-3301

Morton Comprehensive Health Services, Tulsa, 918-587-2171

OREGON

SE Oregon Rural Health Network, Chiloquin, 503-783-2171

Virginia Garcia Memorial Health Center, Cornelius, 503-359-5925

White Bird Clinic, Eugene, 503-342-8255

La Clinica del Carino FHC, Hood River, 503-386-6380

La Clinica del Valle FHC, Phoenix, 503-535-6239

Multnomah County Health Division, Portland, 503-248-3676

NW Human Services, Salem, 503-588-5828

Salud Medical Center, Woodburn, 503-982-1622

PENNSYLVANIA

North Pennsylvania Comprehensive Health Services, Blossburg, 717-638-2141

Broad Top Area Medical Center, Broad Top City, 814-635-2917

Community Medical Center of NW WA County, Burgettstown, 412-947-2255

Pennsylvania Rural Opportunities, Camphill, 717-731-8120

ChesPenn Health Services, Chester, 215-874-1635

Glendale Area Medical Center, Coalport, 814-672-5141
Keystone Rural Health Consortia, Emporium, 814-486-1115
Primary Health Care Services of NW PA, Erie, 814-453-5744
Centerville Clinics, 412-757-6801
Southeastern Greene Community Health Center, Greensboro, 412-943-3308
Hamilton Health Center, Harrisburg, 717-232-9971
Hyndman Area Health Center, Hyndman, 814-842-3206
Southeast Lancaster Health Services, Lancaster, 717-299-6371
Sto-Rox Health Center, McKees Rocks, 412-771-6462
Welsh Mountain Medical/Dental Center, New Holland, 717-354-4711
Esperanza Health Center, Philadelphia, 215-634-4673
Spectrum Health Services, Philadelphia, 215-471-2750
Covenant House Health Services, Philadelphia, 215-844-1020
Philadelphia Health Management Corp., Philadelphia, 215-985-2553
Quality Community Health Care, Philadelphia, 215-227-1003
Greater Philadelphia Health Action, Philadelphia, 215-288-9200
Philadelphia Health Services, Philadelphia, 215-235-9600
Primary Care Health Services, Pittsburgh, 412-244-4700
Scranton Primary Health Care Center, Scranton, 717-344-9684
Shenango Valley Primary Health Care, Sharon, 412-342-3002
B-K Health Center, Susquehanna, 717-853-3135
Rural Health Corp of NE PA, Wilkes-Barr, 717-825-8741
York Health Corp., York, 717-845-2209

RHODE ISLAND

NW Community Nursing and Health Services, Harmony, 401-949-3801
Wood River Health Services, Hope Valley, 401-539-2461
Blackstone Valley CH Care, Pawtucket, 401-723-3117
Providence Ambulatory Health Care, Providence, 401-861-6300
Travelers Aid Society, Providence, 401-521-2255
Thundermist Health Associates, Woonsocket, 401-767-4100

PUERTO RICO

Barceloneta Primary Health Services, Barceloneta, 809-846-4412
Camuy Health Services, Camuy, 809-898-2660

Castaner General Hospital, Castaner, 809-829-5010
Ciales Primary Health Care Services, Ciales, 809-871-0601
Cossma Corporacion, Cidra, 809-739-8182
Florida Primary Health Center, Florida, 809-822-2454
Corp. Servs. Med. Prim. y Prev., Hatillo, 809-898-3935
Lares Health Center, Lares, 809-897-2727
Concilio de Salud Integral de Loiza, Loiza, 809-876-2042
Migrant Health Center-Western Region, Mayaguez, 809-833-1868
Central Areawide Comprehensive Health Services Project, Naranjito, 809-869-5900
Patillas Primary Health Service, Patillas, 809-839-4260
Centro de Diagnostic y Treatment, Playa-Ponce, 809-843-9393
Rincon Rural Health Initiative Project, Rincon, 809-823-5500
San Juan Mental Health Division/Homeless Project, Santurce, 809-721-3233
Jose S. Belaval Community Health, Santurce, 809-726-7373

SOUTH CAROLINA

Calhoun Falls Area Medical Services, Calhoun Falls, 803-447-8578
Charleston Interfaith Crisis Ministry, Charleston, 803-577-6667
Franklin C. Fetter Family Health, Charleston, 803-722-4112
Margaret J. Weston Health Center, Clearwater, 803-593-9283
SC Dept. of Health, Columbia, 803-737-3995
Britton's Neck Health Care Assn., Conway, 803-248-3495
Midlands Primary Health Care, Eastover, 803-353-8741
Allendale County Rural Health Program, Fairfax, 803-632-2533
Little River Medical Center, Little River, 803-249-3424
Sandhills Medical Foundation, McBee, 803-335-8291
St. James-Santee Rural Health Program, McClellanville, 803-887-3274
Family Health Centers, Orangeburg, 803-531-6905
Beaufort-Jasper Comprehensive Health Services, Ridgeland, 803-726-7148
Pee Dee Health Care Consortia, Society Hill, 803-378-4501
Carolina Health Centers, Trenton, 803-275-3218

SOUTH DAKOTA

Union County Health Foundation, Elk Point, 605-356-3317
Northwest SD Rural Health Services, Faith, 605-967-2644
East River Health Care, Howard, 605-772-4574
Isabel Community Clinic, Isabel, 605-466-2120
Rural Health Care, Pierre, 605-224-3114
Sioux River Valley Community Health Center, 605-339-7075
Tri-County Health Care, Wessington Springs, 605-539-1778

TENNESSEE

Benton Community Medical Corp., Benton, 615-338-2831
Chattanooga-Hamilton HCHP, Chattanooga, 615-265-5708
Alton Park and Dodson Avenue Community Health Centers, Chattanooga, 615-267-4591
Laurel Fork-Clear Fork Health Centers, Clairfield, 615-784-8492
Upper Cumberland RHI Primary Care Project, Cookeville, 615-528-7531
Stewart County Primary Care, Dover, 615-232-5329
Mountain People's Health Council, Huntsville, 615-663-2740
Perry County Medical Center, Linden, 615-589-2104
Memphis Health Center, Memphis, 901-775-2000
Union Grainger Primary Care, Morristown, 615- 586-5031
United Neighborhood Health Services, Nashville, 615-228-8902
Matthew Walker Comprehensive Health Center, Nashville, 615-327-9400
Parrottsville Community Health Center, Parrottsville, 615-625-1377
Rural Health Services Consortium, Rogersville, 615-272-9163
Lake County Primary Care Center, Tiptonville, 901-253-9954
Morgan County Medical Center, Wartburg, 615-346-6201

TEXAS

Amarillo Hospital District, Amarillo, 806-378-4692
Chaparral Health Clinic Corporation, Benavides, 512-256-3322
Brownsville Community Health Clinic, Brownsville, 512-548-7499
South Texas Rural Health Services, Cotulla, 512-879-3047
Vida Y Salud Health Systems, Crystal City, 512-374-2301
Dallas/HHS-Homeless Health Care, Dallas, 214-670-3968

Martin Luther King Jr. Family Clinic, Dallas, 214-426-2686
Los Barrios Unidos Community Clinic, Dallas, 214-651-8691
Community Or. Primary Care/Parkland Hospital, Dallas, 214-590-8007
Cross Timbers Health Clinics, De Leon, 817-893-5895
United Medical Center, Eagle Pass, 512-773-8917
Centro de Salud Familiar La Fe, El Paso, 915-545-4550
Centro Medico Del Valle, El Paso, 915-859-6403
Ft. Worth Health Dept. Ft. Worth, 817-870-7363
Gonzales County Health Dept., Gonzales, 512-672-6511
Community Health Service Agency, Greenville, 903-455-5986
Su Clinica Familiar, Harlingen, 512-428-4345
Su Clinica Familiar Dental Project, Harlingen, 512-428-4345
Harris County Hospital District, Houston, 713-7465800
Galveston County Coordinated CCs, La Marque, 409-938-7221
Laredo-Webb County Migrant/UHI Program, Laredo, 512-723-2051
South Plains Rural Health Clinics, Levelland, 806-894-7842
Guadalupe Economic Services Corp., Lubbock, 806-744-4416
East Texas Community Health Services, Nacogdoches, 409-560-5668
Deep East Texas Regional Health Care, Newton, 409-379-4244
Hidalgo County Health Care Corp., Pharr, 512-787-8915
South Plains Health Provider, Plainview, 806-293-8561
Atascosa RHI Health Clinic, Pleasonton, 512-569-5521
Port Arthur Health Dept., Port Arthur, 409-983-6163
Community Action Council/South Texas, Rio Grande City, 512-487-2585
Centro del Barrio, San Antonio, 512-434-0513
Ella Austin Health Center, San Antonio, 512-224-2112
Uvalde County Clinic, Uvalde, 512-278-6604

UTAH

Wayne County Medical Clinic
Bicknell, 801-425-3744
Enterprise Valley Medical Clinic, Enterprise, 801-878-2281
Green River Medical Center, Green River, 801-878-2281
Weber Community Health Center, Ogden, 801-393-5355

Salt Lake Community Health Center, Salt Lake City, 801-973-0493

VERMONT

Community Health Center of Burlington, Burlington, 802-862-9011

Northern Counties Health Care, St. Johnsbury, 802-748-9405

VIRGIN ISLANDS

Frederiksted Health Center, St. Croix, 809-772-1992

East End Family Health Center, St. Thomas, 809-775-4388

VIRGINIA

Brunswick Health Care, Alberta, 804-949-7211

Blue Ridge Medical Center, Arrington, 804-263-4752

Sandy River Medical Center, Axton, 804-685-7095

Tri-County Medical Corp., Aylett, 804-769-3022

Bland County Medical Clinic, Bastian, 703-688-4331

Boydton Medical Center, Boydton, 804-738-6975

Clinch River Health Services, Dungannon, 703-467-2201

Western Lee County Health Clinic, Ewing, 703-445-4826

Ivor Medical Center, Ivor, 804-859-6161

Tri-Area Health Clinic, Laurel Fork, 703-398-2292

Central Virginia Community Health Center, New Canton, 804-581-3271

Peninsula Institute for Community Health, Newport News, 804-380-8709

Eastern Shore RH System, Onancock, 804-787-7373

Daily Planet (HCH), Richmond, 804-783-0678

Saltville Medical Center, Saltville, 703-496-4421

St. Charles Community Health Clinic, St. Charles, 703-383-4428

Stoney Creek Community Health Center, Stoney Creek, 804-246-6100

Lunenburg Medical Center, Victoria, 804-696-2165

WASHINGTON

NEW Health Programs, Chewelah, 509-935-6001

West Coast Health Care Consortium, Copalis Beach, 206-289-3877

Okanogan Farmworkers Clinic, Okanogan, 509-422-5700

Columbia Basin Health Assn., Othello, 509-488-5256

La Clinica S. Columbia Rural Health, Pasco, 509-547-2204
Puget Sound Neighborhood Health Centers, Seattle, 206-461-6935
Central Seattle Community Health Center, Seattle, 206-461-6910
Pike Market Medical Clinic, Seattle, 206-728-1687
International District Community Health Center, Seattle, 206-461-3617
Seattle Indian Health Board, Seattle, 206-324-9360
Country Doctor Community Clinic, Seattle, 206-461-4513
Health Care for the Homeless, Seattle, 206-296-5088
Sea-Mar Community Health Center, Seattle, 206-764-4736
Metropolitan Development Council/HCHP, Tacoma, 206-627-8588
Community Health Care Delivery System, Tacoma, 206-627-8067
Yakima Valley Farm Workers Clinic, Toppenish, 509-865-5600
Columbia Valley Community Health Services, Wenatchee, 509-662-5163

WEST VIRGINIA

E.A. Hawse Health Center, Baker, 304-897-5915
Community Health Systems, Beckley, 252-8324
Clay-Battelle Community Health Center, Blacksville, 304-432-8211
Camden-on-Gauley Medical Center, Camden-on-Gauley, 304-226-5725
Clay County Primary Health Care, Clay, 304-587-7301
Monongahela Valley Assn. of Community Health Centers, Fairmont, 304-366-0700
Tug River Health Assn., Gary, 304-448-2101
Minnie Hamilton Health Care, Grantsville, 304-354-9244
Valley Health Systems, Huntington, 304-525-3334
Preston-Taylor Community Health Centers, Kingwood, 304-454-2423
Shenandoah Community Health Center, Martinsburg, 304-263-4956
Bluestone Health Assn. WV, Matuaka, 304-425-8067
Rainelle Medical Center, Rainelle, 304-438-6188

Tri-County Health Clinic, Rock Cave, 304-924-6262
New River Family Health Center, Scarbro, 304-469-2905
Roane County Family Health Care, Spencer, 304-927-1495
Monroe Health Center, Union, 304-772-3064
Northern Greenbrier Health Clinic, Williamsburg, 304-645-7872

WISCONSIN

Northern Health Centers, Lakewood, 715-276-6321
Marshfield Family Health Center, Marshfield, 715-389-3440
Sixteenth Street Community Health Center, Milwaukee, 414-672-1353
Milwaukee Indian Health Board, Milwaukee, 414-931-8111
Coalition for Community Health, Milwaukee, 414-226-8883
Isaac Coggs Health Connection, Milwaukee, 414-265-7608
North Woods Community Health Center, Minong, 715-466-2201
La Clinica de los Campesinos, Wild Rose, 414-622-4206

WYOMING

Tri-County Development Corp., Guernsey, 307-836-2751
NOWCAP Migrant Health, Worland, 307-347-6185

SOUTH PACIFIC

Pohnpei Community Health Center, Kolonia, Pohnpei, 619-320-2438
Ministry of Health Services, Majuro, Marshall Islands
Bureau of Health Services, Koro, Palau, 680-488-1757
Commonwealth Community Health Center, Saipan, Northern Mariana Islands 670-234-8950
Southern Region Community Health Center, Agana, Guam, 671-828-8611

CONTACT LENSES (See EYE CARE.)

CONTRACEPTION (See BIRTH CONTROL.)

CORNELIA DE LANGE (See also RARE DISEASES.)

Tip # 1: Contact the Cornelia de Lange Syndrome Foundation at 1-800-223-8355 in Connecticut.

CORONARY ARTERY BYPASS SURGERY

Tip # 1: Get a second opinion on the necessity for bypass surgery.

How it works: Research published in the *Journal of the American Medical Association* found that 14% of coronary artery bypass surgery in three hospitals was deemed inappropriate. Get a second opinion before agreeing to this surgery even if your insurance does not require it.

Tip # 2: Compare doctors' fees for performing the surgery and average hospital costs at different hospitals.

How it works: Bypass surgery will include a doctor's fee and a hospital fee. Consider only qualified, recommended doctors with whom you feel comfortable. Among these, compare fees and the average total fees of the hospitals where they operate for a comparison of total costs to you. For purposes of rough illustration only, the average charge for a coronary bypass with cardiac catherization in Dade County, Florida, in 1990 at different hospitals ranged from $36,325 to $61,709. Even with insurance coverage, that represents a substantial difference in the patient's costs between the least expensive and most expensive hospitals. The average charge for a bypass without cardiac catherization ranged from $30,477 to $55,200 in Dade County in 1990. (These figures were supplied by the Florida Health Care Cost Containment Board.)

COSMETIC SURGERY (See PLASTIC SURGERY.)

COUGH (See also COLDS and SMOKING.)

Tip # 1: If you have a chronic cough and smoke, consider giving up smoking.

How it works: Chronic cough is a very common result of smoking. Coughing may occur all day or just part of the day, for example, early in the morning. Cough caused by smoking will disappear if you quit. For help quitting, see SMOKING.

Tip # 2: Ask your doctor if an unexplained chronic cough may be caused by your medication.

How it works: Chronic cough may be a side effect of some medications. One of the most common medicines that may cause coughing are some kinds of ACE inhibitors used to control high blood pressure. If you cough and you are on one of these drugs, DO NOT STOP TAKING THE MEDICINE, but call your physician and discuss the relationship between this drug and your cough and be guided by his/her advice.

Tip # 3: Among over-the-counter remedies for cough, look for those containing dextromethorphan.

How it works: Many over the counter remedies for cough are ineffective. One ingredient that may be effective for you is dextromethorphan.

Quality check: Check with your pharmacist or doctor about taking drugs containing dextromethorphan with other medications as it can be very harmful taken with certain other drugs such as a class of anti-depressants called MAOIs.

Tip # 4: For unexplained, chronic cough consult your doctor.

How it works: A cough that does not go away may be a sign of some treatable disorder such as tuberculosis, allergy, or respiratory disorder. Consult your doctor for diagnosis.

CREUTZFELD-JAKOB DISEASE (See RARE DISEASES.)

CRI DU CHAT SYNDROME (See RARE DISEASES.)

CROHN'S DISEASE (See also COLITIS AND ILEITIS.)

Tip # 1: Contact the Clearinghouse for Digestive Disorders at 301-468-6344 and the Crohn's and Colitis Foundation of America at 1-800-343-3637.

How it works: Both these organizations send free information on Crohn's Disease. The Crohn's and Colitis Foundation sponsors a mail order pharmacy program and promises savings, convenience, and an information sheet with each prescription.

Tip # 2: Try to get into an experimental study of Crohn's Disease treatment. See also STUDIES.

How it works: Experimental treatment studies often offer free treatment to patients who qualify as subjects. In particular, the Clinical Center of the National Institutes of Health in Bethesda, Maryland, has ongoing studies of Crohn's Disease. For information on getting into a study of experimental treatment at this and other institutions, see STUDIES.

Tip # 3: Contact the National Foundation for Ileitis and Colitis for information on Crohn's disease.

How it works: You can get brochures and other information on Crohn's disease from the National Foundation for Ileitis and Colitis by calling 1-800-343-3637 and referrals to support groups by calling 1-800-932-2423.

CUSHING SYNDROME (See RARE DISEASES.)

CUTIS LAXA (See RARE DISEASES.)

CYSTIC FIBROSIS

Tip # 1: Contact the Cystic Fibrosis Foundation at 1-800-344-4823.

How it works: The Cystic Fibrosis Foundation (CFF) will send you free information. You can also be put in touch with local CF centers where social workers may be able to help you get diagnosis and treatment without cost, regardless of your income, and state aid for your medical bills.

CYSTICERCOSIS (See RARE DISEASES.)

CYSTINOSIS (See RARE DISEASES.)

CYSTINURIA (See RARE DISEASES.)

CYSTITIS

Tip # 1: Drink a lot of fluids, especially cranberry juice, to head off an early cystitis attack.

How it works: Reoccurring attacks of cystitis, a urinary tract infection, plague many women. Often they can feel one coming on. Flushing the system out by drinking an extra large amount of fluids and urinating frequently may be all that's necessary to head the infection off. Cranberry juice is a particularly effective liquid for preventing cystitis because, by raising the acid level, it discourages growth of bacteria that causes cystitis.

Quality check: If you do have a bacterial infection, it may get worse without treatment with antibiotics. Also, sometimes more extensive evaluation is needed to determine the cause of repeated infections which, if not corrected, could lead to serious kidney disease.

CYTOMEGALOVIRUS

Tip # 1: For information on Cytomegalovirus (CMV), call the Centers for Disease Control at 404-332-4555 24-hours a day.

How it works: CMV infects a majority of Americans and is the most frequent virus acquired before birth. It is usually not serious in adults but is a danger to high risk groups like the unborn infant and people whose immune system is compromised by HIV or drugs used to suppress immunity in organ transplant donors. Those at risk can hear recorded messages on different aspects of CMV diagnosis and treatment by calling the CDC. Call the 24-hour line when rates are cheapest during evenings and weekends.

DEAFNESS (See HEARING LOSS)

DENTAL CARE

Tip # 1: Call your local health department for free or low cost dental care for children.

How it works: Children in families with low income can, in some communities, receive free dental care from the local health department. Look up Family and Children's Services or Social Services or Health Department under the name of your county or community in the phone book. Or call your state general information number listed under GENERAL INFORMATION, Tip # 1.

Tip # 2: Take care of your teeth on a daily basis to prevent expensive problems.

How it works: While prevention is important in any health area, nowhere will prevention more clearly keep costs down than in dental care. Toothbrush, floss, and a massaging pick used regularly will do much to prevent gum disease and cavities as will keeping sugar in the diet to a minimum. Ask your dentist or hygienist to critique your style of home care and then stick with it.

Tip # 3: Get treatment for dental problems early to prevent more costly problems.

How it works: The filling of a cavity may cost $45; left unfilled the cavity may result in the need for a $1200 root canal and a crown a year later. Similarly, tooth sealants and fluoride treatments for children in areas where there is not enough fluoride in the water may save more expensive treatment later.

Quality check: Overprevention as well as underprevention can be a problem. If you think your dentist is doing unnecessary procedures discuss your concern with him/her and ask if there are alternatives. Before agreeing to extensive treatment, get a second opinion. For recommendations on frequency of dental procedures, write for consumer information from the American Dental Association at East Chicago Ave., Chicago, IL, 60611-2678 or call 1-800-621-8099.

Tip # 4: Compare dentists' fees in your community and in a more rural location.

How it works: Dentists charge different amounts for their treatment because of many factors including the costs of maintaining an office. Within one neighborhood there may be a range worth investigating. Also, the average of rural fees is significantly less than the average for urban fees, so consider a ride in the country for your dental care. Delta Dental of Pennsylvania provided these figures for a 1992 issue of *Parade Magazine*:

Treatment	Rural	Urban
Check-up	$16	$42
2 small X-rays	$16	$35
Medium amalgam filling	$20	$60
Complete acrylic dentures	$980	$1600

Quality check: Confidence and trust in your dentist, as with your physician, is of prime importance. If your relationship and experience with a dental care provider over a period of time has been satisfying, think twice before going "shopping" for another.

Tip # 5: Consider getting routine care through a managed dental care plan.

How it works: For a monthly payment of $8 a month in one community, families enrolled in a managed dental care plan get cleaning and X-rays for all members. This rate, equivalent to $48 for a 6-month period turns out to be a bargain compared to a typical fee of $48 for basic cleaning for just one person in the same period.

Fillings and other dental treatment are extra. Find managed dental care plans by looking up "Dentists Information and Referral Services" in the yellow pages and asking specifically for such a plan.

Quality check: The managed dental care plan is a source through which dentists may attract patients who will then use them for the fillings and other dental treatment priced closer to market rates. Beware that, unlike dentists who charge more for basic care, dentists participating in managed dental care plans have an incentive to suggest more expensive treatment to help make up for the lower priced care. Some patients have complained of unnecessary treatments being recommended. A patient who goes outside the managed dental care plan for other kinds of treatment has to weigh the advantages of this maneuver against having a one-dentist relationship.

Tip # 6: Consider getting routine dental care through a dental hygienist school.

How it works: Schools for training dental hygienists are often part of a college. The students may get supervised practice in dental hygiene in clinics open to the public. A typical clinic in a state or community college system provides a complete teeth cleaning, bite-wing X-rays, fluoride treatment, and hygiene counseling for $10 a visit. A similar service in a private dentist's office might cost $35-$60 plus the cost of the X-rays.

Quality Check: The student hygienists may be slower and less confident than the experienced hygienist in a dental office, but they are typically graded on their performance so they do their best, and their treatment is checked by a supervisor.

Tip # 7: Go to a dental school of a university for low cost or free treatment by supervised dental students.

How it works: Dental schools need patients on whom students can practice. If you are lucky and have a dental school clinic in your community, consider checking it out. If a school is not near by, for extensive treatments it would be worth a trip of some distance. One young woman whose teeth were all damaged as a child was welcomed enthusiastically at a school because her damage was unusually extensive and a particularly valuable learning experience for the students. The woman had all of her teeth capped without charge, saving thousands of dollars. Some schools in more remote locations actually have trouble getting enough patients. These areas may be pleasant, inexpensive vacation spots where you and your family can combine a break from school and work with needed dental treatment.

Quality check: All the treatment by dental students is supervised by the staff and is likely to be state of the art. However, it may be slower as the students are learning by working on your teeth.

Tip # 8: Find a young dentist beginning his/her practice and negotiate a fee.

How it works: Young dentists setting up their practice need ways to attract new patients but they are limited in what they may or will do to market their services. You can make a reasonable offer that is less than the going price for the treatment and the dentist may find your offer a lot more attractive than an empty chair. When the practice is full, don't be surprised if the deal is off. (But then you could find another new dentist.)

Tip # 9: If you have dental coverage on an insurance plan, consider having your children's improperly positioned wisdom teeth extracted *before* they become ineligible for your insurance, sometimes at age 18.

How it works: Many young people have one or more wisdom teeth that are impacted or in a position to threaten nearby molars and gum structures. Dentists are often recommending extraction of the poorly positioned teeth before they cause problems. This determination may be made at about age 17 or 18, but many people wait a few years because the procedure does not seem urgent. When your child is over 18, however, it may be too late for your policy to pay for the procedure unless your child is a fulltime student. Once your child is off your policy, the expense for the procedure (which costs about $1000) may have to come out of your pocket or out of the young person's income.

Quality check: There is usually no need to extract a wisdom tooth in a proper position unless the gums are unhealthy or the tooth is opposite a tooth that is to be extracted. When extraction is recommended, doing it in the late teens is often less complicated than later.

Tip # 10: Take the whole mouth approach and consider the long term.

How it works: In an effort to save money, people sometimes focus only on the short term. Fixing a cavity now is still cheaper than extracting a tooth later. A lost tooth may cause all kinds of problems in the long run, including a need for a bridge or denture which are expensive and sometimes an inconvenience. But there are other kinds of gains to be made by asking your dentist or orthodontist to tell you problems he/she foresees down the line and the treatment that would prevent or solve them. For example, one woman, in danger of losing a tooth, spent $1500 on gum treatment, a crown, and other procedures to save the tooth. Later she went to an orthodontist about other problems involving spacing. He pulled the $1500 tooth to relieve overcrowding and put braces on her teeth. Asking her dentist for an overview of her dental future might have prevented this costly double treatment. Sometimes the more expensive treatment is a bargain in the long run. For example, one man had several teeth that did not meet properly. The bad bite bothered him but he did not want to go to the trouble and expense of having it corrected. One day he had a cavity that needed filling. The dentist persuaded him to put a cap on the cavity that would also change the surface of the tooth and correct the bite. The patient had to pay more for the cap but his bite feels much better and he thinks he has saved on time, comfort, and money in the long run.

Tip # 11: When your dentist suggests braces, consider getting a second opinion.

How it works: There is a controversy among dentists as to when braces are necessary to save teeth. Hearing more than one point of view may save you the cost of unnecessary braces.

Tip # 12: If you have dental insurance and your children's teeth need straightening, consider having the necessary orthodontia done before they are ineligible for your coverage.

How it works: Straightening of teeth is sometimes considered cosmetic and optional. But some defects in positioning cause a poor bite and problems such as cheek biting, headaches, jaw pain later. Overcrowding can increase the chances of decay and gum disease. If you are ever going to seek orthodontics for your children, consider doing it while they are still on your plan even though they may be willing to put it off. Orthodontics in childhood is an easier and less expensive process than in adulthood and time off for appointments may be less costly.

Tip # 13: Ask several orthodontists for a free evaluation.

How it works: The more you know about your options the better choices you can make. Many orthodontists will give you an appointment to evaluate your or your children's teeth without charge. They will discuss whether braces are necessary and the costs of an entire treatment at that time. Many treatments, braces, for example, take a period of years and you are charged for the whole treatment rather than for individual visits. This allows you to plan for payments on a monthly basis. By seeking several free evaluations from different orthodontists you can compare opinions, prices, and options without initial cost.

Quality check: Listening to different opinions may help you choose the highest quality approach at the lowest cost.

Tip # 14: Compare the costs of plastic braces with metal braces.

How it works: Plastic braces are more the color of teeth and therefore less noticeable than shiny metal braces. They usually cost considerably more. If you are an adult to whom appearance makes a big difference psychologically or in your work, the less noticeable kind may be worth the difference in money to you. But so many kids these days have braces that it's not something to hide; some even are proud to get them. So you may choose to save some money and go with metal for your kids or for yourself.

Tip # 15: If you have a medical health policy but no dental coverage, consider with your doctor the general health aspects of any dental treatment. Can it be covered under your medical policy?

How it works: Some dental treatment is related to general health and if so stated can be covered under your medical policy. For example, a child injured her gums by falling on a stick. The wound required no treatment at first, but when it did not heal quickly, she was found to have a congenital periodontal problem. This problem may have contributed to the wound not healing. Minor periodontal surgery corrected the problem and was paid for under medical coverage only because the claim stated its contribution to the wound situation that was covered. Similarly dental treatment that results from any accident or from a medical problem like a tumor may be covered under medical insurance even though the treatment is done by a dentist.

Tip # 16: Some categories of veterans may receive dental care without charge or for a modest co-payment.

How it works: While eligibility for dental care is generally more limited than for medical services, some groups of disabled veterans or veterans with service related dental problems may receive dental care without cost or for a modest co-payment if their incomes are above a certain level. These include totally disabled veterans and veterans in vocational rehabilitation programs. Dental care for conditions related to medical problems may also be treated. For more precise information, contact the Department of Veterans Affairs, Washington, DC 20420 or look up Veterans Affairs under Federal Government in your phone book for a regional office or your nearest VA facility.

Tip # 17: Consider having your dentures made in England but CHECK CURRENT PRICES FIRST.

How it works: A full set of acrylic dentures in the U.S. was recently reported to cost from $980 to $1600. In the United Kingdom, a set was reported to cost an average of $376 through a private dentist. The difference might be enough to pay for your round trip airline ticket—you might have a great vacation and get your new dentures both at one great price. Remember that prices change and the value of the dollar against any foreign currency fluctuates, so check out current prices in British pounds and convert to dollars. The British tourism office may be able to help you contact an appropriate dentist. DO NOT PLAN TO GO TO ENGLAND FOR DENTURES

WITHOUT FIRST GETTING A FIRM COMMITMENT ON PRICE FROM A DENTIST THERE.

Quality check: Get the same kind of references for a dentist abroad as you would here. Remember if the dentures need adjusting, you might not be able to go back easily to have them worked on.

Tip # 18: Try to get into an experimental study of dental or oral treatment. See also STUDIES.

How it works: Experimental treatment studies often offer free treatment to patients who qualify as subjects. In particular, the Clinical Center of the National Institutes of Health in Bethesda, Maryland, has ongoing studies of several dental and oral disorders including salivary gland dysfunction, taste and related sensory disorders, oral motor dysfunction, recurrent herpes, impacted third molars (wisdom teeth), chronic facial pain, TMJ (jaw disorder), painful diabetic neuropathy, reflex sympathetic dystrophy, and oral endosseous implants.

For information on getting into a study of experimental treatment at this and other institutions , see STUDIES.

Tip # 19: For free brochures on oral health and disease, contact the Epidemiology and Oral Disease Prevention Program at 301-496-4261.

DEPRESSION (See also Mental Health.)

Tip # 1: Contact the National Foundation for Depressive Illness at 1-800-248-4344.

Tip # 2: For depression after childbirth, call a support organization for post-partum depression.

How it works: Mothers often feel depressed after delivery. When this condition lingers more than a few days, call an organization that is concerned with this distinct illness. Call Depression after Delivery at 1-800-944-4773 or 215-295-3994 on Monday, Tuesday, or Thursday mornings Pacific time. Or call Post-Partum Support International at 805-967-7636 or the Family Resource Coalition at 312-341-0900.

Tip # 3: Contact the National Counseling Center of the Humanistic Foundation at 1-800-333-4444.

How it works: A counselor will respond personally to your inquiry about a problem involving alcohol or drug abuse and depression. Referrals may be made to the for-profit treatment centers which sponsor this information line. Referrals are also made to non-foundation treatment centers and financial help is available at the Foundation's own holistic treatment centers.

DERMATOLOGY (See also ACNE, ECZEMA, DYSTROPHIC EPIDERMOLYSIS, PSORIASIS, and SKIN CANCER.)

Tip # 1: Wearing sun screen rated SPF 15 is probably the best care for the money for the health of your skin.

How it works: Direct sun on the skin is a major factor in skin aging, burning damage, and skin cancer. Sun block or sun screen products are very effective and an important protection against sun damage to skin.

Tip # 2: Don't buy sun screen rated higher than 15 unless you need extra water resistance.

How it works: The higher the SPF rating of a sun screen or sun block, the better protection—up to a point. Beyond an SPF rating of 15, there is often no improvement in the sun blocking characteristic even though products with higher ratings usually cost a lot more. However, high SPF rated products are more often waterproof and may resist water and perspiration longer. So consider buying the 15 SPF, and avoid paying for any higher rating unless you need strong water and sweat resistance.

Tip # 3: When buying cosmetics, remember that cosmetics are usually not of medical benefit to your skin.

How it works: Advertisements for many expensive cosmetics make lavish claims of "nourishing" or "rejuvenating" or "repairing" your skin. If you are willing to pay high prices for up-scale cosmetics, do it because they make you look good, not because of any claim of medical benefit. Hypoallergenic cosmetics are worth paying more for only for those who are allergic to regular cosmetics. Note that some cosmetics with additives such as sun screen may have some of the same benefits as the additive but you rarely know how much of the active ingredient (and therefore how much benefit) you are getting. See Tip # 2.

Tip # 4: Avoid very expensive and glamorous moisturizers and preparations for dry skin.

How it works: Dry skin lotions and creams help hold in the moisture and make the skin feel better, but, contrary to many advertisements, they may not prevent aging of the skin or other grand claims. So don't waste your money because of false claims; buy the least expensive preparation that keeps your skin moist.

Tip # 5: Contact the American Academy of Dermatology at 708-330-0230 for information and referral.

Tip # 6: Consider buying generic medications for the skin.

How it works: As with any medication, generic products are usually less expensive than the corresponding name brand ones. In the case of oral antibiotics for acne, such as tetracycline, some generics are many times cheaper than their name brand equivalents.

Quality check: Ask your dermatologist if the generic form of a pharmaceutical product is as effective as a name brand. Some generic topical medications are not as effective as the name brand medication, not because of differences in the active ingredient, but because of differences in the ointment or cream that make the active ingredient less effective.

Tip # 7: For unexplained rashes and other skin irritations, temporarily stop using newly acquired cosmetics, soaps, household products.

How it works: A large portion of unexplained rashes and skin irritation are cases of contact dermatitis or an allergic reaction to something you touched, often a new product or material you have recently introduced into your home. Cosmetics and household cleaners are among the most likely causes of contact dermatitis, but plants, new fabrics, or other materials may also have set off an allergic reaction. You may be able to cure the rash by discontinuing use of the product.

Tip # 8: Contact the FDA for information on contact dermatitis or mysterious rashes.

How it works: The Food and Drug Administration (FDA) provides current information in booklet form on a wide range of subjects. For the booklet called "Contact Dermatitis: Solutions to Rash Mysteries," order publication FDA91-1166. Write FDA, 5600 Fisher's Lane, Mail Code HFE-88, Room 1663, Rockville MD 20857 or call 301-443-3170.

Tip # 9: Contact the Skin Cancer Foundation at 212-725-5176.

How it works: The Skin Cancer Foundation will send you information on different types of skin cancer.

Tip # 10: Consider participating in an experimental study on your skin disorder.

How it works: Studies of experimental treatment often give free treatment to those who qualify as subjects. In particular, on-going skin disease research at the Clinical Center of the National Institutes of Health includes studies in basal cell carcinoma, benign mucosal pemphigoid, flat warts, epidermolysis, bullous pemphigoid, dermatitis herpetiformis, herpes gestationis, granuloma faciale, disorders of keratinization, pemphigus foliaceous, pemphigus vulgaris, psoriasis, Sezary syndrome, vasculitis, and xeroderma pigmentosa.

For information on how to get into a study of experimental treatment at this and other institutions, see STUDIES.

DIABETES

Tip # 1: Ask your state health department if it administers local diabetes treatment and management programs for those with limited resources.

How it works: About half the states have diabetes treatment and management programs administered through local health departments. Treatment may be low cost or free for those without resources. Call your local health department or look for a diabetes or chronic disease section under Community Health, Public Health, or Human Resources in the state directory in your telephone book. Or look under GENERAL INFORMATION in this book to locate the general information number for your state government.

Tip # 2: Contact the American Diabetes Association at 1-800-232-3472.

How it works: The American Diabetes Association will send information and will refer you to local groups which offer support, quarterly seminars promoting lifestyle changes, and educational materials.

Tip # 3: For children with diabetes, contact the Juvenile Diabetes Foundation (JDF) at 1-800-223-1138.

How it works: The JDF will send you information and referrals and support group contacts. Members of the staff speak Spanish.

Tip # 4: Contact the National Diabetes Information Clearinghouse at 301-468-2162.

How it works: The National Diabetes Information Clearinghouse is a service of the National Institute of Diabetes and Digestive and Kidney Diseases (NIDDK) of the National Institutes of Health (NIH). The Clearinghouse has bibliographies, a newsletter called "Diabetes Dateline," a diabetes dictionary of over 300 diabetes related terms, publications, and an on-line data base.

Tip # 5: Consider participating in an experimental study of diabetes treatment. See also STUDIES.

How it works: Experimental treatment studies often offer free treatment to patients who qualify as subjects. In particular, the Clinical Center of the National Institutes of Health in Bethesda, MD, has ongoing studies of both insulin- and non-insulin-dependent diabetes mellitus.

For information on getting into a study of experimental treatment at this and other institutions, see STUDIES.

DIET PROGRAMS (See also NUTRITION.)

Tip # 1: To get information about the safety of diet programs, contact the Food and Drug Administration or the Federal Trade Commission.

How it works: Diet books abound and diet products are widely advertised, but they are not all safe, especially for individuals with certain health problems. To ask about the safety of diets write

Consumer Affairs Information, FDA, 5600 Fishers Lane HFC-110, Rockville, MD 20857 or call Office of Consumer Inquiries at 301-443-3170.

For consumer information about diet products, write Federal Trade Commission, Correspondence Branch, Washington DC 20580.

DIGESTIVE DISORDERS

Tip # 1: Contact the Digestive Disease Information Clearinghouse at 301-468-2162.

How it works: The Clearinghouse provided by the National Institute of Diabetes and Digestive and Kidney Diseases (NIDDK) of the National Institutes of Health (NIH) can answer questions on digestive disorders, send literature, and inform you of experimental studies of the disease.

Tip # 2: Consider participating in an experimental study of treatment of your digestive disorder. See also STUDIES.

How it works: Experimental treatment studies often offer free treatment to patients who qualify as subjects. In particular, the Clinical Center of the National Institutes of Health in Bethesda, MD, has on-going studies of digestive disorders including Zollinger-Ellison Syndrome and islet cell tumors. For information on getting into a study of experimental treatment at this and other institutions, see STUDIES.

DISABILITY (See also BLINDNESS, DYING, EQUIPMENT, HANDICAPPED CHILDREN, HOME HEALTH CARE, HOSPICE, and LONG TERM CARE.)

Tip # 1: If you become disabled or responsible for a disabled person, consider consulting an attorney and an accountant.

How it works: If you or someone you are responsible for becomes mentally or physically disabled, consider consulting an attorney who specializes in law for the aging and/or disabled immediately. If you have assets and/or several sources of income, consider also engaging an accountant. The fees may be well worth every penny. The laws change state by state concerning which assets of the family (family home, other property, annuities, retirement funds, etc.) can or must be available to pay for long term care or charges for catastrophic illness before any government assistance is made available. Capital gains taxes apply to assets sold to pay bills. Disability benefits provided by an employer's contribution are also subject to regular income tax. Because of the complex impact of changes made necessary by disability, consult an attorney and/or accountant before making any major financial decisions.

Tip # 2: Contact your insurance company quickly.

How it works: Explain your situation to your insurance carrier immediately after disability occurs. In many cases, the carrier will assign a personal contact to be your aide and intermediary with the carrier. That person can be a gold mine of help with claims and expenses.

Tip # 3: Consider applying for disability benefits under Social Security. Note two basic types of disability programs.

How it works: The two basic types of disability programs under Social Security (SS) are Social Security disability benefits and Supplemental Security Income (SSI). Eligibility for Social Security benefits is based on money you may have paid into the Social Security system while you worked. Eligibility requires Social Security work credits. Tips # 4 through # 10 apply to Social Security disability benefits. Eligibility for Supplemental Security Income (SSI) is based on having low income and low assets and does not require Social Security work credits. (For specific income limits for eligibility, see SUPPLEMENTAL SECURITY INCOME.) Tips # 11 through # 14 apply to SSI. In some cases, you may receive both Social Security benefits and SSI as long as your total income is not so high that you are ineligible for SSI. Social Security rules are complex, lengthy, and subject to change. Do not rely solely on advice from social workers, health care providers, or this book. This tip and those that follow are only an overview. Contact Social Security (with your number in hand) at 1-800-772-1213 to discuss your particular situation or to set up an appointment with your local SS office.

Tip # 4: If you are disabled and if you have paid into the Social Security system during a certain number of years of work, you and sometimes other members of your family may be eligible for disability benefits.

How it works: You may be eligible for Social Security Disability benefits (1) if you meet SS definition of disability and (2) if you have enough work credits to qualify. Social Security considers you disabled if you are unable to do *any kind of work for which you are suited* and if this inability is expected to last for at least a year or to result in death. Social Security does not pay for partial or short-term disability. The Disability Determination Office in your state determines whether your disability meets its definition. If you are now working and earning $500 or more a month you are generally not considered disabled. Your condition must be severe. Also, certain kinds and degrees of impairment are on a list of conditions that automatically qualify as disabilities. If your condition is not on that list, the Disability Determination Office will determine if you can do the same work you did in the last fifteen years and if you can do any other kind of work considering your age, education, experience and skills. If you cannot, your claim of disability will usually be approved. If you worked in the past and paid into the Social Security system through payroll deductions, you may have earned enough credits to be eligible for disability benefits. In 1992, you receive one Social Security credit for every $570 of earnings with a maximum of 4 credits per year so that full-time workers generally earn 4 credits a year. If you are 31 years or older you would need the same number of credits as you would need for retirement—for most people that totals 40 credits—and you generally must have earned 20 of the credits in the last 10 years before you were disabled. If you were younger than 31 when you became disabled, fewer credits are necessary. The amount of your Social Security benefits depends on how much you have paid into the system.

For more information or to apply for Social Security disability benefits, call, visit, or write your local Social Security office. Or call toll-free 1-800-772-1213 between 7 a.m. and 7 p.m. Central time on business days to speak to a Social Security representative. Have your Social Security number ready. Also, for more details ask for the Social Security publication called "Disability," available free of charge.

Tip # 5: Children or spouses of those who qualify for Social Security disability benefits may often receive benefits.

How it works: Unmarried children including step-children, adopted children and, in some cases, grandchildren of those who qualify for Social Security disability benefits may also receive benefits. To qualify, a child must be under 18 years old or under 19 if a full time high school student. Disabled children over age 18 who became disabled before age 22 may also receive benefits based on a parent's eligible disability. A spouse who is 62 or older may receive benefits or a spouse of any age who is caring for a child under 16 or disabled and also receiving disability checks. Family members who qualify for benefits based on the eligibility of a disabled worker do not need work credits of their own.

Tip # 6: If you are disabled, aged 50 or more, and your spouse or ex-spouse has died, you may be eligible for Social Security disability benefits based on your deceased spouse's work credits.

How it works: If your spouse had sufficient work credits before he/she died, and you are disabled and 50 years old or more, you may qualify for Social Security disability benefits. Your disability must have started before your spouse died or within seven years after his/her death. (If you have been caring for the children and receiving disability checks, you are eligible if you become disabled before those checks end or within seven years after they end.) If you are divorced from your deceased spouse, you are also eligible for the same benefits as a widow or widower provided the marriage lasted ten years or longer.

Tip # 7: Apply for Social Security disability as soon as you are disabled and plan for a waiting period.

How it works: You should apply for Social Security disability benefits as soon as you are disabled or foresee being disabled within several weeks. The application process takes from 60 to 90 days. You must be considered disabled for a five month waiting period before you are entitled to benefits. Benefits start with the date of entitlement, which is the first month after the five month waiting period has been served. Once disability is approved, benefits will be paid back to the date of entitlement. To avoid further delays, have these items ready when you apply: your social security number, proof of age for you and any family members applying for benefits based on your disability, names, addresses, and phone numbers of doctors and health providers that treated you and dates of treatment, a summary of your work for the last 15 years, a copy of your W-2 form or federal tax return for the last year, and dates of former marriages if your spouse is applying.

Tip # 8: If your claim of disability is denied, you can appeal.

How it works: If your claim of disability is denied and you disagree with the decision, there are four levels of appeal and the Social Security office will help you with the paperwork. You have 60 days from the time you receive a decision to file an appeal to the next level. First, you may ask for a reconsideration by evaluators who did not make the original decision. If still unsatisfied, you may apply for a hearing before a judge. Third, an Appeals Council will review your case to decide if there was an issue the judge did not address. Finally, you may appeal to a Federal Civil Court.

Tip # 9: You can earn money working and still receive Social Security disability benefits under certain circumstances.

How it works: Social Security disability rules include work incentives so that people on disability whose conditions are improving can begin to work again. For example, a Trial Work Period allows you to earn as much as you can in 9 months (not necessarily consecutive) without affecting your benefits. After the Trial Work Period your earnings are evaluated. If your earnings do not average more than $500 a month, benefits will usually continue. If earnings do average more than $500 a month, benefits will continue for another 3-month grace period before they stop. For an additional 36 months, if you are still disabled, you will be eligible to receive a monthly benefit without a new application for any month your earnings drop below $500 and continued Medicare coverage.

For more information about SS work incentives ask your local Social Security office for the booklet "Working While Disabled...How Social Security Can Help." Or order it by calling 1-800-772-1213.

Tip # 10: If you are eligible for Social Security disability benefits, prepare for a possible gap in medical insurance coverage.

How it works: When you have been getting disability benefits for two years, you will automatically be enrolled in Medicare regardless of your age. (See MEDICARE.) However, your total wait for Medicare coverage will be almost two and a half years from the onset of disability because you must wait five months from onset of disability to receive your first check. In this gap, you may have difficulty maintaining insurance coverage. Note that coverage from a group medical insurance you may have had through your previous employer may be extended under COBRA regulations. (See COBRA.) Extended coverage under COBRA, when available, is not required to cover more than 18 months (36 months for dependents) after the change in employment so you may still have a year to cover in some other way. Another possibility may be an individual, group, or HMO plan which does not deny coverage to people with pre-existing conditions. (See INSURANCE and HMOs.) Also, if your financial need is great, you may qualify for Supplemental Security Insurance (SSI) and/or Medicaid for which there is no waiting period. (See Tip # 9 and MEDICAID.)

Tip # 11: If you are eligible for Medicare and have little income or resources, ask about the Qualified Medicare Beneficiary (QMB) program.

How it works: If you get Medicare for any reason including disability and you have low income and few resources, you may have your Medicare Part B premiums paid for under the Qualified Medicare Beneficiary (QMB) program. (QMB generally has higher qualifying income than Medicaid, which also pays Medicare Part B premiums.) Ask your local Social Security office for the fact sheet "You Should Know About QMB," Publication No. 05-10079. Or call 1-800-772-1213.

Tip # 12: If you are 65 and older, disabled, or blind and have low income and few assets, you may be eligible for Supplemental Security Income (SSI).

How it works: Medical requirements for disability benefits are the same for SSI as for Social Security and the procedures for determining disability are the same. Children as well as adults can get SSI benefits because of disability or blindness. There is no work credit requirement and no waiting period before you may receive disability benefits under SSI. However, processing your claim sometimes takes as long as six months. Apply immediately upon eligibility because, in contrast to Social Security disability payments which pay for the time the disability prevented you from working, SSI pays only from the date you filed. It is good to send a letter to Social Security establishing a protected filing date while you are waiting for your appointment. For the address and to make application and arrange an appointment, call 1-800-772-1213. Eligibility for SSI requires demonstration of financial need. SSI looks at your income and what you own. It does not usually count all of your income nor does it count food stamps and certain other assistance. It does not count the home you live in or some of your possessions including, usually, your car. You may also set aside some money for a work goal without reduction of your SSI payments. (See Tip # 14.) And you may work as long as your total income does not exceed a certain amount. The amount of income you may have each month and still qualify for SSI depends upon where you live. Call 1-800-772-1213 to find out the income limits in your state.

For more information ask your local Social Security office for Publication no. 05-11000 called "SSI," or order it by calling 1-800-772-1213.

Tip # 13: If you are eligible for SSI, you may be able to get Medicare premiums paid, Medicaid, food stamps, and/or other social services. (See MEDICAID and FOOD STAMPS.)

How it works: If you qualify for SSI, you may also qualify for Medicaid. In some states, application for Medicaid is done automatically for all SSI applicants and the eligibility criteria are the same; in other states SSI applicants have to make separate application for Medicaid. You may also apply for Food Stamps and other social services and these will not count as income in figuring SSI eligibility.

Tip # 14: If you are eligible for SSI, consider setting up an SSI approved plan to become self-supporting.

How it works: Generally, if the money you save becomes higher than a certain amount, you may become ineligible for SSI. But this should not discourage you from saving toward a job goal, because money set aside for a job goal may not be counted when SSI eligibility is figured. If you make a plan to become self-supporting and it is approved by the Social Security Administration, then you can set aside money to help you reach the goal. For example, you could set aside money to buy a computer to start a business at home or to get training for a job you could do even with your disability. That money would not affect your eligibility for SSI. Social Security staff will even help you write an acceptable plan.

Tip # 15: Look into all disability programs for which you may be eligible.

How it works: Look into all disability programs for which you may be eligible such as workers' compensation (including black lung) or disability benefits from certain federal, state, local governments, civil service, or military programs. Note that, according to federal regulations, total combined payments to you and your family from Social Security and any of these other programs may not exceed 80% of your average current earnings before becoming disabled. If your combined income from disability benefits totals more than this limit, Social Security disability payments will be reduced so that your disability income is within the limit. You may have a private disability plan that you have paid for. Any benefits you derive from such a plan is not considered in figuring your maximum benefit allowable under Social Security. A private disability plan may have a different and possibly more liberal definition of disability and may pay benefits when Social Security will not. (See INSURANCE.)

Tip # 16: If your need for Medicaid/SSI (Supplemental Security Income) is urgent, ask for special expediting of your application and establish a protected filing date.

How it works: The process of evaluating your disability may take six months. If you are very ill or dying or have other urgent need, call the Social Security toll-free number 1-800-772-1213. Explain your urgency and ask that your application receive special expediting. The Social Security staff can make an appointment for you near where you live and arrange for special handling to speed up the process.

Tip # 17: If you are not eligible for Medicare or Medicaid, use all your resources to find financial help.

How it works: If you are not eligible for either Medicare or Medicaid, use your insurance carrier contact, your lawyer and/or accountant, your employer benefits contact and your local Human Resources Department to find out exactly what is the extent of financial help. Then use those benefits to buy time to figure out the best long term solution for your family. Start early. These things take time to work out. Don't do anything in haste. (Your Human Resource Department is listed under your state listings in the phone book or use the general information number for your state listed under GENERAL INFORMATION, Tip # 1.)

Tip # 18: If there are two incomes in the family, consider filing separate income tax returns.

How it works: If there are two incomes in the family, consider filing separate tax returns so that all medical expenses can be charged to the disabled income and significantly reduce the tax bill. Ask your doctor to write a prescription for every health care need—equipment, home health care, home modification, everything related to the disability—and save these as documentation to support your tax claims.

Tip # 19: Consider writing an advance directive or other legal document to guide caretakers in making health care decisions in the event you cannot.

How it works: Advance directives make known to family and health care providers what measures you want taken about your health care and/or financial affairs in case you are unable mentally or physically to make these decisions now or in the future. Consider making a legally binding durable power of attorney, a separate medical power of attorney, a temporary power of attorney and/or a living will or health care declaration. These documents may protect the caregiver against unwanted "extraordinary measures" to keep you alive and allow the caregiver to continue to take care of financial obligations when you cannot because of disability. Make any document detailed, extensive, and all inclusive. Laws concerning these legal documents vary from state to state. Consult an attorney.

Tip # 20: NETWORK!

How it works: Don't be bashful, proud, private, or wimpy! Develop and use a network of people in the same boat as you—disabled or families of the disabled. Get hints for how to cope and emotional support. Share resources. Go to see someone else's house adapted for the disabled before you adapt yours. Get and give tips. Ask for names or recommendations for nursing or home health care aides so you won't have to pay an agency to find one. Also, touch base with every friend you have and tell them what you need—visits, an hour of time off for the caretaker, or a gift of their professional service you may need. When friends say, "Tell me what I can do to help," tell them.

DOCTORS, CHOOSING (See also COMMUNITY HEALTH CENTERS.)

Tip # 1: For primary adult care, choose a doctor in family, general practice, or internal medicine, not a specialist. For children choose a pediatrician.

How it works: Specialists usually charge more than doctors in primary care. Specialists are usually more experienced in the areas of their specialty than in seeing "the big picture." A specialist is not a "better" doctor but a different kind of doctor that you generally don't need for most illnesses.

Quality check: If, however, you have a persistent condition that defies treatment or an unusual condition your doctor cannot identify or does not seem to know much about, seek a referral to a specialist.

Tip # 2: If you are choosing a new doctor, consider asking him/her to postpone a complete physical exam, when appropriate.

How it works: Some doctors want to give you a complete physical exam before they take you on as a patient. This exam may cost from

$150 to $800 and it may not be covered by your insurance. The exam gives doctors important information which, in some cases, they may need to treat you, but it may not turn up any new information that was not in the records from your previous doctor or from your files. If you don't have money for this exam or if you're not sure you want to stay with this doctor, consider asking the doctor to postpone the exam. A less expensive way to start a relationship with a new doctor is with a short office visit, either when you are sick or when you are not sick but want to get to know the doctor. If this doctor turns out to be one you want to stay with, you can then consider a physical exam at an appropriate time.

Quality check: A physical exam if you have not had one in several years may be part of maintaining good health. The extent and frequency of routine physical exams is controversial even among doctors.

Tip # 3: Consider a doctor whose offices are in unpretentious buildings or in areas where rents and other costs may be lower.

How it works: A doctor may charge lower fees if his/her office expenses are lower. Very swanky new offices in the high rent district may not mean better care but they may mean higher fees. If you are considering driving several miles into town or to a new suburban office complex, consider driving in a different direction, into a small town or rural area, for example, to a doctor who can make a living charging less. Compare fees carefully because the relationship between total office costs and individual fees are unpredictable. Compare the fees you are most likely to use often, for example, simple office visits, because a fee may be relatively high for one procedure and relatively low for another.

Quality check: Wherever you look for a doctor, make your list from recommendations from patients and health care providers.

Tip # 4: Ask for a list of fees per procedure in the office of a doctor you are considering.

How it works: You will not know, of course, what procedures you and you family may need in the future, but you will expect to pay the basic office visit fee many times. Compare this fee and fees for any other specific services you anticipate using with the fees of other doctors. The American Medical Association (AMA) has recommended its members post fees where patients can see them; if fees are not posted ask for them. This inquiry may require a trip to the doctor's office. (Phone inquiries are not always welcomed.) A visit may be desirable so you can judge the atmosphere and efficiency of the office before selecting a doctor.

Quality check: Fees are based less on the quality of care you get from a doctor than on the doctor's office expenses, debts, etc. Compare fees, however, only from those doctors who have been recommended to you by other patients or medical providers and have appropriate training for the services you are seeking. See also Tip # 8.

Tip # 5: If you have health insurance or Medicare, compare the fees of doctors you are considering with the "reasonable and customary" fee scale your insurance company uses for several basic services you might use.

How it works: If your policy pays, for example, 80% of the doctor's "reasonable and customary" charges, the difference between "reasonable and customary" charges and your doctor's fees will be your responsibility to pay (along with copayments and deductibles). Ask your insurance company for a sampling from their "reasonable and customary" list.

Tip # 6: If your income is limited, consider getting primary care from a community health center.

How it works: Since 1975 the federal government has funded qualified community health centers and migrant health centers in hundreds of communities. Primary health care is made available to all community residents, regardless of their financial or insurance status. Usually, charges are reduced on a sliding scale for patients with incomes less than a certain amount. Patients who can afford to pay are expected to pay. Insurance companies are billed on behalf of patients with coverage. Medicare and Medicaid patients are welcome. Federally subsidized health centers must, by law, serve populations that are identified by the Public Health Service as medically underserved such as those living in certain low income or rural areas or populations with special needs such as homelessness or AIDS.

To find a community health center near you see the list of the more than 650 federally funded community health centers and migrant centers under COMMUNITY HEALTH CENTERS. For more information, write to the National Association of Community Health Centers at 1330 New Hampshire Ave., NW, Suite 122, Washington, DC 20036.

Tip # 7: For free printed information on primary care, call Primary Care Information at 703-821-8955.

How it works: Primary Care Information offers materials on primary health care, Migrant Health Centers, and clinical care, ambulatory care, and financial management.

Tip # 8: To review a doctor's qualifications, contact the American Medical Association (AMA).

How it works: The AMA will provide information about a doctor's professional qualifications if a consumer identifies the doctor by full name, office address, and specialty. Write to AMA Physician Data Services, 515 N. State St., Chicago, IL 60610.

DOCTOR, FEES

Tip # 1: Ask your doctor if he/she will treat you for the amount considered "reasonable and customary" by your insurance company.

How it works: Ask your doctor if he/she will treat you for what your insurance considers "reasonable and customary" fees so that you can get the maximum coverage for that treatment. If not, perhaps another doctor will.

Tip # 2: Negotiate fees. Ask to pay less.

How it works: Don't be afraid to tell your doctor you are unable to pay stated fees. If fees seem unreasonably high or if you cannot pay them in any case, tell the doctor. He/she would probably prefer to take less than to lose your business. Negotiating fees is particularly fruitful if the doctor is starting out and still has a skimpy practice or if he/she is in an area or community where fewer patients are available, for example, a pediatrician in a neighborhood where families that used to have children have grown older or a general practitioner in an area of town from which families have moved further out. Medicine is a business and some doctors will make deals, but you have to ask—preferably before you receive the doctor's service.

Tip # 3: Ask for "professional courtesy."

How it works: Many doctors offer "professional courtesy" to others in the health care professions, another way of saying doctors offer professional discounts. Nurses, medical technologists and technicians, social workers, and others in the industry have received discounts of 10% to 20% from doctors, just by mentioning their profession. If your job is remotely connected to health care, ask if you are eligible for a discount.

Tip # 4: Work for a doctor.

How it works: If you can type, file, enter data, make appointments, you may be able to get a job in a doctor's office. If you have health care training so much the better. The doctor you work for will generally give you his/her services free of charge. Pick a highly recommended physician in general practice or in a specialty you need.

Tip # 5: Get advice—and maybe a prescription from your doctor by telephone.

How it works: Sometimes you are sick and you know what you have because you have had it several times before. All you need is a prescription. Or sometimes your symptoms are very specific and easy for the doctor to diagnose. In such cases, the doctor may be comfortable advising and/or prescribing by phone. This service is almost always free and also saves the time and trouble of any office visit.

Quality check: If you can't state clearly what is wrong or your ailment seems very serious, you may be better off seeing your doctor. The doctor cannot give any better treatment by phone than the information you give him/her.

Tip # 6: Tell the doctor's office nurse your problem by phone.

How it works: Nurses are very familiar with medical treatment and in routine cases may suggest an easy or inexpensive alternative to a doctor's visit. Nurses can help you make the decision whether to come in to the office or not. Also, sometimes they may offer office services that do not require a consultation with the doctor, such as changing dressings on wounds or checking blood pressure. Physicians assistants and nurse practitioners also may be available for similar consultation and, in some cases, may be able to make an appointment to see you without a doctor at a lower cost.

Quality Check: While nurses can be very helpful and sometimes save you a trip to the doctor, when in doubt, be safer and see the doctor.

DOWNS SYNDROME

Tip # 1: Contact the National Downs Syndrome Congress at 1-800-232-NDSC.

How it works: The NDS Congress provides a journal ten times a year, pertinent publications, a hotline with up-to-date information on care of Downs Syndrome patients, and a yearly convention which offers education and networking experience.

Tip # 2: Contact the National Downs Syndrome Society at 1-800-221-4602.

How it works: The Society offers free information packets and will make referrals to local programs for the newborn and older child.

DRUG (See DRUG ABUSE or MEDICATIONS.)

DRUG ABUSE (See also ALCOHOL ABUSE.)

Tip # 1: Contact Cocaine Anonymous at 1-800-347-8998.

How it works: Cocaine Anonymous is a national organization with a program of self-help for users of cocaine who want help for recovery. The national office can give you the number of a chapter near you and send you literature about the program.

Tip # 2: Contact Narcotics Anonymous at 818-780-3951.

How it works: Narcotics Anonymous (NA) is a national organization with a program of self-help users of narcotics who want help for recovery. The national office can give you the phone number of a chapter near you and send you literature about the program.

To get the number of a local chapter of Narcotics Anonymous without paying for a call, call the Cocaine Hotline at 1-800-CO-CAINE and ask for a chapter of NA in your area.

Tip # 3: Contact the National Drug Information and Referral Line of the National Institute on Drug Abuse at 1-800-662-HELP.

How it works: Counselors at the National Drug Information and Referral Line give callers individual recommendations, information, and referral for prevention, treatment, and rehabilitation of drug abuse.

Tip # 4: For publications on drug abuse, contact the National Clearinghouse for Alcohol and Drug information at 1-800-729-6686.

How it works: The National Clearinghouse for Alcohol and Drug Information is a service of the National Institute on Drug Abuse. Ask for the most recent catalog of publications free of charge or publications on specific subjects related to drugs, for example, drug testing. Free information is available from the National Clearinghouse and you can speak to a specialist about a specific problem. Lists of support organizations by state and by special emphasis are also provided.

Tip # 5: Contact the American Council for Drugs at 1-800-488-DRUG.

How it works: The Council offers information on drug education and has a catalog of materials available.

Tip # 6: For information about drugs in the workplace, contact the Drug-Free Workplace Helpline at 1-800-843-4971.

How it works: You can get a free consultation in which counselors walk you through the steps of establishing a drug-free work environment according the size and type of business you are in.

Tip # 7: Contact the "Just Say No" Kids' Club at 1-800-258-2766.

How it works: The national Club office can show you how to start a local club for 7-14 year olds, which offers education and support for resisting the temptation to use drugs.

DRUGS (See DRUG ABUSE or MEDICATIONS.)

DUANE SYNDROME (See RARE DISEASES.)

DUBOWITZ SYNDROME (See RARE DISEASES.)

DUHRING DISEASE (See RARE DISEASES.)

DYING (See also HOSPICE.)

Tip # 1: Consider caring for a terminally ill loved one at home.

How it works: On the average, the largest amount people are ever charged for health care is for the last 10 days of life. Intensive care and last resort procedures are often the most costly, running into tens of thousands of dollars. When a patient is terminally ill, many procedures are known to be of no use except to make the family feel they have done everything. Sometimes all that is needed and wanted by the patient is medication for uncomfortable symptoms and pain which can often be administered at home. Necessary services by home medical programs or hospice care are usually far less costly than hospitalization. Even if family members have to take a leave of absence from work to care for a dying person, the savings realized through home care often are greater than the loss of wages for that time period.

Quality check: The terminally ill usually want two things: freedom from pain and to be at home. The quality of life at home is often not only better but far less costly. The presence of family and friends is a comfort that cannot be bought.

Tip # 2: Consider hospice care for the terminally ill patient.

How it works: Once a patient is considered a few months from death, usually six, by a doctor, hospice care may be appropriate. Generally, the patient must not be on radiation or chemotherapy because the focus of hospice care is on dying in peace and dignity rather than on attempts at recovery. Drugs are given only to ease symptoms and keep the patient comfortable. Also, the patient is not subjected to repeated blood tests or being moved to diagnostic or treatment centers. The hospice program director can talk with the patient's doctor about whether it is time to abandon more aggressive treatment and seek more peaceful final months without stating a specific life-expectancy for the patient. Hospice care is sometimes home treatment by visiting nurses and other trained personnel. A full range of services may also be provided including counselors to help plan for changing needs, chaplains, and volunteers. Some provide 24-hour emergency service as well as periodic visiting care. A relative or other caretaker is sometimes required to be with the patient on a full-time basis and work with the visiting hospice workers. Other hospice programs are home-like in-patient facilities where the patient lives and dies. Hospice care is less expensive than hospitalization. Accredited hospices accept private insurance, Medicare, and Medicaid. In addition, many hospices are non-profit and charge on a sliding scale; services are rendered regardless of ability to pay. Find hospice programs in your community by consulting with the local hospital social worker, by interviewing hospices found in the yellow pages of the phone book, or by referral from national organizations concerned with hospice care. (See Tips #3 and #4.) Investigate several hospice programs. At in-patient facilities, ask about the waiting list and consider putting a patient with little hope of recovery on the waiting list even before such care is necessary.

Quality check: Ask the hospice program you are considering about their licensing as a hospice. Ask also if it is Medicare certified; if so, it has been approved by federal standards. Look for accreditation with the National Hospice Organization (NHO). Or call the NHO at 1-800-658-8898 to ask for accredited hospice programs in your community. If the patient is a child, Children's Hospice International can give you appropriate information. Call 1-800-242-4453.

Tip # 3: For information and referrals call Hospice Link at 1-800-658-8898.

How it works: Hospice Link is a referral line of the Hospice Education Institute, a non-profit organization which offers training seminars to hospice professionals and books on the subject. Hospice Link staff will answer questions and refer to hospice programs in your area.

Tip # 4: Contact the National Hospice Organization at 1-800-658-8898.

How it works: The National Hospice Organization sets accreditation standards for hospices in the U.S. and makes referrals to accredited hospices by location. Staff will answer individual questions and mail information on request.

Tip # 5: Look for other hospice-like programs in your community.

How it works: Only programs that meet certain definitions and requirements may use the designation "hospice," but other programs for the dying may be appropriate for you. For example, in one community a Catholic charity facility provides a home for those dying from cancer only. It is not considered a hospice because it does not meet the requirement of treating other terminal conditions, but its program is excellent. Ask the local hospital social worker for suggestions.

Tip # 6: Consider writing "advance directives" concerning your health care should you become unable to make such decisions yourself.

How it works: Enormous unnecessary bills mount up when a person who is dying is given futile treatment to prolong life even when there is no hope of recovery. You can write "advance directives" or documents that specify what kinds or levels of medical care you want for yourself if you are terminally ill and unable to make a lucid decision at the time. In such documents you may instruct your family and medical health providers not to use specific measures or equipment to sustain your life. You may ask that you not be resuscitated if your heart stops or that you not be put on a breathing machine, for example. By limiting extreme measures to prolong life, you will also limit the burden of unnecessary costs to your estate. There are several kinds of documents that can be drawn up to assure that your wishes be respected concerning health care in terminal illness. Such documents include "durable power of attorney," "temporary power of attorney," "medical power of attorney," and a "living will." All of them may let your family and doctor know your wishes. Laws vary by state as to which documents, if any, are legally binding and which are merely instructive and under what conditions. Consult an attorney for individual advice. A source of information on advance directives is Choice in Dying, Inc., 250 West 57th St., New York, NY 10107. Or call 212-246-6973.

Quality check: Although hospital personnel may ask if you have made a living will, you are under no obligation to have one or to limit your treatment in terminal illness. However, if you worry that you will live on in suffering and meaninglessness, having control over the final medical procedures by means of a living will may relieve you of that concern. It will also relieve family members of the anguish of making such decisions themselves.

Tip # 7: Consider asking an objective knowledgeable person to help make decisions about health care for the terminally ill.

How it works: Sometimes the decisions about prolonged care for a terminally-ill patient are agonizing for a family. Sometimes some members of the family want to let a person die in peace and others want to do "whatever is possible." The family may feel enormous guilt for "giving up." Ask the patient's doctor for help with the decision. Also, the chaplain at a hospital is prepared to help resolve such conflict in a family; the social services department can also advise. Or ask a trusted family friend or clergyperson to lead the family to a decision.

Tip # 8: When a patient dies, the family is usually not responsible for unpaid medical bills.

How it works: When a patient dies, the estate will be billed for medical treatment not paid by health insurance or the patient. If the estate does not cover the remaining medical bills, family such as children or siblings are usually not responsible for paying, even though hospitals sometimes send bills to family members. In some states, however, the spouse is responsible.

DYSLEXIA (See also LANGUAGE DISORDERS.)

Tip # 1: Contact the Orton Dyslexia Society at 1-800-ABCD-123 (410-337-9459 in Maryland).

How it works: The Orton Dyslexia Society is a clearinghouse for information on dyslexia and gives referrals to local chapters.

DYSPHONIA, CHRONIC SPASMODIC (See RARE DISEASES.)

DYSTROPHIC EPIDERMOLYSIS

Tip # 1: Contact the Dystrophic Epidermolysis Association at 212-995-2220 for information specific to this disease.

DYSTROPHY, DUCHENNE MUSCULAR (See RARE DISEASES.)

EATING DISORDERS

Tip # 1: Contact the National Association of Anorexia and Related Disorders at 708-831-3438.

How it works: The Association will send you free information, referrals, and support groups contacts.

Tip # 2: Check your insurance policy to see what coverage you have for treatment of eating disorders.

How it works: Although hospitalization or acute care for the physical aspects of an eating disorder like anorexia or bulimia may be covered, many insurance policies do not cover long-term treatment of the underlying disorder. Check your insurance policy before signing up for a program and ask program directors what assistance they can give you in planning payment.

ECZEMA

Tip # 1: Contact the Eczema Association for Science and Education at 503-228-4430 for information specific to this disease.

EDUCATION, PATIENT (See GENERAL INFORMATION or specific disease.)

ELDERLY (See AGING, HOME CARE, EMERGENCY, especially Tips 10-14)

EMERGENCY, DROP-IN, AND AFTER-HOURS (See also WALK-IN CLINIC.)

Tip # 1: Do not use the emergency room for non-emergencies.

How it works: The emergency room is the most expensive facility in which to seek medical care. When you are admitted to an emergency room at a hospital there is an immediate charge for use of the facility. A minimum of $50 to $79 is charged in one community in addition to charges for seeing a physician and for the treatment provided. It has been estimated that well over a third of minor medical problems have been handled unnecessarily—

and at unnecessary cost—at emergency rooms equipped for much more serious emergencies. Many people think the emergency room will provide quicker care, but for non-urgent problems, this is unlikely. People entering the emergency room go through a *triage* evaluation whereby the most urgent problems are treated first and the less urgent cases must wait. You will get quick service in an emergency room only if your case is very urgent or the staff at that time is not very busy. The average wait for emergency treatment nationwide has been reported to be two hours. Consider that non-emergency traffic in the emergency area clogs the facility and makes it harder to render treatment for true emergencies. An estimated 60% to 80% of emergency traffic is for procedures that could have been done at a doctor's office.

Quality check: There are certain symptoms such as chest pain or disorientation and confusion which can be warning signs of a true emergency. In such cases an immediate visit to an emergency room may save your life.

Tip # 2: Familiarize yourself *now* with what your insurance policy says about emergencies.

How it works: Your insurance policy may treat emergencies differently from non-emergency problems. It may pay 100% of emergency costs compared to a smaller amount, usually 80%, of non-emergency treatment. Establishing the situation as an emergency is therefore important whether you go to an emergency room or a doctor's office. Your policy may require notification within a certain number of hours of admission in order for you to qualify for full insurance coverage. You and other responsible persons should be familiar with these provisions to make the best decisions in an emergency.

Tip # 3: Familiarize yourself *now* with your nearest emergency center *before* you have a truly urgent need for treatment.

How it works: Knowing where your nearest hospital is may not be enough in a true emergency. You may have to circle the hospital to find the emergency entrance, impeded by traffic and lights. Learning the best approach could save precious seconds. Actually driving up to the emergency room and seeing the actual doors could also help. Go in and locate the admissions clerk. Know what you should do in an emergency all the way to the point when a medical staff member would take over.

Quality check: Emergency centers are rated Level 1, Level 2, and Level 3 by the Joint Commission on Health Care Organizations (JCHO). A comprehensive trauma center, Level 3, the best equipped facility for a serious emergency, will have specialists such as cardiologists and brain surgeons on the premises at all times. Emergency centers rated 1 and 2 can handle many kinds of emergencies but may not have specialists on hand for some needs. An estimated one-third of the nation's serious injuries are handled each year in medical facilities that were not adequately equipped or staffed. Find out which is which in your community by calling nearby facilities and asking what rating they have received for emergency treatment. Or call the Emergency Health section of your state health department.

Tip # 4: Familiarize yourself *now* with all the emergency and after-hours options available to you for use outside of office hours.

How it works: In some communities there are only two options: doctors' offices, which are closed evenings, nights, and weekends, and the emergency room at local hospitals where a stiff fee is charged upon admission. More and more however, communities are offering other clinic situations less costly than the emergency room.

Free-standing minor emergency centers, both private and public, are found in almost any community. Hospitals are also offering lower cost alternatives to the emergency room. One community hospital has an emergency room staffed with physicians and equipped to handle urgent and serious medical problems, a "quick track" emergency service, and a family care center. The "quick track" area is the best place to go for minor emergencies that would receive low priority in the emergency room. In the "quick track" facility, nurse practitioners or physician's assistants see and treat common, uncomplicated problems under the supervision of a physician. The family care center provides after-hours care from a physician on a drop-in basis. The "quick-track" facility and the family care center charge similar fees; the hours are different, one operating from 8 a.m. to 8 p.m., the second from 11 a.m. to 11 p.m. The only period that medical care at regular daytime prices is not available at this hospital is from 11 p.m. to 8 a.m. Knowing the hours, prices, and kinds of treatment available at all the facilities in your community and putting a chart of these on your family bulletin board or refrigerator could help you select the most appropriate care for unexpected medical problems.

Quality check: Many people, even doctors, will tell you horror stories about missed diagnoses by personnel at various medical facilities, adding "Don't go to a minor emergency center (or wherever) because I know someone who died from ...." Unfortunately, there are also horror stories about going to regular doctors' offices, to emergency rooms, and to specialists. Some of the problems cited—whether involving a para-medic or a specialist—actually stem from patients not telling the physician or para-medic all pertinent information such as other conditions they have or other medications they are taking or some activity associated with the disorder. No one is a mind-reader. If you have a medical condition, carry a copy of a doctor's description of your problem in your wallet to show any medical person who treats you. Also, tell medical personnel in an emergency facility all the medicines you are taking (either prescriptions or over-the-counter medicines), any alcohol or other substance you may have taken, and unusual activity or food you have recently been exposed to.

Tip # 5: Call your regular family physician for less urgent emergencies, even after hours.

How it works: Your family physician may be the best person to call after business hours. The problem is, of course, the office is closed evenings, weekends, and holidays, when, it often seems, you are most likely to get sick or injured. But almost all doctors have emergency numbers, beepers, and other ways to be reached. Your doctor or a trusted substitute should always be on call. You may be reticent to take advantage of a doctor's after-hours availability, but that's what the doctor on call is for. He/she may advise you or prescribe over the phone.

Quality check: It was a physician specialist who told us to call your regular doctor before going to a clinic where no one knows you. He said, "If your doctor won't talk to you or see you after hours in an emergency, get another doctor." He preferred a regular doctor prescribing over the phone without seeing you to an emergency doctor who sees you but does not know your case. Of course, in urgent emergencies such as severe bleeding, losing consciousness, or chest pain, go directly to an emergency room and have someone call your doctor while you are on the way.

Tip # 6: In an emergency room, give the admitting clerk the most urgent description of your problem that is truthful to qualify your treatment for insurance coverage as an emergency.

How it works: Many insurance policies pay 100% of costs associated with an emergency but less for a non-emergency. The emergency status often depends on what you first tell the admitting clerk in an emergency room. The admitting clerk, in the interest of speed and priority, tends to write down the first thing you say. If you come in with chest pains, fearful you are having a heart attack, but say apologetically, "It may just be indigestion, but I'm having chest pains and I'm afraid it may be the beginning of a heart attack," the clerk may write down *"Indigestion, chest pains."* If it turns out you have indigestion or some other minor problem, your insurance is not likely to consider that an emergency. On the other hand if you come in and say assertively to the clerk, "I think I'm having a heart attack," which is what you truly fear or you wouldn't be there, the clerk may write down "heart attack." The insurance company, no matter what the outcome, will more likely pick up on the original label and pay 100% as for an emergency.

Tip # 7: Notify—or allow another responsible person to notify— your insurance company immediately about your use of an emergency service.

How it works: Many insurance policies require precertification, that is, a statement of your intention to use a hospital in time for the insurance company to evaluate the procedure and affirm that it is covered. In the case of emergencies, policies are somewhat more lenient, giving you a certain number of hours (typically 48 hours) to let the company know what you have done. But if you do not let them know you are having emergency treatment within the time allowed, the company may not pay for the procedure or may pay a lesser amount of the bill. Exceptions may be made for life-threatening emergencies.

Tip # 8: Carry your insurance card at all times.

How it works: In an emergency you may be unconscious or at least distracted and you will not be thinking about insurance coverage or medical costs. The hospital personnel, however, will have these things on their mind. Carrying your insurance card will enable you, first of all, to obtain treatment readily at the nearest or most appropriate hospital. Your insurance card will also enable you, another responsible person, or the hospital to obtain the best insurance coverage for the emergency procedure.

Tip # 9: Obtain documentation for any emergency treatment denied payment as an emergency and resubmit it to the insurance company.

How it works: If you have had treatment for an emergency denied, the higher degree of coverage usually given a true emergency, and you think the lower coverage is not justified, explain this to the physician who treated you and ask him/her to redefine the treatment more accurately or to add additional information to reflect the emergency situation.

Tip # 10: For calling help in an emergency, use your local emergency number, 911 where the 911 system is in operation, or a private ambulance service.

How it works: The 911 system, where it is in operation, is considered the best single system for calling for emergency help and an ambulance. Never call it nine-eleven because small children will waste time searching for the eleven on the phone dial. Call your doctor only after 911 has answered because the call to a doctor can take precious time. A doctor's office is not set up for reporting emergencies.

Quality check: Check the average response time to 911 numbers in your area by calling the emergency medical system (EMS) at your fire department. If the fire department does not have this information, call the state EMS office which is probably found through your state health department. If the response time is more than nine minutes for 90% of its calls, you may want to consider using a private ambulance service and keep that number posted by your phone or taped to your phone.

Tip # 11: For an elderly or disabled person staying alone, consider subscribing to a personal emergency response system (PERS) to get help in an emergency.

How it works: A personal emergency response system is a calling system whereby pressing a button alerts a telephone center that a person is in trouble. Help can be called just from the one signal; talking is not necessary (though preferable). The personal emergency response system may help put off the day when more expensive custodial care may be necessary.

Quality check: The most uncertain part of the personal response system is whether the person who needs it actually attaches the button to him/herself or keeps it within easy reach at all times. Also, sometimes the service is slower than expected and actually causes a delay compared to 911 or other direct service. The button must be checked often for proper functioning, battery changes, etc. Sometimes the distance is too great from the system center for the radio waves from the button to make the proper contact. Be sure the system you are considering works *from the location you intend to use it.* A report comparing the features and prices of 20 devices is available from the American Association of Retired Persons (AARP). Ask for AARP's Product Report: PERS, order # D-12905. Mail your request to AARP Fulfillment (EE291) P.O. Box 22796, Long Beach, CA 90801-5796.

Tip # 13: Consider a portable telephone and/or speaker phone with remote control instead of a personal emergency response system for an elderly or disabled person staying alone.

How it works: A portable telephone whose receiver can be carried into the bathroom, down in the basement, out in the yard by an elderly or disabled person is often a less expensive but useful way to keep the person in touch with emergency facilities and other parties. Placed beside the tub or carried in the pocket, a portable phone can be a lifeline to an emergency service or other helpful person. One can be purchased for under $75 with no extra monthly charge. A speaker phone with a remote button the elderly or disabled person can carry in a pocket or around the neck may also provide phone service for emergencies.

Quality check: Portable phones are quite reliable; one needs only to remember to recharge them overnight. If the phone is not carried around, of course, it is less useful as an emergency calling device so people staying alone must remember to keep it beside them or carry it in a pocket or tied to a belt. Rental of portable phones is more expensive but the phone will be replaced free of charge periodically or when not working well, no questions asked. Note that a portable phone will not work if your electric power is out, while a regular phone will.

Tip # 14: Contact Medic Alert Foundation International at 1-800-ID-ALERT or 1-800-344-3226.

How it works: The Medic Alert Foundation provides a bracelet or necklace which a medic, ambulance attendant, or emergency room doctor can read. On the bracelet or necklace there is an 800 number to call to get your full health history and special precautions to be taken in your case. The initial fee for this service is $36.

Tip # 15: Get information on making an escape plan for a disabled person in case of fire.

How it works: All households should have an escape plan in case of fire. Such a plan is especially critical for a disabled person. A discussion of what a disabled person should do can be found in an article entitled "Staying Alive" from *Accent on Living*, volume 33, number 4, spring issue 1989, pages 74-78. To get this article call NARIC (National Rehabilitation Information Center) at 1-800-346-2742 or 301-588-9284. Ask for NARIC Accession Number J11221.

ENCEPHALITIS (See also TRAVEL.)

Tip # 1: For information on St. Louis encephalitis, call the Centers for Disease Control and Prevention (CDC) at 404-332-4555.

How it works: Outbreaks of this mosquito-borne virus occur occasionally in the United States. The CDC will give you recorded information on this serious but rare disease.

Tip # 2:. For information on Japanese encephalitis, call the Centers for Disease Control and Prevention (CDC) at 404-332-4555.

How it works: Japanese encephalitis is a mosquito-born disease common in rural areas of China, India, and other parts of Asia. Usually, only travelers need be concerned. Information on immunization is available through the CDC.

ENDOCRINE DISORDERS

Tip # 1: Consider participating in an experimental study of treatment of your endocrine disorder. See also STUDIES.

How it works: Experimental treatment studies often offer free treatment to patients who qualify as subjects. In particular, the Clinical Center of the National Institutes of Health in Bethesda, MD, has ongoing studies of many endocrine disorders including pituitary tumors, ambiguous genitalia, Cushings Syndrome, Nelson's Syndrome, congenital adrenal hyperplasia, adrenal insufficiency, growth hormone deficiency, premature ovarian failure, Turner Syndrome, hypophosphatamic rickets, precocious puberty, delayed puberty, hirsutism, and infertility. For information on getting into a study of experimental treatment at this and other institutions, see STUDIES.

ENDOCARDIAL FIBROELASTOSIS (See RARE DISEASES.)

ENDOMETRIOSIS

Tip # 1: For information contact the Endometriosis Association at 1-800-992-ENDO.

Tip # 2: Order the FDA reprint of "Endometriosis—Coping with a Mysterious Disease."

How it works: The Food and Drug Administration (FDA) provides current information in printed form on a wide range of subjects. For a copy of an article on endometriosis, order Publication # FDA92-1191. Write FDA, 5600 Fisher's Lane, Mail Code HFE-88, Room 1663, Rockville MD 20857 or call 301-443-3170.

EPIDERMOLYSIS BULLOSA (See RARE DISEASES.)

EPILEPSY

Tip # 1: Contact the Epilepsy Foundation of America at 1-800-332-1000.

How it works: The Epilepsy Foundation provides referrals to local affiliates, counseling, and support groups. Trained medical personnel may ask for a customized literature search. The Foundation also helps with legal problems involving rights of epileptics.

Tip # 2: Contact the National Easter Seals Society at 1-312-243-8400.

How it works: The National Easter Seals Society can advise you on treatment and other issues relevant to epilepsy. Write 2023 W. Ogden Ave., Chicago, IL 60602.

Tip # 3: Consider participating as a subject in a medical research study of epilepsy.

How it works: The National Institute of Neurological Disorders and Stroke (NINDS), one of the National Institutes of Health, supports an epilepsy research program at eleven centers across the country which occasionally seek patients for treatment studies. Contact the NINDS at 301-496-5924.

EPSTEIN-BARR VIRUS

Tip # 1: Call the Centers for Disease Control at 404-332-4555.

How it works: Recorded information about Epstein-Barr virus and about Epstein-Barr's relationship to chronic fatigue syndrome is available at this number 24-hours a day. Also, one of your phone menu options is to be put directly in touch with physicians who study this disease if you call between 8 a.m. and 4:30 p.m. Eastern time weekdays except federal holidays.

EQUIPMENT, HEALTH CARE (See also PHYSICAL THERAPY and REHABILITATION.)

Tip # 1: Consult a physical therapist about equipment needs and sources.

How it works: The physical therapist (PT) has access to books of equipment and sources both local and regional besides a wealth of experience. Talk to him/her about what equipment you will need, ways to cut costs, resources for getting equipment, what modifications of the house will be necessary. Other members of the medical team also have years of training and experience—use it!

Tip # 2: For free fact sheets and information on medical and rehabilitative equipment, call 1-800-346-2742.

How it works: ABLEDATA is a database that includes information on 15,000 assistive devices, both commercially produced and customized. In addition, ABLEDATA Fact Sheets on equipment are available free from the National Rehabilitation Information Center of the Department of Education. Fact sheet topics include van lifts, car seats, bath lifts, reclining bath seats, powered scooters, ramps, stairlifts, patient lifts, tilt-in-space wheelchairs, seat cushions, standing aids, modular seating components, assistive devices for arthritis, and funding for assistive technology. Most ABLEDATA publications are available in large-print, braille, cassette, and computer diskette.

For fact sheets or to ask individual questions, call the toll-free number above or 301-588-9284 between 8 a.m. and 6 p.m. Eastern time.

Tip # 3: Before buying equipment, talk to your insurance contact.

How it works: Insurance companies often have a list of local suppliers who will give a discount as a result of an insurance company's referral. You pay less and the insurance carrier pays less. Start with this list of suppliers and then shop for price.

Tip # 4: Get how-to information for modifying your house for a disabled person.

How it works: Needs assessors connected with a rehabilitation program have a lot of experience and can give you good suggestions. But don't accept every piece of advice without question. After all, it's your house. Modifications are expensive and affect the resale value of the house. Always ask why. Some suggestions may not apply to your lifestyle. For example, if you love wall to wall carpeting and you are advised to take it up so the wheel chair can roll, don't take it up, just get different wheels on the wheel chair. Before you buy equipment or adapt your house, go to someone else's house and see what works for them and what doesn't. Network!

Less Restrictive Housing Environments: Examples, Methods, Designs, and Guidelines for Improving New and Existing Housing is a how-to book on adapting the house and environment for the disabled person. Diagrams and descriptions cover vehicles, parking, doors, windows, kitchens, bathrooms, and bedrooms. For information on ordering this book, contact NARIC (National Rehabilitation Information Center at 1-800-346-2742 or 301-588-9284. Ask for NARIC Accession Number RO5715.

Tip # 5: Equipment or modifications to your house to accommodate a disabled person may represent a tax deduction. Get your doctor's prescription for them.

How it works: Medical expenses that total more than a certain amount may be used as deductions from your income when you pay income tax. Equipment and household modifications necessary for medical reasons count as medical deductions. Call the Internal Revenue Service for free details. Get your doctor's prescription for all equipment and modifications and save these as documentation for your tax returns.

Tip # 6: Medicare and, in most states, Medicaid cover some medically necessary home medical equipment but be sure the supplier accepts Medicare or Medicaid as payment in full.

How it works: Those 65 and older or under 65 but disabled enough to qualify for Social Security Disability Insurance (SSDI) are eligible—after two years of disability—for Medicare coverage which covers "durable medical equipment" (DME) like braces, artificial limbs and eyes, and internal devices. Needy persons who qualify for Supplemental Security Income (SSI) or Aid to Families with Dependent Children (AFDC) and, in some states, others whose medical expenses make them indigent may qualify for Medicaid. Medicaid coverage varies from state to state but in many states Medicaid covers prosthetics. If you qualify for and are enrolled in either Medicare or Medicaid, be sure that your dealer in prosthetics accepts Medicare or Medicaid (along with any copayments that may apply) as payment in full. Not all dealers accept Medicare or Medicaid assignment. Consider finding one that does. See also MEDICARE and MEDICAID.

Tip # 7: The Veterans Administration (VA) pays for equipment related to rehabilitation for eligible veterans.

How it works: For service-connected veterans, equipment necessary for overall medical or rehabilitative intervention is provided free. For non-service connected veterans with incomes below a certain level, such equipment is provided as available without charge or (for some categories of veterans) for a small copayment. Such equipment includes prosthetics, wheelchairs, hearing aids and other kinds of sensory or mobility equipment.

Tip # 8: Check your state's Workers' Compensation laws for help with equipment.

How it works: Many states require rehabilitation benefits of workers covered under Workers' Compensation policies. These benefits may include prosthetics and other equipment which might help return an injured person to work.

Tip # 9: Ask your state rehabilitation department if you qualify for equipment under the Rehabilitation Act of 1973 and its amendments.

How it works: The federal government through the states provides equipment to help working age people work again or to live independently. Some of these programs are called Federal/State Rehabilitation Title I, Vocational Rehabilitation Services Title VI, Supported Employment Title VII, Independent Living Title VIIC, and Independent Living (for the elderly blind). Ask which of these programs might apply to you. If you have difficulty finding the right number in the phone book, call the general information number for your state listed in this book under GENERAL INFORMATION, Tip #1.

Tip # 10: For young disabled children, equipment may be available through the Tax Equity and Fiscal Responsibility Act of 1982.

How it works: The Tax Equity and Fiscal Responsibility Act of 1982 (TEFRA) provides help for children from birth to age 6 who are disabled by the Supplemental Security Income (SSI) definition but who would be financially ineligible for SSI because of their parents' income. (See also DISABILITY.) This program provides services and equipment necessary to help the child remain in the home instead of an institution.

Tip # 11: Be creative.

How it works: Many self-help devices are quite simple to duplicate in a home work shop or by substitution with things you already have in your home but have been using for something else. Consult your physician for ideas and cautions when making equipment.

ERYTHROMELALGIA (See RARE DISEASES.)

EXAMINATION, PHYSICAL (See CHECK-UP, ROUTINE.)

EXERCISE (See FITNESS)

EXPERIMENTAL TREATMENT (See STUDIES OF EXPERIMENTAL TREATMENT.)

EXSTROPHY OF THE BLADDER (See RARE DISEASES.)

EYE CARE (See also BLINDNESS and DISABILITY.)

Tip # 1: Understand the difference between an optometrist and an ophthalmologist.

How it works: An ophthalmologist is an M.D. who specializes in diseases of the eye, their treatment, and eye surgery. An ophthalmologist will also prescribe corrective glasses. An optometrist is not an M.D. and specializes in fitting corrective glasses and contact lenses. An optometrist may be considerably less expensive than an ophthalmologist and as experienced in vision exams and lens fitting. So for routine vision checks or new glasses, consider going to the optometrist. And if any findings by the optometrist suggest disease, he/she should refer you to an ophthalmologist.

Quality check: A complete eye exam by an ophthalmologist every few years may detect a developing disease that an optometrist might not see.

Tip # 2: Consider getting vision screening tests from a health fair.

How it works: Health fairs held at hospitals, churches, drug stores, schools, and even shopping malls, advertised in the newspaper, very often include free vision screening. Make a point of checking your family's eyes once a year at a health fair free if you have no symptoms of eye problems.

Quality check: Usually health fair screenings are only vision checks and do not detect eye diseases that are not currently impairing vision.

Tip # 3: If you get a red area in the white of your eye indicating a hemorrhage, it will usually heal without treatment.

How it works: Hemorrhage in the white of the eye is one of the most common complaints that cause patients to visit their eye doctors but usually no treatment is necessary. It looks bad but it is usually not dangerous and it will heal on its own.

Tip # 4: If you have a sty on your eyelid, usually you can treat it as effectively with a hot compress as with medication.

How it works: Medications are usually less effective than moist heat and they cost more.

Tip # 5: For dry eyes, consider using over-the-counter drops for dry eyes instead of expensive medicine.

How it works: Over-the-counter medicine, some ophthalmologists say, is currently as effective as more expensive medicine, but avoid drops with a preservative.

Tip # 6: If you are a new user of contact lenses, consider lens insurance; if you are veteran, consider passing up lens insurance.

How it works: On the average, a new wearer of contacts loses or tears about two pairs of lenses in the first year and each lens on the average costs about $40. If you lose two pairs in the first year, you've lost $160—more than the price of insurance. On the other hand, someone who has worn lenses for a year without losing or tearing them may save money by passing up insurance.

Tip # 7: Compare buying disposable contact lenses with buying regular lenses.

How it works: A three-month supply of disposable contact lenses, that is, a package of six lenses, costs about $45, that is $180 a year. At the same time, you save money on cleaning solution because you only clean them once a week. You also will not be considering insurance on them as you might for non-disposables. The disposables are convenient, easy to use, and you can change the prescription easily from one purchase to the next. The average person replaces one pair a year of the more expensive permanent lenses, so compare the yearly costs of the two kinds of lenses before making your decision.

Quality check: Some people complain of eye irritation from protein build-up when using disposable lenses. Some serious eye infections have been observed related to the use of disposable lenses.

Tip # 8: The National Eye Care Project provides free diagnosis and follow-up for eye problems for the elderly who would not otherwise get care.

How it works: Over 7000 members of the American Academy of Ophthalmology contribute to the project by donating their services to U.S. citizens and legal residents over 65 whose previous eye doctor is no longer available or who cannot pay for eye care. Call 1-800-222-EYES for a referral to a local participating eye doctor. Professional services—but not drugs, hospital care, and eyeglasses—are donated to those in need.

Quality check: Their affiliation with the American Academy of Ophthalmology indicates these doctors are fully trained.

Tip # 9: Contact the Lions Club if you cannot pay for eye care or glasses.

How it works: The Lions Club helps low-income people obtain eye glasses. A Lions Club project, Light House for the Blind, offers money for treatment. Contact your local chapter or the national headquarters:

Lions Club International
300 Second Street
Oak Brook, IL 60570

Tip # 10: Contact the National Retinitis Pigmentosa Foundation at 1-800-683-5555 for information and referrals.

Tip # 11: Contact the National Society to Prevent Blindness at 1-800-331-2020.

How it works: The National Society to Prevent Blindness provides information and referrals to local chapters. It has English- and Spanish-speaking staff. Direct service programs vary; some branches run STAR programs of enrichment for blind children, vision screenings, and referral service.

Tip # 12: Try to get into an experimental study of treatment of your eye disorder.

How it works: Experimental treatment studies often offer free treatment to patients who qualify as subjects. In particular, the Clinical Center of the National Institutes of Health in Bethesda, MD, has ongoing studies of glaucoma, neuro-ophthalmology, ophthalmic congenital disease, vision deficiency, retinal degeneration, uveitis, and other eye disorders. The National Eye Institute of the National Institutes of Health is also supporting clinical trials all over the country in which participants receive free care. Ongoing studies involve advanced glaucoma intervention, age-related eye disease, central vision occlusion study, collaborative ocular melanoma, endophthalmitis virectomy, herpetic eye disease, cataracts, essential iris atrophy, ocular hypertension, retinitis pigmentosa, juvenile macular degeneration, fundus flavinaculatus, gyrate atrophy of the choroid and retina, Reiger's Syndrome, Peter and Axenfeld Syndrome, aniridia, oculocutaneous albinism, ocular albinism, alteration of color vision, vitreo-tetinal disease, disorders of the macula, and uveitis. Call the National Eye Institute at 301-496-5248 or write to:

National Eye Institute
Information Office
Bldg. 31, Room 6 A32
Bethesda, MD 20892

For more information on getting into these and other studies of experimental treatment, see STUDIES.

EYEGLASSES (See EYE CARE.)

FABRY DISEASE (See RARE DISEASES.)

FACIAL INJURY OR DISORDER (See also CLEFT PALATE, HEAD CAN-
CER, PLASTIC SURGERY.)

   Tip # 1: Consider contacting the National Association for the
   Cranio-Facially Handicapped.

   How it works: The Association is concerned with all aspects of
   cranio-facial handicap. Write to National Association for the
   Cranio-Facially Handicapped at P.O. Box 11082, Chattanooga, TN
   37401 or call 615-266-1632.

   Tip # 2: For psychological support for facial deformities, contact
   Let's Face It at 508-371-3186.

FACTOR XIII DEFICIENCY (See RARE DISEASES.)

FAIRBANK DISEASE (See RARE DISEASES.)

FAMILY PLANNING (See BIRTH CONTROL.)

FASCIOLIASIS (See RARE DISEASES.)

FELTY SYNDROME (See RARE DISEASES.)

FERTILITY (See also GYNECOLOGY.)

   Tip # 1: Contact the American Fertility Society.

   How it works: The American Fertility Society will provide booklets
   on reproductive health and fertility. Call 205-933-8494.

FETAL ALCOHOL SYNDROME (See RARE DISEASES.)

FIBROMYOSITIS (See RARE DISEASES.)

FIBROSITIS (See RARE DISEASES.)

FILARIASIS (See RARE DISEASES.)

FISH (See FOOD POISONING Tips # 3, 4, and 6.)

FISSURED TONGUE (See RARE DISEASES.)

FITNESS (See also SPORTS MEDICINE.)

   Tip # 1: Exercise. It provides valuable medical prevention.

   How it works: Lower rates of heart disease, high blood pressure,
   osteoporosis, stroke, and certain kinds of cancer have been observed for people who exercise regularly than for people who lead

a sedentary lifestyle. Exercise decreases your risk of diabetes. Stress reduction and lowered body fat are other benefits. Exercise like walking, stair climbing, and aerobic dancing is almost cost free, although you can run the price of exercise up if you spend a lot of money on health clubs and exercise equipment.

Quality check: Certain types of exercise may be inappropriate. If you have a medical problem, seek a physician's advice. If you exercise for your health but over-do it or do it improperly, you may incur a costly injury. Read the next four tips.

Tip # 2: Begin an exercise program slowly and progress gradually.

How it works: More harm than good is done to your health if you decide to take up running (or tennis, or basketball, or rowing....) and you go out the first day and do it as hard as you can. Injury or exhaustion from starting too fast has ended many exercise programs the first week.

Start out the first day with very mild exercise and stay at that level the first week. Each week increase the intensity/duration only a little bit, for example, about 10% increase in distance for runners and walkers. Slow progress pays off in fitness.

Tip # 3: Every time you exercise, warm up first.

How it works: Before each exercise session, warm up your muscles and other systems. Sudden stress on muscles or too much exercise too soon can injure cold muscles and strain joints. Your heart and lungs perform more efficiently when they have a warm-up. Begin whatever form of exercise you have chosen at half-intensity. For example, walk slowly before you stride out fast; walk before you jog, jog before you run, and gently stretch out your arms and legs several minutes before playing tennis. During warm-up you will also find that your heart and lungs adapt to the increased oxygen demand so that you will become less winded during full exercise.

Tip # 4: Exercise at a comfortable rate.

How it works: Too intense exercise is likely to cause injury and exhaustion. One way to assure a healthy work intensity is to figure your target heart rate. Subtract your age from 220. Your heart rate during exercise should be only 60% to 70% of that figure. The best way to check your heart rate is by feeling your pulse with your finger on the inside of your wrist for ten seconds and multiply the number of heart beats by six. Slow down if your heart rate exceeds your target heart rate. Speed up if your heart rate is less than your target heart rate and you can do so comfortably. Another way to tell if you are exercising too hard is the Talk Test: If you are unable to carry on a conversation as you exercise, you are doing it too hard.

Tip # 5: Cool down after exercise.

How it works: Your muscles during exercise are putting out waste products and your body is creating heat. When you stop exercising, your body needs a way to dissipate the waste materials and the heat. Reducing the intensity of your exercise slowly—just as you built it up slowly—gives your body a chance to adjust chemically and to cool off. Failure to cool down slowly can result in muscle tightness or cramps and faintness. In addition, do not take a hot shower right after exercise when you should be cooling down. When you have just exercised, your body is sending proportionately more blood away from your heart towards the outside surface where it can be released with the help of sweat evaporation. Hot water counteracts this cooling effect and the body may respond by sending more blood away from the heart toward the surface with the result that you may faint. Hitting your head as you fall in the shower may be more unhealthy and more costly than the benefits of exercise!

Tip # 6: Combine aerobic and anaerobic exercise for fitness.

How it works: There are two basic types of exercise: aerobic and anaerobic. Aerobic exercise builds endurance and improves cardiovascular fitness. Duration is the important measure of aerobic exercise. Some aerobic exercises are walking, running, biking, aerobics, and swimming. Weight bearing aerobic exercise such as running, walking, and jumping rope helps prevent osteoporosis. Anaerobic exercise builds strength and flexibility. Intensity is the important measure of anaerobic exercise. Anaerobic exercises involve quick bursts of energy in speed or strength as in sports like weight lifting, sprinting, diving, and gymnastics. Both aerobic and anaerobic fitness will improve health and the quality of life. Most of the disease prevention aspects of exercise come from aerobic exercise, but the strength and flexibility built up through anaerobic exercise can do much to prevent the frailty associated with old age. A fitness program that features both types of activity is recommended.

Tip # 7: For cardiovascular fitness, aerobic exercise is necessary for a minimum of twenty minutes a day at least three times a week.

How it works: An exercise session of less than twenty minutes simply is not a cardiovascular work-out and does not lead substantially toward fitness. To build and sustain cardiovascular health, exercise must occur long enough and often enough—three times a week minimum. Remember this acronym: FIT.

F= Frequency: at least three times a week.

I= Intensity: moderate.

T= Time: at least twenty minutes.

Tip # 8: Combine exercise and diet programs for weight maintenance or reduction.

How it works: For every mile you walk or run, you burn approximately 100 calories. Therefore, it takes running or walking 35 miles to burn one pound of fat! (A pound of fat equals 3500 calories.) So exercise alone is not likely to wipe out all-you-can-eat gravy and dessert. But if you eat a diet that just maintains your current weight, the addition of exercise will gradually take off the pounds.

Tip # 9: For more information on fitness contact:

Presidents' Council of Physical Fitness and Sports
Department of Health and Human Services
450 5th Street NW, Suite 7103
Washington, DC 20001
Phone: 202-272-3430 or 202-272-3421.

FLU SHOTS (See also INFLUENZA)

Tip # 1: Flu shots are usually given in local health departments often at much lower costs than at doctors' offices.

How it works: Flu (influenza) shots are recommended for high risk persons including the elderly and those with chronic health problems. Every year the flu shots are formulated to protect against the strain of flu virus predicted to be the most prevalent in your area by the Centers for Disease Control and Prevention (CDC). All health departments are provided a supply in the fall.

FOLIC ACID

Tip # 1: Women of child-bearing age should take extra folic acid.

How it works: The U.S. Public Health Service recommends women of child-bearing age take supplements of folic acid, a B vitamin, to prevent neural tube birth defects such as spina bifida and anencephaly that affect one or two out of every 1000 babies born. A supplement of .4 mg. a day taken by all mothers-to-be, research shows, would cut the numbers of babies suffering from neural tube defects by one-third. If you might become pregnant, ask your doctor about the amount you need. Folic acid is often included in multiple vitamin supplements.

FOOD POISONING

Tip # 1: Take precautions to prevent food poisoning.

How it works: Milk and other dairy products, eggs, meat, poultry, and seafood are the most likely sources of food poisoning. To prevent growth of germs, buy these products last in the grocery store and refrigerate at home immediately. Do not buy or use eggs that are cracked; do not eat food made with raw egg. Keep meat and meat juice away from other foods during transporting and storage. Cut meat on acrylic cutting boards rather than on wood because germs that may be in meat will hide and grow in wood whereas acrylic boards can be washed and dried more efficiently, especially if you use a dishwasher. Don't use a rag you have wiped meat juice with to wipe other dishes or surfaces without washing and drying first. That rag can spread germs from meat, especially raw meat, so that whole areas are infected. Do not eat meat, poultry, or seafood raw. These products also need to stay cold while they thaw. Do not leave food out unrefrigerated more than the one or two hours necessary for a meal. Discard any canned goods that have bulging ends because bulges mean the food inside may be spoiled; both ends of metal cans should be flat or slightly concave.

Tip # 2: Call the Department of Agriculture Meat and Poultry Hotline for information on food poisoning from meat or poultry.

How it works: Tips on spotting and preventing food poisoning from meat and poultry are available from the Department of Agriculture's Office of Public Awareness. Call the Hotline at 1-800-535-4555.

Tip # 3: Call the FDA toll-free seafood hotline at 1-800-332-4010.

How it works: The FDA hotline will answer questions on seafood buying, handling, and storage for safe home consumption and on seafood labeling. Questions will be answered by experts from 10 a.m. to 2 p.m. weekdays. You can order publications and hear pre-recorded information on seafood safety on the hotline 24 hours a day.

Tip # 4: To report illness from eating seafood, call 1-800-886-FISH.

How it works: Public Voice for Food and Health Policy, a private research and educational organization, gathers information from callers about the extent to which contaminated seafood is reaching consumers and shares this information with appropriate federal agencies.

Tip # 5: For home canning, freezing, and preserving instructions, call the County Extension Service of your state's Department of Agriculture.

How it works: Home canning can be an economical, safe way to feed your family, if you follow processing instructions carefully. Your County Extension Service agent will send written instructions and conduct demonstrations. Home canned, frozen, or preserved food should be discarded without tasting if it looks or smells wrong or if canning jar seals are broken.

Tip # 6: Call the Centers for Disease Control and Prevention (CDC) Hotline for detailed information on protection from germs (organisms) that cause food poisoning.

How it works: The CDC hotline gives detailed information on disease from botulism, salmonella, campheiobactur, e. coli, shellfish poisoning, and figella. Call 404-332-4555 and push the touchtone numbers that lead to "Food-borne enteric diseases."

FOOD STAMPS (See also NUTRITION and WIC.)

Tip # 1: Consider applying for Food Stamps if your income is low.

How it works: Contact your local Family and Children's Services or health department to see if you qualify for food stamps. The program for low income households in effect reduces costs of food items. Medicaid recipients are usually eligible.

FOOT CARE (See BUNION and PODIATRY.)

FORBES-ALBRIGHT SYNDROME (See RARE DISEASES.)

FORBES DISEASE (See RARE DISEASES.)

FREY'S SYNDROME (See RARE DISEASES.)

FROELICH'S SYNDROME (See RARE DISEASES.)

FRUCTOSE INTOLERANCE, HEREDITARY (See RARE DISEASES.)

GALACTOSEMIA (See RARE DISEASES.)

GALLBLADDER AND GALLSTONES

Tip # 1: Consider finding a surgeon and a facility that offers laparoscopic removal of the gallbladder or gallstones instead of conventional surgery.

How it works: Traditionally, when the gallbladder or gallstones had to be removed, the abdomen was opened surgically. The patient risked infection, was a long time in the hospital and typically was not able to work for six weeks. Through laparoscopy, the stone or gallbladder can be removed through a tiny incision. The physician is guided by a tiny viewing scope. The average hospital stay for patients treated by laparoscopy at one hospital is 1.3 days and work can be resumed soon after.

Quality check: This surgery, when appropriate, is usually better for the patient than conventional surgery. Ask several hospitals in your area how many such surgeries have been successfully done at that facility, which surgeons perform it, and what training and certification they have in that procedure.

GAMMA GLOBULIN (See also TRAVEL.)

Tip # 1: Consider getting gamma globulin at a local health department before you travel to certain foreign countries.

How it works: Gamma globulin by injection provides a degree of immunity against a wide range of diseases and will help protect you from some diseases prevalent in some foreign countries. The shot, taken before travel, may cost about $12 in a county health department compared to two or three times that in a private doctor's office. Check with your local health department or call the CDC at 404-332-4555 (Travel) to see if gamma globulin is advised for travel in the country you plan to visit.

GANGLIOSIDE SIALIDASE DEFICIENCY (See RARE DISEASES.)

GARDNER SYNDROME (See RARE DISEASES.)

GASTRITIS, GIANT HYPERTROPHIC (See RARE DISEASES.)

GAUCHER DISEASE (See RARE DISEASES.)

GENERAL INFORMATION, GENERAL SOURCES
(Elsewhere in this book sources of information are given for specific topics. The following general sources offer a wealth of information on a wide range of health-related subjects.)

Tip # 1: To contact any state agency or state administered program, call the state's general information number listed below.

How it works: State agencies and state administered programs of federal agencies are listed in the phone book under the name of the state. However, it is often hard to find these agencies because their names may vary from state to state and an agency may be listed under another heading you may not recognize. Or you may not know if your state has a certain program. The person who answers the general information number should be able to give you the number you want. This number is usually listed first under the state heading in a box labeled "Frequently Called Numbers." The general information numbers by state are also listed below:

Alabama........205-242-8000	Montana..........406-444-2511
Alaska.........907-465-2111	Nebraska.........402-471-2311
Arizona........602-542-4900	Nevada...........702-885-5000
Arkansas.......501-371-3000	New Hampshire....603-271-1110
California.....916-322-6740	New Jersey.......609-292-2121
Colorado.......303-866-5000	New Mexico.......505-827-4011
Connecticut....203-566-2211	New York.........518-474-2121

Delaware.......302-736-4000

D.C............202-727-1000

Florida........904-488-1234

Georgia........404-656-2000

Hawaii.........808-586-2211

Idaho..........208-334-2411

Illinois.......217-782-2000

Indiana........317-232-3140

Iowa...........515-281-5011

Kansas.........913-296-0111

Kentucky.......502-564-2500

Louisiana......504-342-6600

Maine..........207-289-1110

Maryland.......301-974-2000

Massachusetts..617-727-2121

Michigan.......517-373-1837

Minnesota......612-296-6013

Mississippi....601-354-7011

Missouri.......314-751-2000

North Carolina...919-733-1110

North Dakota.....701-224-2000

Ohio.............614-466-2000

Oklahoma.........405-521-2011

Oregon...........503-378-3131

Pennsylvania.....717-787-2121

Rhode Island.....401-277-2000

South Carolina...803-734-1000

South Dakota.....605-773-3011

Tennessee........615-741-3011

Texas............512-463-4630

Utah.............801-538-3000

Vermont..........802-828-1110

Virginia.........804-786-0000

Washington.......206-753-5000

West Virginia....304-558-3456

Wisconsin........608-266-2211

Wyoming..........307-777-7220

Tip # 2: Contact NORD for literature on any of 1000 diseases.

How it works: NORD (National Organization for Rare Diseases) compiles fact sheets on hundreds of rare and not so rare diseases from Aarskog Syndrome to Zollinger-Ellison Syndrome. (See RARE DISEASES for more information, and see Appendix B for a complete list of diseases.) Useful materials on better known disorders such as acne, anemia, hiccups, hypertension, and sickle cell disease are also available from NORD and rare forms may be described in the material. Each fact sheet contains the disease name, synonyms, a general description of the disorder, symptoms, causes, affected population, standard treatments, investigational treatments, and a list of resources that can be contacted for further information. The first fact sheet you order from NORD is free; subsequent orders are $3.25 per copy including postage and handling. Written orders only are accepted with payment but you can call NORD toll-free at 1-800-999-6673 to ask if a particular disease fact sheet is available and what its order number is. NORD's address is P.O. 8923, New Fairfield, CT 06812-1783. For those of you with personal computers and modem, you can access the database directly. You can reach NORD Services section of CompuServe by typing "GO NORD" at any prompt on the CompuServe Information System.

Tip # 3: Contact the Food and Drug Administration (FDA).

How it works: 1) Health professionals can order a free Medical Bulletin, information for health professionals, published three times a year on new medical developments and controversies. Write to Department of Health and Human Resources, Public Health Service, FDA, Medical Bulletin (HFI-42), 5600 Fisher's Lane, Rockville, MD 20857. (No phone orders are accepted.) 2) For free reprints of articles on many health topics (available in Spanish as well as English) write FDA, 5600 Fisher's Lane, Mail Code HFE-88, Room 1663, Rockville, MD, 20857 or call 301-443-3170, specifying which topic you are interested in. These articles are reprints from a ten-times-a-year publication "FDA Consumer," which you may subscribe to at this same number or address. 3) You may address individual consumer/patient questions on food, drugs, cosmetics, and medical devices to the public information specialist at the nearest FDA district office listed in your phone book. The national FDA Public Affairs office can also provide information and make referrals to specific FDA sources. Call 301-443-4166 or write FDA, Public Affairs, Room 13-88, 5600 Fishers Lane, Rockville, MD 20857.

Tip # 4: Call the National Health Information Center at 1-800-336-4797.

How it works: Call between 9 a.m. and 5 p.m. Eastern time for short recorded messages on these topics: lyme disease, cancer, AIDS, medicare and medicaid, and health insurance. A health counselor is also available to answer individual questions on a broad spectrum of health topics. They can also refer you to other appropriate sources. If the toll-free line is busy, you can call 301-565-4167, or if you do not want to wait on the line for a counselor, write to the National Health Information Center at P.O.Box 1133, Washington, DC 20013-1133.

Tip # 5: Call the CDC's Voice Information System at 404-332-4555.

How it works: The Centers for Disease Control and Prevention (CDC) and the Agency for Toxic Substances and Disease Registry (ATSDR) have developed a Voice Information System that allows anyone using a touchtone phone to obtain prerecorded information on certain diseases or health areas, symptoms, prevention methods, immunization requirements, current statistics, and recent disease outbreaks. A complex system of several hundred messages provides information on health issues to travelers to specific foreign countries. Health topics covered in great detail include AIDS, chronic fatigue syndrome, cytomegalovirus, infection control in dentistry, encephalitis, enteric diseases, Epstein Barr, hepatitis, immunizations, influenza, hospital-acquired infections, Lyme disease, malaria, rabies, Rocky Mountain Spotted Fever, vaccine-preventable diseases, and yellow fever. Other topics are being added. Since the CDC's Voice Information System is accessible 24-hours a day, you can save money by calling when rates are low. Since long-distance phone calls to this information system are not free except in the Atlanta area, you may have better luck finding the lines free than you do when you call toll-free 800 numbers to other information systems.

Tip # 6: Contact the Office of Disease Prevention and Health Promotion Center (ONHIC) at 1-800-336-4797.

How it works: ONHIC helps the public and health professionals locate health information resources, an information and referral system, and publications. The staff uses a database to find the most appropriate organizations and materials. You may also call ONHIC at 301-565-4167 or write ONHIC, P.O. Box 1133, Washington, DC 20013-1133.

Tip # 5: To locate the appropriate federal agency for your need, contact the Federal Information Center (FIC.)

How it works: The FIC provides a one-stop source of assistance for callers with inquiries about any federal government agency, program, or service. Residents of 72 metropolitan areas can dial an FIC on a local-call basis. Residents of four states may dial an FIC toll-free number. To see if your area has a FIC number, look up Federal Information Center under Frequently Called Numbers at the top of the U.S. government listings in your phone book. A complete list of FIC numbers and addresses is available free from the Consumer Information Center (CIC), General Services Administration, Pueblo, CO 81009. Or call the CIC at 202-501-1794.

Tip # 6: Subscribe to or read regularly in your library one or more newsletters on health issues published by a reliable medical source.

How it works: For example, the Mayo Clinic publishes a monthly newsletter called "Reliable Information for a Healthier Life." Single copies are available for $3 each and a yearly subscription for $24. Call 1-800-333-9037 or write Mayo Clinic Newsletter, Subscription Services, P.O. Box 53889, Boulder, CO 80322-3889. Also, the "Harvard Medical School Health Letter" interprets medical information for the public in a timely and accurate fashion. For copies or a subscription write to Harvard Medical School Health Letter, 164 Longwood Ave., 4th Floor, Boston, MA 02115 or call 617-432-1435. "Health After 50" is the name of a monthly medical newsletter from Johns Hopkins University School of Medicine. Call 1-800-829-9170 for a year's subscription for $24.

Tip # 7: Use the National Medical Library by phone, mail, and computer.

How it works: The National Medical Library is the largest medical library in the world and its books, journals, and databases are available to the public. Many materials (books, journals, photographs, audiovisual materials, and databases) are located at the main library in Bethesda, MD, (near Washington, DC), and can be used on site by the public. Additional materials are also available at eight Regional Libraries, 131 Resource Libraries, and 3300 Primary Access Libraries (mostly at hospitals) that may be more conveniently located. Some materials can be borrowed; most materials are on loan only to other libraries, for example, in hospitals and medical schools where the lending policies of those institutions apply. Most of the information provided by the library is through its computer reference resources. Most medical information you would want is available in public libraries, hospital libraries, and medical school libraries. The National Library of Medicine is the resource of last resort to help professionals and informed consumers access hard-to-find materials. Research assistance is available by calling 1-800-272-4787 and, for persons with touchtone phones, using the menu provided on the following page to reach an area of interest. A staff specialist will speak with callers about their research needs in particular medical areas. Researchers will try to fill requests by mail as well. Write National Library of Medicine, 8600 Rockville Pike, Bethesda, MD 20894. The National Library of Medicine's MEDLARS® system provides the public on-line information retrieval accessed by means of a terminal or microcomputer, telecommunications software, a modem, a telephone line and a printer. Its most-used data base is MEDLINE covering twenty years of 3500 journals, but there are more than twenty other databases ranging from AIDSTRIALS, a record of clinical trials of substances being tested for use against AIDS, to TOXLINE®, a record of effects of drugs and other chemicals. A user-friendly software package called GRATEFUL MED® for use in the MEDLAR system is sold for $29.95 plus $3 shipping. With the exception of CHEMLINE and TOXLIT (which charge royalties), all databases accessible by Grateful Med are charged at the rate of about $36/hour during prime time (10 a.m. to 5 p.m., Eastern time weekdays) and $29 during non-prime time. The average cost of a Grateful Med search of these files is between $2 and $4. The newest feature is "Loansome Doc," a printout capability for full-text articles. The Grateful Med order number for IBM is PB86-158482; the order number for Macintosh is PB89-196083/GBB. An application form for a User ID code is enclosed in the package. To purchase, call 703-487-4650 or write:

National Technical Information Service
U.S. Department of Commerce
5285 Port Royal Road
Springfield, VA 22161

Tip # 8: Use the CHID database at most hospitals and universities for research on health topics.

How it works: CHID or Combined Health Information Database, maintained by the National Institutes of Health, has a unique ability to search through files of over 65,000 abstracts in 17 different medical areas: AIDS and school education; AIDS education;

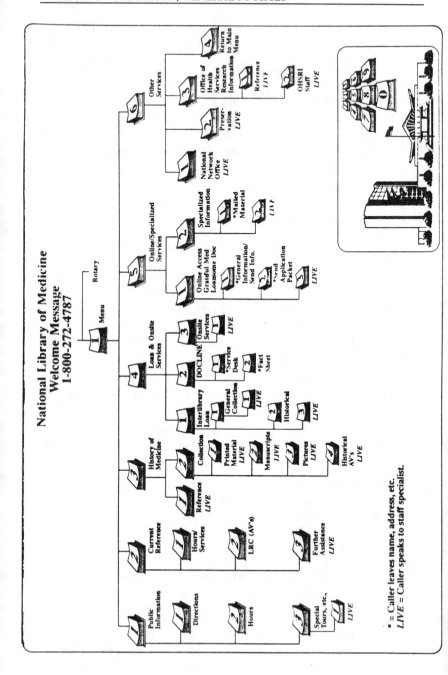

National Library of Medicine
Welcome Message
1-800-272-4787

* = Caller leaves name, address, etc.
LIVE = Caller speaks to staff specialist.

Alzheimer's disease; arthritis, musculoskeletal, and skin diseases; asthma education; blood resources; cancer patient information; cholesterol, high blood pressure, and smoking education; deafness and communicative disorders; diabetes; digestive diseases; disease prevention/health promotion; eye health education; kidney and urologic disease; post traumatic stress disorder; VA patient health education.

For more information on CHID, call 301-368-6553 or write:

National Institutes of Health
Mr. Richard Pike
Box CHID
9000 Rockville, MD 20892

Tip # 9: Individuals and groups can obtain copies of audiovisual cassettes on various medical topics from the National AudioVisual Center at 1-800-788-6282.

Tip # 10: Read newsletters and publications of health-oriented consumer groups.

How it works: Some consumer groups publish books, newsletters, and other publications on health-related services and products. Some groups have a non-establishment viewpoint which serve to balance more "official" information from government or medical organization sources. The Consumers Union, a non-profit organization founded in 1936, does independent research on consumer services and products and reports its findings in its monthly *Consumers Reports*. Many of its articles concern health-related services, for example, HMOs, long term care insurance, drugs, and health care products. Consumers Union also publishes *Consumer Reports on Health,* a periodical devoted to health information, as well as books such as *The Woman's Guide to Good Health, The Man's Guide to Good Health, The Prostate Book, Treating Acne, The Complete Drug Reference,* and *Allergies. Consumer Reports* and some related books are available at most libraries. To order Consumer Reports, write Customer Services, P.O. Box 53029, Boulder, CO 80322-3029. To order Consumer Union books, write 9180 LeSaint Drive, Fairfield, OH 45014-5452 or call 513-860-1178.

People's Medical Society is a consumer organization which

deals exclusively with health issues. Membership is $15 a year and includes a subscription to the *People's Medical Society Newsletter.* The Society publishes inexpensive books on specific topics, for example, *Take This Book to the Gynecologist With You* and *Take This Book to the Hospital With You.* You can order these plus condition updates, bibliographies and information packs from the People's Medical Society Health Library. For membership or order forms, write Peoples Medical Society, 462 Walnut St., Allentown, PA 18102. Phone orders may be made by credit card at 1-800-624-8773.

GENETIC DISEASES

Tip # 1: Consider participating in an experimental study of treatment of your genetic disorder. (See STUDIES.)

How it works: Experimental treatment studies often offer free treatment to patients who qualify as subjects. In particular, the Clinical Center of the National Institutes of Health in Bethesda, MD, has ongoing studies of many genetic disorders including amino aciduria, lysosomal storage disease, carbohydrate metabolic disorders, disorders of secreted proteins, bone and connective tissue disorders, disorders of copper metabolism, cystinosis, Fanconi Syndrome, Lowe Syndrome, Menkes disease, osteogenesis imperfecta, Ehlers-Danlos Syndrome, and ectodermal dysplasia. For information on getting in a study at this or other institutions, see STUDIES.

Tip # 2: Contact the Alliance of Genetic Support Groups at 1-800-336-GENE.

How it works: The Alliance is a clearinghouse for organizations relating to genetic disorders and will put you in touch with support groups and other resources pertaining to genetic disorders in general or a particular kind of disease.

GIANOTTI-CROSTI SYNDROME (See RARE DISEASES.)

GIARDIASIS (See RARE DISEASES.)

GILBERT SYNDROME (See RARE DISEASES.)

GLIOBLASTOMA MULTIFORME (See RARE DISEASES and CANCER.)

GLUCO-6-DEHYDROGENASE DEFICIENCY (See RARE DISEASES.)

GLUCOSE-GALACTOSE MALABSORPTION (See RARE DISEASES.)

GLUTARICACIDURIA I and II (See RARE DISEASES.)

GLYCOGEN STORAGE DISEASE VIII (See RARE DISEASES.)

GONORRHEA (See also SEXUALLY TRANSMITTED DISEASES.)

Tip # 1: Consider going to your local health department for a test for gonorrhea if you have any symptoms or reason to believe you may be infected with any sexually transmitted disease.

How it works: Most health departments test for and treat gonorrhea and other sexually transmitted diseases free of charge. Penicillin is usually provided free of charge. It is very important to take the medication for as long as directed, getting refills before the supply is gone. Also, consider seeking birth control, disease protection counseling, and assistance from the health department in stopping the spread of the disease to other persons.

Tip # 2: Call the STD Hotline at 1-800-227-8922.

How it works: The Sexually Transmitted Diseases (STD) Hotline gives callers information and referrals.

GORDON SYNDROME (See RARE DISEASES.)

GORHAM'S DISEASE (See RARE DISEASES.)

GRAVES' DISEASE (See RARE DISEASES.)

GROWTH DISORDERS

Tip # 1: Patients on growth hormone therapy who cannot afford the hormone medication may contact the manufacturer for a free supply.

How it works: Genentech, Inc., the manufacturer of Protropin®, and Eli Lilly Co., manufacturer of Humatrope®, both have a program of free medication for uninsured patients who cannot pay for treatment with growth hormone medications. Contact Genentech at 1-800-879-4747, Ext. 2287, 2272, and 6008; contact Eli Lilly at 317-276-2950.

Tip # 2: Contact the Human Growth Foundation at 1-800-451-6434.

How it works: The Human Growth Foundation is interested in people with growth disorders of all origins. The Foundation sends free booklets, makes referrals to local chapters which sponsor parent support groups, and publishes a monthly newsletter. It serves as a clearinghouse of resources.

Tip # 3: Read *Understanding Growth Hormone*.

How it works: *Understanding Growth Hormone* (1993) is a comprehensive book on growth hormone, its role in growth and growth therapy, and growth disorders including those not currently treatable by growth hormone. The book by Neil Shulman M.D. and Letitia Sweitzer is available in book stores or from the publisher, Hippocrene Books, 171 Madison Avenue, Suite 1602, New York, NY 10016. Telephone 212-685-4371.

GUILLAIN-BARRE SYNDROME

Tip # 1: Contact the Guillain-Barre Syndrome (GBS) Foundation International at 215-667-0131.

How it works: The Foundation supplies literature and offers patients assistance in finding a local chapter from a list of chapters world-wide. It provides referrals to physicians experienced in GBS, publishes a newsletter, and sponsors an educational symposium for the medical community and the public.

GYNECOLOGY (See also BIRTH CONTROL, ENDOMETRIOSIS, FERTIL-ITY, HYSTERECTOMY, MAMMOGRAMS, PAP TEST, PREGNANCY, SEXU-ALLY TRANSMITTED DISEASES, WOMEN'S HEALTH, and specific diseases)

Tip # 1: Ask the American College of Obstetricians and Gynecologists (ACOG) for a list of pamphlets.

How it works: ACOG will send you a list of pamphlets you can order by subject. Send an stamped, self-addressed envelope to ACOG, 409 12th St., SW, Washington, DC 20024.

HAGEMAN FACTOR DEFICIENCY (See RARE DISEASES.)

HAND-FOOT-MOUTH DISEASE (See RARE DISEASES.)

HANDICAPPED ADULT (See also DISABILITY, EQUIPMENT, HOME HEALTH CARE, REHABILITATION, and WORKPLACE.)

Tip # 1: Contact Higher Education and Adult Training for People With Handicaps Resource Center at 1-800-544-3284.

How it works: This organization advises on post-secondary education for people with handicaps. Although an organization for adults, it is a good resource for handicapped children approaching adulthood. Information for this resource center can help individuals and families set goals.

HANDICAPPED CHILD (See also DISABILITY, PEDIATRICS.)

Tip # 1: Contact the state agency concerned with handicapped children *immediately* after the birth of a handicapped child.

How it works: Sometimes a state will take full financial responsibility for a handicapped child from birth. If you wait before seeking help you may accumulate insurmountable medical debts. Ask the social worker at the hospital where the child was born or any hospital where to call for help. Look up your state government in the phone book and find an office named "crippled children" or "handicapped children" under Department of Health or Department of Human Resources or Department of Education. It may also be under Family and Children's Services. Many states have financial aid for handicapped children whose parents cannot pay for their care.

Tip # 2: If your family has limited income and resources, your disabled child may qualify for Supplemental Security Income (SSI).

How it works: In recent years, there has been a growing concern that parents are unaware of the disability benefits available for their disabled children. Children may qualify as disabled by the same determination process that disabled adults go through to receive Social Security disability benefits and SSI (See DISABLED) except the medical criteria are not related to ability to work. A child, that is, a person under 18 years of age, will be considered disabled if he or she is not working and has an impairment that is as severe as one that would disable an adult. If the child's condition is on a listing of impairments contained in Social Security regulations he/she will be considered disabled for SSI purposes. This list describes symptoms, signs, or laboratory findings of such physical and mental problems as cerebral palsy, mental retardation, or muscular dystrophy that are severe enough to disable a child. If the child's condition is not on the list, a disability evaluation team will assess the child's ability to function in the ways that children of a similar age normally do. The evaluation process takes several months. However, in the case of severe disabilities such as AIDS, blindness, or amputation of limbs, SSI payments will be made for six months while the evaluation is being made. If later the child does not qualify as disabled, the money will not have to be paid back. The child's resources and some of the parents resources will be evaluated to see if they meet the criteria of low resources.

For more information, call 1-800-772-1213 any business day from 7 a.m. to 7 p.m. Central time and ask specific questions or request the booklet, "Social Security and SSI Benefits for Children with Disabilities."

Tip # 3: If your disabled child receives a back payment under the Zebley court case, consider spending it within six months.

How it works: If your disabled child is now receiving SSI and is receiving a large back payment under the Zebley court case, note that any money left from this payment after six months will count as a "resource" and may cause you to become ineligible for SSI. Consider spending this back payment on the child's needs within six months.

Tip # 4: Contact the National Information Center for Children and Youth with Handicaps (NICHCY) at 1-800-999-5599.

How it works: NICHCY assists parents, educators, caregivers, advocates and others working to improve the lives of children with disabilities. Services include personal responses to specific questions, referrals to other organizations, sources of help, and technical assistance to parent and professional groups. NICHCY distributes fact sheets on specific disabilities and general information on vocational/transitional issues, legal rights, and advocacy.

Tip # 5: Call the National Center for Youth with Disabilities at 1-800-333-NCYD for information, referrals, and bibliographies.

Tip # 6: Call the National Resource Library at 1-800-333-6293.

How it works: An information specialist at the National Resource Library will do an information search for you on chronic conditions, employment, education, psychosocial issues, and finances based on the information you give about your child's needs. Call between 8 a.m. and 4:30 p.m. Central time.

Tip # 7: Contact Higher Education and Adult Training for People With Handicaps Resource Center at 1-800-544-3284.

How it works: This organization advises on post-secondary education for people with handicaps. Although an organization for adults, it is a good resource for handicapped children approaching adulthood. Information from this resource center can help individuals and families set goals.

HASHIMOTO'S SYNDROME (See RARE DISEASES.)

HEAD CANCER (See also CANCER.)

Tip # 1: Contact Heads Up at 619-543-3456.

How it works: Heads Up is a support group for people faced with emotional or physical challenge as a result of head and neck cancer. It provides educational materials and practical tips.

HEAD INJURY

Tip # 1: If, after you hit your head, one pupil looks larger than the other under equal lighting, go to an emergency center.

How it works: Increased pressure inside your skull from bleeding and swelling may put pressure on the nerve to one of your eyes. Unequal pupils is therefore a sign of internal injury that may require immediate treatment.

Quality check: Some people are born with unequal pupils and this harmless condition should be taken into consideration. Also, some serious brain damage can occur without affecting the pupils.

Tip # 2: Contact the National Head Injury Foundation at 202-296-6443.

How it works: The National Head Injury Foundation has a Family Helpline to answer questions and provide referrals and contacts with support groups. Staff members can look up rehabilitative services available for your situation in a comprehensive national directory or you can buy the directory for $70. Foundation staff can advise on how to get family services from government or private agencies or funding for legal assistance.

HEADACHE (Also, see MIGRAINE.)

Tip # 1: Contact the National Headache Foundation at 1-800-843-2256 or 1-800-523-8858 in Illinois.

How it works: The Foundation will send free literature on headaches and their treatment if you send a self-addressed envelope stamped with two first-class stamps to National Headache Foundation, 525 Northwestern Ave., Chicago, IL 60625.

Tip # 2: For information on serious chronic headaches, contact the National Institute of Neurological Diseases and Stroke (NINDS) of the National Institutes of Health.

How it works: The NINDS provides printed information on headaches and other disorders related to the head and nerves, answers questions about the program, and can refer you to appropriate researchers. Call 301-496-5924.

Tip # 3: For cluster headache, see also RARE DISEASES.

HEARING AIDS (See also HEARING IMPAIRMENT.)

Tip # 1: If you cannot afford a hearing aid, consider contacting Hear Now for help.

How it works: An organization in Denver, CO, called Hear Now sponsors the National Hearing Aid Bank. Hear Now reconditions donated hearing aids and gives them, as appropriate, to needy people with a hearing loss. Call Hear Now at 303-758-4919.

Tip # 2: Call the National Hearing Aid Helpline at 1-800-521-5247.

How it works: The Helpline provides information and distributes a directory of hearing aid specialists certified by the National Hearing Aid Society. Call weekdays from 8 a.m. to 5 p.m.

HEARING IMPAIRMENT (See also HEARING AIDS.)

Tip # 1: For a free screening test of your hearing at home, dial 1-800-222-EARS, Monday through Friday, 9 a.m. to 5 p.m. Eastern Standard Time.

How it works: At this toll-free number, an operator at Occupational Hearing in Philadelphia will ask you what area of the country you live in. The organization has numbers for 230 centers all over the country. The operator will give you the number of the one nearest you. You will be advised to be in a quiet room for the test and to use a good, clear telephone. When you dial this local number you will be instructed to place the receiver firmly against your right ear and listen for four tones. These tones are very soft in order to test hearing sensitivity near your hearing threshold. Then you will be told to put the receiver firmly against your left ear to listen for four more tones. If you do not hear all eight tones, you may have some hearing loss and may want to seek further evaluation. It may be helpful to repeat the test until you become comfortable with the procedure. Only you will know whether you passed or failed the screening test. For those who have failed, the recording will give the number of the sponsoring hearing clinic where you may make an appointment for a detailed hearing evaluation, if you wish, but you may, of course, go to any hearing center or ear doctor. This test is aimed primarily at adults, as children are not reliable at performing the test, but if you train your small child to use this test reliably when his/her hearing is at its best, then when he/she has a cold or is recovering from an ear infection, you can check to see if the child's hearing is reduced. A reduction in hearing suggests fluid in the middle ear. The telephone hearing test also can be used before and after a rock concert or other experience with loud noise to demonstrate noise-induced hearing loss. Although this loss may be temporary, repeated assault by loud noise may lead to permanent loss. A demonstration of temporary loss on the telephone test may impress a teenager or other skeptic of the dangers of prolonged loud noise.

Quality check: This telephone test is a screening test only. It cannot tell you what kind of hearing loss you may have or whether it is correctable or not. Also, there are several factors involved in understanding speech. The test only identifies one of them, the ability to hear pure tones. The test is also dependent on the quality of the telephone and telephone connection.

Tip # 2: Hearing tests are sometimes given free at local health departments and at some health fairs.

How it works: Free hearing screenings are often offered at health departments and health fairs. If you pass the test, you probably need go no further. If you do not pass the criteria for normal hearing, you need to go to a hearing clinic or physician to test for degree of hearing loss and diagnosis of cause.

Tip # 3: Consider getting a TDD (telephonic device for the deaf, also called a TTY).

How it works: TDDs are special computers that transmit written conversations by telephone. Anyone with a TDD can type messages on the TDD keyboard and send them instantly by telephone to another person with a TDD and receive an immediate answer displayed on the TDD screen. Emergency agencies such as police and fire departments have TDD access as well as many businesses such as banks, investment firms, airlines, and insurance companies. Many hearing impaired people also have them. A TDD can be bought for as little as about $100 but many cost more depending on features such as small travel size, built-in printers, and answering machines. For purchasing information, contact a hearing aid dealer or your telephone equipment dealer. See also Tip # 8.

Tip # 4: Ask AT&T about lowered long distance telephone rates for individuals using telephonic devices for the deaf (TDD).

How it works: For individuals using telecommunications devices for the deaf (TDD) and using AT&T as their long distance carrier, AT&T will lower long distance telephone rates to accommodate the longer time period needed for communication. Day time phoning will be billed as evening phoning; evening phoning will be billed at the night and holiday rate. AT&T also sells TDDs. Call AT&T on a TDD at 1-800-833-3232 for information on how to activate this discount through your local phone company.

Tip # 5: To carry on a telephone conversation between a hearing- or speech-impaired person who has a TDD and a person without a TDD, call a relay service for the deaf.

How it works: In many states a relay service operates 24 hours a day, seven days a week, assisting conversations between hearing- or speech-impaired people with a TDD and callers without TDDs. To contact the relay in your state, look up Consumer Information and/or Services for Disabled Customers near the front of your phone book or look for the name of your state followed by the words Relay Center, for example, Georgia Relay Center. A relay service has two numbers, one for callers with a TDD and a voice line for callers without a TDD. An operator of a relay service listens to the spoken messages and transmits these via TDD to the hearing impaired caller then transmits TDD replies back to the speaking caller. Conversations are transmitted word for word by trained communications assistants and in the strictest confidence. Local calls are free of charge and long distance calls within states may be discounted.

Tip # 6: Consider buying a closed captioning device for your television, or a new TV with a built-in decoder.

How it works: Most prime time, news, and public television programming has captioning for the deaf on a closed circuit line. When the captioning device is in use, every word spoken and other sounds are displayed in captioning near the bottom of the picture. When the captioning feature is not in use, the captioning is unseen. Captioning for the deaf is a very effective way for hearing impaired persons to improve language and reading skills as well as receive information and entertainment. It may also help foreign language speakers learn English. All television sets made after July 1, 1993, must have built-in captioning decoders.

For purchasing information, contact a hearing aid dealer, television and electronics dealer, or call the National Captioning Institute at 1-800-533-9673.

Tip # 7: Call the Better Hearing Institute at 1-800-EAR-WELL for information on financial assistance for the purchase of hearing aids.

How it works: Financial assistance for the purchase of hearing aids is available from local and national government and social service organizations.

Tip # 8: For money-saving tips, contact the Tele-Consumer Hotline at 1-800-332-1124 (voice and TDD.)

How it works: The Tele-Consumer Hotline is a nonprofit, independent and impartial telephone consumer information service which provides free telephone assistance and publications on special telephone equipment. Call the Hotline for money-saving tips, TDD directories, troubleshooting, selecting a telephone, telephone fraud, relay services, and more.

Tip # 9: For instruction in teaching a very young deaf child by correspondence, contact the John Tracy Clinic at 1-800-522-4582 (voice or TDD for the deaf).

How it works: The John Tracy Clinic offers a highly personalized teaching service for families of young deaf children to use in the home. The Clinic provides materials and instructions and parents are encouraged to report progress in writing to the assigned teacher who writes back, encouraging and addressing individual concerns. The correspondence course is free of charge; donations are welcome. Write the John Tracy Clinic at 806 W. Adams Blvd. Los Angeles, CA 90007. The Clinic offers a similar program for the deaf/blind child.

Tip # 10: Contact an organization concerned with hearing impairment.

How it works: Here is a sampling of the many national organizations which can provide information, referrals, and support on subjects relating to hearing impairment.

Alexander Graham Bell Association for the Deaf,
3417 Volta Place NW
Washington, DC 20007
Voice/TDD (202) 337-5220

Conference of Educational Administrators Serving the Deaf
P.O. Box 5545
Tucson, AZ 85703
Voice/TDD (602) 628-5261

Deafness and Communicative Disorders Branch
Department of Education
330 C Street SW, Room 3303
Washington, DC 20202

Hear Now
4001 S. Magnolia Way, Suite 100
Denver, CO 80237
Voice/TDD (303) 758-4919
Voice/TDD (303) 648-HEAR

Lion's Clubs International
300 22nd Street
Oak Brook, IL 60570

National Congress of Jewish Deaf
13580 Osborne Street
Arleta, CA 91331
Voice/TDD (818) 896-6721

The National Easter Seals Society
2023 West Ogden Avenue
Chicago, IL 60612

National Institute on Deafness and Other Communication Disorders
National Institutes of Health
Building 31, Room 1B-62
9000 Rockville Pike
Bethesda, MD 20892
Voice (301) 496-7243
TDD (301) 402-0252

Quota International Inc.
Suite 908
1828 L Street, NW
Washington, DC 20036
(202) 331-9694

For other organizations concerned with hearing impairment and the deaf, see the next tip.

Tip # 11: Contact the National Information Center on Deafness (NICD).

How it works: The NICD is a centralized source of information about hearing loss and deafness. For answers to questions, literature, and order forms for inexpensive pamphlets and other publications, call 202-651-5051 (voice) and 202-651-5052 (TDD). Or write the NICD at Gallaudet University, 800 Florida Ave. NE, Washington, DC 20002-3695. Ask the National Information Center on Deafness for their current list of more than sixty national, non-profit organizations concerned with a wide range of groups and issues pertaining to deafness. Some organizations relate to deafness irrespective of methods of communication and education while others emphasize certain methods or aspects. Some are connected with churches or ethnic groups, and some are consumer groups. A description of the work of each organization is included in the NICD list.

HEART DISEASE

Tip # 1: The best way to keep a heart healthy for little money is through diet, exercise, and other preventive measures.

How it works: A low-fat diet, that is, one that derives no more than 30% of its calories from fat, is associated with significantly lower risk of coronary heart disease. Remember that is not 30% of the *weight* of a meal but 30% of the *calories.* A gram of fat has 9 calories whereas a gram of carbohydrate has only 4 calories. A different but related risk to the heart is cholesterol. A cholesterol level associated with lower risk of coronary disease is below 180 with twice as much HDL or "good" cholesterol to LDL or "bad" cholesterol. (See also (CHOLESTEROL.) Maintain normal blood pressure to reduce risk of coronary artery disease. (See HIGH BLOOD PRESSURE.) Maintain your weight within the normal range. (See NUTRITION.) And...QUIT SMOKING. (See SMOKING.)

Tip # 2: Women after menopause, ask your gynecologist about taking hormone supplements to reduce the risk of heart disease.

How it works: The lower level of risk of heart disease that women seem to enjoy when compared to men disappears after menopause when the supply of certain hormones is dramatically diminished. Supplements of these hormones may be associated with fewer heart attacks as well as other benefits. Ask your gynecologist if hormone supplements are appropriate for you.

Tip # 3: Ask your doctor about aspirin as a means of reducing your risk of heart attack.

How it works: A low daily dose of aspirin (usually half a tablet) may be associated with lower risk of heart attack in both men and women. Ask your doctor if a low dose of aspirin would be appropriate for you to take daily. For those who can not tolerate aspirin, there are substitutes that may have the same effect.

Tip # 4: Contact The American Heart Association.

How it works: The American Heart Association (AHA) provides information, referrals and contact with local chapters as well as educational programs. Call 214-373-6300. Or write the AHA at 7272 Greenville Ave., Dallas, TX 75213.

Tip # 5: Consider joining Mended Hearts.

How it works: Mended Hearts is an organization of people who have gone through heart attack, heart surgery, or angioplasty. They offer support to each other and to others who are about to go through treatment for heart disease. Local groups provide social events, speakers, and a monthly newsletter.

To contact a Mended Hearts group, contact the American Heart Association branch nearest you (listed in the phone book) or write The Mended Hearts Inc., 7320 Greenville Ave., Dallas, TX 25231.

Tip # 6: Consider participating in an experimental study of treatment of your heart disorder (See also STUDIES.)

How it works: Experimental treatment studies often offer free treatment to patients who qualify as subjects. In particular, the Clinical Center of the National Institutes of Health in Bethesda, MD, has ongoing studies of many heart disorders including coronary heart disease, microvascular angina hypertrophic cardiomyopathy, valvular heart disease, and hypertension. For information on getting in a study in this or other institutions, see STUDIES.

Tip # 6: Contact the National Heart, Lung, and Blood Institute (NHLBI) Education Programs Information Center.

How it works: The NHLBI serves as a source of free information and materials on cholesterol, smoking, asthma, and high blood pressure—major risk factors for cardiovascular health for professionals and consumers. Call 301-951-3260 or write NHLBI Education Programs Information Center at 4733 Bethesda Ave., Suite 530, Bethesda, MD 20814.

HEMOPHILIA

Tip # 1: Call the National Hemophilia Foundation at 1-800-42-HANDI.

How it works: The National Hemophilia Foundation makes referrals for treatment, to support groups, and to local chapters which may have financial help available. In addition, the Foundation sends out information on hemophilia and HIV infection, which is a special danger for hemophiliacs who have received blood transfusions during a period of time in the past when donated blood was not screened for HIV contamination. English and Spanish speaking staff are available.

HEPATITIS (See also LIVER DISEASE.)

Tip # 1: Call the Centers for Disease Control and Prevention (CDC) at 404-332-4555 for current and detailed, recorded information on hepatitis 24-hours a day.

Tip # 2: Ask your doctor about the immunization of adults and children for hepatitis B.

How it works: Hepatitis B is a serious viral disease for which there is a vaccine. At-risk people should ask their doctors or health department about immunization. Attempts to vaccinate at-risk populations have not been effective in bringing the disease under control, however. Recently, therefore, the Advisory Committee on Immunization Practices of the U. S. Public Health Service has recommended that hepatitis B vaccine be integrated into the regular childhood immunization program on a flexible schedule of three doses between birth and six to eighteen months of age. For more detailed, recorded information on the new recommendations, call the CDC at 404-332-4555 from a touchtone phone. For free or low cost immunization contact your local health department.

HERPES

Tip # 1: Call the National Herpes Hotline or the National STD Hotline.

How it works: The National Herpes Hotline at 919-361-8488 is answered by staff that can send you information, direct you to local or other organizations, or answer individual questions. The STD (Sexually Transmitted Diseases) Hotline provides similar services on a broader range of topics from minor STDs to chronic viral infections as well as pelvic inflammatory disease, syphilis and gonorrhea. Its number is toll-free: 1-800-227-8922. Both hotlines are operated by the American Social Health Association through contracts with the Centers for Disease Control and Prevention (CDC).

HIB (Haemophilus Influenza type b)

Tip # 1: Have your child immunized against Hib infections.

How it works: Hib or haemophilus influenza type b is a virus that causes serious diseases including meningitis. It is recommended that all children receive Hib conjugate vaccine beginning at 2 months of age. The vaccine is usually offered at local health departments free or at low cost as well as in private doctor's offices and clinics.

HIDRADENITIS SUPPURATIVA (See RARE DISEASES.)

HIGH ALTITUDE

Tip # 1: Take precautions against high mountain sickness at high altitude.

How it works: High mountain sickness is characterized by headache, nausea, fatigue, shortness of breath, and insomnia. Not immediately apparent, it may become a problem 6 hours to 2 days into your mountain stay. Here are some tips for avoiding illness at high altitude: Avoid alcohol a few days prior to and during a high altitude stay, drink lots of fluids, avoid over-exertion, eat lightly, eat a high carbohydrate diet. High mountain sickness can be serious and if it persists, consider returning to a lower altitude and seeing your doctor.

HIGH BLOOD PRESSURE (Hypertension)

Tip # 1: Exercise regularly as directed by your physician, keep your weight appropriate through diet, and avoid salt, alcohol, and cigarettes.

How it works: Although many people have high blood pressure because of other factors such as heredity and race, lifestyle factors play an important role in high blood pressure and its complications. Overweight, excessive alcohol consumption, excessive salt intake, and stress all contribute to high blood pressure. You may be able to avoid treatment with expensive drugs or at least reduce the amount of necessary medication by losing weight, and avoiding salt and excessive alcohol. Smoking does not raise blood pressure but it increases the risk of complications from high blood pressure. Exercise, by helping to control weight and reduce stress, can indirectly lower blood pressure. (See FITNESS.)

Quality check: The lifestyle changes described above may significantly increase the quality of life as well as reduce the costs of medication. However, certain types of exercise such as weight lifting and certain types of rapid-weight-loss diets may actually be too stressful for the patient with high blood pressure. Ask your doctor which kinds of exercises and diets are best for you.

Tip # 2: Eat foods rich in potassium but low in salt.

How it works: Inadequate potassium makes salt even more dangerous for people with high blood pressure. To get adequate potassium, eat daily portions of potassium-rich, low salt food such as orange juice, grapefruit, and bananas. Do not take potassium supplements without your doctor's approval because it can be unsafe for some hypertensive patients with kidney damage or for those who are taking certain types of high blood pressure drugs.

Tip # 3: Ask your doctor to keep costs in mind when prescribing medicine for high blood pressure.

How it works: There are many kinds of blood pressure medicine. An average year's therapy with one medication alone can range from $131 for a diuretic to $466 for one of the more expensive classes of drugs. Often patients may require two or even three drugs for high blood pressure. Some drugs are more appropriate for you than others. Among the drugs that your doctor considers appropriate, ask him/her to prescribe the least expensive one or one with a guaranteed price or other offer.

Tip # 4: See MEDICATIONS in this book for more hints on saving money on drugs.

Tip # 5: Get free blood pressure tests to monitor your condition without going to the doctor.

How it works: Blood pressure monitoring is basic to treatment whether you are on drugs or managing your situation with exercise and diet. Save a trip to your doctor's office by taking advantage of free tests. Some drug stores have a free automatic blood pressure machine. You sit down, put your arm in a cuff and press a button. A computer screen shows your blood pressure and heart rate. Some patrons come daily to use the machine. Many hospitals offer free blood pressure screenings at convenient hours each week. County health departments often test blood pressure without charge any time during office hours. Other blood pressure screenings are offered at shopping centers. Notices of such screenings are advertised frequently in local newspapers under headings such as "Health briefs" or "Health watch." Or call your local hospital, social worker, American Heart Association office, or health department to find the nearest testing sites.

Quality check: An out-of-order machine or a poorly calibrated one may give you inaccurate results. Ask the pharmacist in a drug store if the machine is in good working order.

Tip # 6: Consider buying a blood pressure measuring device and learn to take your own blood pressure, if frequent monitoring is necessary.

How it works: The measurement of blood pressure requires two pieces of equipment: an arm cuff that has a pressure gauge attached and a listening device. The blood pressure measuring equipment may save money in the long run and may be more convenient by lengthening the time between visits. (Coordinate this arrangement with your doctor.) To learn how to take your own blood pressure at home, ask the nurse in your doctor's office to show you. For good, easy-to-follow instructions on measuring blood pressure, you may wish to consult the book *High Blood Pressure* by Shulman, Saunders, and Hall (Dell Publishing, NY 1993) or other patient education books on the subject.

Quality check: Your blood pressure cuff can be out of calibration, or you may not be using it properly, or you may experience a hearing loss that would make your measurement inaccurate. Blood pressure cuffs that go around your finger instead of your arm may not be reliable, according to *Consumer Reports*, 1992. Take your blood pressure equipment with you periodically when you do go to the doctor or nurse or blood pressure screening and compare your measurement with the professional measurement at the same time.

Tip # 7: Contact the High Blood Pressure Information Center.

How it works: The High Blood Pressure Information Center provides free patient information and referrals to blood screening programs. Call 301-951-3260 or write 120/80 National Institutes of Health, Bethesda, MD 20892.

Tip # 8: Consider participating in an experimental study of treatment of high blood pressure. (See also STUDIES.)

How it works: Experimental treatment studies often offer free treatment to patients who qualify as subjects. In particular, the Clinical Center of the National Institutes of Health (NIH) in Bethesda, MD, has ongoing studies of high blood pressure including idiopathic hypertension, familial hypertension, renovascular hypertension, steroid hypertension, hypokalemia, and lipid disorders. For information about getting into a study at this or other institutions, see STUDIES.

Tip # 9: For information about high blood pressure in black people, contact ISHIB.

How it works: The International Society for Hypertension in Blacks (ISHIB) will send free patient information. Write ISHIB at 185 Edgewood Ave., Atlanta, GA 30303 or call 404-616-3810. You may join ISHIB for a $50 annual membership fee and receive updated scientific information and a quarterly journal. An annual conference is held by ISHIB.

Tip # 10: Consider reading the book *High Blood Pressure* by Shulman, Saunders, and Hall.

How it works: The recently updated book *High Blood Pressure* from Dell Publishing (New York, 1993) is written by physicians for ordinary readers. It is a concise reference for those with high blood pressure. The price of the paperback is $3.95.

HILL-BURTON HOSPITAL FREE CARE

Tip # 1: If you are indigent, consider contacting hospitals that fall under the federal Hill-Burton bill.

How it works: Hospitals that have been built with federal grants under the Hill-Burton plan are obligated by law to provide some free services for indigent patients without cost. Many hospitals fall under this category. Some offer certain free services, others offer other free services. To locate the help you need, call 1-800-638-0742 (1-800-492-0359 in Maryland) and see which ones near you can help.

HISPANIC HEALTH

Tip # 1: For health information for Spanish-speaking people, call COSSMHO at 202-387-5000.

How it works: COSSMHO, the National Coalition of Hispanics and Health and Human Services Organization, is a non-profit organization dedicated to improving the health of Hispanic citizens. It puts out a newsletter six times a year and offers help and information to the Spanish-speaking community through community-based intervention.

HISTIOCYTOSIS-X (See also RARE DISEASES.)

Tip # 1: Contact the Histiocytosis-X Association of America at 1-800-548-2758 or 609-881-4911 in New Jersey.

How it works: The Association offers printed material and emotional support for persons with histiocytosis.

HIV (Human Immuno-deficiency) (See also AIDS.)

Tip #1: Consider taking an *anonymous* test for HIV.

How it works: Most HIV testing is confidential, that is, no one will tell your HIV status to people near you or make it public. But your name and status is on record and may be on a list filed with the state; individuals along the way may see your name. *Anonymous* testing, by contrast, is done without any reference to your name. You get a code, take the test, and when you return, you give your code and get your results. Your name is not on any record. Complete privacy on the HIV issue is the safest route to take while you are planning your future. Call a national or local AIDS organization for referrals to anonymous testing sites. (See AIDS.)

Tip #2: If you are HIV positive, get the best job and insurance situation you can while you are healthy and your status is not known by anyone else.

How it works: You may realize you are in a job you had not planned to stay in. If you have insurance provided by your employer, consider keeping this job anyway because insurance coverage may have to be your first priority. On the other hand, you may have a job that provides no insurance. In that case, consider seeking a job with a company that offers group insurance without testing for HIV. (These are increasingly rare.) The best thing you have going for you is that you are now healthy and productive as a worker. Do everything the regular way, joining the health plan at the usual time, asking for no special favors, asking no unusual questions because anything that sets you apart from the pack of other employees may result in an individual examination. Be aware that some otherwise firm job offers are contingent on passing a physical.

Tip # 3: Order a booklet especially for those recently identified as HIV positive.

How it works: "Positive Living" is a 27-page booklet written especially for those recently identified as HIV positive. It can be obtained free from the American Social Health Association by sending a self-addressed business-sized envelope with 52-cents postage on it to P.O. Box 13827-PL, Research Triangle Park, N.C. 27709.

HMO

Tip # 1: Consider a good HMO (health maintenance organization).

How it works: An HMO or health maintenance organization charges members a monthly or quarterly fee. Whether or not the patient uses the HMO plan, the fee is the same. For that fee, the HMO offers patients a wide array of health care services from hospitalization to prescriptions for a very small copayment, typically about $2 to $10 per doctor's office visit and $2 to $5 per prescription. An HMO may operate in a group setting in one location or it may be a network of providers in individually located offices. An advantage of HMO coverage over most insurance policies is that the HMO favors preventive care and usually covers well-baby care, immunizations, screening tests, and yearly examinations. Another advantage is that very little paperwork is necessary in using an HMO plan in contrast to most health insurance plans. The best thing about a certified HMO for many consumers may be that it is not as likely to exclude pre-existing conditions as insurance programs are. HMO members must use doctors affiliated with the organization to get coverage except in emergency situations and other special cases. This limitation is cited as the major drawback of an HMO, but many users find that the selection of affiliated doctors is large enough and includes the same quality of professional as is found outside the HMO. An HMO with its monthly fee is a pay-as-you-go plan with protection against unexpected or overwhelming costs of serious medical problems. In that way HMO membership is like a very low-deductible health insurance plan but tends to be less expensive because the HMO keeps costs low. Here's how: The HMO pays the doctor rather than reimbursing the patient. The HMO sometimes refuses to pay doctors or hospitals for procedures it deems unnecessary or charges it considers excessive. It may drop doctors who have a record of more lab tests or other procedures than other doctors with the same kinds of patients and specialty. HMOs put the pinch on doctors and other providers to save money rather than on patients. HMOs generally have been out of favor with some doctors because of the restrictions on them, but as HMOs have become increasingly popular with patients, even the most sought-after doctors have felt pressured to join an HMO in order to be where the patients were going.

Quality check: Because HMOs will not pay for treatment they consider unnecessary, the incentive to doctors is to undertreat. A doctor might not do a test even though he/she might want to because of the risk of not being paid. The fear of litigation should he/she fail to treat, however, tends to balance the incentive to undertreat.

Tip # 2: Compare the terms and reputations of different HMOs.

How it works: Compare monthly fees and copayments and deductibles if any. Get a complete description of coverage in writing. Ask particularly about coverage of pre-existing conditions. Ask for rules about pre-notification and approval. Ask about coverage if you get treatment outside of the networks as in emergencies or for care from a specialist. Ask if coverage is limited or denied for certain procedures such as mental health or optional procedures. Ask doctors you are considering on the lists if they are happy with their HMO experience and if they are taking new patients. Ask about continuity of care and coverage (being allowed to see the same doctor) if your company drops the plan or your doctor leaves the organization in the middle of your treatment. Some issues which most affect patient satisfaction besides costs and coverage are the choice of primary care doctors and specialists, the freedom to use specialists, and the method by which the HMO pays doctors. Patients are most satisfied when there is a lot of choice, that is, more primary care doctors (family doctors, internists, and pediatricians) to choose from at a centralized HMO site and/or long lists of primary care and specialists in an HMO network. Happy enrollees say their HMO has "all the best doctors." Providing "all the best doctors" may be a function of the HMO checking formal accreditation and malpractice records and informal patient satisfaction surveys. HMO members are most satisfied when fewer restrictions are placed on the use of specialists. The method of payment of doctors is not often a patient's concern but it correlates heavily with patient satisfaction. Some HMOs pay primary doctors in their organization a straight salary or a salary plus a bonus if the HMO makes a profit. Others pay per-patient, that is, according to the number of HMO members who sign up for that primary care doctor. Others pay set fees based on services rendered. In general, a 1992 *Consumers Report* found HMO members are more satisfied with organizations that paid participating doctors on a fee-for-service basis rather than a salary, salary-plus-bonus, or per-patient sign-up basis.

Quality check: A lengthy discussion of differences in HMOs in general and patient-satisfaction ratings for specific plans can be found in *Consumer Reports*, August 1992 issue.

HOME CARE, HOME HEALTH CARE (See also AGING, DISABILITY, HOSPICE and LONG TERM CARE.)

Tip # 1: Consider home care to keep an elderly person living independently, to keep an ill person out of an institution, to keep children and families together.

How it works: The term "home care" describes a wide range of services including house calls by physicians, nurses, nurses aides, therapists and other health care professionals, homemaking services, child care, meals-on-wheels (see Tip # 9), transportation, visiting and telephoning reassurance, pastoral counseling, and equipment services. Home care services may be all that is necessary to keep an elderly person from having to move into assisted living or skilled nursing care institutions. Home care services may provide medical care for a patient who would otherwise have to be hospitalized. Home care can be critical to a family with children with working parents or special problems. Keeping families together and patients at home may be very desirable for the emotional well-being of those involved. Home care involving only a few or infrequent services can be less expensive than care in a hospital, nursing home, or other institution where you must pay for all available services on a 24-hour basis. On the other hand, home care involving several skilled services on a frequent basis can be more costly than care in an institution. Use the following tips to evaluate your options.

Tip # 2: Locate home care through national organizations, local referral services, and the phone book.

How it works: The National HomeCaring Council makes referrals to most of the homemaker and home health aide services in the country including those it accredits. Call 212-674-4990 or write National HomeCaring Council, 235 Park Avenue South, New York, NY 10003. The National League for Nursing will refer you to agencies it accredits. Call 212-582-1022 or write National League of Nursing, American Public Health Association, 10 Columbus Circle, New York, NY 10019. If you are in a hospital or nursing home and are considering home care, talk to the social worker or discharge planner who will make a plan for home care, if appropriate, and make referrals. Call the local United Way, Area Agency on Aging, county or state Health Department, Family Services, Social Services, Visiting Nurse Associations, Catholic Charities, Jewish Family Services, or other organizations listed in the white pages for free or inexpensive home care services for eligible people. In the yellow pages, call agencies listed under Home Care, Home Health Care, Hospice, Nurses, Visiting Nurses. Also, call agencies and organizations set up to help people with specific diseases or situations such as the local office of the American Cancer Society or AIDS organizations.

For meals on wheels, see Tip # 8.

Tip # 3: Compare service and cost of different kinds of home care providers.

How it works: Home care services may be provided by for-profit home care agencies, non-profit home care agencies, governmental tax-supported home care agencies, and employment agencies and nurses' registries. Each has its own characteristics. For-profit or proprietary home care agencies may be the most expensive home care option per service, but as such they may provide care most closely suited to your need. A good agency will draw up a plan of service after a careful evaluation of your situation and will give you the level of service you need, no more and no less. A non-profit home care agency may be less expensive than a for-profit agency and may charge on a sliding scale. It may also use trained volunteer help for some of its services. A good non-profit agency will draw up a plan of service after evaluating your situation. States, counties, and other government units often provide tax-supported home care services such as visiting nurses and housekeeping services. For example, the federal Older American Act Funds and Social Security Block Grants to States provides homemaker-home health aide services and home-delivered meals to the eligible elderly. Social workers in a government program should evaluate your needs and provide a plan for what can be provided as well as advice on other programs you may need. Government agencies sometimes, but not always, restrict their services to certain groups such as the elderly or those with low income or with certain disabilities. Employment agencies and nurses' registries place nurses or other health care personnel in your home for a fee. As the employer, you are fully responsible for the supervision of the person hired. Support services offered by another kind of agency might not be available. For example, if you ask for a nurse when a less expensive nurse's aid might do, there is no evaluation service to advise you. If you are knowledgeable, assertive, and a good supervisor, you might consider this arrangement, but it should not cost as much as full-service from a for-profit agency.

Tip # 4: Network for nursing or home health care aides. If you go through an agency, you pay the agency and you pay the professional. If you can find someone privately, it's cheaper and can mean the difference between at-home care and institutional care. (See the next tip.)

Quality check: If you employ nursing or home health care aides on your own, you will have more tax papers to file such as social security, state unemployment, withholding taxes, etc.

Tip # 5: Employ health care students to give respite care.

How it works: If you live near a university or professional school with a nursing or physical therapy program, contact the school for students willing to give respite care. Students usually need spending money and they can give the care giver some needed time off as well as some skill level.

Tip # 6: Arrange for the least skilled care appropriate.

How it works: Sometimes an elderly person incapacitated by stroke is attended by a registered nurse (RN) because the family only knew to ask for "a nurse." Many such patients can be cared for just as well and much less expensively with a personal care attendant. An RN is, however, necessary to administer complex treatment. (See next tip.) Choosing the least skilled care level appropriate and the fewest hours necessary is important for saving money and can be facilitated by good evaluation and planning by a home care agency. Less expensive than Registered Nurses (RN) are Licensed Practical Nurses (LPN), who have less education in the field than RNs, and who can take care of less complex nursing tasks. Nursing assistants, home health aides, or attendants are not nurses but should have had 60 hours of training as recommended by the National HomeCaring Council. Specialists such as respiratory therapists, speech therapists, and nutritionists can be called in as needed. When nursing care is lengthy or constant or when several different services are necessary, home care may not be the most cost-effective choice. Assisted living facilities or nursing homes because they provide housing, nutrition, supervision, nursing care, and specialized therapy under one roof, may be the less expensive option.

Tip # 7: Learn to give medications yourself.

How it works: Nurses (RNs and LPNs) are allowed to give medications but nurses are expensive. Less expensive home health care aides are not allowed to give medications. So, if a patient needs simple medications or even injections, learn to give it yourself.

Tip # 8: Look for certification and accreditation of home health care agencies.

How it works: If your state requires licensing of home care agencies, be cautious about dealing with an unlicensed organization. However, licensing often does not indicate quality. Agency bonding does not indicate quality but only that an agency has protected itself in the case of suits against it. Certification and accreditation, however, are indications of quality. State health department certification is important because it indicates that an agency has met basic federal and state standards and is therefore eligible for payment for Medicare and some Medicaid home health services. Accreditation means that an agency has met the basic requirements of certain non-profit organizations that are concerned with the quality of home care. Two of these accrediting organizations are the National HomeCaring Council and the National League for Nursing. Their numbers and addresses can be found in Tip # 2.

Tip # 9: Contact the National Association for Home Care for a directory.

How it works: The National Association for Home Care, a trade association, provides an annual National Homecare & Hospice Directory listing 12,000 home care provider organizations and 1200 hospices nationwide. The directory is available for $5 by writing: Attention: 1993 Directory, 519 C Street NE, Washington, DC 20002-5809.

Tip # 10: Ask for a booklet "All About Home Care: A Consumer's Guide" from the Council of the Better Business Bureaus.

How it works: The Better Business Bureau publishes a very useful consumer's guide to home care. It tells how to find and evaluate home care services. It discusses financing, sources of aid, taxes, security problems, and it lists questions to ask in several areas of concern. To receive this booklet, write Council of Better Business Bureaus, 1515 Wilson Blvd., Arlington, VA 22209.

Tip # 11: Contact the Foundation for Hospice and Homecare.

How it works: The Foundation for Hospice and Homecare will send you the booklet mentioned in Tip # 7 and other materials. The staff can answer individual questions on all aspects of home care. Call 202-547-6586 or write the Foundation for Hospice and Homecare at 519 C Street NE, Washington, DC 20002-5809.

Tip # 12: Consider a "meals on wheels" program.

How it works: Meals on wheels programs deliver one or two meals a day to people at home who find it difficult to shop for or prepare food for themselves. Churches, synagogues, organizations concerned with specific diseases like cancer groups or AIDS support organizations, and other community groups operate similar services. Some deliver a hot meal at noon plus a sack supper for later.

Those who receive the service often pay to defray costs, which are low because delivery and sometimes preparation is done by volunteers. In some cases of need, non-profit organizations may be able to waive or reduce payment. The Older American Act Funds and Social Security Block Grants to States also funds home-delivered meals to the elderly. For more information, call the local office on aging or health department for federally funded programs. To find a meals on wheels program, call a local chapter of United Way for referrals. In some communities there is a listing under Meals on Wheels in the white pages of the phone book, although similar programs may go by a different name. Also, contact the National Association of Meals Programs at 202-547-6157 for referrals to member programs. Consider also arranging with local restaurants for carry-out and delivery service, a growing practice. Meals of every kind, not just pizza and Chinese food, can be available delivered to the customer's door. Cost for restaurant food is at restaurant prices, but, if this is all it takes to keep a home-bound person out of a nursing home or institution, it may be a health care bargain. If home delivery is not advertised in your community, call neighborhood restaurants and discuss individual arrangements.

Tip # 13: Enlist the help of visiting volunteers.

How it works: Churches, synagogues and other community organizations offer programs of visiting volunteers who go into homes of the elderly, disabled, or chronically ill on a regular basis to help. They may bathe and dress the patient or write letters and engage in conversation. They may fix a meal and do light housekeeping tasks. Usually they will do anything they are qualified to do in a short period of time to make living at home more possible and pleasant for the patient. Most programs provide training programs for the volunteers; some volunteers are retired health care professionals. To find visiting volunteer programs in your area, call the local office of United Way, individual churches and community organizations, and hospice care listed in your phone book. Also, see next tip.

Tip # 14: Contact the National Federation of Interfaith Volunteer Caregivers at 1-914-331-1358.

How it works: The National Federation of Interfaith Volunteers will put you in touch with local projects affiliated with over 1000 church and synagogue congregations across the nation. Interfaith Volunteers, trained by the National Federation, transport the sick or elderly to and from the hospital, doctor's office, and clinic. They also provide personal care, telephone check-ups, and patient visits. In addition, they will provide respite care for caregivers for disabled children. Be aware that Interfaith Volunteers, like most volunteers, do not give out medicine.

Tip # 15: Buy home care supplies in bulk.

How it works: Strike a deal with the local pharmacy to buy home care supplies in bulk. These might include diapers, pads, disinfectants, syringes, bandages, and whatever else you use in quantity. Usually there is a discount from the shelf price when you buy by the case. Bulk buying also means fewer trips to the drug store for the caregiver.

Tip # 16: Ask your doctor for a prescription for everything, not just prescription medication.

How it works: Ask your doctor for prescriptions for medicine, even over-the-counter medicine, supplies, equipment, home modification. All these expenses may be itemized as medical deductions on your tax return if documented by doctor's prescriptions.

HOMELESS (See also MENTAL HEALTH, Tip # 5, and COMMUNITY HEALTH CENTERS.)

HOSPICE CARE

Tip # 1: Consider hospice care for the terminally ill patient.

How it works: Once a patient is considered a few months from death, usually six, by a doctor, hospice care may be appropriate. Generally, the patient must not be on radiation or chemotherapy because the focus of hospice care is on dying in peace and dignity rather than on attempts at recovery. Drugs are given only to ease symptoms and keep the patient comfortable. Also, the patient is not subjected to repeated blood tests or being moved to diagnostic or treatment centers. The hospice program director can talk with the patient's doctor about whether it is time to abandon more aggressive treatment and seek more peaceful final months without stating a specific life-expectancy to the patient. Hospice services are provided in the least restrictive environment possible. Hospice care is often home treatment by visiting nurses and other trained personnel. A full range of services may also be provided including counselors to help plan for changing needs, chaplains, home-maker/home health aide services, and volunteer assistance. Some provide 24-hour emergency service as well as periodic visiting care. A relative or other caretaker is sometimes required to be with the patient on a full-time basis and work with the visiting hospice workers. Other hospice programs are home-like in-patient facilities where the patient lives and dies. Hospice care is less expensive than hospitalization. Accredited hospices accept private insurance, Medicare and Medicaid where applicable. (See Tip #2.) In addition, many hospices are non-profit and charge on a sliding scale; services are rendered regardless of ability to pay. Find hospice programs in your community by consulting with the local hospital social worker, by interviewing the staff at hospices found in the yellow pages of the phone book, or by referral from national organizations concerned with hospice care. (See Tips #3 and #4.) Investigate several hospice programs. At in-patient facilities, ask about the waiting list and consider putting a patient with little hope of recovery on the waiting list even before such care is necessary.

Quality check: Ask the hospice program you are considering about their licensing as a hospice. Ask also if it is Medicare certified; if so, it has been approved by federal standards. Look for accreditation with the National Hospice Organization (NHO). Or call the NHO at 1-800-658-8898 to ask for accredited hospice programs in your community. If the patient is a child, Children's Hospice International can give you appropriate information. Call 1-800-242-4453.

Tip #2: Hospice services may be paid for by Medicare, Medicaid in some states, or private insurance. Check your policy.

How it works: It is important to read the provisions of your Medicare, Medicaid, or private insurance policy to see what coverage is offered for hospice care. Medicare now covers hospice services but regulations require the patient or family member to sign a statement saying that he/she waives the right to Medicare coverage for other types of treatment for the terminal illness. Most of the hospice care must be in the home with only short stays in an in-patient facility. The hospice must also be accredited for Medicare. Medicaid covers hospice care in about 32 states. See MEDICAID, Tip #3 for services covered or, for an update, call state Medicaid office to see if your state does. Private insurance may cover hospice care. Check your policy. In general, insurance companies approve hospice care because the alternatives are usually more expensive. If hospice care is not specifically mentioned in your policy, ask for your case to be reviewed by the company and an agreement made in writing to cover hospice care.

Tip # 3: For information and referrals call Hospice Link at 1-800-658-8898.

How it works: Hospice Link is a referral line of the Hospice Education Institute, a non-profit organization which offers training seminars to hospice professionals and books on the subject. Hospice Link staff will answer questions and refer to hospice programs in your area.

Tip # 4: Contact the National Hospice Organization at 1-800-658-8898.

How it works: The National Hospice Organization sets accreditation standards for hospices in the U.S. and makes referrals to accredited hospices by location. Staff will answer individual questions and mail information on request.

Tip # 5: Look for other hospice-like programs in your community.

How it works: Only programs that meet certain definitions and requirements may use the designation "hospice," but other programs for the dying may be appropriate for you. For example, in one community a Catholic charity facility provides a home for those dying from cancer only. It is not considered a hospice because it does not meet the requirement of treating other terminal conditions, but its program is excellent. Ask the local hospital social worker for suggestions.

Tip # 6: Contact the Foundation for Hospice and Homecare.

How it works: The Foundation can answer individual questions and also send you a free booklet, "All About Hospice: A Consumer's Guide." Call 202-547-6586 or write Foundation for Hospice and Homecare, 519 C Street NE, Washington, DC 20002-5809.

HOSPITAL-ACQUIRED INFECTIONS

Tip # 1: Call the Centers for Disease Control and Prevention (CDC) at 404-332-4555 for current information on hospital-acquired infections.

How it works: The CDC provides very detailed, recorded information on hospital-acquired infections 24 hours a day including information on prevention, symptoms, diagnosis, treatment, and prevalence. To save money, call during low telephone rate hours. To receive written information on hospital-acquired infections and answers to other questions ONLY AFTER listening to the recorded information, call the CDC public inquiry number 404-639-3534 weekdays except federal holidays 8:30 a.m. to 5 p.m. Eastern time.

HOSPITAL STAYS

Tip # 1: Ask your doctor to send you to the least expensive hospital that can give you quality care.

How it works: Your doctor may be on the staff of several hospitals. Or choose a recommended specialist from the list of staff at the particular low-cost/high-quality hospital you choose. See the following tips.

Quality check: Ask someone in the administration office of a hospital you are considering if it is accredited by the Joint Commission on Accreditation of Healthcare Organizations or call the Joint Commission in Oak Brook, IL at (708) 916-5800 to ask about the accreditation of a hospital you are considering. For other questions concerning quality of hospitals, call the American Hospital Association at 312-280-6263.

Tip # 2: Shop around for room-rates.

How it works: A semi-private room in an accredited suburban hospital on Long Island, NY, recently cost $407 a night. In a large metropolitan New York City hospital it was $650 a night. Location is a major cost factor for hospitals just as for other businesses. The more lengthy your hospital stay the more relevant room-rate comparisons may be although room rates are just one cost factor to compare.

Quality check: Differences in the range of services may affect your choice of hospital. If a hospital does not have services you may need, it is no bargain.

Tip # 3: Shop around for average costs per day for the procedure you are considering. Also ask how many days of hospitalization are usually required for the procedure.

How it works: For new, cutting-edge procedures with high-tech equipment, choose a large hospital that provides these services and does them efficiently. For routine procedures check prices at smaller, less prestigious hospitals. Large and expensive hospitals do wonderful things with the latest technology and often are more expensive across the board than smaller hospitals. If you are having an ordinary surgical procedure by traditional methods, however, you have no use for the latest laser brain surgery capabilities and no desire to pay for these special capabilities. Note that some hospitals are cheaper per day but less efficient in scheduling and take more days to get something done. Estimate total costs and compare.

Tip # 4: Use comparative information from a cost containment board to shop around.

How it works: Different hospitals typically charge different amounts for different procedures. It's very hard for an individual to compare costs as no two hospitalizations are alike and accounting methods vary. Charts of figures on the following pages, however, illustrate differences in costs for common procedures undertaken in Dade County (Florida) hospitals as compiled by the Florida Health Care Cost Containment Board for 1990. These prices may no longer be current, but they do reflect the range of costs and the value of shopping around. See if your state has a cost containment board to provide you with comparable figures for your area.

Quality check: Quality of hospital care varies from institution to institution. The relationship between cost and quality is not

AVERAGE CHARGE PER PATIENT BY

	Normal Childbirth- The Baby RDRG 3910	Normal Childbirth- The Baby (Complications) RDRG 3911	Normal Childbirth- The Mother RDRG 3730	Cesarean Section- The Mother RDRG 3700	Angina Pectoris RDRG 1400
					(Dollars)
DADE COUNTY					
AMI Palmetto General Hospital	900	1.313	2,922	6.013	6,265
Anne Bates Leach Eye Hospital	—	—	—	—	—
Baptist Hospital of Miami	842	1.176	2.678	4,810	4,487
Cedars Medical Center	—	—	—	—	6,145
Coral Gables Hospital	1,937[1]	—	—	—	4,724
Deering Hospital	—	—	—	—	4,222
Doctors Coral Gables	474	686	2,641	5,516	3,685
Golden Glades Regional Medical Center	—	—	—	—	5.036
Hialeah Hospital	853	1,231	3,394	6.587	6.625

HOSPITAL AND ILLNESS CATEGORY

Heart Failure & Shock (Complications) RDRG 1271	Stroke RDRG 0141	Chest Pain RDRG 1430	Hyster-ectomy RDRG 3580	Digestive System Problems (Complications) RDRG 1821	Back Problems (Non-surgical) RDRG 2430	Simple Pneumonia & Pleurisy RDRG 0890
11.359	14.028	5.334	8.407	5.792	4.784	7.555
—	—	—	—	—	4.405[1]	—
8.125	9.857	3.435	6.408	4.622	4.453	4.609
11.009	10.764	5.528	8.764	7.244	5.561	9.068
7.392	9.365	4.324	7.427	5.107	4.887	6.265
8.124	9.655	3.842	7.771	5.671	4.574	4.122
7.164	7.610	3.376	6.202	4.567	3.694	5.024
9.907	9.741	4.046	7.930	4.588	4.997	5.514
11.664	15.547	5.703	7.521	4.940	5.087	6.768

	Normal Childbirth- The Baby RDRG 3910	Normal Childbirth- The Baby (Complications) RDRG 3911	Normal Childbirth- The Mother RDRG 3730	Cesarean Section- The Mother RDRG 3700	Angina Pectoris RDRG 1400
					(Dollars)
Humana Hospital Biscayne	—	2.031[1]	—	—	5.011
Jackson Memorial Hospital	1.172	1.613	2.124	4.977	3.755
James Archer Smith Hospital	695	1.080	2.232	5.598	4.288
Kendall Regional Medical Center	—	—	—	—	5.571
Larkin General Hospital	—	—	—	—	4.824
Mercy Hospital	960	1.466	3.064	5.714	4.878
Miami Children's Hospital	3.964[1]	3.465[1]	—	—	—
Miami Heart Institute	—	—	—	—	4.877
Mount Sinai Medical Center	838	1.337	3.025	5.805	6.119
North Gables Hospital	—	—	—	—	3.988
North Miami Medical Center	Closed	2nd Qtr. 1990			
North Shore Medical Center	546	959	2.241	4.300	5.655
Palm Springs Hospital	—	—	—	—	5.337
Pan American Hospital	3.220[1]	—	—	—	4.859
Parkway Regional Medical Center	826	1.195	2.928	6.032	4.342
South Miami Hospital	1.045	1.463	3.157	5.536	4.045
South Shore Hospital	—	—	—	—	4.618
St. Francis Hospital	615	734	3.289	6.201	5.542
University of Miami Hospitals and Clinics	—	—	—	—	—
Victoria Hospital	—	—	—	—	4.216
Westchester General Hospital	—	—	1.950[1]	—	5.108

NOTES:

- No discharges were reported for this diagnosis.

1. The hospital reported 10 or fewer discharges for this diagnosis, or had 10 or fewer discharges after excluding cases of unusually high cost.

2. Differences in corresponding mother/baby data may be related to diagnostic

Heart Failure & Shock (Complications) RDRG 1271	Stroke RDRG 0141	Chest Pain RDRG 1430	Hyster- ectomy RDRG 3580	Digestive System Problems (Complications) RDRG 1821	Back Problems (Non- surgical) RDRG 2430	Simple Pneumonia & Pleurisy RDRG 0890
9.429	12.371	4.479	10.104	6.012	5,723	7,620
7.368	11.117	3.340	8.571	4.835	4.328	5.030
8.208	15.919	4.073	6.449	4.925	4.796	5.138
9.691	12.785	4.943	9.819	6.109	5.067	7.386
8.487	8.011	3.412	7.551	5.708	3.482	7.167
8.170	11.748	3.899	8.179	5.929	5.473	5.931
6.877[1]	15.109[1]	2.581[1]	6.234[1]	4.475	2,037	6.624
8.823	8.503	3.717	7.739	5.071	4.629	7.516
11.282	12.871	5.088	6.349	6.054	6.437	8.303
7.841	7,957	2.788	9.031	6.365	4.373	7.258
9.184	11.015	4.677	6.866	4.936	4.565	6.054
9.804	9.906	4.813	7.491	5.641	5.548	7.207
8.818	11.525	3.858	7.704	5.427	5.372	6.398
8.596	10.341	3.501	9.484	6.334	6.161	6.097
8.511	9.099	3.458	7.186	5.340	4.496	6.510
8.352	7.779	3.584[1]	4.865[1]	5.519	8.123	6.466
9.371	11.704	4.330	6.936	7.534	5.344	8.476
11.607[1]	3.330[1]	—	—	6.358	907[1]	4.078[1]
8.508	10.685	2.774	8.248	6.559	4.801	5.739
11.466	17.319[1]	5.943	7.409	6.434	5.506	6.174

categories not included in this publication.
3. No discharges for this diagnosis after excluding cases of unusually high cost.

The averages shown are submitted by Florida hospitals to the Florida Health Care Cost Containment Board for the reporting period January 1, 1990 through December 31, 1990. All averages have been verified as accurate by the submitting hospitals.

constant. Some higher priced hospitals may offer the best care; on the other hand, some very expensive hospitals are not so much higher quality as inefficiently run. An excellent hospital with a good handle on costs may give you the best care. Ask your doctor for an opinion on the quality of care for the procedure you need at the hospitals with which he/she has an affiliation. Also, ask other knowledgeable people who have been recently hospitalized.

Tip # 5: Some hospitals will offer a set fee for a certain treatment.

How it works: Some hospitals offer a set fee guarantee for certain procedures such as delivery of a baby so that a patient knows the limits and doesn't have to worry about additional costs. Ask hospitals in your area if they have such a policy or if they will offer this guarantee to you individually.

Tip # 6: Consider using a Veterans Administration (VA) hospital if you qualify.

How it works: There are currently about 26 million living veterans. Almost one third of the nation's population, approximately 71 million persons who are veterans, dependents, and survivors of deceased veterans, are potentially eligible for VA medical benefits. The VA recognizes two categories of patients. Those in the "mandatory" group are those in the "service-connected" category (veterans who were injured or contracted a disease during active duty) and those veterans who, although not in the "service-connected" category, have an income less than a certain level (as of 1992, $18,844 if single and without dependents and $22,613 if married or with a dependent). Those in the "discretionary" category will be given hospitalization if resources are available and if the patient agrees to pay a deductible equal to what would have been paid under Medicare. Adjusted annually, the deductible in 1992 was $652 for the first 90 day period, and half of that for each additional 90 days. For those in the latter category needing a hospitalization not available in their region, it may be worthwhile to seek out a less crowded facility. For example, VA hospitals in the northeastern region of the nation currently have more resources available for "discretionary" patients than the VA hospitals in Florida where there is an enormous demand.

For a full description of eligibility write the Department of Veterans Affairs, Washington DC 20420 and ask for the latest edition of *Federal Benefits for Veterans and Dependents*. Local counselors are available. Offices are listed in your phone book under U.S. Government—Veterans Affairs.

Quality check: Treatment can be excellent in a VA hospital and cutting edge procedures are often available. Innovations in kidney and heart transplants, for example, were developed in VA hospitals. Among the 171 VA hospitals, 127 are linked with teaching centers. Often the best care at VA facilities is found in highly specialized treatment. Different VA hospitals are leaders in different procedures. One reputable source recommends going to the VA's Palo Alto, CA, or Seattle hospitals for prosthetics, to Pittsburgh or Portland for organ transplants, Washington for a pacemaker for your heart. Consider getting orthopedic surgery in Indianapolis, Denver, or Boston. Boston and San Antonio are noted for cancer treatment. The best AIDS programs are reported to be in New York, Miami, West Lost Angeles, and San Francisco. Overall quality of treatment at VA hospitals is equal to treatment in civilian facilities. A study conducted by the Joint Commission of Accreditation of Healthcare Organizations showed the rate of death and complications following surgery in 1991 at VA hospitals was equal to figures from non-VA hospitals. The VA slightly outscored civilian counterparts by 10 points on a 1-100 scale of overall quality. A VA hospital, as a government institution, is more likely to suffer from bureaucratic red tape, however, than a private hospital in the competitive market. There may also be more of a problem in continuity of care, seeing the same doctor each visit, at a VA hospital than at another hospital.

Tip # 6: Go to a public or charity hospital if you have a very low income.

How it works: Some hospitals are supported by tax money or by charitable donations. These institutions usually have a sliding scale or special arrangement so that hospitalization costs are low or free for certain groups who cannot afford hospitalization. Tax supported institutions may offer lower rates only to residents of their counties or states and they may have other restrictions. Proof of low income will be required. If your income is not low enough to qualify you for a reduced rate at a public or charity hospital, note that the full cost of hospitalization there may be *more* than in your neighborhood hospital. For the names of public hospitals near you, call or visit your library and ask for information from the *American Hospital Association Guide to Health Care*.

Quality check: Many such institutions are affiliated with medical schools; their physicians are often residents supervised by physicians/professors. The residents are often fresh and enthusiastic though less experienced. The supervisors may be on the cutting edge of medical research. Waiting lines and bureaucracy, however, may be excessive in hospitals with sliding scales and, if you are admitted, waiting days for tests and other procedures while in the hospital may add to your total bill.

Tip # 7: If you are indigent, consider contacting hospitals that fall under the federal Hill-Burton bill and demonstrate that you need indigent care.

How it works: Hospitals that have been built with federal grants under the Hill-Burton plan are obligated by law to provide some free services for indigent patients without cost. Many hospitals fall under this category. Some offer certain free services, others offer other free services. To locate the help you need, call 1-800-638-0742 (1-800-492-0359 in Maryland) and see which ones near you can help.

Tip # 8: Consider less expensive out-patient services but first compare in-patient and out-patient coverage on your insurance policy before making decisions. Sometimes the less expensive procedure is the least covered by insurance.

How it works: To save money for the patient, one doctor sent his patient home from the hospital between in-patient treatments and had the patient return for diagnostic tests on an out-patient basis. The outpatient service was at a lower cost, but it turned out that the patient's insurance would cover the diagnostic test only if they were part of a hospitalization. The "money-saving" choice cost the patient more. Go over your insurance policy with your doctor before making such decisions.

Quality check: You may be monitored more closely in a hospital setting than in an out-patient setting. On the other hand, the possibility of being exposed to a contagious disease may be greater in a hospital.

Tip # 9: Find a cooperative care unit in a local hospital where a friend or family member can help provide care at lower cost.

How it works: Hospitals are beginning to develop cooperative care units that require family members or friends to help care for patients. This is especially appropriate for people with long-term illnesses, chronic conditions, or even mothers of new babies. The costs in these units are lower than in the hospital's regular facilities.

Quality check: Your friends or relatives may be untrained but their attention may be more constant and may give you a boost in morale. Trained staff should always be nearby when help is needed.

Tip # 10: Inform your insurance company about any proposed hospitalization.

How it works: Many insurance policies require that a hospitalization be pre-certified, that is, approved for coverage. Without this step, the company may not pay or may not pay as much for your hospitalization. In addition, there may be some surprises that will affect your choices. For example, one patient needed an EKG and selected a clinical situation where a computer read the EKG results. This was possibly the less expensive option but the insurance company would not pay because its policy paid only for EKG results read by a human. You cannot retain all the provisions of a policy in your head, so if possible before scheduling a procedure, check your insurance.

Tip # 11: If your insurance will not pay for a hospital treatment because it is experimental treatment, consider enlisting your doctor and perhaps a lawyer to convince the insurance company the treatment should be covered.

How it works: Many insurance companies refuse to pay for experimental treatment. They do not want to pay for treatments that are not of proven value. However, if the treatment can be shown to be effective or likely to be effective, the company may change its mind. Ask your doctor to show the insurance company the latest research indicating expected good results of the treatment or good results already demonstrated.

Tip # 12: Ask your insurance company how many days the insurance company considers allowable for the procedure you plan to have.

How it works: Some insurance companies do not expect to pay for more than a certain number of days it considers standard for each procedure. After you have found out the number of days covered by your insurance company, ask your doctor to aim for no more than that duration or help you demonstrate to your insurance company why more days were necessary.

Tip # 13: If you have insurance but can't pay the copayment, consider bargaining with a hospital before admission.

How it works: Some hospitals would prefer to negotiate a bill than lose your business. If your insurance policy will pay a portion, for example, 80% of the hospital charges and you have trouble paying the remaining copayment, ask hospital billing representatives if they will accept the 80% and waive the co-payment. Consider choosing a hospital that says Yes and get a written agreement before you check in. A hospital that is not filled to capacity is, of course, a better bet than an overcrowded facility.

Tip # 14: Ask your doctor about the value of tests prior to admission to a hospital.

How it works: Before a procedure is done in a hospital (surgery for example), a battery of tests is often given to each patient, like blood work and heart tests. The test battery is intended to determine if the patient can stand the procedure and to uncover any potential problems. But the standard battery may include tests unnecessary in your case. Perhaps your doctor has already tested you for these conditions or perhaps they are irrelevant. For example, a PAP screening test is often done as part of pre-hospitalization testing. As valuable as the test is for screening for cancer, if you have recently had a PAP there may be no need to do it again for hospitalization. Discuss admission testing with your doctor and eliminate unnecessary tests.

Tip # 15: Get necessary preoperative or pre-treatment tests outside the hospital if your insurance will cover it and save a day in the hospital.

How it works: For many treatments, especially surgery, the first day of hospitalization is spent getting tests. If you ask for a list of tests your doctor has ordered and if these can be done on an outpatient basis, you can get this part of the procedure done without paying for a day in the hospital. But first check to see that your insurance will cover the tests on an out-patient basis.

Tip # 16: Avoid going into the hospital (when you have a choice) on a weekend or a Friday.

How it works: If you have a choice about what day you enter a hospital for non-emergency or elective admission, consider that many kinds of tests, diagnostic and preoperative, are not done routinely on the weekend. If you need some tests before you are treated and you enter the hospital during or right before the weekend, you may spend costly time waiting for the staff to begin these procedures on Monday. It is most efficient to enter on a Monday and have a full work week to get what you need done.

Quality check: In spite of what people say about Mondays, the staff is fresh and ready to get down to work.

Tip # 17: Consider drawing up "advance directives" before going into a hospital.

How it works: Advance directives are legal documents that state what kinds of treatment you would want, especially limitations on extreme measures, in the event that you were terminally ill and unable to make such decisions yourself. A Durable Power of Attorney for Health and a Living Will are two of the most common advance directives. It varies by state whether these documents are legally binding. With an advance directive in hand, hospital officials may be able to limit your treatment according to your stated wishes if you are beyond the point of recovery. Such a document can prevent draining a terminally ill patient's resources on useless treatment. (See also DYING.)

Tip # 18: If you know you are unable to pay a hospital bill, soon *after* admission contact the hospital's social worker for help with Medicaid or other financial resources.

How it works: Every accredited hospital has a social worker. Seek this person out or have a friend or relative contact the social worker so that he/she can start your application for Medicaid immediately. This is important because the process is usually a lengthy one. The social worker may be able to advise you if you qualify or if there are special ways by which you can qualify. If not, he/she can advise you about other resources which deal specifically with your situation or your particular disease.

Tip # 19: Don't accept unnecessary supplies in a hospital.

How it works: Hospitals provide many items to patients—and may charge them for the items—that they don't want or need. Beginning with the admissions package which may contain a plastic cup and plastic washing basin that few ever use, hospital supplies provided automatically may include run from a $4 pack of facial tissues to a $40 foam mattress pad. Ask the nurse not to leave these items you don't want and not to charge for them. But don't break the plastic wrap and open them up or they're yours for keeps.

If you do choose to accept a non-perishable item, it will go home with you. If you come back to the hospital for a similar procedure, bring the item back or you'll have to buy it all over again. At one hospital, all the patients admitted for angioplasty automatically get the $40 mattress pad, pay for it, and take it home. Some patients have three, four, and five angioplasties without bringing the pad back to the hospital.

Tip # 20: When you need a personal item, bring it from home or ask a family member or friend to buy it for you outside of the hospital.

How it works: Every personal item you receive you will be charged for and usually at a rate much higher than the usual retail value. For example, if you ask for a comb, you will get one—and be charged for it, probably much more than you would pay retail. So bring your own comb or send someone out to buy one. Similarly, a patient who needs frequent changes of elastic support stockings, for example, can ask the hospital for new ones, usually at premium prices, or can save money by having a relative take the old ones home, wash and return them. Vaseline swabs for your lips, sanitary napkins, tooth brushes—these small items add up. Patients tend to leave large things at home, too, and then have to buy them at the hospital. Nurses say patients who regularly use walkers or raised toilet seats or other essentials forget to bring them. Consider also bringing with you vitamins, regular medicines—both prescription and non-prescription. Consult with your doctor about what medication you intend to bring. Don't take medicines in the hospital until your doctor has approved them and turned the medicines over to the nurse with instructions to administer and record them on your chart.

Tip # 21: Don't ask for a private room unless one is medically necessary unless you are willing to pay more.

How it works: Private rooms cost more than semi-private rooms. And if you have insurance, your insurance policy probably will not pay the difference between a private room and a semi-private room unless medical necessity is proven, for example, when a patient has a contagious disease. If your doctor advises you to have a private room, ask him/her to demonstrate its necessity to your insurance company. Sometimes, if there is a problem with a roommate, you can ask to be moved to a different semi-private room to alleviate the problem.

Tip # 22: Record or have someone record the occasions for tests, therapy sessions, X-rays, and other treatments not only to watch for overcharges but to have documentation if your insurance company disputes the frequency.

How it works: Sometimes a patient has repetitive tests to monitor a situation or frequent treatments and the insurance may pay for some but not all of one type. Having a record of time and date can help convince the insurance company that these procedures were actually done in the numbers billed and your doctor can verify that they were also necessary. This record can also be helpful if you are contending that certain tests were not performed for which the hospital charged you.

Tip # 23: Ask the hospital soon after your admission to let you pay just a little bit of your bill every month.

How it works: If you have a big hospital bill and you don't have the money to pay, work out a plan with the hospital billing department to pay a little every month. If you pay even a very little every month by arrangement, your account usually will not go into the bill collecting department or agency and you will not be pressured to pay. It's like borrowing from the hospital but usually hospitals don't charge any interest so it's cheaper than borrowing elsewhere to pay the hospital. You may wish to work this out soon after you are admitted rather than before you are admitted or the hospital may not admit you. The advantage of working it out before admission is that you know what to expect, for example, what the hospital considers a reasonable monthly payment.

Tip # 24: Check out before check-out time on the day of your departure from the hospital.

How it works: Just as in a hotel, after check-out time another day is often added to your bill. So officially end your stay with the hospital by checking out in the business office before check-out time. Just vacating the room is not enough if the hospital does not note your departure.

Tip # 25: Review the bill carefully before paying or submitting to the insurance company and have errors corrected.

How it works: Always check the bill before paying or allowing it to be submitted to the insurance company. Many people allow the hospital to file insurance claims without ever checking the bill. Then they pay their portion of the bill without question. Independent studies have shown there are errors on a majority of hospital bills. Many are keying errors. Even a misspelling of your name may result in part of your records being filed as another person's or vice versa. Overcharges to look for are whole bottles of pills such as pain pills from which you only took a few, accessories such as lambskin pads you never ordered and never used, charges for tests done four times when they were only done two times, services such as whirlpool therapy or even anesthesia that you never had, etc. Note that a test or procedure that was ordered and canceled may still appear on your bill. If it is re-scheduled it may appear on your bill a second time. Also, tests or procedures are occasionally done in error. You may find you are billed for these occasional mistakes just as if they were intended. Especially check to see that you were not billed for the day you left before check-out time because that is a frequent billing error. Report all errors immediately to the billing department. Ask for a "patient inquiry" person in the business office or a patient advocate to help you sort things out. Some insurance companies offer a patient who finds an error in a bill a percentage of the savings! Ask if yours does.

Tip # 26: Ask your doctor to review your hospital bill before paying or submitting to your insurance company and have errors corrected.

How it works: Your doctor can check for errors you could not recognize. For example, he or she can quickly identify procedures on the bill that are not relevant to your case and convince the hospital to remove them. The doctor can judge far better than you if a procedure or medication was charged more often or in higher quantity than is correct. If you let the hospital bill go on automatically to the insurance company before the doctor reviews it, it will be harder to correct later.

Tip # 27: Ask the hospital to audit your bill *against the medical record* if you think you have been overcharged.

How it works: If you think you have been charged for procedures that were not done or materials you did not use or other inaccuracies, ask the billing department to compare their charges with the *medical* record including the patient charts where everything that happened during your hospital stay should be recorded. Procedures and medications that are not on the chart are not billable.

Tip # 28: Look for inappropriate "up-coding" of procedures on your bill.

How it works: Many hospitals use DRG codes for billing. These are standard fees for standard procedures. There may be one fee for an uncomplicated hysterectomy, for example, and another, larger fee for a hysterectomy with complications which is designated by a different DRG code. If you think your procedure was simple— ask your doctor—and if it was up-coded (changed to a code for a more complicated procedure), ask why. Sometimes a hospital may up-code for something as simple as a rash that required no special treatment. Up-coding brings in more money for the hospital and costs you more if you are uninsured or paying a percentage of the bill. If you think the up-coding is inappropriate, get the facts from your doctor and protest to the hospital.

Quality check: Up-coding is a judgment call and it may be difficult to prove an up-coding is inappropriate.

Tip # 29: Ask your health insurer to review your case, if you think you have been underpaid.

How it works: Mistakes happen. If you see something on your claim you think should have been paid but was not, ask your health insurer for a review. The reviewer will check for coding mistakes, misinterpretation, or some category of coverage that was over-looked. Mistakes discovered should be rectified.

Quality check: Remember, mistakes go both ways. A review may turn up an overpayment.

Tip # 30: See if your insurance company offers to split savings with you for finding errors on your bill.

How it works: Insurance companies would like to have someone check all medical bills for errors. Who would do better than you? Many if not most patients with good insurance that pays, for example, 100% of charges over a certain amount have little incentive to even look at the bill. To make sure you actually do read your bill critically, some insurance companies offer to split the savings with the patient if the patient finds an error that saves the insurance company money. If the insurance company is going to pay the costs anyway, why not accept their offer and get a little back for yourself?

Tip # 31: If you get a bill from the hospital indicating your insurance company refuses to pay a certain charge, ask your insurance company why?

How it works: An insurance company may refuse to cover certain items; you may have an argument with the insurance company in which case you will have to ask your doctor to prove that the item was necessary and chargeable. Or you may have an argument with the hospital. Some charges the insurance company refuses to pay are because of errors the company thinks the hospital has made. The hospital won't necessarily tell you there is an ongoing dispute; you may only be told you are now responsible. By asking the insurance company why an item is not being paid for you can tell where the hitch is and, if warranted, help your insurance company in the dispute by providing documentation or information.

Tip # 32: The family of an adult patient who dies (except, in some cases, the spouse) is usually not responsible for hospital bills not covered by the patient's insurance or estate.

How it works: When an adult is admitted to a hospital, usually someone is asked to state or sign a statement saying who is responsible for the cost of treatment. An adult is generally responsible for his/her own debts. Don't sign that you are responsible for a parent or other adult family member. (A parent is generally responsible for minor children, however.) If a patient dies, his/her estate is responsible for bills not covered by insurance. However, hospitals often bill adult children and siblings of patients who died, but these family members are usually under no legal obligation to pay.

Tip # 33: If you have a big hospital bill and a little too much money to qualify for Medicaid, you may become eligible for three months of Adult Medical Aid.

How it works: You may have big hospital bills and some money coming in. You make too much to qualify for Medicaid but not enough to pay off the bills and take care of your other obligations too. You could try to pay off a substantial part of the hospital bills and struggle for as long as you can with the rest of your expenses, getting behind on your rent, etc. Or you could pay just enough on your hospital bills to stay off the hospital's collection list and let the rest accumulate. When you have accumulated a medical debt equal or greater than three times your monthly income, you may then qualify for temporary Adult Medical Aid under Medicaid. If you had paid the hospital and let the rent go, you may not have been eligible for any kind of help.

HUNTER SYNDROME (See RARE DISEASES.)

HUNTINGTON'S DISEASE

Tip # 1: Contact the Huntington's Disease Society of America at 1-800-345-4372.

How it works: The Huntington's Disease Society gives information and referrals. English and Spanish speaking staff are available.

HURLER SYNDROME (See RARE DISEASES.)

HYDROCEPHALUS (See RARE DISEASES.)

HYPOGLYCEMIA

Tip # 1: Contact the Hypoglycemia Foundation.

How it works: The Foundation provides information and referrals and sponsors related research. Write Hypoglycemia Foundation, 153 Pawling Avenue, Troy, NY 12180. Or call 518-272-7154.

HYPOPLASTIC LEFT HEART SYNDROME (See RARE DISEASES.)

HYSTERECTOMY

Tip # 1: Ask your gynecologist if a less extreme treatment would be just as effective as a hysterectomy.

How it works: In the case of cancer and other serious diseases, a hysterectomy may be the only safe procedure. But consider some other approaches to these disorders commonly treated by hysterectomy:
- Fibroids may cause bleeding, pressure and frequent urination. Because fibroid growth is stimulated by estrogen, fibroids may shrink during menopause and cease causing problems on their own. Consider limiting the intake of estrogen by not taking birth control pills. If fibroids must be removed, consider a myomectomy which removes only the fibroid and leaves the uterus, but choose a surgeon with a lot of experience in this new procedure.
- Abnormal bleeding from the uterus is often caused by hormonal

imbalance and may often be treated successfully with hormone supplements. A D&C (dilation and curettage), often performed on an out-patient basis, may solve the problem without removing the uterus.

- Urinary stress incontinence, the loss of normal bladder control when there is sudden pressure on the bladder, may, in some cases, be corrected by Kegel exercises which strengthen the muscles controling urination.
- Hyperplasia, a build-up of the tissue lining the uterus which may cause irregular bleeding, can often be corrected by hormone treatment. It should be treated to reduce the risk of uterine cancer.
- Menstrual pain can often be relieved by medication.
- Non-invasive cervical cancer may often be treated by removal of the diseased tissue by a freezing technique called cryo-surgery or by a cone biopsy which removes only a small portion of the cervix.

Quality check: Many people feel that alternatives to hysterectomy are far more healthful. Any surgery has risks. Some conditions, however, are so troublesome that relief is worth the surgery and many women who have had a hysterectomy say they wish they had had one years before.

Tip # 2: When hysterectomy is the best option, ask your doctor about laparoscopic hysterectomy.

How it works: Excising the uterus through a tiny incision and removing it via the vagina is less invasive than traditional surgery. The surgeon is guided by a tiny light and microscope. Although the physician's fee for laparoscopic procedures may not be less (and may be more) than fees for traditional surgery, the shorter hospital stays and a shorter recovery time may result in lower total medical costs and time off from work. Not all surgeons or all facilities offer laparoscopic hysterectomy, which has been done for only a few years. Ask for referral to a team that has performed this operation successfully many times.

Quality check: Some situations are not appropriate for laparoscopic surgery. New procedures are not necessarily the safest during the early years of availability.

Tip # 3: Compare the price of the average hysterectomy at different hospitals in your area.

How it works: As illustration, during 1990 average hospital costs in 25 different hospitals in Dade County, FL, ranged from $6202 to $10,104. The average from the region was $7584. These figures were reported by the hospitals themselves and were published by the Florida Health Care Cost Containment Board. Get current cost averages from hospitals you are considering or from your state cost containment board if one exists.

Quality check: Be sure you are comparing apples to apples when you collect figures. Cost averages should all apply to procedures labeled DRG or RDRG, abbreviations used to indicate procedures described in a standard way by the medical community.

Tip # 4: Compare your doctor's fees for hysterectomy with the national average.

How it works: The physician's fee in 1992 for a total hysterectomy, with or without removal of tubes and ovaries, cost an average of almost $1900 nationally. 90% of doctors fees were less than $3000. Fees for hysterectomies involving surgical correction of other complications as part of the hysterectomy were more than fees for simple, complete hysterectomies. If your doctor's fees are out of line with these figures, ask for an explanation and/or a reduction.

I-CELL DISEASE (See RARE DISEASES.)

IMMUNE SYSTEM

Tip # 1: Try to get into an experimental study of treatment of disorders related to the immune system. (Also, see STUDIES.)

How it works: Experimental treatment studies often offer free treatment to patients who qualify as subjects. In particular, the Clinical Center of the National Institutes of Health in Bethesda, MD, has ongoing studies of many disorders relating to the immune system including eosinophilic syndromes, Epstein Barr, sarcoidosis, granulomatous hepatitis, hyperimmunoglobin and recurrent infections, immunodeficiency diseases, mycoses, neutropenia, parasitic diseases, recurrent bacterial infections, varicella-zoster, vasomotor rhinitis, vasculitis, and autologous bone marrow transplants. For information on getting into a study at this or other institutions, see STUDIES Tip # 2.

IMMUNIZATIONS

Tip # 1: Consider getting immunizations at your local health departments where all childhood immunizations and most adult immunizations are free or very inexpensive.

How it works: Immunizations, by preventing serious diseases, are perhaps the most cost-effective measure you can take with your health care dollar. Children by the age of two years should be immunized against at least nine childhood diseases: measles, mumps, and rubella; diphtheria, pertussis (whooping cough), and tetanus (together called DPT); polio; and meningitis and other diseases caused by haemophilus influenza type B (Hib). Recently the Advisory Committee on Immunization Practices of the U.S. Public Health Service has added vaccination against hepatitis B to its list of recommended immunizations for infants and unimmunized children and adolescents. (See also HEPATITIS.) Many local health clinics give the series of shots which cover these diseases free or on a sliding scale according to the patient's income. Florida for example gives all immunizations to children under the age of two free to encourage early immunizations. In a large city in another state, the cost of one DPT shot (out of a series of three) at the various county health departments surrounding the city ranges from $8 to $10 for people who can pay and is free for people who cannot. In a doctor's office in the same city, the cost of one DPT shot in the series ranges from $25 to $35 in addition to the fee for the office visit. Similar savings are usual for the other immunizations. You can go to the health department for the immunizations and take the records to your regular pediatrician to sometimes save about $200 total for the complete immunization series. Check with your health department when your baby is very young. Adults can get free or low cost immunizations or booster shots also. Flu shots, hepatitis B vaccine, and gamma globulin injections to provide immunity to a variety of diseases are all typically provided at health departments for about a fourth the cost of a doctor's visit.

Quality check: Doctors' offices keep full records of immunizations and you can call and easily get records. There may be more red tape in getting similar information from a health department. Waiting time may be greater at a health clinic than at a private doctor's office. The immunizations themselves, however, are just the same as in any doctor's office.

Tip # 2: Get free immunizations at immunization drives held annually in many communities.

How it works: Children's hospitals, health departments, and other organizations in some communities hold annual drives to immunize all children. They offer free immunizations at schools, health centers, and even shopping centers. Watch your local newspaper or call local health departments for schedules.

Tip # 3: Call the Centers for Disease Control and Prevention (CDC) at 404-332-4555 for current and detailed, recorded information on immunizations 24-hours a day.

How it works: The CDC gives up-to-date and detailed information on their information line. You can also order a copy of "Parents' Guide to Immunization" to keep for reference and a Stay Well card, a little coloring book pamphlet with a place for records in the back.

IMPOTENCE

Tip # 1: Consider contacting the Impotence Information Center at 1-800-843-4315.

How it works: The center provides free information to prospective patients on the causes and treatment for Impotence. Call from 8:30 to 5:30 Central time or leave a recorded message after hours. Note that the information line is operated by a manufacturer of penile implants.

Tip # 2: Contact Recovery of Male Impotence at 313-357-1216 in Michigan.

How it works: Recovery of Male Impotence is a self-help group which assists patients and distributes an information packet. It is a service of Grace Hospital in Detroit, MI, and is affiliated with 23 hospitals nationwide.

INCONTINENCE (See BLADDER PROBLEMS.)

INDIAN HEALTH

Tip # 1: Native American Indians may be entitled to free health care through the Indian Health Service.

How it works: Members of federally recognized tribes or those who have proof they are a descendant of a member may be entitled to free health care if they go to their reservation to receive care from the Indian Health Service. There are also urban Indian Health Services located in New York City (212-598-0100) and Boston (617-232-0343), and an alcohol treatment program in Baltimore (301-675-3535).

INFECTIOUS DISEASES

Tip # 1: Call the Centers for Disease Control and Prevention (CDC) at 404-332-4555 for current and detailed, recorded information on infectious diseases.

How it works: The CDC specializes in tracking and studying infectious diseases. The CDC was among the first to do massive work on AIDS, Legionnaire's Disease, Lyme Disease, toxic shock syndrome and other diseases that have broken into the news as "new" threats to health. The CDC is also a major source of information on traditionally feared infectious diseases including those that are rare in this country. Detailed current information on infectious diseases, their symptoms, and treatment is available by phone 24-hours a day. Call evenings and weekends for the lowest rates.

INTERSTITIAL CYSTITIS (See BLADDER PROBLEMS, CYSTITIS, and RARE DISEASES.)

INSURANCE

Tip # 1: Keep in mind how insurance works.

How it works: Insurance companies pay some portions of medical bills for people who hold health insurance policies when those people become sick or disabled. Many policy holders pool their money (in the form of regularly paid premiums) so that those who face medical expenses can get financial help when they need it. If you and your family stay relatively healthy, you will pay more money into an insurance company than you get out. But you will protect yourself from overwhelming expenses should you or your family have serious medical problems. Insurance is protection from the risk of overwhelming medical expenses. If it weren't for that risk, you would do better to use the money you pay for your insurance for paying your routine medical bills. Keeping this in mind in itself may help you make money saving decisions.

Tip # 2: Keep in mind the different kinds of health-related insurance and get the coverage you can afford but no more than you need.

How it works: There are several kinds of health insurance to consider:

1) Hospital-surgical policies cover hospitalization for covered conditions and many services received in a hospital, in-patient or out-patient, such as doctors' fees, lab tests, and radiation treatment but not services outside of the hospital.

2) Major medical or comprehensive policies cover hospital treatment and medical costs outside of a hospital as well as in a hospital.

3) Excess major medical policies can provide coverage of costs beyond the lifetime limits of your other insurance policies.

4) Hospital indemnity policies pay you directly a specified amount per day for every day you are hospitalized. You can use it to pay your medical bills or for anything else, for example, paying your rent.

5) Medicare supplement called MedSup or Medigap covers the co-payments or deductibles or uncovered expenses that Medicare does not pay. Medicare supplements, like Medicare itself, apply only to people over age 65 and the disabled. (See MEDICARE SUPPLEMENT.)

6) Long term care policies pay for nursing home care or custodial care in the home. Typically payment is a certain amount for each day in a nursing home or custodial care. (See also LONG TERM CARE.)

7) Disability policies pay a certain amount to help you make up for lost wages when health problems prevent you from working. (See also DISABILITY.)

You would probably not want hospital/surgical and comprehensive policies together since they overlap. Excess major medical could be combined with hospital/surgical or comprehensive policies if the lifetime limits of either are too low. Hospital indemnity policies would help you if you are otherwise uninsured for hospital stays or if you need extra money while you are sick. It is not paid when medical problems are handled on an outpatient basis. Medigap or Mediplus applies to people eligible for Medicare only. Coverage from long term care policies varies widely and must be carefully considered. Everyone who needs wages should consider disability insurance along with medical insurance.

Quality check: Look up any insurance company whose policies you are considering in Best's ratings (found on the reference shelves of any library) to see how their ability to pay claims is rated in the industry. Also, call your state insurance commissioner's office to see that an insurance company is licensed to do business in your state and what is its record of paying claims.

Tip # 3: Compare what health insurance policies offer and not just what they cost.

How it works: When you say "I have insurance" you are not saying much. Policies can vary from the most meager coverage of very limited medical treatments (at very low premiums) to almost total coverage of all medical problems (at astronomical premiums).

Questions to ask for each policy you are considering should explore (1) *Benefits*: How do they apply to your unprotected risk areas? (2) *Exclusions*: How could these hurt you? (3) *Definitions*: Each policy includes definitions to protect the *company* in case of a suit. What do they mean? The Health Insurance Association of America (HIAA) publishes *The Consumer's Guide to Health Insurance* to help you make good decisions in health coverage. The following pages from the HIAA Guide are used with permission. For a complete guide, write HIAA at 1025 Connecticut Avenue, NE, Washington, DC 20036-39981, or call 202-223-7780.

Tip # 4: Sign up for group insurance with your employer as soon as you are eligible. Or seek an employer with a good group insurance program as part of its benefits.

How it works: Many employers offer group insurance (several

Comparing plans

Think carefully about your own particular situation. Do you want coverage for your whole family? Or just yourself? Do you want protection from a catastrophic illness? From disability? Are you concerned with preventive care and checkups? Do you want to choose your providers? Or would you be comfortable in a managed care setting that might restrict your choice somewhat but give you the coverage and convenience that you want? These are questions that only you can answer.

Here are some of the things to look at when choosing and comparing health insurance plans.

Health Insurance Checklist
Covered medical services

- Inpatient hospital services
- Outpatient surgery
- Physician visits (in the hospital)
- Office visits
- Skilled nursing care
- Medical tests and X-rays
- Prescription drugs
- Psychiatric and mental health care
- Drug and alcohol abuse treatment
- Home health care visits
- Rehabilitation facility care
- Physical therapy
- Hospice care
- Maternity care
- Chiropractic
- Preventive care and checkups
- Well-baby care
- Dental care
- Other covered services

Are there any medical service limits, exclusions, or pre-existing conditions that will affect you or your family?

_____

What cost containment and quality assurance procedures are included (e.g., utilization review, precertification, second surgical opinions)?

_____

Costs

How much is the premium?

$_____ ☐ month ☐ quarter ☐ year

Are there any discounts available for good health or healthy behaviors (e.g., non-smoker)?

_____

How much is the annual deductible?

$_____ per person

$_____ per family

What co-insurance or co-payments apply?

_____ percent after I meet my deductible

$_____ co-pay or % co-insurance per office visit

$_____ co-pay or % co-insurance for "wellness" care (includes well-baby care, annual eye exam, physical, etc.)

_____ % co-insurance for inpatient hospital services

Is there an annual "out-of-pocket" maximum amount of co-insurance I pay per year for covered services? How much?

$_____

Is there a lifetime maximum benefit?

$_____

Service

How will service needs be handled? Is there a local or toll-free phone number?

_____

Will you fill out claim forms? How long will it take for claims to be processed?

_____

Is the insurance company a solid one?

Good references_____

Licensed in my state_____

Company financial stability/rating_____

months of employment may be required before you are eligible), and some pay a substantial portion of the costs. When the company pays part of insurance costs that is an important benefit; even if the company does not pay part, group insurance rates are still more economical than individual policy rates. Sometimes you are required by an employer to sign up for the insurance as soon as you are eligible, but if you are not you are probably safer doing so anyway as soon as it is offered. If you turn it down for any reason (for example, if your spouse has an insurance policy that covers you) and then later decide to sign up, you will most likely have to prove that you are insurable, that is, a good risk. If you have gotten a medical disease or injury since you turned down insurance, you may not be eligible for the group insurance at all.

Tip # 5: When both spouses are eligible for insurance policies, examine them for the best coverage for the money.

How it works: Insurance policies will not pay double for medical costs so there is no point in having two similar policies unless one or both are likely to be terminated. Choose the one that seems to have the best coverage for you for the money, but consider also the stability of the two jobs. If a wife has a better policy with an employer but is likely to quit to raise a family, the husband's policy may be safer. If a company is laying off or facing instability, that company's policy may not be the best.

Tip # 6: Find group insurance even if you are an unaffiliated individual.

How it works: Group insurance is by far the least expensive insurance and if your employer pays part of the cost as a benefit, so much the better. Individual insurance is far more costly but almost everyone is or can be affiliated with a group. For example, if you are 50 or older you can join the American Association of Retired Persons for a very small annual fee and buy insurance offered by that group to its members. If you are self-employed, there are organizations for you. Look for local organizations, too. For example, The Kennedy Center sponsors a group insurance plan for Washington, DC, area artists. Almost everywhere there are organizations that offer group plans for particular categories of people. Professional groups often negotiate for insurance group plans. You may have to offer credentials to qualify for membership but interest (in the form of a membership check) is sometimes all it takes.

Quality check: When signing up with a professional or interest group that offers insurance, check the rating of the insurance carrier just as you would if you were buying insurance on your own. Also, investigate thoroughly what coverage you are getting for your money.

Tip # 7: Consider taking college courses for the college's insurance program.

How it works: Some colleges offer their students health insurance. It is not often very comprehensive but it is relatively inexpensive and may be available to students who are not able to get insurance otherwise because of a pre-existing condition. Sometimes a student need only enroll in one course to qualify.

Tip # 8: Save money on premiums by selecting a relatively high deductible.

How it works: Consider insurance as protection against catastrophe, not a way of paying small day-to-day bills. If you had a surgery, for example, that cost more than your house, you would probably be financially wiped out. Insurance can save you from that catastrophe by paying for treatment of your serious illness and injury. If you are more healthy than average, however, you probably pay considerably more for your insurance than you would if you paid your own bills. Only if you have larger than average medical expenses do you actually get back in payment more than you put in. That is why insurance should be regarded as protection against unusually large expenses but not as a way to save money on day-to-day health costs.

In sum, consider assuming small risks. Share large risks with other policy holders of your insurance company. Many people however, have come to regard insurance as a way to pay routine bills—$35 for a visit to the doctor with a sore throat, $42 for a tooth filling, or $120 for a few stitches. Only if someone else—like your employer—pays a very substantial amount for your insurance is this approach a good deal for you. The best choice for someone who is paying for his/her own insurance is usually to have a high deductible and, because of that, lower rates. Then you pay your own routine medical bills that are less than the deductible and keep the insurance for those really expensive things. You may save a lot of money on premiums.

Quality check: The high deductible approach may not be a money saver if you or someone in your family has a chronic medical condition for which the accumulated debts do constitute a major medical crisis. Take a pencil and paper and write down how many trips to the doctor or hospital you are likely to need per year and at what cost. You might project from last year's expenses. Then, for several different levels of deductibles, figure out the totals of what you would pay in a year by adding the cost of a year's insurance payments and the projected medical expenses left unpaid by insurance in a year. For which level of deductibles do you pay less?

Tip # 9: Ask the office of the insurance commissioner in your state if the state has a program of low cost basic insurance for those with limited incomes.

How it works: Several state governments offer or are considering offering basic insurance plans for low income people who are not eligible for Medicaid. Look up Insurance Commissioner in the phone book under the name of your state.

Tip # 10: Buy insurance or join a medical plan with no pre existing condition clause even if it costs more unless you and your dependents have never sought medical care for a serious problem.

How it works: Many insurance policies will not cover "pre existing conditions" for a period of three, six months or a year after signing up—if ever. If you have an old health problem flare up during that period of restriction, treatment for that problem will not be covered. If you know you or a family member have heart trouble, or cancer, a congenital defect, for example, insurance with a pre-existing condition clause may not cover you. You will have to find an insurance policy without the clause even though it costs more. Consider also an HMO which often does not have pre-existing condition clauses.

Tip #11: Look for "inside limits" before buying insurance and before getting treatment.

How it works: Inside limits are limitations on coverage of certain kinds of medical treatment inside a policy that may be quite liberal in its coverage of most treatment. Treatment often limited in coverage includes mental health and physical therapy. When buying insurance, compare the disadvantage of such limitations with the premiums you would be paying. Is the policy worth the money? Consider what treatments you or your family is most likely to need. If you are an avid polo player, physical therapy just might be in your future. If you are having some family problems that may lead to the need for mental health treatment, avoid a policy with tight limits on mental health coverage. Once you have your insurance, re-read it before seeking treatment. One woman injured her knee. After arthroscopic surgery, she started on a program of frequent physical therapy. After several months when her insurance claims were filed she discovered she had run up a bill of several thousand dollars and her policy only covered a total of $500 of physical therapy. If she had noticed the limitation earlier, she would have had fewer physical therapy sessions in which she would ask for more instruction for training on her own between therapy sessions. Similarly, spacing out mental health appointments to once a month instead of once a week may be enough to solve a problem while keeping the costs under the yearly or total limits on mental health coverage.

Tip # 12: When buying life insurance, consider a whole life policy that allows you to receive substantial benefits during severe but not necessarily terminal illness.

How it works: Some life insurance policies allow you to draw out a portion of your life insurance during certain serious illnesses. This is not borrowing on the insurance (which is another useful possibility) because no interest is charged. Some policies require a doctor to sign a statement that the illness is terminal before the early payment is allowed, but at least one does not. One policy, for example, allows withdrawals of up to 25% of a policy's worth to cover costs of stroke, serious renal disease, cancer, heart attack, or by-pass surgery regardless of the prognosis. The premium for this policy is about 10% higher than the company's policies without early withdrawal clauses and a rider makes term insurance available to keep death benefits up.

Tip # 13: When buying disability insurance, look for the words "non-cancelable" and "guaranteed renewable."

How it works: An individual policy can be canceled by an insurance company after a claim is paid, if the insurance company does not want to cover your health claims further. A group policy cannot be cut nor the premiums raised unless the whole group's coverage is cut or premiums raised. So unless the group as a whole is unprofitable, you are safer in a group than on an individual policy.

Quality check: Unfortunately, group insurance increasingly is applied to much smaller groups than before (one small company, for example) with less spreading of risk. Consequently, one large claim from that group has more of an influence on rates than if the group were larger.

Tip # 14: Consider school insurance policies for children.

How it works: School insurance policies are usually very inexpensive and not very comprehensive. Some cover accidents only during school hours or school sponsored trips and are carried by the school itself. Some offer optional 24-hours-a-day accident coverage which can be purchased by parents for very little money. These sometimes cover 100% of costs for accidents and may be worthwhile for families who are underinsured otherwise.

Tip # 15: Consider splitting your disability insurance dollar among several insurance companies.

How it works: Companies differ widely as to what they consider a payable disability. One company may pay for a certain problem and another won't, so it's a good idea to be enrolled on several plans. For example, a salesman got a rare disease called dysphonia in which his ability to talk became limited. One of his policies would not pay disability, claiming there were a lot of work options open to him not involving talking. Another of his policies conceded that his income would be limited because he was unable to continue in his current employment. He received partial disability from the second company.

Quality check: Compare the costs of two separate policies versus the costs of one policy with the same total payout to see what extra, if anything, you would be paying for dual protection.

Tip # 16: Consider the financial standing of an insurance company you are considering buying a policy from.

How it works: The insurance company from which you buy needs to be in solid financial condition. Companies are rated by *Best's Guides* (available in almost every library and insurance office) according to their potential ability for paying claims. Other raters evaluate insurance companies from an investor's point of view which may not be as relevant to you. Many insurance companies make much of their money from investing premiums. Those that invest well will be better able to pay your claim, but they may choose to reward their investors more conscientiously than their customers. Actually, insurance companies in each state contribute to a fund so that you are protected against loss of coverage due to the failure of a company licensed in that state. The differences in financial standing between companies, however, affect how liberal the company can be in interpreting your claim and paying. Some insurance policies pay almost any reasonable claim while others are very stingy in payment. Non-profit companies, though they may seem better for the consumer because they do not require a profit on their transactions, are also barred from making some of the kinds of investments for-profit companies do.

Tip # 17: Ask the billing clerks at your provider which companies pay the best.

How it works: Sometimes word of mouth accounts of what a company has paid and not paid are a guide to how liberal a company is. It would take a long time, however, to poll an adequate sample of customers about insurance companies payment practices. So ask the billing specialists at your providers (insurance collection personnel) which companies and policies come through the best for patients in their experience and which ones offer more hassles and less coverage.

Tip # 18: Avoid policies with lengthy benefits schedules.

How it works: When a policy states that it covers usual and customary charges across the board, you only have to worry about how "usual and customary" compares to your doctor's bills. A policy that states actual schedules (payment limits) for named disorders is limiting its liability in specific instances for the life of the policy and will not necessarily be giving as full coverage as the one with the "usual and customary" blanket coverage which does fluctuate with actual fee averages.

Tip # 19: Before you move from one state to another, reconsider your health insurance policy, its costs, and its payment record in both states.

How it works: There are variations in payment policy from state to state. A good policy in one state may not be so good in another. A man in Pennsylvania, for example, had a disease requiring shots which cost $500 every 3 months. The very large insurance company which covered him paid these bills. When the man moved to Georgia, however, the same company on the same policy would not honor his claim because the shots were considered experimental treatment. The company is simply more liberal in Pennsylvania than in Georgia on the matter of experimental treatment. The man did not want to change policies, however, because his illness would then be a preexisting condition not covered for a period of time on most new policies.

Tip # 20: Be wary of cancer policies or other dreaded disease policies.

How it works: Cancer and other dreaded disease policies may play on your fear of a particular disease. They cover you only if you get that disease. Why spend money on insurance for only one disease when you could use the money to buy or upgrade your insurance for any disease, condition, or injury? Cancer insurance may be a little cheaper than general insurance, reflecting the lower risk the company is taking. It may, however, be appropriate if you have a high risk of developing cancer.

INTERNATIONAL HEALTH (See TRAVEL)

IRRITABLE BOWEL SYNDROME (See RARE DISEASES.)

JOB RELATED HEALTH OR ACCOMMODATION (See OCCUPA-
TIONAL HEALTH and WORKPLACE.)

JOSEPH'S DISEASE (See RARE DISEASES.)

JOUBERT SYNDROME (See RARE DISEASES.)

KAWASAKI DISEASE (See RARE DISEASES.)

KETOTIC HYPERGLYCINEMIA (See RARE DISEASES.)

KIDNEY

Tip # 1: Dialysis for kidney failure is covered under Medicare at any age.

How it works: End stage renal failure, the stage at which dialysis is needed, is the only specific disease covered by Medicare which otherwise serves as insurance for those over 65 and the disabled. At any age, a patient on dialysis can file for Medicare assistance by contacting the local Social Security office.

Tip # 2: Contact the American Kidney Fund at 1-800-638-8299 for financial assistance.

How it works: The American Kidney Fund offers one time grants to eligible people to assist with needs relating to dialysis such as medication or transportation. English and Spanish speaking staff.

Tip # 3: Contact the National Kidney Foundation at 1-800-622-9010.

How it works: The National Kidney Foundation offers information on kidney disease and treatment and on financial resources for health care. The Foundation will also put you in touch with local branches.

Tip # 4: Contact the National Kidney and Urologic Diseases Information Clearinghouse (NKUDIC).

How it works: The NKUDIC provides education and information on kidney and urologic diseases to patients, professionals, and the public. It makes referrals to other organizations. It maintains a subfile of the Combined Health Information Database (CHID) and provides bibliographies on diabetes and kidney disease, audiovisual materials, brochures, and fact sheets. Call 301-468-6345 or write Box NKUDIC, 9000 Rockville Pike, Bethesda, MD 20892.

Tip # 5: Try to get into an experimental study of treatment of kidney disease. (See also STUDIES.)

How it works: Experimental treatment studies often offer free treatment to patients who qualify as subjects. For information about getting into a study, see STUDIES.

KLINEFELTER SYNDROME (See RARE DISEASES.)

KORSAKOFF'S SYNDROME (See RARE DISEASES.)

LACTOSE INTOLERANCE (See RARE DISEASES.)

LANGUAGE DISORDERS

Tip # 1: Contact an organization concerned with different language disorders.

How it works: The following organizations give information and other forms of support to those seeking help for language disorders:

American Speech-Language-Hearing Association
10801 Rockville Pike
Rockville MD 20852
1-800-638-TALK or 301-897-5700 (TDD)

National Aphasia Association
P.O. Box 1887
Murray Hill Station
New York, NY 10156-0611

Orton Dyslexia Society
724 York Rd.
Baltimore, MD 21204
1-800-ABCD-123 or 301-296-0232

Veterans Administration Audiology and Speech
Pathology Services
50 Irving St. NW
Washington, DC 20422
202-745-8270

LASER SURGERY

Tip # 1: Compare costs of laser surgery with that of conventional surgery.

How it works: Because of the costs of equipment and training, laser surgery may be more expensive than traditional surgery. However, if better results are expected through laser surgery or if laser surgery requires less time in the hospital and out of work, laser surgery may be a bargain. Ask your doctor to compare these important factors for you.

Quality check: Ask your surgeon what training he/she has had in laser surgery and how many procedures similar to yours he/she has done.

LEAD POISONING

Tip # 1: Call the federal Environmental Protection Agency (EPA) Water Hotline at 1-800-426-4791 for information about lead in water.

How it works: The EPA information specialists will answer individual questions about water quality, direct you to local sources of information about your local water quality, and send you printed information on lead in water.

Tip # 2: Call your state government about lead in paint and other sources.

How it works: For information about the danger of lead ingestion or exposure, especially to young children, call the department of environmental health or public health of your state government. The number may be listed under the name of your state in the phone book or call your state general information number listed under GENERAL INFORMATION, Tip # 1.

LEGIONNAIRE'S DISEASE (See RARE DISEASES.)

LEPROSY (See RARE DISEASES.)

LEUKEMIA

Tip # 1: Contact the Leukemia Society of America.

How it works: The Leukemia Society offers information and referrals and contact with support groups as well as financial aid.

Write to the Leukemia Society at 800 Second Avenue, New York, NY 10017 or call 212-573-8484.

LICE

Tip # 1: Ask for treatment for head lice at your local health department.

How it works: Most health departments offer medication and directions for treatment of head lice. Successful treatment depends on your diligence in applying medication and washing linens. Follow the directions closely.

LIP, HARE (See CLEFT PALATE, FACIAL INJURY OR DISORDER, PLASTIC SURGERY.)

LIVER DISEASE

Tip # 1: Avoid or limit the use of alcohol.

How it works: Alcohol abuse is a leading cause of liver failure. Sometimes patients with liver disease, even recipients of liver transplants continue to consume alcohol, making their health problems more serious and more costly. See ALCOHOL ABUSE for information on treating alcoholism.

Tip # 2: Contact the American Liver Foundation at 1-800-223-0179.

How it works: The Foundation offers information on various forms of liver disease, treatment, and fund-raising ideas for liver transplant patients. English and Spanish speaking staff.

Tip # 3: Try to get into an experimental study for treatment of your liver disorder. (See also STUDIES.)

How it works: Experimental treatment studies often offer free treatment to patients who qualify as subjects. In particular, the Clinical Center of the National Institutes of Health in Bethesda, MD, has ongoing studies of many liver disorders including granulomatous hepatitis, chronic viral hepatitis, primary biliary cirrhosis, and cholestatic liver disease. For information about getting into a study at this or other institutions, see STUDIES.

LONG TERM CARE (See also DISABILITY, HOME HEALTH CARE and IN-SURANCE)

Tip # 1: Compare the costs of long term care in the home with costs of long term care in an assisted living or skilled care facility.

How it works: Long term care in the home by family members and others may be cheaper than in an institution if frequent visits by skilled health care professionals are not required. To compare costs, estimate the costs and frequency of professional home care visits, respite care, and other paid supplementary care. If daily care is given by a family member who otherwise would be earning wages outside the home, loss of those wages and other benefits of employment must be factored into the total cost. Also, count in the costs of modifications of a family home which may be necessary for patient care. Services which may make long term care in the home possible include "meals on wheels" programs, adult day care, home care services, and visiting volunteer programs. For more information on these services, see HOME CARE.

Quality check: In any case, long term care at home is very taxing on the caregivers and the degree of mental and physical disability of the patient must be major considerations in the decision to give long term care at home. Home care providers may help you assess your options.

Tip # 3: Consider adult day care to supplement long term care at home. (See also ADULT DAY CARE.)

How it works: Adult day care gives supervision and therapeutic programs outside the home to those adults who need them. Such services give much needed respite to caregivers and may make long term care at home possible.

Tip # 4: Consider home care services to make long term care in the home more feasible. See HOME CARE SERVICES.

Tip # 5: Keep itemized records of modifications to your home to accommodate an elderly or chronically ill person.

How it works: Expenses for widening doors, modifying bathrooms, installing lifts or special alarms are all medically related work and should be deductible from taxable income as medical expenses if they total enough to qualify. Ask your doctor to write a prescription for modifications.

Tip # 6: Consider licensing your home as a home for the disabled.

How it works: When you, as the patient or caregiver, are at the point of needing to hire professional health workers to provide long term care in your own home, consider licensing your home according to state and local laws as a home for the disabled. You then can find one or two other medically disabled people to keep and help defray the costs. Also, modifications of the home then become business expenses. The licensed home can continue to provide care to the family member after the original caregivers become unable to continue.

Tip # 7: Set up a "special needs" trust for a chronically ill person.

How it works: Since caregivers themselves may die or be unable to care for a chronically ill person, planning for the patient's future needs is important. Engage an attorney experienced in such trusts to be sure its benefits won't affect his/her future eligibility for federal or state aid.

Tip # 8: Consider life and disability insurance for the caregiver.

How it works: Since caregivers themselves may die or be unable to care for a chronically ill person, consider insuring the caregiver with adequate life insurance and disability insurance to support the home in either event.

Tip # 9: Consider contributing the maximum allowable and affordable to non-taxable retirement plans of the caregiver.

How it works: Contributing to a retirement plan for the caregiver not only gives the working caregiver help for retirement but reduces the adjusted gross income so that medical deductions may be greater.

Tip # 10: When choosing long term care in a nursing facility, choose the least intense level of care that is appropriate.

How it works: When custodial care and supervision is all that is required, consider assisted living facilities. These are less restrictive environments and are less expensive than skilled nursing facilities. Some assisted living facilities operate skilled nursing units nearby for those who may later find them necessary.

Tip # 11: Check licensing, accreditation, and inspection reports of long term nursing facilities.

How it works: A state license should be posted near the entrance to every long term nursing facility and it should be current. If not, ask why not and beware. A report of the most recent state inspections including any deficiencies noted should also be posted. Ask to see them. Ask if the facility is accredited by the Joint Commission on Accreditation of Health Care Facilities. Accreditation indicates a certain level of quality, but many excellent facilities do not seek such accreditation because the evaluation costs thousands of dollars.

Tip # 12: Review a list of charges before admission to a nursing facility.

How it works: Each facility is required by law to post a list of charges that you can review before admission. Also it is illegal for nursing care facilities to require advance deposits while waiting for Medicare approval. However, they can require a deposit for individual comfort and convenience items not covered.

Tip # 13: If you are admitted for skilled care under Medicare and later Medicare payment is denied, you may not be responsible for payment.

How it works: If you are admitted for temporary skilled care under Medicare and later Medicare denies payment because Medicare does not consider you in need of skilled care, the cost is usually the nursing facility's responsibility because admission staff is supposed to recognize those who do not need skilled care. You should not have to pay the fees.

Tip # 14: Ask for advice on financial assistance for nursing care.

How it works: The staff at a nursing facility should be able to advise on sources of financial assistance including Medicare, Medicaid, and private insurance. You may also consult the state department of human resources or a local family services office for advice on financial assistance for nursing care facilities.

Tip # 15: If several different therapies are prescribed while the patient is in a nursing home or care facility, talk to the insurance carrier about how those services should be billed. Often, if the facility bills all therapies on one bill along with other services, insurance companies won't pay the maximum for therapy. If therapy services are billed separately each month, however, insurance covers a larger portion of the charge. Insist the facility accommodate your request for separate bills for each kind of therapy.

LOWE'S SYNDROME (See RARE DISEASES.)

LUNG DISEASE

Tip # 1: Call the Lungline at 1-800-222-5864.

How it works: The National Jewish Hospital and Research Center operates the Lungline which provides a nurse qualified to answer many callers' questions about respiratory infections and immune system diseases including asthma, emphysema, chronic bronchitis, allergies, juvenile rheumatoid arthritis, and smoking. Literature is also available.

Tip # 2: Contact the American Lung Association.

How it works: The American Lung Association provides information and referrals to programs. Call the local chapter listed under American Lung Association followed by the name of your state or city. Or call the national office at 212-315-8700 for a referral.

Tip # 3: Try to get into an experimental study of treatment of your respiratory disorder. (See also STUDIES.)

How it works: Experimental treatment studies often offer free treatment to patients who qualify as subjects. In particular, the Clinical Center of the National Institutes of Health in Bethesda, MD, has ongoing studies of many respiratory disorders including interstitial lung disease, emphysema, chronic bronchitis, and cystic fibrosis. For information about getting into a study at this or other institutions, see STUDIES.

LUPUS

Tip # 1: Contact the Lupus Foundation of America at 1-800-558-0121.

How it works: The Lupus Foundation offers information and referral to doctors, treatment centers, and support groups. For Spanish speaking staff, call 301-670-9292.

Tip # 2: Contact the American Lupus Society.

How it works: The ALS provides a 24-hour recording for callers to leave their names and addresses to receive information on services offered.

Tip # 3: Contact the Terri Gotthelf Lupus Research Institute at 1 800-82-LUPUS for information and referrals.

LYME DISEASE

Tip # 1: Call the Centers for Disease Control and Prevention (CDC).

How it works: The CDC gives current and detailed, recorded information on Lyme disease 24-hours a day at 404-332-4555. To save money, call during low telephone rate hours. Also, a pamphlet on Lyme disease available from the CDC has a color picture of the characteristic rash of Lyme disease and of the tick that carries it. The pamphlet also includes information on causes, prevention, diagnosis and treatment. To request this pamphlet, call CDC public inquiry at 404-639-3534.

LYMPHEDEMA, HEREDITARY (See also RARE DISEASES.)

Tip # 1: Contact the National Lymphedema Network at 1-800-541-3259.

How it works: The Network provides information on lymphedema and other venous disorders. It gives referrals to treatment centers. Call between 8 a.m. and 6 p.m. Pacific time.

LYMPHOMA, GASTRIC (See RARE DISEASES.)

MACULAR DEGENERATION (See RARE DISEASES and EYE CARE.)

MACROGLOSSIA (See RARE DISEASES.)

MALARIA

Tip # 1: Call the Centers for Disease Control and Prevention (CDC) at 404-332-4555 for current information on malaria.

How it works: The CDC has very detailed, recorded information on malaria 24 hours a day including information on prevention, symptoms, diagnosis, treatment, and prevalence of malaria. To save money, call during low telephone rate hours. To receive written information on malaria and answers to other questions ONLY AFTER listening to the recorded information, call the CDC public inquiry number 404-639-3534 weekdays except federal holidays 8:30 a.m. to 5 p.m. Eastern time.

MALIGNANT HYPERTHERMIA (See RARE DISEASES.)

MAMMOGRAMS

Tip # 1: Be aware that the Medicare program now covers mammograms for women aged 65 and older.

How it works: In previous years Medicare did not cover the costs of mammograms to detect breast cancers even though 80% of all breast cancers occur in women over age 50. For this reason, many women did not have the screening mammograms which, according to the National Cancer Institute, could reduce breast cancer deaths for older women by 30%. Now the need for such coverage under Medicare has been recognized, but many women are unaware of the new coverage. Consider having a mammogram at the frequency your doctor recommends for your age and history. The American Cancer Society recommends women have a baseline mammogram between ages 30 and 39. a mammogram every two years from age 40 to 49 and a yearly mammogram age 50 and over.

Tip # 2: See if your insurance covers mammograms. There may have been a recent change.

How it works: Some insurance policies cover mammograms while some do not. Some states have recently changed their laws to require policies issued in the state to cover mammograms. Yours may be one. Consider having a mammogram done at the frequency your doctor recommends for your age and history.

Tip # 3: Shop around for a lower-priced mammogram including radiologist's reading.

How it works: To detect breast cancer at an early more treatable stage, have a mammogram done once a year if you are over fifty or more often if so advised by your doctor. Shop around for a less expensive mammograms at an accredited centers.

Within one metro area in the southeast and on the same city rapid transit line, mammogram costs (including reading by a radiologist) ranged from $89 to $123. The lower price was at a hospital in a small town/suburb; the higher figure was for a hospital in a high rent neighborhood. The savings by going to the less expensive location would be well worth the bus fare.

Similarly, in one mid-western city, the average cost of a mammogram (four views) and interpretive reading at a large university hospital was $87.50 for the X-rays themselves and an additional $38 for the reading, for a total of $125.50. The cost at a radiology center in the same city was only $78 for both the X-rays and reading—a difference of $47.50. Be sure and ask if the radiologist's reading fee is included in the price.

Quality check: When you make an appointment, ask if the mammography center is certified by the Mammography Accreditation Program of the American College of Radiology (ACR) or call the American Cancer Society at 1-800-ACS-2345 for a verification of accreditation.

Tip # 4: Look for reduced cost screening programs which are available in most areas several times a year or other reduced cost programs.

How it works: A mammogram at a hospital or medical center nationally costs between $75 and $160. A common price for a mammogram from a health fair or other screening program is $60. A consortium of hospitals in one city offered a $50-off coupon to any woman who would watch a video explaining breast care. Such programs are announced in newspapers and by posters in drug stores and shopping centers.

One non-profit program in New York offers a mammogram with a reading by a radiologist for just $45 for people without medical insurance and whose yearly family income is under $50,000. If your annual family income is between $50,000 and $100,000 and you have no insurance the fee is $100. For others the regular charge of $155 is charged directly to your health insurance company. There is no charge for people who cannot afford to pay.

Quality check: Mammograms and their interpretation by a radiologist are only as good as the individual operating the machine and the radiologist reading the results. Many health fairs are sponsored by local hospitals and use hospital equipment and personnel. Before going to the screening, call the sponsor and check to see that the sponsor's program is certified by the Mammography Accreditation Program of the American College of Radiology (ACR) or call the American Cancer Society at (800) ACS-2345 for a verification of accreditation.

Tip # 5: Order an FDA publication on mammograms.

How it works: The Food and Drug Administration (FDA) provides current information in booklet form on a wide range of subjects. To receive the free booklet "Why Women Don't Get Mammograms (And They Should)," order Publication # FDA90-1137. Write FDA, 5600 Fisher's Lane, Mail Code HFE-88, Room 1663, Rockville, MD, 20857 or call 301-443-3170.

Tip # 6: Read up on breast care.

How it works: The more you know about breast care, the better you can make cost-conscious decisions. A good source of information is *Dr. Susan Love's Breast Book* by Susan M. Love, M.D., with Karen Lindsey (Addison-Wesley, 1991, $12.95).

MANNOSIDOSIS (See RARE DISEASES.)

MARFAN SYNDROME (See RARE DISEASES.)

MATERNITY (See BREAST FEEDING, PREGNANCY.)

MCCUNE-ALBRIGHT SYNDROME (See RARE DISEASES.)

MEASLES (See IMMUNIZATIONS.)

MEDICAID

Tip # 1: Find out if you qualify for Medicaid assistance.

How it works: Medicaid is a program providing health care services for individuals and families with low incomes and limited resources. In many states, patients must also be elderly, disabled, or a single parent. It is funded by state and federal dollars. Every state determines its own eligibility requirements. Eligibility is generally determined by income, assets and other resources, and certain circumstances such as age, disability, or pregnancy.

In most states those who are eligible for Supplemental Security Income (SSI) or Aid to Families with Dependent Children (AFDC) benefits are also eligible for Medicaid. In some states, overwhelming medical bills may permit eligibility for limited periods even though an individual's income is too high to qualify otherwise. This eligibility option is referred to as "medically needy" coverage.

The eligibility requirements are very complicated; there are different income limits for different circumstances, and they change from time to time. Call your state Medicaid office to ask where you can apply for Medicaid benefits in your state. (See phone numbers in Tip # 2.)

Many states have special Medicaid programs for infants and pregnant women. These pregnancy-related programs may have names that differ from the general state Medicaid program. Programs for pregnant women may have higher income allowances than other Medicaid programs in the state.

Applications are often taken at your community public assistance, Family and Children's Services, welfare, human services, or health department office. You can apply for Medicaid by telephone or letter in some states, in others you or an authorized representative must appear in person. You can apply at the nearest Social Security office for SSI (including Medicaid). Another resource to help you get started is the social worker in any hospital.

At some point you may have to provide a birth certificate or other proof of age, your social security number, citizenship status, wage records, forms and documents showing your income and assets. Certain programs may require proof of pregnancy, specific medical conditions, or proof of medical expenses. If you qualify for Medicaid you will be given a card to show to every medical provider.

Tip # 2: To get more information about Medicaid or referral in your state, call the state Medicaid office.

How it works: While Medicaid enrollment is handled through local social service agencies, every state has a state Medicaid number, listed below:

Alabama	205-277-2710 Ext. 200
Alaska	907-465-3355
American Samoa	011-684-633-4559
Arizona	602-234-3655 Ext. 4053
Arkansas	501-682-8487
	501-682-8487 (long term care)
California	916-657-1496
Connecticut	203-566-2934
Colorado	303-866-5901
Delaware	302-577-4400
D.C.	202-727-0735
Florida	904-488-3560
Georgia	404-656-4479
Guam	671-734-7269 or 7264
Hawaii	808-586-5392
Idaho	208-334-5795
Illinois	217-782-2570
Indiana	317-233-4448
Iowa	515-281-8794
Kansas	913-296-3981
Kentucky	502-564-4321
Louisiana	504-342-3891
Maine	207-289-2674
Maryland	301-225-6535
Massachusetts	617-348-5691
Michigan	517-335-5001
Minnesota	612-296-2766
Mississippi	601-359-6050
Missouri	314-751-6922
Montana	406-444-4540
Nebraska	402-471-9147
Nevada	702-687-4378
New Hampshire	603-271-4314
New Jersey	609-588-2600
New Mexico	505-827-4315

New York	518-474-9132
North Carolina	919-733-2060
North Dakota	701-224-2321
Northern Mariana Islands	670-234-8950 Ext. 2905
Ohio	614-644-0140
Oklahoma	405-557-2539
Oregon	503-378-2263;
	503-378-4728 (seniors and disabled)
Pennsylvania	717-787-1870
Puerto Rico	809-765-1230
Rhode Island	401-464-3575
South Carolina	803-253-6100
South Dakota	605-773-3495
Tennessee	615-741-0213
Texas	512-450-3050
Utah	801-538-6406
Vermont	802-241-2880
Virginia	804-786-7933
Virgin Islands	809-774-4624;
	809-773-2150
Washington	206-753-1777
West Virginia	304-926-1700
Wisconsin	608-266-2522
Wyoming	307-777-7531

Tip # 2: Find Medicaid providers.

How it works: Not every doctor or clinic accepts Medicaid patients. Through an arrangement between Medicaid and health care providers, Medicaid pays a certain fee for covered services and a doctor, hospital, clinic, or other provider must accept that fee and charge the patient no more. In almost half the states you may be responsible for a small copayment, usually less than $3.

Some providers do not want to accept Medicaid fees because they may be lower than what they otherwise charge. Be sure the doctor or other health care provider you choose does accept Medicaid payments before you make an appointment.

Almost all hospitals, however, accept Medicaid because any provider that accepts federal funds (as most hospitals do) is required by law to accept Medicaid. Note that doctors in federally designated Community Health Centers, located in hundreds of poorly served communities, provide primary health care to Medicaid recipients and others. To find a Community Health Center near you, see COMMUNITY HEALTH CENTERS.

Quality check: In some areas, patients have been unable to find a physician, nursing home, or other health provider reasonably near their home who accepts Medicaid.

Tip # 3: See what services are covered by Medicaid in your state.

How it works: The costs of certain medical services are covered by Medicaid in all fifty states and other U.S. territories, according to federal law. These are inpatient hospital services, outpatient hospital services, rural health clinic services, other laboratory and x-ray services, nurse practitioners' services, nursing facility services and home health services for individuals 21 and older, early and periodic screening, diagnosis, and treatment for individuals under age 21, family planning services and supplies, physician services, and nurse-midwife services.

In addition, other optional services may be covered by Medicaid on a state-by-state basis. For example, in some states Medicaid covers dentures; in other states it does not. Similarly, some states cover hospice care, physical therapy, adult vision care, or private duty nursing. Others do not. Even pharmacy services are optional although covered in all but the Virgin Islands and Puerto Rico. Get up-to-date information about what your state covers by calling your state Medicaid number listed in Tip # 2.

Whenever possible, choose services covered by Medicaid. For example, choose a physician or a physical therapist rather than a podiatrist in states where a podiatrist's services are not covered by Medicaid but a physician's or physical therapist's are.

The following list, used for illustration only, shows Medicaid coverage of optional services across the country as of October 1991. Remember that coverage changes; states from time to time drop coverage of services because of financial pressure and some services are added. For this reason, the chart may no longer be totally accurate for your state.

Optional Services Covered by State Medicaid Programs

Services are listed in alphabetical order followed by the abbreviated names of states or territories where that service is covered. No asterisk after a state or territory name indicates the service is covered in that state only for the *Categorically Needy*, that is, those individuals who are receiving federally supported financial assistance. An asterisk after a state name indicates the service in that state is covered both for the *Categorically Needy* and also for the *Medically Needy*, those individuals who are eligible for medical assistance but not for general financial assistance.

Case management services:
AL, AR*, CA*, CO, CT*, FL*, GA*, HI*, ID, IN, IA*, KS*, KY*, LA*, ME*, MD*, MA*, MI*, MN*, MS, MO, NE*, NV, NH*, NM, NY*, NC*, ND*, OH, OK*, OR*, PA*, RI*, SC*, SD, TN*, TX*, UT*, VT*, VA*, WA*, WV*, WI*.

Chiropractors' services:
AK, AS*, AR*, CA*, CT*, FL*, ID, IL*, IN, IA*, ME*, MN*, NE*, NV, NH*, NJ*, NC*, ND*, OH, OR*, PA*, SD, TX*, VT*, WA, WV*, WI.

Christian Science nurses:
CA*, IN, ME*.

Christian Science sanitoriums:
CA*, CT*, IL*, IN, ME*, MI*, MN*, MS, NJ, OH, OR*, TN*, TX*, VA*, WI*.

Clinic services:
AL, AK, AS*, AZ, AR*, CA*, CO, CT*, DE, DC*, FL*, GA*, GU, HI*, ID, IL*, IN, IA*, KS*, KY*, LA*, ME*, MD*, MA*, MI*, MN*, MS, MO, MT*, NE*, NV, NH*, NJ*, NM, NY*, NC*, ND*, NMI*, OH, OK*, OR*, PA*, PR*, SC*, SD, TN*, TX*, UT*, VT*, VI*, VA*, WA*, WV*, WI*, WY.

Dental services:
AK, AS*, AZ, AR*, CA*, CT*, DC*, FL*, GA*, GU, HI*, IL*, IN, IA*, KS*, KY*, ME*, MD*, MA*, MI*, MN*, MS, MO, MT*, NE*, NV, NH*, NJ*, NM, NY*, NC*, ND*, NMI*, OH, OK*, OR*, PA*, RI*, SC*, SD, TN*, UT*, VT*, VA*, WA*, WV*, WI, WY.

Dentures:

AS*, AZ, AR*, CA*, CT*, DC*, FL*, GA*, HI*, IL*, IN, IA*, KS*, LA*, ME*, MD*, MA*, MI*, MN*, MO, MT*, NE*, NV, NJ*, NM, NY*, NC*, ND*, NMI*, OH, OR*, PA*, RI*, SD, UT*, VT*, WA*, WV*, WI.

Diagnostic services:

AS*, CA*, CT*, DE, DC*, HI*, IL*, IN, KY*, ME*, MA*, MI*, MN*, MS, MT*, NH*, NJ*, NY*, NC*, ND*, NMI*, OR*, TX*, UT*, WA, WI.

Emergency hospital services:

AK, AZ, AR*, CA*, CO, DE, DC*, FL*, GU, HI*, ID, IL*, IN, KS*, KY*, MD*, MA*, MI*, MN*, MS, MT*, NE*, NV, NH*, NJ, NM, NY*, ND*, OH, OR*, PA*, SC*, SD, TN*, TX*, UT*, VT*, VA*, WA*, WV*, WI*, WY.

Eyeglasses:

AL, AK, AS*, AZ, AR*, CA*, CO, CT*, DE, DC*, FL*, GA*, GU, HI*, IL*, IN, IA*, KS*, ME*, MD*, MA*, MI*, MN*, MS, MO, MT*, NE*, NV, NH*, NJ*, NM, NY*, NC*, ND*, NMI*, OH, OK, OR*, PA*, RI, SC*, TX*, UT*, VT*, VA*, WA*, WV*, WI, WY.

Hospice care:

AL, AZ, CA*, CO, DE, FL*, GA*, HI*, ID, IL*, IA*, KS*, KY*, MD*, MA*, MI*, MN*, MO, MT*, NM, NY*, NC*, ND*, OH, PA*, RI*, TN*, TX*, UT*, VT*, VA*, WA, WI*.

Mental disease, inpatient hospital services for persons aged 65 or older:

AK, AR*, CA*, CO, CT*, DE, DC*, FL, IL*, IN, IA, KS*, KY*, LA, ME*, MD*, MA*, MI*, MN*, MO, MT*, NE*, NV, NH*, NJ, NY*, NC*, ND*, OK, OR*, PA*, RI*, SC*, TN*, UT*, VT*, VA, WA*, WI, WY.

Mental disease, nursing facility services for persons aged 65 or older:

AL, AR, CA*, CO, CT*, DC*, ID, IL*, IA, KS*, KY*, MD*, MA*, MI*, MN*, MT*, NE*, NV, NH*, NJ, NM, NC*, OH, PA*, RI*, SC*, SD, TN*, UT*, VT*, VA, WA*, WI*.

Mentally retarded, intermediate care:

AL, AK, AZ, AR, CA*, CO, CT*, DE, DC*, FL, GA*, HI*, ID,
IL*, IN, IA, KS*, KY*, LA, MD*, MA*, MI*, MN*, MO, MT*,
NE*, NV, NH*, NJ, NM, NY*, NC*, ND*, OH, OK, OR*, PA*,
RI*, SC*, SD, TN*, TX*, UT*, VT*, VA, WA*, WV*, WI, WY.

Nursing facilities for individuals under age 21:

AL, AK, AZ, AR, CA*, CO, CT*, DC*, DE, FL, GA*, HI*, ID,
IL*, IN, IA, KS*, KY*, LA, ME*, MD*, MA*, MI*, MN*, MS,
MO, MT*, NE*, NV, NH*, NJ, NM, NY*, NC*, ND*, OH, OK,
OR*, PA*, RI*, SC*, SD, TN*, TX*, UT*, VT*, VA*, WA*, WV*,
WI*, WY.

Occupational therapy:

AK, AS*, AZ, AR*, CA*, DC*, FL*, HI*, IL*, IN, IA*, KS*, KY*,
ME*, MA*, MI*, MN*, MS, MT*, NE*, NV, NH*, NJ*, NM,
NY*, ND*, NMI*, OH, OR*, SC, VT*, VA*, WA*, WI*.

Optometrists' services:

AL, AK, AZ, AR*, CA*, CO, CT*, DE, DC*, FL*, GA*, GU, HI*,
ID, IL*, IN, IA*, KS*, KY*, LA*, ME*, MD*, MA*, MI*, MN*,
MO, MT*, NE*, NV, NH*, NJ*, NM, NY*, NC*, ND*, OH, OK*,
OR*, PA*, RI*, SC*, TN*, TX*, UT*, VT*, VA*, WA*, WV*, WI,
WY.

Other practitioners' services:

AL, AS*, AZ, AR*, CA*, CO, CT*, DE, DC*, FL*, GA*, HI*, ID,
IN, IA*, KS*, KY*, LA, ME*, MD*, MA*, MI*, MN*, MS, MT*,
NE*, NV, NH*, NJ*, NM, NY*, NMI*, OH, OK*, OR*, SC*,
TN*, TX*, UT*, VT*, VA*, WA*, WV*, WI, WY.

Personal care services:

AK, AZ, AR, DC*, FL*, ID, KS*, ME*, MD*, MA*, MI*, MN*,
MO, MT*, NE*, NV, NH*, NJ, NY*, NC*, OK*, OR*, SD, TX*,
UT*, WA, WV*, WI*.

Physical therapy:

AK, AS*, AZ, AR*, CA*, CT*, DC*, FL*, HI*, ID, IL*, IN, IA*,
KS*, KY*, ME*, MD*, MA*, MI*, MN*, MS, MT*, ME*, NV,
NH*, NJ*, NM, NY*, ND*, NMI*, OH, OR*, SC, SD, TX*, UT*,
VT*, VA*, WA*, WV*, WI*, WY.

Podiatrists' services:

AZ, CA*, CO, CT*, DE, DC*, FL*, GA*, HI*, ID, IL*, IN, IA*, KY*, LA, ME*, MD*, MA*, MI*, MN*, MO, MT*, NE*, NV, NH*, NJ*, NM, NY*, NC*, ND*, OH, OK*, OR*, PA*, RI, SC*, SC, TN*, TX*, UT*, VT*, VA*, WA*, WV*, WI*

Prescription drugs:

AL, AK, AS*, AZ, AR*, CA*, CO, CT*, DE, DC*, FL*, GA*, GU, HI*, ID, IL*, IN, IA*, KS*, KY*, LA*, ME*, MD*, MA*, MI*, MN*, MS, MO, MT*, NE*, NV, NH*, NJ*, NM, NY*, NC*, ND*, NMI*, OH, OK*, OR*, PA, RI*, SC*, SD, TN*, TX*, UT*, VT*, VA*, WA*, WV*, WI*, WY.

Preventive services:

AS*, CA*, CT*, DC*, HI*, IL*, IN, KY*, ME*, MA*, MN*, MS, NE*, NH*, NJ*, NY*, NC*, ND*, NMI*, OR*, UT*, WA*, WI.

Private duty nursing

AS*, AZ, AR*, CA*, CO, DE, DC*, FL*, IL*, IN, KS*, ME*, MD*, MA, MN*, MT*, NE*, NV, NH*, NY*, NC*, ND*, OH, OR*, UT*, WA*, WV*, WI.

Prosthetic devices:

AL, AK, AS*, AZ, AR*, CA*, CO, CT*, DE, DC*, FL*, GA*, HI*, IL*, IN, IA*, KS*, KY*, LA*, ME*, MD*, MA*, MI*, MN*, MS, MO, MT*, NE*, NV, NH*, NJ*, NM, NY*, NC*, ND*, NMI*, OH, OK, OR*, PA*, RI*, SC*, SD, TN*, TX*, UT*, VT*, VA*, WA*, WV*, WI*, WY.

Psychiatric inpatient services for individuals under age 21:

AL, AK, AR*, CA*, CO, CT*, DC*, HI*, IL*, IN, IA, KS*, KY*, LA, ME*, MD*, MA*, MI*, MN*, MO, MT*, NE*, NV, NH*, NJ, NY*, NC*, ND*, OK*, OR*, PA*, RI*, SC*, TN*, UT*, VT*, WA*, WV*, WI.

Rehabilitative services:

AL, AS*, AR*, CA*, CO, CT*, DE, DC*, FL*, HI*, ID, IL*, IN, KS*, KY*, LA*, ME*, MA*, MI*, MN*, MS, MO, MT*, NV, NH*, NJ*, NY*, NC*, ND*, NMI*, OH, OK*, OR*, PA*, RI*, SC*, SD, TN*, TX*, UT*, VT*, VA*, WA*, WI, WY.

Respiratory care:

AZ, CA*, FL*, HI*, IN, MI*, NV, OR*, TN*, TX*, VI*, WA*, WV*, WI*.

Screening services:

AS*, CA*, CT*, DC*, HI*, IN, KY*, ME*, MA*, MN*, MS, MT*, NE*, NH*, NJ*, NY*, NC*, ND*, NMI*, OK, OR*, UT*, WI.

Speech, hearing, and language disorders:

AK, AS*, AZ, AR*, CA*, CT*, DC*, FL*, GU, HI*, IL*, IN, IA*, KS*, KY*, ME*, MD*, MA*, MI*, MN*, MS, MT*, NE*, NV, NH*, NJ*, NM, NY*, ND*, NMI*, OH, OR*, SD, UT*, VT*, VA*, WA, WV*, WI*, WY.

Transportation services:

AL, AK, AS*, AZ, AR*, CA*, CO, CT*, DE, FL*, GA*, HI*, ID, IL*, IN, IA*, KS*, KY*, LA*, ME*, MD*, MA*, MI*, MN*, MS, MO, MT*, NE*, NV, NH*, NJ, NM, NY*, NC*, ND*, NMI*, OH, OK*, OR*, PA*, RI*, SC*, TN*, TX*, UT*, VT*, VA*, WA*, WV*, WI*, WY.

NOTE: American Samoa (AS) and the Northern Mariana Islands (NMI) operate special Medicaid waivered programs. In Puerto Rico all services are provided through public health facilities. In Oregon, all services shown to be available to the medically needy are not available to all medically needy groups.

Tip # 4: Apply early for Medicaid.

How it works: Because it might take a month or more in some states for a decision to be made on your eligibility, it's important to apply early for Medicaid so you can receive timely treatment and avoid accumulating medical bills. This is particularly important for pregnant women who should seek Medicaid or a change in Medicaid coverage early in their pregnancy so their babies can get important prenatal care. Medicaid will pay for bills incurred up to three months before the date of application if the applicant was eligible during that time period. If you failed to get treatment because you couldn't pay, your baby is at risk. Also, if you got treatment from a provider that does not accept Medicaid payment, the retroactive Medicaid payment cannot be applied to those bills.

MEDICAL BILLS (See also, HOSPITAL STAYS, DOCTOR, Choosing, DOCTOR, Fees, MEDICAID, MEDICARE, and listings of individual diseases by name)

Tip # 1: If you are unable to pay for medical care, go to any accredited hospital and ask to see the social worker for advice.

How it works: Every accredited hospital has a social worker to whom you can usually talk whether or not you are admitted to that hospital. The social worker can help you understand Medicaid, start the application process, or advise you of your other options whether or not you qualify for Medicaid. Be forewarned that some hospitals have tried to separate the counseling duties of the social worker from the financial advice function and may reserve such advising for inpatients under another name. Some hospitals require admission to the hospital before you can see the social worker. Many hospitals, however, allow public access to the social workers. Just ask to see the social worker and offer as little explanation as possible.

Tip # 2: Some clinics and hospitals will allow patients to pay bills on a monthly plan.

How it works: It may be easier for you to pay medical bills if they are spread out over a longer period. Talk to the billing office of the doctor, clinic, or hospital soon. Some clinics allow you to pay on a monthly basis and do not charge interest on the unpaid balance. Paying this way would be cheaper than paying by credit card at a high interest rate or by borrowing with interest.

Tip # 3: See if you qualify for Medicaid on account of your overwhelming medical bills even if your income is otherwise too high.

How it works: Income, assets, and other circumstances determine your eligibility for Medicaid. Some states have a special condition under which some people are declared Medically Needy Adults because of accumulated medical bills and are thereby eligible. Call your Medicaid office and ask where to apply. See also MEDICAID.

Tip # 4: Ask local charities for help with payment of medical expenses.

How it works: Many charities such as churches and organizations related to a disease offer assistance. For example, your church may have a short term aid program for people overwhelmed financially by health problems. Catholic churches help people especially through the St. Vincent de Paul Society which offers help for prescriptions. The Salvation Army may also provide short term assistance. The American Cancer Society may give up to $150 for travel to get treatment or for anti-nausea drugs. The Muscular Dystrophy Association helps provide needy patients with wheel chairs, doctor's visits, physical and occupational therapy, and transportation to therapy. The Leukemia Society may pay up to $700 a year to help patients with medical expenses. (See also specific disease listings.)

Tip # 4: If you have insurance that pays a percentage of your doctor's bills, say 80%, and you cannot pay the remaining copayment, tell the doctor.

How it works: The doctor may agree to charge you the full amount but accept only the insurance payment and let the copayment go. It may be better to discuss this with your doctor during your first visit. A doctor is more likely to be sensitive to your situation if you explain the problem honestly up front rather than accept the service and then bring up the issue of your inability to pay. Also, talking to the doctor who ultimately makes the decisions is usually better than talking to the staff who do not usually have the authority to waive or reduce fees.

MEDICARE (If disabled, see also DISABILITY.)

Tip # 1: Apply for Medicare if you are 65 or older or if you are younger and are disabled or have end-stage kidney disease.

How it works: When you turn 65 or become disabled or in need of dialysis for kidney failure, make application for Medicare at your local Social Security office.

Medicare Part A covers most hospitalization and some inpatient nursing care. Medicare Part B covers most doctors' fees and outpatient treatment. Most people have to pay premiums to get Part B just as you would to a private insurance company but Medicare Part B premiums are generally much smaller. You also must pay deductibles and copayments under Medicare Part B as you usually do for private insurance. (You do not have to pay premiums if you receive benefits or are eligible to receive benefits under Supplemental Security Income (SSI) or the Railroad Retirement System or if you or your spouse had Medicare-covered employment.)

Many but not all medical costs are covered by Medicare. For details, see the most recent Medicare handbook. (To order the handbook, see Tip # 4.) Coverage for Medicare, unlike Medicaid, is uniform throughout the United States.

Medicare is available to those who have a wage history or are eligible for Social Security. If you are over 65 but not eligible for Social Security, you may still be able to BUY into Medicare insurance for less than a private policy. As of 1993, Medicare Part A coverage costs $197 a month, and Part B costs $36.60 a month; the amount is subject to change yearly. Call your Social Security local office and discuss the possibility of buying in and compare Medicare with other options.

Tip # 2: If you are about to become eligible for Medicare, you can save money by enrolling in Part B of Medicare NOW.

How it works: Part B, the portion of Medicare that covers many outpatient services including physical therapy and rehabilitation, requires a premium (unlike Part A which covers hospital stays and is provided free to qualified recipients). Part B costs a certain amount determined yearly ($36.60 a month, as of 1993); you take Part B from the time of your initial eligibility. But if you are not covered by an employee plan and you delay in enrolling in Part B, there will be a 10% penalty for each 12 months you wait. So unless you already have an employee health plan, it may be better to sign on now.

Tip # 3: Consider a Medicare Coordinated Care Plan for savings.

How it works: Medicare contracts with health maintenance organizations (HMOs) or competitive medical plans to provide prepaid, managed care plans to those enrolled in Medicare Part B. You pay a fixed monthly premium and only small co-payments for each service.

Many beneficiaries find coordinated care plans are a good way to get more health care for their dollar. Your out-of-pocket costs are usually more predictable and less paperwork is involved. Coordinated care plans may also offer benefits not covered by Medicare for little or no additional cost. As with most HMOs, your care will be provided mostly by health care professionals who have contracted with that HMO.

For more information, order Booklet 509-X, "Medicare and Coordinated Care Plans," by writing Consumer Information Center, Department 59, Pueblo, CO 81009.

Tip # 4: Get the current Medicare handbook.

How it works: To get the current Medicare Handbook for information on benefits, participating physicians, health insurance supplements to Medicare, and limits to coverage, call 1-800-772-1213 or write for Publication HCFA 10050 at:

U.S. Department of Health and Human Services
6325 Security Blvd.
Baltimore, MD 21207

Tip # 5: For answers to questions about enrollment in Medicare A and B, call 1-800-772-1213.

How it works: Social Security staff answer individual questions about Medicare. Have your Social Security number ready. The service operates from 7 a.m. to 7 p.m. Eastern time, Monday through Friday. When staff members are busy a recording will tell you an accurate estimate of how many minutes you may have to wait, usually not long. The best hours to call for an available staff member are before 9 a.m. and after 4 p.m. Wednesday through Friday.

Recorded information and pamphlets are also available at the above number on these subjects: disability and survivorship, qualified Medicare beneficiary program, legal rights to appeal, the effect of working on benefits, taxation of Social Security income, and other topics.

Tip # 6: If you are eligible for Medicare and also for Medicaid, Medicaid will pay your premiums for all Medicare benefits as well as other costs.

How it works: If you have applied and have been accepted for Medicaid, the Medicaid program will pay all the premiums for Medicare Part 1 and 2 and all deductibles and co-payments you would have had to pay under Medicare alone.

Tip # 7: If you qualify for Medicare and have limited income and resources, apply for the Qualified Medicare Beneficiary Program (QMB).

How it works: If you have limited income and resources, you may be eligible for the Qualified Medicare Beneficiary Program which will pay your premiums, deductibles, and co-insurance payments. Call your local or state social services or welfare office to see if you qualify.

Tip # 8: Consider buying supplemental coverage on your insurance plan or Medigap plan to cover what Medicare does not. (Also, see MEDICARE SUPPLEMENT INSURANCE.)

How it works: If you are enrolled in or about to enroll in Medicare, consider a supplemental policy, also called Medigap or Mediplus, which would cover the part of the bills your policy does not cover such as the 20% co-payment and the costs of medication.

Quality check: While supplemental policies can save you a lot of money if you have surgery or other expensive procedures, remember that supplemental policies are like having a low deductible on regular insurance: it may cost more than it's worth.

Tip # 9: Be sure your doctor or medical provider accepts Medicare "assignment" or Medicare's "limiting charge" fee schedules.

How it works: The Medicare program pays doctors and other health providers for their services to patients enrolled in Medicare. Medicare patients pay an annual $100 deductible. After that, for each medical service covered by Medicare, the patient pays a 20% co-payment and Medicare picks up the other 80%. Medicare has a fee schedule for each medical service and providers who agree to charge no more than the Medicare fee limit are said to "accept Medicare assignment" or be Medicare "participating physicians."

The amount set by Medicare for each procedure is often less than what medical providers usually charge non-Medicare patients. For this reason, many doctors and health care providers do not accept Medicare assignment. Be careful when someone in a medical office says "Yes, we accept Medicare." They may mean they accept Medicare payment plus additional charges.

When a provider who does not accept Medicare assignment charges more than the Medicare limit for a procedure, that is called "balance billing." In many cases, patients pay the difference or balance in addition to their co-payment. A section of the Physician Payment Reform Law of 1991 sets limits on what even a non-participating physician can charge a Medicare patient. The Medicare balance-billing was limited (in most cases) to 20% over the Medicare fee. These federal regulations on balance billing have been interpreted differently in different states and enforcement of the law has been lax.

In any case, ask if your doctor and other providers will accept Medicare payment along with your 20% co-payment as payment in full BEFORE you consider accepting services. (See the following tips.)

Tip # 10: Find doctors and medical providers near you who do accept Medicare assignment.

How it works: To find doctors who accept Medicare assignments as payment in full, call the office of the insurance company that administers Medicare in your state. This toll-free number and a mailing address are printed on your explanation of benefits. For your convenience, these numbers are listed below by state:

ALABAMA
Blue Cross-Blue Shield of Alabama—1-800-292-8855

ALASKA
Aetna—1-800-452-0125

ARIZONA
Aetna—1-800-352-0411

ARKANSAS
Arkansas Blue Cross and Blue Shield—1-800-482-5525

CALIFORNIA
In the counties of Los Angeles, Orange, San Diego, Ventura, Imperial, San Luis Obispo, and Santa Barbara—Transamerica

Occidental—1-800-675-2266; in the rest of the state—Blue Shield of California—1-800-952-8627 or 1-800-952-8627 depending on the area code.

COLORADO
Blue Cross and Blue Shield of Colorado—1-800-332-6681 and in metro-Denver 303-831-2661.

CONNECTICUT
The Travelers—1-800-982-6819, in Hartford 203-728-6783, and in Meriden 203-237-8592

DELAWARE
Pennsylvania Blue Shield—1-800-851-3535

DISTRICT OF COLUMBIA
Pennsylvania Blue Shield—1-800-233-1124

FLORIDA
Blue Shield of Florida—1-800-666-7586

GEORGIA
Aetna—1-800-727-0827

HAWAII
Aetna—1-800-272-5242

IDAHO
CIGNA—1-800-627-2782

ILLINOIS
Blue Cross & Blue Shield of Illinois—1-800-642-6930

INDIANA
AdminaStar Federal—1-800-622-4792

IOWA
IASD Health Services—1-800-532-1285

KANSAS
Counties of Johnson and Wyandotte—Blue Shield of Kansas City—1-800-892-5900; rest of state—Blue Cross-Blue Shield of Kansas—1-800-432-3531

KENTUCKY
Blue Cross & Blue Shield of Kentucky—1-800-999-7608

LOUISIANA
Arkansas Blue Cross-Blue Shield—1-800-462-9666, in Baton Rouge—504-927-3490; in New Orleans-504-529-1494

MAINE
C and S Administrative Services—1-800-492-0919

MARYLAND
In the counties of Montgomery and Prince Georges—Pennsylvania Blue Shield—1-800-233-1124; in the rest of the state—Maryland Blue Shield—1-800-492-4795

MASSACHUSETTS
C and S Administrative Services—1-800-882-1228

MICHIGAN
Michigan Blue Cross & Blue Shield—In area code 313, 1-800-482-4045, in area code 517, 1-800-322-0607, in area code 616, 1-800-442-8020, in area code 906, 1-800-562-7802, in Detroit, 313-225-8200.

MINNESOTA
in Counties of Anoka, Dakota, Fillmore, Goodhue, Hennepin, Houston, Olmstead, Ramsey, Wabasha, Washington, and Winona—The Travelers—1-800-352-2762; in the rest of state, Blue Shield of Minnesota—1-800-392-0343

MISSISSIPPI
The Travelers—1-800-682-5417

MISSOURI
In the counties of Andrew, Atchison, Bates, Benton, Buchanan, Caldwell, Carroll, Cass, Clay, Clinton, Daviess, DeKalb, Gentry, Grundy, Harrison, Henry, Holt, Jackson, Johnson, Lafayette, Livingston, Mercer, Nodaway, Pettis, Platte, Ray, St. Clair, Saline, Vernon, Worth—Blue Shield of Kansas City—1-800-892-5900; in the rest of the state, General American Life—1-800-392-3070.

MONTANA
Blue Cross and BLue Shield of Montana—1-800-332-6146

NEBRASKA
Blue Shield of Nebraska—1-800-633-1113

NEVADA

Aetna—1-800-528-0311

NEW HAMPSHIRE

C and S Administrative Services—1-800-447-1142

NEW JERSEY

Pennsylvania Blue Shield—1-800-462-9306

NEW YORK

In the counties of Bronx, Kings, New York, Richmond—Empire Blue Cross and Blue Shield—516-244-5100; in the counties of Columbia, Delaware, Dutchess, Suffolk, Sullivan, Ulster, and Westchester—Empire Blue Cross and Blue Shield—1-800-442-8430; in Queens County—212-721-1770; in the rest of the state—Blue Shield of Western New York—1-800-252-6550

NORTH CAROLINA

Connecticut General—1-800-672-3071

NORTH DAKOTA

Blue Shield of North Dakota—1-800-247-2267

OHIO

Nationwide Mutual—1-800-247-2267

OKLAHOMA

Aetna—1-800-522-9079

OREGON

Aetna—1-800-452-0125

PENNSYLVANIA

Pennsylvania Blue Shield—1-800-382-1274

RHODE ISLAND

Blue Cross and Blue Shield of Rhode Island—1-800-662-5170

SOUTH CAROLINA

Blue Cross and Blue Shield of South Carolina—1-800-868-2522

SOUTH DAKOTA

Blue Shield of North Dakota—1-800-437-4762

TENNESSEE

Connecticut General—1-800-342-8900

TEXAS

Blue Cross & Blue Shield of Texas—1-800-442-2620

UTAH

Blue Shield of Utah—1-800-426-3477

VERMONT

C and S Administrative Services—1-800-447-1142

VIRGINIA

In the counties of Arlington and Fairfax and in the cities of Alexandria, Falls Church, and Fairfax—Pennsylvania Blue Shield—1-800-233-1124; in the rest of the state—The Travelers—1-800-442-3423

WASHINGTON

Washington State—In Seattle—1-800-422-4087; in Spokane—1-800-572-5256; in Tacoma—206-597-6530

WEST VIRGINIA

Nationwide Mutual—1-800-848-0106

WISCONSIN

WPS—1-800-362-7221; in Madison—608-221-3330; in Milwaukee—414-931-1071

WYOMING

Blue Shield of Wyoming—1-800-442-2371

AMERICAN SOMOA

Hawaii Medical Services—808-944-2247

GUAM

Aetna-808-524-1240

NORTHERN MARIANA ISLANDS

Aetna—808-524-1240

PUERTO RICO

Seguros De Servicio De Salud De Puerto Rico—In Puerto Rico metro area—809-749-4900; in the rest of Puerto Rico—1-800-462—7015; in U.S. Virgin Islands—1-800-474-7448

VIRGIN ISLANDS

Seguros De Servicio De Salud De Puerto Rico—1-800-474-7448

Tip # 11: If your doctor accepts Medicare assignments and you think he/she is charging you more than the Medicare-approved fee, call your Medicare carrier.

How it works: Your Medicare insurance carrier is the same company to which your doctor or medical provider submits claims. This company has all the limits for every service and should address your complaint. Its phone number is on your explanation of Medicare Benefits form.

Tip # 12: Contact an office of your Area Agency on Aging for information on Medicare counseling help available in your area.

How it works: The federal government provides for Area Agencies on Aging which may be administered by local governments. The Agency near you can give you information about Medicare and will refer you to a counselor for your particular problem. To find an Area Agency on Aging, call Administration on Aging listed in the phone book under United States Government, Health and Human Services Department. Tell this office where you live for a referral.

Tip # 13: For help with overcharging for Medicare services or to report abuse of Medicare, call 1-800-368-5779.

How it works: The Department of Health and Human Services Inspector General's Hotline takes calls from people who have been overbilled or billed for services not received. In the latter case the operator will take the information and begin investigating. In cases of overbilling mistakes, the operator will advise you to write and explain what is wrong with the bill and mail your letter to the address at the top of your bill. The Hotline is answered from 10 a.m to 4 p.m. Eastern time but messages may be left after hours.

If you prefer to write, the address is

HHS OIG HOTLINE
P.O. Box 17303
Baltimore, MD 21203-7303

Tip # 14: For legal help collecting correct payments or refunds from Medicare, write Medicare Beneficiaries Defense Fund.

How it works: The Medicare Beneficiaries Defense Fund can help when you have been unable to get deserved payments from

Medicare and cannot afford legal fees to pursue a resolution. Write to the organization at 130 W. 42 St., 17th Floor, New York, NY, 10036-7803

MEDICARE SUPPLEMENT INSURANCE

Tip # 1: Consider buying supplemental insurance coverage within six months of enrolling in Medicare Part B.

How it works: If you are enrolled in or about to enroll in Medicare Part B, consider buying a private health insurance supplemental policy, also called Medigap or Mediplus, which would cover the part of the bills Medicare Parts A and B do not cover such as co-payments and deductibles and non-covered services.

If you are about to turn 65 or have just turned 65, it's important to make your decision immediately because Medigap policies will accept all applicants without rejecting anyone for pre-existing conditions for six months following age 65. After six months, an insurance company may reject you because of a pre-existing condition.

Under recent federal regulations, insurance companies in most states now offer up to ten standard Medigap policies generally rated A to J according to how much additional coverage they offer. A policy type A reimburses policy-holders for the 20% co-payment required for physicians and laboratory fees (after $100 deductible) and for hospital stays beyond the number of days covered by Medicare up to 365 days in a lifetime. These are among the core benefits. Policy types B through J offer core benefits plus certain additional coverages such as skilled nursing facility co-payments, deductibles, and, in the most comprehensive plans, prescription drugs. Premiums vary according to coverage level and by company.

All the new standard policies are guaranteed renewable as long as the policyholder pays premiums and has answered application questions accurately. Those who hold old policies before the recent standardization may switch to new ones if there is any advantage. New regulations forbid insurers to sell more than one Medigap policy to the same person.

Quality check: While supplemental policies can save you a lot of money if you have surgery or other expensive procedures, remember that supplemental policies are like having a low deductible on regular insurance: it may cost more than it's worth.

When considering switching to a new standard policy from an old policy, remember the new ones may not be a better deal than your older one and once you've changed you can't go back. The new standard policies were devised primarily to eliminate the confusion of many, sometimes overlapping policies previously sold. Also, be sure you are ACCEPTED by a new policy before dropping your old one.

Tip # 2: In some states, consider Medicare SELECT for savings on Medicare Supplement Insurance premiums.

How it works: Medicare SELECT is a new kind of Medicare Supplement or Medigap insurance. Medicare beneficiaries who buy a Medicare SELECT policy will be charged lower premiums in return for agreeing to use the services of certain designated health care professionals called "preferred providers." Insurers, including some HMOs, offer Medicare SELECT in the same way standard Medigap policies are offered. They are required to meet certain federal standards and are regulated by the states.

Tip # 3: If you choose a Medicare Coordinated Care plan for your Medicare Part B coverage, you may get supplementary coverage through that plan at little or no extra cost.

How it works: One of the ways to get Medicare Part B benefits is through a Medicare Coordinated Care Plan. (See MEDICARE, Tip #3.) One of the advantages of a Coordinated Care Plan is that, since care is provided through an HMO or competitive medical plan, you may be eligible for additional services not covered by Medicare such as dental care, preventive care, hearing aids or eyeglasses. These additional benefits may make supplemental insurance or Medigap less necessary in your case.

Tip # 4: Get free information on what to look for in Medicare supplement insurance.

How it works: For free tips on choosing a supplement to Medicare, write for "The Consumer's Guide to Medicare Supplement Insurance," The Health Insurance Association of America, P.O. Box 41455, Washington, DC 20018.

Or get a copy of "Guide to Health Insurance for People with Medicare." This guide explains how supplemental insurance works, tells how to shop for Medigap insurance, gives information on new standard plans and on Medicare SELECT and lists names and contact information of state insurance departments and state agencies on aging. Ask for Publication 518-Y by writing Consumer Information Center, Department 59, Pueblo, CO 81009.

MEDICAL DEVICES, FRAUD

Tip # 1: If you have doubts about the effectiveness of an advertised medical device, contact the FDA.

How it works: Sales people and advertisements for medical devices that don't work especially target teenagers and the elderly. Many ineffective devices are fraudulently sold for weight loss and as cures for arthritis, cancer, AIDS, and baldness. Inquire about specific products or treatments by contacting the FDA. Call 301-443-3170 or write to

U.S. Department of Health and Human Services
Public Health Service
Food and Drug Administration
Center for Devices and Radiological Health, Rockville, MD 20857.

MEDICATIONS

Tip # 1: Ask your doctor if there is an equally effective drug that costs less.

How it works: Compare three antibiotics for infections such as those causing earache or strep throat: A ten-day supply of Antibiotic A at one drug store costs under $20; a comparable ten-day supply of Antibiotic B costs about $60; a ten-day supply of Antibiotic C costs over $90. For an otherwise healthy person with an upper respiratory infection who has not been treated for such an ailment in six months, Antibiotic A is the cheapest effective drug. If a doctor prescribes one of the other two drugs instead, you or your insurance company is picking up the tab for the $40-$70 difference in price. Questioning whether this is the cheapest effective drug may guide the doctor to the most cost effective solution.

Quality check: Effectiveness is more important than price. Consider the example above. While Antibiotic A is very effective against the most common bacteria causing upper respiratory infection, Antibiotic B is a broader spectrum drug and may be effective against some bacteria that Antibiotic A does not attack. If Antibiotic A does not work, a broader spectrum drug may be necessary. Also, if you have been treated with Antibiotic A recently, a new infection may indicate a change in medicine because the bacteria may be resistant to the first drug. After raising the price issue, let your doctor guide you.

Tip # 2: Ask the doctor for free samples.

How it works: All doctors are given free samples by drug company representatives. These must be used or they go to waste. It doesn't hurt to ask for some to defray at least part of the cost of your prescription. In the situation described above comparing Antibiotic A and Antibiotic B, a doctor might give you samples of the first to last several days, saying, "If it works, call me and I'll prescribe the rest. If not, I'll prescribe Antibiotic B."

If you are starting a new medication, taking free samples for a few days to see if the drug works and if there are any side effects may eliminate having to throw away unused medicine you bought.

Quality check: Samples physicians give out may not be the full regime necessary so you may need to have a prescription in addition to the samples.

Tip # 3: Consider buying generics instead of name-brand drugs.

How it works: A doctor prescribes 30 capsules of a name-brand medication for acne, for example. The cost is $78.68 for a month's supply at a particular pharmacy. One generic brand, however, sells at the same drug store for $68.99 and another generic brand sells for $50.34. The pharmacist thinks highly of the drug manufacturer that sells the least expensive generic and recommends you purchase that.

Quality check: The amount of active ingredient in a capsule or tablet varies somewhat; the FDA regulates this variability for all approved drugs in this country. Certain name brands are known to have very little variability while the variability of an unspecified generic might be greater although within the FDA limits.

In addition, even when the amount of active ingredient in a medication may be the same for name-brand drugs and generics, the fillers and binders may be different. This means the absorbability of the active ingredient may be different. Some binders, for example, do not dissolve as readily as others.

Generic drugs are a better buy when small variations in concentration and absorption do not matter. However, for some medications, the predictability of certain name-brand products is important. Some drugs which pharmacists we interviewed did <u>not</u> recommend buying as generic products were seizure medication, some heart medicine, birth control pills and certain other hormones. There may be others. Ask the pharmacist if he or she recommends generic substitutions for each prescription. Or ask the pharmacist to consult your doctor by phone before making a substitution. Some doctors may specify no generic substitutions.

(By the way, drugstores generally make more profit on generics than name-brand drugs where competition is greater so drug stores are usually happy to carry a large line of generics.)

Tip # 4: Buy more less often.

How it works: Pharmacies charge a dispensing fee each time they fill or refill a prescription. If you buy more at one time, you will save the dispensing fee for frequent refills.

For example, a certain acne medicine seemed to be effective for one teenager for over a year. At each visit, the dermatologist prescribed 30 capsules with 3 refills allowable. That totaled 120 capsules before another prescription would be necessary. The lowest cost generic at one chain pharmacy store was $50.34 for 30 capsules; at that rate (4 X $50.34), the 120 capsules would cost $201.36. BUT 120 capsules purchased at one time costs only $177.00, for a savings of $24—$96 for a whole year. Even if your physician has prescribed the drug in several small refills, most pharmacists will sell you all the capsules at once.

Occasionally, a pharmacy has almost run out of the medication you need. The pharmacist may suggest you take what the pharmacy has and come back later for the rest. In that case, consider having the whole prescription filled at another pharmacy because at the first pharmacy you will end up paying the dispensing fee twice. You can ask the pharmacist to waive the second fee.

A few drug stores figure the dispensing fee as a percentage of the cost of the drug. At these stores, buying in quantity does not save money.

Quality check: Ask your pharmacist about shelf life of the medication. Buying more than you can use before the quality expiration date means waste or reduced quality. In the case above, the 120-day supply fell well within the shelf life of the medicine. Also, buying larger quantities is not such a good idea when the condition for which the drug was prescribed is expected to clear up or when the drug causes side effects or doesn't work.

Tip # 5: Consider buying prescriptions taken regularly by mail order.

How it works: Mail order prices are generally cheaper than those at local drugstores. There are many catalogs. The AARP Pharmacy Service for members of the American Association of Retired Persons (AARP) is a good example. (Membership in AARP is $8 a year. Call 1-800-441-AARP.) Some organizations for people with particular diseases offer members mail-order service especially for the drugs they especially need. For example, the Crohn's and Colitis Foundation of America, the National Spinal Cord Injury Association, and some AIDS groups offer pharmaceutical services. Ask the organization associated with your illness about pharmacy services. (See also particular disease headings.) Some insurance companies that reimburse prescription costs sponsor mail-order purchase to help keep their costs down.

Quality check: Make price comparisons between the mail order price and the price you actually pay elsewhere (not the price a catalog says is the "regular" price).

Compare mail-order suppliers with those of local pharmacies. For example, your local drugstore may keep a computer record of all your medications and may warn you if you are purchasing a drug that is incompatible with another drug you are also taking. Or the local pharmacist may provide good medical records for tax reports or other information that you need.

Tip # 6: Buy larger dosage tablets and cut tablet in half.

How it works: The amount of medication in two small tablets sometimes costs more than the same amount of medication in one larger or more concentrated tablet. For example, a bottle containing 200 tablets of 2.5 mg. of Hormone A, a product often taken daily, in one drugstore costs $74, whereas 100 tablets containing 5.0 mg costs only $51. If you are taking 2.5 mg. daily, ask your doctor to prescribe 5.0 mg. and then take half a tablet a day for a savings of about $7 a month. Drug stores sell little kits to help cut tablets in half accurately.

Quality check: You must be careful to divide pills equally in half. Dividing is easier if the pill is scored with a line down the middle. Do not split capsules or time release medication.

Tip # 7: Take advantage of hold-the-price, money-back, or other guarantees and promotional offers from drug companies.

How it works: For example, one company offers a lifetime fixed price for one medication. The guarantee says that all patients who are prescribed the drug by December 3, 1995, and who are enrolled in the Lifetime Guarantee will never have to pay more than the Lifetime Fixed Price.

Another example of a money-saving promotion offers satisfaction-or-your-money-back. Some companies will refund your money if one of their medications does not work and you return what is remaining in its original bottle along with a retail return goods form. This guarantee allows you to try a medication without being stuck with a bill if it does not prove useful. Other manufacturers offer you a second medication free if you need two different drugs to control your medical problem.

After one pharmaceutical company makes a promotional offer, others often follow. The offers come and go and doctors are not always up to date. Don't hesitate to call the company's customer service number, often toll free, or the local manufacturers representative whose number your doctor or pharmacist will know, to ask a drug company what incentives they can give you. Your pharmacist or doctor may know of other special offers.

Quality check: Obviously, the most important consideration is getting an appropriate medicine for your condition.

Tip # 8: Don't be fooled by "loss leaders." Compare prices for each drug you buy.

How it works: Drug stores often advertise commonly used drugs at very low—even below cost—prices to attract you. That's fine if you are going to buy the advertised special while its price is reduced. But remember that other products in the same store may be the same or more expensive than those products at other pharmacies. And the special low price may also go back up later.

Tip # 9: Shop around and leave your name for the best price.

How it works: When people call pharmacies and ask for prices of certain medications, the pharmacies recognize that many of the callers are comparing prices. Sometimes the store will quote a very attractive price to win your business. If you leave your name, it will go into the computer and you will get that price when you come in. It may be a lower price than the price you would have paid if you had come in without calling. If drug stores play this game, you can play too. Call ahead for each prescription. And remember that impulse buying once you get there may be no bargain.

Tip # 10: Take advantage of "We'll match any price" offers.

How it works: Some drug stores advertise something like "You will be amazed by our low prices. In fact, if you can find a lower price anywhere in town, we will match it." The advertiser may in fact have average or even higher than average regular prices but the store will match the lower price if you get a lower legitimate price quote from another drug store in that community.

We tried out one chain drug store whose television advertisements offered such a price match. First, we telephoned several drug stores and got price quotes for a very expensive drug commonly used to treat persistent acne. We found the store's regular price for a 30-day supply was about $20 more than a very nearby family-owned store and about $40 more than the cheapest store in town. We concluded the chain drug store's claim about low prices was incorrect but the price matching offer was real. The store cheerfully sold us the medication at the lowest price available in town, saving us about $40 and a trip across town.

Tip # 11: Consider negotiating a price with your pharmacist.

How it works: Drug stores are competitive and the pharmacist may be willing to negotiate the price of a medication. Make an offer. Or ask him/her to match the lower price of another drug store even if the drug store does not advertise price-matching. It won't hurt to ask.

Tip # 12: If you are over 60, ask for a senior citizens' discount.

How it works: Many pharmacies offer 10% to 20% discount to people over age 62 or 65. Some will give you the discount because you ask and are "close enough" to their age of eligibility.

Tip # 13: When a mail-in information card is attached to your medication, fill it out and mail it in.

How it works: Some medications have attached mail-in cards offering newsletters or bulletins and asking you for information that may guide their response. It may be useful for you to be in contact with the manufacturer of a medicine you take.

Tip # 14: Order the free FDA publications on buying and taking medicines.

How it works: The Food and Drug Administration (FDA) provides current information in booklet form on a wide range of subjects. For information on buying medicine, order Publication # FDA91-1175.

For information on how to take your medicines, order FDA91-3188 for acetaminophen-codeine, FDA91-3180 for antihistamines, FDA91-3183 for beta blockers, FDA92-3191 for cephalosporins, FDA92-3167 for diuretics, FDA92-3192 for erythromycin, FDA91-3186 for estrogens, FDA90-3176 for nonsteroidal anti-inflammatory drugs, and FDA91-3184 for penicillins. Add an S to the end of each order number above to get the brochure in Spanish.

Write FDA, 5600 Fisher's Lane, Mail Code HFe-88, Room 1663, Rockville, MD 20857 or call 301-443-3170.

Tip # 15: Some drugs approved in foreign countries may be bought by U.S. citizens for their own use when under a physician's care. Restrictions apply.

How it works: Some very effective drugs used in some foreign countries are not available in the U.S. because the Food and Drug Administration (FDA) has not approved them for general use. There are two ways you may get such a drug.

If the drug is approved for use by a foreign country but is not approved for general use in the U.S. by the FDA, individuals may import up to a three months supply for their personal use only and must be under a physician's care. Other restrictions may apply. News of such drugs is often reported in the newspaper or in medical publications such as *The Medical Letter* (1000 Main St., New Rochelle, NY 10801). Importing for personal use is usually done by mail-order. (See also AIDS, Tip # 6 and MIGRAINE.)

Another way to receive treatment with a drug not approved for general use in the U.S. is for your doctor to present a proposal to the FDA asking permission to do an investigational study of treatment with the drug for your particular case. The FDA decides on a case-by-case basis.

For more information, call your regional FDA office listed in your phone book under U.S. Government and ask for the Compliance Department. Or contact the FDA national office at 301-443-4166 or write FDA, Public Affairs, Room 13-88, Rockville, MD 20857 for referral.

How it works: When you use a drug approved for use in another country you are relying on that country's regulatory agency to determine safety and effectiveness. Many other countries are less conservative than the U.S. in making such judgments.

Tip # 16: Consider asking for state assistance to pay for medication you can't afford.

How it works: A substantial number of states have special funds (in addition to Medicaid) for providing medication free or at low cost to people who can't afford it. Some of these programs are exclusively for the elderly or for people with AIDS, high blood pressure, diabetes, or some other particular disease. Other programs may have few limitations other than need. Call your public health department or state medical assistance program to see what your state offers.

Tip # 17: If you cannot afford the drug that is prescribed, you may qualify for free drugs from the manufacturer.

How it works: Many drug companies offer free or reduced costs to those who demonstrate they cannot pay. For information on prescription drug programs for the medically indigent, your doctor can write Pharmaceutical Manufacturers Association, 1100 Fifteenth Street NW, Washington, DC 20005. A toll-free hotline for physician inquiries is available at 1-800-PMA-INFO (202-393-5200 in Washington, DC, area). Your pharmacist can give you the name of the manufacturer of your medication or you can look it up in the *Physician's Desk Reference* (PDR) at your library.

Also a great deal of information on indigent programs is provided by an September 1992 Status Report prepared by the staff of the Special Committee on Aging, United States Senate; portions of this are reprinted in Appendix A. First, there is a list showing which medications are made by which manufacturers. Second, there is a description of the programs of some of the drug companies that provide at least some of their products free to the medically indigent.

MEDIGAP or MEDIPLUS (See MEDICARE SUPPLEMENT)

MENIERE'S DISEASE

Tip # 1: Contact the Meniere's Network at 1-800-545-4327.

How it works: The Meniere's Network is sponsored by the Ear Foundation and provides literature including a newsletter about the hearing disorder. The phone is answered from 8 a.m. to 5 p.m. Central time and you may leave a recorded message after hours.

MENTAL HEALTH

Tip # 1: For information on mental health or specific mental disorders, call the National Mental Health Association Information Center at 1-800-969-6642.

How it works: The NMHA number is answered 24 hours a day and you can order printed information on warning signs of mental health problems or on specific mental disorders such as post-trau-matic stress syndrome, depression, manic-depression, or schizo-phrenia and others. A person will talk with you, if you can get a free operator, Monday through Friday, 9 a.m. through 4:30 p.m. Eastern time.

Tip # 2: Contact the National Alliance for Mental Illness at 1-800-950-NAMI for information and referral.

Tip # 3: For help with depression call the National Foundation for Depressive Illness at 1-800-248-4344.

How it works: A 24-hour recorded message at the National Foundation for Depressive Illness describes symptoms of depres-sion and offers reassurance that 80% of cases of depression can be successfully treated.

Tip # 4: Contact the OC (Obsessive-Compulsive) Foundation at 203-772-0565.

How it works: The OC (Obsessive-Compulsive) Foundation offers information and treatment referrals as well as videos, booklets, and other publications.

Tip # 5: For help for homeless mentally ill, call 1-800-444-7415.

How it works: The National Resource Center on Homelessness and Mental Illness provides technical assistance and information about services and housing for the homeless mentally ill population. This program is sponsored by the National Institute of Mental Health. The number is answered from 8 a.m. to 5 p.m.

Tip # 6: Consider enrolling in a course at a university that offers student counseling.

How it works: Some colleges and universities, especially large ones that offer graduate programs in psychological counseling, offer free counseling to students, even those who are enrolled in only one course. If you are enrolled, you are entitled to this service.

It may even be worthwhile to enroll for one course just to have this opportunity. At one state university, enrollment in a course costs $75 per hour per quarter credit for in-state students. So a five-hour credit course that meets five hours per week costs $375. Once-a-week counseling for 12 sessions during the quarter you are eligible at regular market price of $60 would total $720, plus you get course credit and your studies may head you in a new direction that is good for your mental health.

Quality check: A therapist's knowledge, interpersonal skills and training as well as cost are all important considerations in selecting a therapist.

Tip # 7: Most state and local health departments have mental health counseling, treatment, and hospitalization charged on a sliding scale.

How it works: Often local health departments offer counseling and day treatment while state health departments run mental health hospitals. There may be waiting lists. Patients are taken on a most-in-need basis, which takes into account ability to pay and other resources available as well as urgency of the problem. Emergencies are almost always accepted for treatment.

Local and state mental health centers often provide their patients with drugs prescribed for mental conditions at far lower prices than a commercial pharmacy. Referrals to other professionals such as neurologists may also be much less expensive than if patients sought out those specialists on their own.

Tip # 8: Consider the difference in fees charged by various kinds of therapists.

How it works: A psychiatrist in one city usually charges over $100 for one 45-55 minute session. A clinical psychologist in the same city typically charges less, about $60. A clinical social worker with a masters degree in social work alone charges even less. A licensed marriage and family counselor may also be a relatively inexpensive choice appropriate for some problems. A minister, priest, or rabbi may counsel without cost. If you have a problem you need help with, the lower priced counselors may be able to help you as well or better than a higher priced counselor, depending on the problem. If you end up taking medication monitored by a psychiatrist and continue counseling with the less expensive level counselor it is still cheaper than having the psychiatrist as the primary counselor.

Another thing to consider is your insurance coverage, its

deductibles and limits. Your policy may cover a psychiatrist but not a clinical social worker, so for you the less expensive counselor may cost you more.

Tip # 9: Consider seeking counseling from your minister, priest or rabbi.

How it works: Your minister, priest, or rabbi may give counseling to congregation members free. If not, the fees are likely to be reasonable and reduced if you cannot pay.

Tip # 10: Consider participating in an experimental study of treatment of your mental health disorder. (See STUDIES.)

How it works: Experimental treatment studies often offer free treatment to patients who qualify as subjects. In particular, the Clinical Center of the National Institutes of Health in Bethesda, MD, has ongoing studies of many mental disorders including depression, mania, manic-depression, bipolar disorders, geriatric depression, seasonal affective disorders, obsessive-compulsive disorders, borderline personality disorder, schizophrenia, tardive dyskinesia, attention and cognition disorders, rapid cyclers, anxiety disorders, night terrors, menstrual and menopausal mood and behavior disorders, eating disorders, Alzheimer's dementia, and depression related to medical illness. For information about getting into a study at this or other institutions, see STUDIES.

MENTAL RETARDATION IN CHILDREN (See also DISABILITY, DOWNS SYNDROME and HANDICAPPED CHILD.)

Tip # 1: Contact the Association of Children with Retarded Mental Development, Inc.

How it works: For information and referral call 212-741-0100 or write to:

Association of Children with Retarded Mental Development
817 Broadway
New York, NY 10003

METABOLIC DISORDERS (See also RARE DISORDERS.)

Tip # 1: Consider participating in an experimental study of treatment of your metabolic disorder. (See STUDIES.)

How it works: Experimental treatment studies often offer free treatment to patients who qualify as subjects. In particular, Clinical Center of the National Institutes of Health in Bethesda, MD, has ongoing studies of many metabolic disorders including agammaglobulinemia, thymoma, ataxia-telangiectasia, di George Syndrome, growth hormone deficiency, panhypopituitarism, hypoammaglobulinemia, dysgammaglobulinemia, Ig A deficiency, severe combined immuno-deficiency syndrome, Sezary Syndrome (cutaneous t-cell lymphoma), human t-cell lymphotrophic virus, and tropical spastic paraparesis. For more information on getting into a study at this or other institutions, see STUDIES.

MIGRAINE (See also HEADACHE.)

Tip # 1: Contact the National Migraine Foundation at 312-878-7715.

How it works: For information and referral, call or write to

National Migraine Foundation
5252 N. Western Ave.
Chicago, IL 60625

MISSING CHILDREN

Tip # 1: Contact the National Hotline for Missing Children at 1-800-843-5678 (202-644-9836 in Washington, DC).

How it works: To report missing children or sightings of missing children call the National Hotline above. The organization offers assistance to law enforcement agencies.

MULTIPLE SCLEROSIS (MS)

Tip # 1: Contact the National Multiple Sclerosis Society at 1-800-624-8236.

How it works: This 24-hour number allows you to leave your name and address so that printed information can be mailed to you. If you need to speak to a staff member, call 1-800-227-3166 Monday through Thursday 11 a.m. to 5 p.m. Eastern time.

The National Multiple Sclerosis Society will put you in contact with local chapters which have limited financial assistance available for medical equipment. Local chapters sponsor support and counseling groups. They have a lending library, an educational program, and an aquatic program.

Tip # 2: Consider participating in an experimental study of treatment of multiple sclerosis (MS). (See STUDIES.)

How it works: Experimental treatment studies often offer free treatment to patients who qualify as subjects. In particular, the Clinical Center of the National Institutes of Health in Bethesda, MD, has ongoing studies of MS. For information about getting into a study at this or another institution, see STUDIES.

MUSCULAR DYSTROPHY

Tip # 1: Contact the Muscular Dystrophy Association (MDA) at 1-602-529-2000.

How it works: Regardless of your financial status, MDA will pay for diagnostic tests to determine if you have MD or if you have one of 40 diseases that fall under the Muscular Dystrophy definition. MDA often will pay for any diagnostic services, medical care, a wheelchair, braces and crutches that your insurance does not cover. The MD Association will put you in touch with a local district organization. It also sponsors summer camp for children with MD.

MYASTHENIA GRAVIS

Tip # 1: Call the Myasthenia Gravis Foundation at 1-800-541-5454.

How it works: Patients in distress or needing immediate help can talk to staff at this number. Also, written material is available. The Myasthenia Gravis Foundation will also put you in touch with local chapters which sponsor patient support groups and may provide diagnostic services, treatment and some financial assistance. For example, the Pennsylvania chapter of the organization helps with providing the drug Mestinon® to those who cannot afford to pay and have no insurance. That number is provided on request by the national office. A program offering medication at reduced prices is also available to myasthenia gravis patients through the national foundation. See Tip #2.

Tip # 2: Contact the mail order prescription service of the Myasthenia Gravis Foundation at 1-800-999-1242.

How it works: The Myasthenia Gravis Foundation sponsors a mail order prescription service which offers drugs most used by MG patients and other medicines at a reduced price. There is a $10 annual participation fee. Normal delivery time is two weeks, but overnight delivery is possible. For information or to participate, write to RX America, Myasthenia Gravis Foundation, 53 West Jackson ST., Suite 660, Chicago, IL 60604.

NARCOLEPSY

Tip # 1: Keep in a safe place a copy of the results of any Multiple Sleep Latency Test (MSLT) you may have had done and show it to each new doctor you may consult.

How it works: A doctor typically will not prescribe medication for a patient for narcolepsy without a definite diagnosis. Because the disorder is difficult to diagnose and many misdiagnoses occur along the way, a doctor will usually not take the patient's word for the diagnosis. The patient will then have to undergo—and pay for—an MSLT. Keep the results of this definitive test in a safe place and take it to each new medical provider.

Tip # 2: Contact the Narcolepsy Network.

How it works: For literature, a newsletter, and referrals to physicians and sleep centers, contact these groups:

Narcolepsy Network
P.O 190
Belmont, CA 94002-0190
(415) 591-7884

American Narcolepsy Assoc.
425 California St.
Suite 201, San Francisco, CA 94104
1-800-222-6085 (8 a.m. to 5:30 p.m. Pacific time)

NATIONAL INSTITUTES OF HEALTH (See listing of NIH under STUDIES.)

NATIVE AMERICAN HEALTH (See INDIAN HEALTH.)

NECK CANCER (See HEAD CANCER.)

NEUROFIBROMATOSIS

Tip # 1: Contact the National Neurofibromatosis Foundation at 1-800-323-7938 or in New York at 212-460-8980.

How it works: The Foundation gives information about the disease and makes referrals to physicians on its clinical advisory board. Local chapters have educational programs and support groups. English and Spanish speaking staff are available.

Tip # 2: Contact the Inter-Institute Genetics Program, National Institutes of Health.

How it works: For information on neurofibromatosis, call 1-301-496-1380 or write to

Coordinator, Inter-Institute Genetics Program Bldg. 10, Room 1D21
National Institutes of Health
Bethesda, MD 20205.

NEUROLOGICAL DISORDERS

Tip # 1: Try to get into an experimental study of treatment of your neurological disorder. (See STUDIES.)

How it works: Experimental treatment studies often offer free treatment to patients who qualify as subjects. In particular, the Clinical Center of the National Institutes of Health in Bethesda, MD, has ongoing studies of many neurological disorders including Gaucher's disease, Niemann-Pick disease, Fabry's disease, Tay-Sachs disease, metachromatic leukodystrophy, Krabbe's disease, heredofamilial acute or progressive ataxias, diurnal dystonia, ceroid liporuscinosic and mucolipidosis IV, neurologic disease related to HTLV-1, sclerosing panencephalitis, Alzheimer's, brain tumors, voluntary movement disorder, Parkinson's cerebellar atasia, post-polio syndrome, polyneuropathies, inflammatory myopathies, brain-behavior disorders, epilepsy, stroke disorders, and transient ischemic attacks. For more information about getting into a study at this or other institutions, see STUDIES.

NIEMANN-PICK DISEASE (See RARE DISEASES.)

NURSING HOMES (See LONG TERM CARE.)

NUTRITION (See also DIET.)

Tip # 1: For a personal answer to questions about nutrition and diet call the American Dietetic Association's free hotline at 1-800-366-1655.

How it works: Call the American Dietetic Association toll-free to have your questions about nutrition answered. The hot line is manned by registered dieticians Monday-Friday from 10 a.m. to 5 p.m. Eastern Standard Time. Taped messages can be heard 24 hours a day.

Tip # 2: Order the latest "Dietary Guidelines for Americans" for $1.50 or borrow a recent book on nutrition from the library.

How it works: Order the government publication, number U0003, "Dietary Guidelines for Americans," from ONHIC, Dept 420W, Pueblo, CO 81009 for $1.50. This Office of Disease Prevention and Health Promotion booklet discusses in detail food values, nutritional needs, healthy eating habits, and weight control for Americans over two years old. Similar information is available in libraries.

Tip # 3: For information on food labeling and nutrition contact the FDA.

How it works: The FDA has free brochures on food labeling and nutrition. Request brochures by subject such as Fat, Cholesterol, Preservatives, Sodium, Fiber, Vitamins, etc.

Write to FDA, 5600 Fisher's Lane, Mail Code HFE-88, Room 1663, Rockville, MD 20857.

Tip # 4: Learn about the new FDA "Daily Values" food labeling.

How it works: The Food and Drug Administration (FDA) plans to replace RDAs (Recommended Daily Allowances) with new "Daily Values" for vitamins and other nutrients. To learn about the new labeling and how the new values compare to the old, write for "FDA's Proposal for New 'Daily Values' for Nutrients." Ask for publication # BG 92-1. Write the FDA at HFE-88, 5600 Fishers Lane, Rockville, MD 20857 or call 301-443-3170.

Tip # 5: Contact the FDA for free information on nutrition for women, babies, or the elderly.

How it works: Order Publication FDA91-2247 for information on women's special nutritional needs, Publication FDA91-2243 for nutrition for the elderly, and FDA91-2236 for feeding a baby.

Write to FDA, Office of Consumer Affairs, 5600 Fishers Lane, Rockville, MD 20857.

Tip # 6: If you have young children or are pregnant and have a low income, contact the WIC (Women, Infants, and Children) program for free nutrition assessment and vouchers for free food.

How it works: WIC, funded by the federal government, provides vouchers weekly for free food for low-income pregnant women, infants, and children five years old and under, after a nutritional assessment is made by WIC staff. Mothers can exchange vouchers for foods such as milk, cheese, eggs, juice, and cereal for children and formula for infants. Vouchers are for certain quantities of products: for example, 8 ounces of cheese (and mothers can get any kind, even more expensive brands, in that quantity). Pregnant mothers also are eligible for food vouchers for themselves.

To make appointments for a nutritional assessment and to apply for WIC assistance, call your local health department or Family and Children's Services. Take to the appointment recent employment check stubs, Medicaid card, or food stamps card, and other indication of income.

WIC's dieticians will answer nutrition questions and help you plan your diet.

Tip # 7: Consider applying for Food Stamps if your income is low.

How it works: Contact your local Family and Children's Services or health department to see if you qualify for food stamps. The program for low income households in effect reduces costs of food items. Medicaid recipients are usually eligible.

Tip # 8: Contact the Department of Agriculture Extension Agent for free lessons in preparing low-cost, healthy meals.

How it works: Often Home Extension Agents of the Department of Agriculture will come into your home without charge to give household tips on how to utilize low cost foods for good nutrition. They also give classes on weight control, health, and budgeting.

Tip # 9: Get no more than 30% of your calories from fat.

How it works: A low-fat diet, that is, one that derives no more than 30% of its calories from fat, is associated with a significantly lower risk of coronary heart disease and certain cancers. Remember that the 30% is not 30% of the <u>weight</u> of the meal but 30% of the <u>calories.</u> A gram of fat has 9 calories whereas a gram of carbohydrate or protein has only 4 calories.

Tip # 10: Beware of the food label "Light."

How it works: Food labeled "light" suggests perhaps fewer calories, less salt, less fat, less sugar, less alcohol, or maybe just a lighter taste. The FDA is currently working on regulations to define and limit the use of the term "light." The fine print of the label on many foods says what aspect of the product is "light," so read the whole label and particularly the nutrition information.

Tip # 11: Learn which cooking oils and other products contribute to high cholesterol levels in your body.

How it works: Many oils sold in the store are marked "NO cholesterol." In fact, all 100% vegetable oils have no cholesterol. (Cholesterol is an animal product.) But having no cholesterol is not the same as having no saturated fat; saturated fat has the same effect on the cardiovascular system as cholesterol. Saturated fat increases the body's cholesterol production and thereby contributes to heart and circulatory disease. The cooking oil with the least saturated fat is probably canola oil made from rapeseed. Avoid oils with the highest amounts of saturated fat, the tropical oils from coconut and palm kernel.

Oils that are solidified or "hydrogenated" so that they are solid at room temperature (margarine, for example) may not have cholesterol but they are more harmful than their liquid counterparts because the process of hydrogenation increases the saturation of fats.

Products such as baked goods and desserts may also be labeled "NO cholesterol." Check these for oils with saturated fat among their ingredients.

Tip # 12: Beware of hidden sodium in processed foods.

How it works: Many processed foods have a great deal of sodium, more than would be expected in food prepared from scratch. Sodium is a substance to be avoided by those with high blood pressure. A low-sodium diet would avoid processed foods. The biggest sources of "hidden" sodium include canned soups and vegetables, pickles, ketchup, baking powder, biscuits, frozen prepared dishes, bouillon, processed lunch meats, cheese, hot dogs, olives, pizza, salted nuts, saltines, sauerkraut, sausage, seasonings such as celery salt, garlic salt, lemon pepper, onion salt, many dry seasoning mixtures, soy sauce, teriyaki sauce, tomato juice, steak sauces, and salsa.

Tip # 13: Be cautious about having your nutritional needs analyzed by an organization that sells nutritional products.

How it works: An expert on nutrition who profits from the sale of nutritional products has an incentive to advise you to buy supplements that you may not need. At the very least, shop around for the products recommended for you.

You also may want to verify counseling information with the American Dietetic Hotline at 1-800-366-1655. See also DIET.

OBESITY (See also DIET, NUTRITION and EATING DISORDERS.)

Tip # 1: Call local chapters of Overeaters Anonymous listed in the phone book.

OBSESSIVE AND COMPULSIVE DISORDERS (See also MENTAL HEALTH.)

Tip # 1 : Contact the OC (Obsessive-Compulsive) Foundation at 203-772-0565.

How it works: The OC Foundation offers information and treatment referrals as well as videos, booklets, and other publications.

OBSTETRICS (See PREGNANCY.)

OCCUPATIONAL MEDICINE

Tip # 1: Contact the National Institute of Occupational Safety and Health at 1-800-356-4674.

How it works: The National Institute of Occupational Safety and Health provides information on noise, stress, chemical and physical hazards, carpal tunnel syndrome, and other occupational health hazards. NIOSH conducts health hazard evaluation at the request of employers or workers who suspect a health hazard.

NIOSH also offers health education for workers and courses in industrial hygiene.

Call NIOSH at 1-800-356-4674 between 9 a.m. and 4:30 p.m. for an information specialist or leave a message at other hours for your call to be returned.

Tip # 2: Contact OSHA (Occupational Safety and Health Administration) for standards and consultation.

How it works: OSHA was founded by an act of Congress in 1970 to set standards for safety in the workplace. Full sets of standards are available from OSHA and additional workplace regulations from individual states. An overview is available in a booklet called "All About OSHA." To request this booklet call 202-523-8615 or TDD 1-800-326-2577 for the deaf.

OSHA provides free consultation to employers who request help in identifying and correcting specific hazards, want to improve their safety and health programs, and/or need further assistance in training and education. For information on consultation programs, contact the appropriate office in your state listed below:

Alabama————205-348-3033
Alaska————907-264-2599
Arizona————602-255-5795
Arkansas————501-682-4522
California——415-737-2843
Colorado————303-491-6151
Connecticut——203-566-4550
Delaware————302-571-3908
D.C.————202-576-6339
Florida————904-488-3044
Georgia————404-894-8274
Guam————671-646-9246
Hawaii————808-548-4155
Idaho————208-385-3283
Illinois————312-814-2339
Indiana————317-232-2688
Iowa————515-281-5352
Kansas————913-296-4386

Kentucky————502-564-6895
Louisiana————504-342-9601
Maine—————207-289-6460
Maryland————301-333-4218
Massachusetts—617-727-3463
Michigan————517-335-8250 (health)
    517-322-1809 (safety)
Minnesota————612-297-2393
Mississippi——601-987-3981
Missouri————314-751-3403
Montana—————406-444-6401
Nebraska————402-471-4717
Nevada—————702-688-1474
New Hampshire—603-271-3170
New Jersey——609-292-0404
New Mexico——505-827-2885
New York————518-457-5468
North Carolina-919-733-3949
North Dakota—701-221-5188
Ohio—————614-644-2631
Oklahoma————405-528-1500
Oregon—————503-378-3272
Pennsylvania—800-382-1241 (toll free in state)
    412-357-2561
Puerto Rico——809-754-2171
Rhode Island—401-277-2438
South Carolina-803-734-9599
South Dakota—605-688-4101
Tennessee————615-741-7036
Texas—————512-440-3809
Utah—————801-530-6868
Vermont————802-828-2765
Virginia————804-786-6613
Virgin Islands-809-772-1315
Washington——206-586-0961
West Virginia—304-348-7890
Wisconsin————608-266-8579 (health)

Wyoming————307-777-7786

ORGAN DONATION

Tip # 1: To donate bone marrow, call Lifesavers Foundation at 1-800-950-1050 or 1-800-24-DONOR.

How it works: Lifesavers Foundation recruits bone marrow donors. The numbers are manned from 8 a.m. to 5:30 p.m. Pacific time. After the preliminary costs of blood tissue typing at a local donor site, costs of donation are borne by the recipient, not the donor. Ask Lifesavers for the nearest place to have blood tissue typed.

Tip # 2: To inquire about donating organs, call The Living Bank at 1-800-528-2971 or Organ Donor Hotline at 1-800-24-DONOR.

How it works: Both organizations offer information and referral for organ donations 24 hours a day. Through them, you can get organ donor cards or exchange information about availability of tissues or vital organs so that the best use can be made of this generous gift.

ORTHOPEDICS, CHILDREN

Tip # 1: For information on free orthopedic care for children under 18 years old, call the Shriner's Hospital Referral Line at 1-800-237-5055 or 1-800-282-9161 in Florida.

How it works: Children under 18 who would benefit from orthopedic treatment and whose families cannot afford that treatment, may be eligible for free treatment at Shriners' Hospitals. Cleft palate and lip repair and correction of orthopedic problems are Shriners' Hospital specialties.

OSTEOPOROSIS

Tip # 1: Contact the National Clearinghouse on Arthritis, Muscular, Skeletal, and Skin Diseases at 301-495-4484 or the National Health Information Center at 1-800-336-4797 for free information.

Tip # 2: For advice on preventing osteoporosis in women, see a physician.

How it works: Physicians often recommend estrogen and calcium supplements to post-menopausal women to prevent osteoporosis.

Ask your physician if hormone and calcium supplements are appropriate for you.

Tip # 3: Get weight-bearing exercise.

How it works: Weight-bearing exercise such as walking, running, stair-climbing, or jumping rope increases or maintains the mass of leg bones and slows loss of calcium from the bones.

Quality check: Set up an exercise program with the advice of your doctor.

Tip # 4: Get plenty of calcium from food.

How it works: Osteoporosis is abnormal loss of calcium from bone. While large amounts of calcium may not cure osteoporosis, too little calcium contributes to the disorder. Many older people do not get enough calcium. Dairy products are major sources of calcium, but stick to the low fat kind like skim milk, cottage cheese, nonfat yogurt. Leafy green vegetables and broccoli have large amounts of calcium and should be included in the daily diet. Calcium from food is used more efficiently than calcium supplements.

OVARIAN CANCER (See also CANCER.)

Tip # 1: Be cautious about having routine ovarian cancer tests unless your heredity suggests you are at risk.

How it works: Tests for ovarian cancer are currently reported to be somewhat unreliable and cost between $30 and $60. At this time, they probably should not be used routinely. BUT if you have a family history of ovarian cancer, the tests, used judiciously, can offer valuable information.

Quality check: Ask your doctor what the possibility of false negative or false positive is for your age group.

PAGET'S DISEASE.

Tip # 1: Contact the Paget's Disease Foundation at 212-229-1582 for information and referral.

PAIN, CHRONIC (See also BACK PAIN.)

Tip # 1: Ask for a list of accredited Chronic Pain Management Programs.

How it works: The Commission on Accreditation of Rehabilitation Facilities maintains a list of Accredited Chronic Pain Management Programs. The 139 programs accredited in 1992 are located in 32 states. Locations, addresses, phone numbers and program emphases are available upon request. Write the Commission at 101 N. Wilmot Rd., Suite 500, Tucson, AZ 85711.

PANIC DISORDER (See also MENTAL HEALTH.)

Tip # 1: Panic attacks can be controlled. Write the FDA for a free summary of symptoms, treatments and ways to avoid panic.

How it works: Panic disorder probably has a biological basis. Certain drugs can block attacks. Avoiding caffeine can help some panic-prone people avoid attacks. These and other medical findings are summarized in the April 1992 FDA *Consumer*. Write the FDA at HFE-88, 5600 Fishers Lane, Rockville, MD 20857 or call 301-443-3170.

PAP TESTS

Tip # 1: Order the FDA publication "The Controversial Pap Test: It Could Save Your Life."

How it works: The Food and Drug Administration (FDA) provides current information in booklet form on a wide range of subjects. For free information on the Pap test, order Publication # FDA90-1159. Write FDA, 5600 Fisher's Lane, Mail Code HFE-88, Room 1663, Rockville MD 20857 or call 301-443-3170.

Tip # 2: If you have had a Pap test recently, avoid unnecessary additional Pap tests in routine testing situations.

How it works: A Pap test may be ordered routinely if you are admitted to the hospital or tested for pregnancy or are seeing a doctor about another matter. If you have recently had a normal Pap test, you may wish not to authorize another one as part of a screening package.

Tip # 3: If you are concerned about the validity of your Pap test, ask your doctor to call a clinical pathology lab and ask for a free consultation.

How it works: Clinical pathology labs usually have a pathologist who will consult with client doctors on questions concerning lab results. You can be reassured about your Pap test by having your doctor discuss testing procedures and your results in detail.

PARALYSIS (See SPINAL CORD INJURY, STROKE, REHABILITATION, DISABILITY, and EQUIPMENT.)

PARATHYROID DISORDERS

Tip # 1: Consider participating in an experimental study of treatment of your parathyroid disorder. (See STUDIES.)

How it works: Experimental treatment studies often offer free treatment to patients who qualify as subjects. In particular, the Clinical Center of the National Institutes of Health in Bethesda, MD, has ongoing studies of many parathyroid disorders including hypercalcemia, hypoposphatemia, nephrocalcinosis, nephrolithiasis, multiple endocrine adenomatosis, familial hypercalcemia, hyperparathyroidism, rickets, and osteoporosis. For information about getting into a study at this or another institution, see STUDIES.

PARKINSON'S DISEASE

Tip # 1: Call the American Parkinson Disease Association at 1-800-223-2732.

How it works: The American Parkinson Disease Association provides information and referrals from 9 a.m to 5 p.m. with answering service after hours.

Tip # 2: Call the National Parkinson Foundation at 1-800-327-4545, or 1-800-433-7022 in Florida, or 305-547-6666 (in Miami).

How it works: Nurses answer questions about the disease. Physician referrals and written materials are also provided.

Tip # 3: Call Parkinson's Education Program at 1-800-344-7872.

How it works: This organization provides newsletters, publications and a video tape. It makes referrals to physicians and support groups. Record your address at the toll-free number to receive an information packet. To speak to a staff member, call 714-250-2975.

PEDIATRICS, PEDIATRICIAN (See also HANDICAPPED CHILD, IMMU-
NIZATION, ORTHOPEDICS.)

Tip # 1: Compare the cost of a single visit for a sick child at different
pediatricians before choosing one.

How it works: In one city a single visit to a pediatrician by a sick
child costs anywhere from $35 to $44, a difference of $9. Location
did not systematically determine whether the pediatric office was
high or low. Usually, the initial visit costs more, from $45 to $60.
Costs of tests, immunizations, or other procedures are extra.

Quality check: Compare prices only among recommended qualified pediatricians and among these consider interpersonal skills,
provisions for after-hours, and other services.

Tip # 2: Consider getting childhood immunizations at your local
health department free or for as little as one-fourth the cost of an
immunization in a doctor's office.

How it works: The costs of one DPT shot in a series of immunizations against diphtheria, whooping cough, and tetanus range from
$25 to $35 in one city in addition to the doctor's visit. The cost of a
DPT shot at the various county health departments near this city
is $8 to $10 and is free for people who cannot pay. Similar savings
are usual for the other immunizations. You can go to the health
department for the immunizations and take the records to your
regular pediatrician to save about $200 total for the complete
immunization series.

Quality check: If you go to a health department for immunizations
for your child instead of going to the doctor you will be missing
valuable check ups. Also, you need to keep track of immunizations
to be sure your child gets all the boosters needed to make the shots
effective. See Tip #3.

Tip # 3: Ask the CDC for a Parents' Guide to Immunization and a
Stay Well card.

How it works: The U.S. Department of Health and Human Services,
Centers for Disease Control and Prevention (CDC), distributes a
free booklet for parents explaining all the immunizations needed
to prevent many childhood diseases and a Stay Well card that helps

explain immunizations to your child. Ask for these materials by calling the CDC public inquiry number, 404-639-3534, listening to directions and leaving a message. You can also be connected to a CDC professional if you need to talk to someone personally.

Tip # 4: Contact the American Academy of Pediatrics at 1-800-433-9016

How it works: The Academy provides informational brochures on child and adolescent health topics. Request a specific topic and send a stamped, self-addressed envelope to the American Academy of Pediatrics, 141 Northwest Point Blvd., P.O. Box 927, Elm Grove Village, IL 60009-0927.

Tip # 5: Contact Care of Children's Health.

How it works: The organization has as its goal humanizing health care for children and their families. Ask for its "Maternal and Child Health Publications Catalog" for listings of resources including materials in Chinese, Korean, Tagalog, Spanish, Vietnamese, Lao, and Thai.

Care of Children's Health is located at 7910 Woodmont Ave., Suite 300, Bethesda, MD 20814-3015, or call 301-654-6549.

Tip # 6: For the Adolescent Fathers' Directory of Services, contact the National Center for Education in Maternal and Child Health.

How it works: The National Center for Education in Maternal and Child Health has not forgotten young fathers. For information write the Center at 38th and R Streets NW, Washington, DC 20057 or call 202-625-8400.

PERSONAL EMERGENCY RESPONSE SYSTEMS

Tip # 1: Consider a personal emergency response system (PERS) for a person living alone.

How it works: Elderly or other persons living alone may be more comfortable if they have a way to call for help in an emergency. A Personal Emergency Response System or PERS consists of an alerting device which automatically signals a number where help can be reached. The American Association of Retired Persons (AARP) has published a report called AARP'S Product Report: PERS which compares the features and prices of 20 PERSs. Order publication D12905 from AARP Fulfillment (EE291), P.O. Box 22796, Long Beach, CA 90801-5796.

PERTUSSIS (WHOOPING COUGH) (See RARE DISEASES, also IMMUNIZATIONS.)

PESTICIDE EFFECTS

Tip # 1: Call the National Pesticides Communication Network for questions about the effects of pesticides at 1-800-858-7378 or 1-806-743-3091 in Texas.

How it works: The network advises callers about toxic effects, symptoms of exposure to pesticides as well as information on environmental effects and safe use and disposal.

PHYSICIAN, CHOOSING A (See DOCTOR, CHOOSING.)

PHYSICAL THERAPY

Tip # 1: Consider physical therapy (PT) after injury, surgery, stroke, or onset of muscular pain.

How it works: Physical therapy by a licensed therapist following surgery, injury, stroke, or onset of muscular pain usually shortens recovery time and helps the patient reach a fuller recovery than would medical treatment alone. In recent years, orthopedists and other doctors have been recommending PT services as a standard part of the overall treatment. The services of a physical therapist are relatively inexpensive compared to other medical services and can provide great health benefits. Physical therapy usually must be done by doctor referral.

Tip # 2: Check your insurance policy <u>before</u> incurring large therapy fees to be sure physical therapy (PT) is covered.

How it works: Physical therapy, unless it is specifically stated as a benefit in your insurance plan, may not be covered. Check with your insurance company before undergoing PT so that you can plan for payment. If you find you are not covered and cannot pay the full costs, you can ask the physical therapist to design exercises and teach them to you so that you can do at least some of your PT on your own.

Tip # 3: Consider home-made physical therapy equipment.

How it works: Physical therapists use special inclines, tables, steps, etc. on which the patient exercises. Many of these can be easily made with a hammer and saw in the home workshop. Some physical therapists can give you diagrams and directions or at least will let you sketch and measure their equipment. Sometimes you can substitute things you already have at home, but be sure heights and other characteristics will really give you the same results. Ask the therapist. Having your own home-built equipment will enable you to continue therapeutic exercises at home on your own and will save you the expense of buying special equipment.

Tip # 4: Use some of your physical therapy (PT) time learning how to do therapy at home.

How it works: Most physical therapists teach you how to do exercises at home to continue the effects of therapy in the PT center. They often give you diagrams and schedules. How much of the PT you do on your own and how much with the therapist may be determined by how much you can pay. Ask the therapist to design a program to be used at home and counsel you on getting the most for what you can pay. For instance, if you can only afford twelve PT sessions, it may be better to have twice-a-month therapy for six months with home exercise in between, for example, than twelve sessions of PT immediately after injury or surgery and none later. On the other hand, if your insurance pays for three months of therapy only, for example, you might want to get intensive PT while it is paid for by insurance and then learn how to continue it on your own for as many remaining months as desirable.

PLASTIC SURGERY

Tip # 1: Consider the possibility of outpatient surgery.

How it works: Outpatient surgery usually costs considerably less than inpatient surgery. (See SURGERY.)

Tip # 2: When having lesions or blemishes removed, consider having as many removed at one time as you can because the excisions will cost less when performed in one office or hospital visit than in several office/hospital visits.

Tip # 3: In cases of injury that are not life-threatening emergencies, consider using a plastic surgeon instead of a general surgeon or emergency staff for stitches that might require cosmetic repair later.

How it works: In cases of injury that are not life-threatening emergencies, consider calling a plastic surgeon if the injury is on the face or if you care about the appearance of the repair. Although the services of a plastic surgeon will probably be more expensive than incision and stitches by general emergency staff or surgeon, calling a plastic surgeon may be less expensive than allowing a non-plastic surgeon to treat an injury and then repairing it for cosmetic reasons later. Of course, an emergency room doctor or general surgeon might do an excellent job of stitching.

Tip # 2: Contact Facial Plastic Surgery Information Service at 1-800-592-4533 in the U.S. and 1-800-523-FACE in Canada.

How it works: The Information Service answers inquiries about all types of facial cosmetic and reconstructive surgeries. It provides free brochures and lists of Board Certified plastic surgeons.

Tip # 3: Contact the American Society of Plastic and Reconstructive Surgeons at 1-800-635-0635.

How it works: The Society offers brochures describing procedures and discussing realistic expectations for each. It provides referrals to Board certified specialists in plastic surgery.

Tip # 4: Call the American Academy of Facial Plastic and Reconstructive Surgery at 1-800-332-3223 or the American Academy of Plastic Surgery at 1-800-592-4533 for information, referrals, and verification of certification.

PMS (Premenstrual Syndrome)

Tip # 1: Consider tracking your symptoms on a calendar for two or three months before you see a doctor about PMS.

How it works: The first thing a doctor consulted about PMS will do is ask you to track your periods and symptoms on a chart or calendar for two or three months. He/she will use this information to advise and treat you. You may save yourself an extra office visit by having this information charted before you visit the doctor.

Quality check: If you are suicidal or deeply depressed or unable to control impulsive behavior, see a doctor immediately rather than wait to track.

Tip # 2: Consider contacting PMS Access at 1-800-222-4767 or 608-833-4767 in Wisconsin.

How it works: PMS Access is a service of a pharmacy which sells nutritional products. It provides a free packet of information and literature on PMS and makes referral to support groups. Charting is available for a fee. A catalog of the pharmacy's nutritional products is included. Consult your doctor before taking any product for PMS.

PODIATRY (See also BUNIONS.)

Tip # 1: For information and referral, contact the Podiatric Medicine Association at 1-301-571-9200.

POISON (See also LEAD and PESTICIDES.)

Tip # 1: Look on the first page of your phone book under Emergency Numbers to get immediate help.

How it works: The emergency number under Poisoning is answered 24-hours a day by experienced staff usually at a nearby hospital. Write this number on your personal list of emergency numbers, especially if you have young children, so you can find it easily.

Tip # 2: Each state has at least one emergency poison control number answered by hospital staff; many are toll-free.

How it works: Here is a list of emergency numbers of Certified Regional Poison Centers by state:

ALABAMA
205-939-9201, 1-800-292-6678 (AL only) or 205-933-4050

ARIZONA
602-253-3334

CALIFORNIA
(Fresno) 1-800-346-5922 or 209-445-1222; (San Diego) 619-543-6000 or 1-800-876-4766 (in 619 area only); (San Francisco) 415-476-6600; (San Jose) 408-299-5112, 1-800-662-9886 (CA only); (Sacramento) 916-734-3692 or 1-800-342-9293 (northern CA

only); (Orange) 714-634-5988 or 1-800-544-4404 (southern CA only)

COLORADO

303-629-1123

DC

202-625-3333 or 202-784-4660 (TDD for the deaf)

FLORIDA

813-253-4444 (Tampa) or 1-800-282-3171 (FL only)

GEORGIA

1-800-282-5846 (GA only) or 404-589-4400

INDIANA

1-800-382-9097 (IN only) or 317-929-2323

KENTUCKY

1-800-722-5725 (KY only) or 502-629-7275

MARYLAND

(Baltimore) 410-528-7701 or 1-800-492-2414 (MD only); (DC suburbs only) 202-625-3333 or 202-784-4660 (TDD for the deaf)

MASSACHUSETTS

617-232-2120 or 1-800-682-9211

MICHIGAN

(Grand Rapids) 800-632-2727 (MI only), 1-800-356-3232 (TDD for the deaf);   (Detroit) 313-745-5711

MINNESOTA

(Minneapolis) 612-347-3141, 612-337-7474 (TDD for the deaf)

MISSOURI

314-772-5200 or 1-800-366-8888

MONTANA

303-629-1123

NEBRASKA

402-390-5555 (Omaha) or 1-800-955-9119 (NE only)

NEW JERSEY

1-800-962-1253

NEW MEXICO

505-843-2551 or 1-800-432-6866 (NM only)

NEW YORK

(East Meadow) 516-542-2323, 2324, 2325, 3813; (New York City) 212-340-4494, 212-POISONS, or 212-689-9014 (TDD for the deaf)

OHIO

(Columbus) 614-228-1323, 1-800-682-7625, 614-228-2272 (TDD for the deaf), or 614-461-2012; (Cincinnati) 513-558-5111 or 1-800-872-5111 (OH only)

OREGON

503-494-8968 or 1-800-452-7165 (OR only)

PENNSYLVANIA

(Hershey) 1-800-521-6110; (Philadelphia) 215-386-2100; (Pittsburgh) 412-681-6669

RHODE ISLAND

401-277-5727

TEXAS

214-590-5000 or 1-800-441-0040 (TX only)

UTAH

801-581-2151 or 1-800-456-7707 (UT only)

VIRGINIA

(Charlottesville) 804-925-5543 or 1-800-451-1428; (DC, northern VA only) 202-625-3333 or 202-784-4660 (TDD for the deaf)

WEST VIRGINIA

1-800-642-3625 (WV only) or 304-348-4211

WYOMING

1-800-442-2702 (WY only) or 303-629-1123 in Denver.

PREGNANCY, PRENATAL CARE (See also CAESARIAN and PREGNANCY, UNWANTED.)

Tip # 1: If you are a student at a college or university, student health care may offer pregnancy tests free of charge or for a nominal lab fee ($3 at one college).

Tip # 2: Use a home-kit for pregnancy testing available in a drug store and follow directions carefully.

How it works: Home testing kits for pregnancy can be bought at a drug store from about $12 to $25; the more expensive ones include materials for two tests, one for now and one for next month or an extra to double check. In either case, the price of testing at home is less than the combined costs of office visits and testing fees.

Quality check: Occasionally, these tests read a false-negative, that is, the test says you are not pregnant when you actually are. Less frequently the opposite is true. The error is usually due to not following the directions. The same results on repeated tests may be more reliable than a single test. You may need to verify results with your doctor.

Tip # 3: Be an informed expectant mother—or father.

How it works: A happy pregnancy involving good nutrition, avoidance of drugs, low stress and a well-prepared delivery is more likely to be the least expensive as well because the chance of complications and health problems for the baby is reduced. Buy or borrow from your library recently published books on pregnancy, nutrition during pregnancy and breast feeding, and childbirth. Expectant fathers should also study this information.

The National Center for Education in Maternal and Child Health offers materials appropriate for preparing parents for childbirth and child rearing including an Adolescent Fathers Directory of Services. Write the Center at 38th and R Street NW, Washington, DC 20057, or call 202-625-8400.

Tip # 4: Contact the International Childbirth Education Association toll-free at 1-800-624-4934.

How it works: The International Childbirth Education Association provides referral to local chapters, support groups, membership information, certification, and mail order service. The number is answered 8:30 a.m. to 4 p.m. Central time.

Tip # 5: For free information on prenatal care, contact several organizations.

How it works: The following organizations will send you brochures on prenatal care: The National Clearinghouse for Maternal and Child Health at 703-821-8955, the Allen Guttmachen Institute at 202-296-4012, and the National Institute of Child Health and Human Development at 301-496-5133.

Tip # 6: Consider the Lamaze approach to child birth. For information, call 1-800-368-4404 or 202-857-1128 in Washington, DC.

How it works: The American Society for Psychoprophylaxis in Obstetrics (ASPO) promotes the Lamaze method of childbirth. Lamaze classes all over the country teach the mother and a support person, usually the father of the baby, psychomotor skills, relaxing skills, and stress management techniques. Lamaze emphasizes a non-invasive, non-pharmaceutical approach so that medication is the last resort rather than the first reaction to discomfort.

Lamaze childbirth can save the pregnant mother money. For example, a very common procedure to eliminate pain during delivery is the epidural block which can cost between $650 and $1200. A Lamaze course which may enable a mother to give birth without an epidural costs only $60 to $250. Lamaze course graduates often use some degree of medication but usually less than a woman who makes a decision for medication or anesthesia prior to delivery.

The ASPO can tell you how to contact Lamaze classes in your area.

Tip # 7: Compare fees of different doctors for complete obstetrical service.

How it works: Varying fees for obstetrical care may not reflect quality of care so much as variations in doctors' costs, for example, for rent or for debt. The average 1992 cost of doctors' fees nationally for a vaginal delivery including routine obstetric care before and after delivery was about $1600; 90% of doctors charge less than $3000 for that service. These fees do not include lab fees for tests run during pregnancy nor hospitalization. A delivery and routine care after delivery without prenatal care costs about $900 on the average, but some doctors charge the same for a delivery whether or not they gave prenatal care to discourage mothers from skipping prenatal care to save money.

Quality check: Prenatal care is important for a safe delivery and a healthy baby, particularly in high risk pregnancies and should not be skipped in order to save money.

Tip # 8: Expectant mothers who cannot afford private prenatal care can usually get this care from local health departments for little or no cost. Prenatal care at a health department often consists of a doctor's exam followed, in the case of low risk pregnancies, by regular examinations and testing by physician's assistants or obstetrical nurses. Patients see a doctor when problems develop. Delivery may take place at a public hospital. Medicaid and insurance is accepted as payment; others who are able may pay a small fee.

Quality check: Many patients report very thorough exams by physician's assistants and obstetrical nurses and very satisfactory experiences in public health department prenatal care.

Tip # 9: Expectant mothers who cannot afford private prenatal care can get care from community health centers charged on a sliding scale.

How it works: Community Health Centers, usually federally funded, offer primary health care often including prenatal care in underserved areas of the country and to underserved populations. Charges are based on the patient's ability to pay. For a center near you, see COMMUNITY HEALTH CENTER.

Tip # 10: Avoid drugs for morning sickness. To minimize morning sickness, eat frequent high carbohydrate low fat meals instead of larger, less frequent ones.

How it works: Drugs are expensive; dietary changes are a cheaper and healthier way to go. Drugs should be avoided except in the most extreme cases because of possible harmful effects.

Tip # 11: Pregnant women and all women of child-bearing age should take extra folic acid.

How it works: The U.S. Public Health Service recommends women of child-bearing age take supplements of folic acid, a B vitamin, to prevent neural tube birth defects such as spina bifida and anencephaly that affect one or two out of every 1000 babies born. A supplement of .4 mg. a day taken by all mothers to be, research shows, would cut the numbers of babies suffering from neural tube defects by one third. If you might become pregnant, ask your doctor about the amount you need. Folic acid is often included in multiple vitamin supplements.

Tip # 12: For high risk pregnancy, consider home care. (See also, HOME HEALTH CARE.)

How it works: Sometimes in a high risk pregnancy, a woman must stay in bed. If she cannot be cared for at home, sometimes she must be hospitalized. To help avoid this expensive option, consider home health care.

Home health care services may include home uterine activation monitor, perinatal nursing, infusion therapy, IV antibiotics, patient education and support to mothers with high-risk pregnancy.

Tip # 13: Consider a home birth with a certified health care professional in attendance for delivery in the case of a low-risk pregnancy.

How it works: You can save thousands of dollars and increase a sense of privacy and family intimacy at the same time by delivering a baby at home. For safety sake, have a licensed physician or certified nurse midwife in attendance. Home births are ideal money-savers for families without insurance. If you have insurance, find out if the fees of professionals assisting at the home birth are covered by your insurance.

For more information on home births and other alternatives, contact the National Association of Parents and Professionals for Safe Alternatives in Childbirth at Route 1, Box 646, Marble Hill, MO, 63764 or call 314-238-2010.

Quality check: High risk pregnancies are best handled in a hospital. Also, ask a mid-wife if he/she is certified and verify certification with the American College of Nurse Midwifery in Washington, DC, by calling 202-289-0171. In rare cases, an emergency does occur in a home setting for which home resources may not be adequate.

Tip # 14: Consider a birthing center instead of a hospital for delivery for a low-risk pregnancy.

How it works: A birthing center is a place designed for delivery in a homelike atmosphere with appropriate childbirth professionals in attendance. Delivery in a birthing center usually costs from one-third to one-half the cost of delivery in a hospital. Cesarian sections and other costly intervention will not be used unless necessary.

For more information on birthing centers, contact the National Association of Childbearing Centers at 3123 Gottschall Road, Perkiomenville, PA 18074 or call 215-234-8068.

Quality check: A birthing center near a hospital with obstetric and neo-natal care (as birthing centers often are) is a safer choice than a center not within easy reach of such a hospital as a back-up.

Tip # 15: If your baby is born in a hospital, stay the least amount of time possible after the baby is born.

How it works: A mother and baby with no complications can, in most cases, safely leave the hospital within 24 hours saving hundreds of dollars over a regular length stay of several days. The baby and mother who leave early are also less at risk of contracting a communicable disease in the hospital.

Quality check: Do not leave the hospital if there is any sign of trouble. If you or the baby needs medical care, it is no bargain to miss it. Also, problems sometimes arise later—jaundice is a frequent complication that becomes severe several days after a baby's birth. Those who go home early are usually given visiting nurse care and home treatment. While this arrangement may cost less than daily charges in the hospital for the baby, if you have insurance you may find your plan pays a smaller portion of the at-home bill than of the hospital bill, sometimes 50% compared to 80%.

Tip # 16: Consider breast-feeding your baby for the first year.

How it works: Not only is mother's milk designed especially to meet the needs of human babies, it is free. It requires only that the mother has the good nutrition she needs and plenty of liquids. Feeding the mother well is less expensive than feeding a mother and buying formula for an infant.

For information on breast-feeding, contact La Leche League International, 9616 Minneapolis Ave., Franklin Park, IL 60131, or call 312-455-7730.

Quality check: Mothers taking certain medicines or with certain diseases such as AIDS should not breast-feed babies. Ask your doctor about medication you are taking or disorders you may have.

Tip # 17: For depression after childbirth, call a support organization for post-partum depression.

How it works: Mothers often feel depressed after delivery. When this condition lingers more than a few days, call an organization that is concerned with this distinct illness. Call Depression after Delivery at 1-800-944-4773 or 215-295-3994 on Monday, Tuesday, or Thursday mornings Pacific time. Or call Post-Partum Support International at 805-967-7636 or The Family Resource Coalition at 312-341-0900.

Tip # 18: If you are pregnant and you have a low income, contact the WIC (Women, Infants, and Children) and food stamps program, and get nutrition planning help.

How it works: For free nutrition assessment and vouchers for free food for you and any small children you may have, contact WIC. See WIC for details. See also FOOD STAMPS and NUTRITION Tip # 8.

PREGNANCY, UNWANTED (Adoption and Abortion Alternatives; see also PREGNANCY.)

Tip # 1: It is usually better to deal with state-licensed, experienced, non-profit adoption agencies.

How it works: The area of adoption offers opportunities for exploitation of both expectant mothers and adoptive parents. Non-profit agencies are more likely to have the good of the baby and parents in mind rather than financial rewards. Licensing is imperative for legitimate agencies and experience in the area helps prevent many tragic mishaps.

Tip # 2: Contact the Christian Adoption Agency at 1-800-522-2193.

How it works: The Christian Adoption Agency provides medical care, legal services, and counseling to the expectant mother free of charge. Free housing and transportation can be arranged also if necessary. After the birth of the baby, the organization finds a loving home for the baby. Arrangements can be made for the expectant mother to meet with and even choose adoptive parents. The agency is as concerned with the mother's welfare as with the baby's.

Tip # 3: Call Pregnancy Counseling Services at 1-800-542-4453 or (in Virginia) 1-800-384-3043.

How it works: Pregnancy Counseling Services run by Family Life Services provides a residential program for expectant mothers which includes room, board, and local education. Church supported, the state-licensed maternity home asks the patient's parents to use insurance, if any, to pay medical bills. Girls under 18 without insurance are helped to get Medicaid in Virginia. A shepherding program, that is, a program of families who care for mothers, is also available through Family Life.

The center is also an adoption agency. Counseling, referrals, and brochures are also available to anyone who calls. Counselors match the young woman according to age and circumstances to an appropriate program in her own state or another one. The organization takes calls 24 hours a day.

Tip # 4: Contact the National Abortion Federation (NAD) for a referral to a clinic that meets the organization's guidelines.

How it works: The National Abortion Federation can give you fees and payment policies for abortions at different trimesters of pregnancy at member clinics nearest your location. These are not the only clinics, however, that do abortions in these locations.
Call 1-800-772-9100.

Quality control: NAF affiliated clinics follow safety guidelines that protect your health. Ask for and use the guidelines of the NAF to evaluate any clinic you consider. Also get advice from doctors, health departments, and patients who have used these clinics.

Tip # 5: Ask clinics and doctors for information about local resources that help people who cannot afford abortions.

How it works: Funding for abortions is hard to find and many programs for those in need get financial help from private rather than public sources. These sources may be local. Telephone a clinic or doctor's office and ask what financial help is available. Personnel at the clinic may be able to direct you to appropriate resources.

Tip # 6: Compare prices at different clinics and doctor's offices.

How it works: Differences in location, facilities, profit or non-profit status, and sources of funding result in different fees for patients who can pay. Non-profit centers tend to charge less; less prestigious locations tend to charge less; quality of service is not necessarily determined by fee differences.

Quality check: In calling different clinics to compare fees, you may use a listing such as the Yellow Pages of the phone book. Note that some of the listings under "Abortion Services" that may say something like "Free pregnancy test, practical help, counseling," but do not specifically say "abortion," may be right-to-life groups that are hoping to have the opportunity to talk you out of an abortion. You should always consider the alternatives to an abortion (keeping the baby, seeking resources for helping to deliver and raise a child, or giving it up for adoption) before making your decision, but if you do not want to talk to anti-abortionists, do not call for an appointment or go to a clinic that does not list abortion among its services.

Also, look for a clinic's membership in the National Abortion Federation.

PRENATAL CARE (See PREGNANCY and PREGNANCY, UNWANTED.)

PROSTATE (See also BLADDER.)

Tip # 1: Look for tests for prostate cancer at reduced prices at health fairs and screenings.

How it works: Prostate cancer is a very common health hazard for older men. One out of ten men will develop prostate cancer at some time in his life. Prostate cancer has no symptoms in the early stages. Yearly screening for men over 40 is very important. Screening for prostate cancer can catch the disease early when effective treatment may be less invasive and less costly. Screening tests for prostate cancer include a digital rectal examination for enlarged prostate and a PSA (prostate specific antigen) test.

Quality check: A finding of an enlarged prostate is very common and not usually cancer. The PSA test for prostate cancer, like many screening tests, may yield false positives and false negatives. If a finding is positive, additional tests can confirm or disprove the finding.

Tip # 2: Consider not treating slow growing, early stage prostate cancers in very old men or those with very limited life expectancies.

How it works: Some types of cancers of the prostate are very slow growing and will cause no trouble within a man's lifetime. Usually, it is only an expensive ordeal to treat a man in his late eighties, for example, for slow growing prostate cancer. Yet with the improved detection now possible with a PSA and other tests, some very old men are going through surgery, radiation, and other treatment unnecessarily.

Moreover, if you are not going to accept treatment for such cancers, which a lot of old men have, the PSA test itself is an unnecessary expense. So if a digital rectal examination and history do not suggest a problem with the prostate for a very old man, you may choose to leave it alone.

Quality check: There are no absolute age levels at which prostate cancer should not be pursued. The health of the individual, life expectancy, and personal preference should all be taken into account.

Tip # 3: Contact the Prostate Health Council at 1-800-242-2383.

How it works: The PHC provides several very clear, detailed patient education booklets on prostate diseases, their diagnosis and treatment. Ask for "Prostate Disease," "Prostate Cancer," "Enlarged Prostate," and/or "Prostatitis." Call or write the PHC care of the American Foundation for Urologic Disease, 1120 North Charles St., Suite 401, Baltimore, MD 21201.

PROSTHESES

Tip # 1: When you buy insurance, be sure your prosthesis is covered by your insurance.

How it works: Some insurance plans and HMO programs do not insure you for prostheses or, if they do, may cover only your first and not replacements. Be aware of this when you choose a plan and when you choose a prosthesis dealer.

Tip # 2: Medicare and Medicaid cover prostheses but be sure the dealer accepts Medicare or Medicaid as payment in full.

How it works: Those 65 and older or under 65 but disabled enough to qualify for Social Security Disability Insurance (SSDI) are eligible for Medicare coverage which covers "durable medical equipment" (DME) like braces, artificial limbs and eyes, and internal devices. Needy persons who qualify for Supplemental Security Income (SSI) or Aid to Families with Dependent Children (AFDC) and, in some states, others whose medical expenses make them indigent, may qualify for Medicaid. Medicaid coverage varies from state to state but in many states Medicaid covers prostheses.

If you qualify for and are enrolled in either Medicare or Medicaid, be sure that your dealer in prostheses accepts Medicare or Medicaid (along with any co-payments that may apply) as payment in full. Not all dealers accept Medicare or Medicaid assignment. Consider finding one that does. See also MEDICARE and MEDICAID.

Tip # 2: The Veterans Administration (VA) pays for prosthetic devices related to rehabilitation for eligible veterans.

How it works: For service-connected veterans, equipment necessary for overall medical or rehabilitative intervention is provided free. For non-service connected veterans with incomes below a certain level, such equipment is provided as available without charge or (for some categories of veterans) for a small co-payment. Such equipment includes prostheses, wheelchairs, hearing aids and other kinds of sensory or mobility equipment.

Tip # 3: Check your state's Workers' Compensation laws for help with prostheses.

How it works: Many states require rehabilitation benefits of workers covered under Workers' Compensation policies. These benefits may include prostheses and other equipment which might help return an injured person to work.

Tip # 4: Ask your state rehabilitation department if you qualify for equipment under the Rehabilitation Act of 1973 and its amendments.

How it works: The federal government through the states provides equipment to help working age people work again or to live independently. Some of these programs are called Federal/State Rehabilitation Title I, Vocational Rehabilitation Services Title VI, Supported Employment Title VII, Independent Living Title VIIC, and Independent Living (for the elderly blind). Ask which of these programs might apply to you. If you have difficulty finding the right number in the phone book, call the general information number for your state listed in this book under GENERAL INFORMATION, Tip # 1.

Tip # 5: For young disabled children, prostheses and other equipment may be available through the Tax Equity and Fiscal Responsibility Act of 1982.

How it works: The Tax Equity and Fiscal Responsibility Act of 1982 (TEFRA) provides help for children from birth to age 6 who are disabled by the Supplemental Security Income (SSI) definition but who would be financially ineligible for SSI because of their parent's income. (See also DISABILITY.) This program provides services and equipment necessary to help the child remain in the home instead of an institution.

Tip # 6: If you need a prosthesis following mastectomy, consider contacting the American Cancer Society.

How it works: The American Cancer Society has groups of "veteran" prosthesis users that help others with fitting prostheses. Poorly fitting prostheses for mastectomy patients are a common cause of discomfort and replacement expense.

Tip # 7: Some breast cancer groups give support for feeling good about your body image after a mastectomy without using a prosthesis.

How it works: Prostheses for mastectomy patients are inconvenient and cost money. "Who needs them?" is the attitude of some women. Therapy or group support that emphasizes enjoying your body as it is may be appropriate for some patients.

PSORIASIS

Tip # 1: Try sunlight for psoriasis.

How it works: Natural sunlight may be the best treatment for psoriasis.

Tip # 9: Contact the Psoriasis Foundation at 1-503-297-1545.

How it works: Call the Psoriasis Foundation between 8 a.m. and 5 p.m. Pacific time for information on research and medication. The Foundation can tell you about new experimental treatments available and can help you get medicine at reduced cost.

Q FEVER (See RARE DISEASES.)

RABIES

Tip # 1: Call the Centers for Disease Control and Prevention (CDC) at 404-332-4555 for current information on rabies.

How it works: The CDC has very detailed, recorded information on rabies 24 hours a day including information on prevention, symptoms, diagnosis, treatment, and prevalence of rabies. To save money, call during low telephone rate hours. To receive written information on rabies and answers to other questions ONLY AFTER listening to the recorded information, call the CDC public inquiry number 404-639-3534 weekdays, except federal holidays, 8:30 a.m. to 5 p.m. Eastern time.

RARE DISEASES

Tip # 1: Contact the National Organization for Rare Disorders (NORD) at 1-800-999-6673.

How it works: NORD (National Organization for Rare Diseases) compiles fact sheets on hundreds of rare and not so rare diseases from Aarskog Syndrome to Zollinger-Ellison Syndrome. Useful materials on better known disorders such as acne, anemia, hiccups, hypertension, and sickle cell disease are also available from NORD and rare forms may be described in the material. New diseases are being added continuously.

Each fact sheet contains the disease name, synonyms, a general description of the disorder, symptoms, causes, affected population, standard treatments, investigational treatments, and a list of resources that can be contacted for further information.

The first fact sheet you order from NORD is free; subsequent orders are $3.25 per copy including postage and handling. You can call NORD toll-free, but written orders only are accepted with payment. NORD's address is P.O. 8923, New Fairfield, CT 06812-1783.

For those of you with personal computers and modem, you can access the database directly. You can reach NORD Services section of CompuServe by typing "GO NORD" at any prompt on the CompuServe Information System.

An order form and a NORD catalog listing are in Appendix B.

Tip # 2: Contact the National Information Center for Orphan Drugs and Rare Diseases at 1-800-456-3505.

How it works: This organization sponsored by the federal government provides free information to patients, health professionals, and the public. Call between 9 a.m. and 5 p.m. Eastern time.

RAYNAUD'S DISEASE (See also RARE DISEASES.)

Tip # 1: For free information on Raynaud's disease, ask for a fact sheet from the National Heart, Lung, and Blood Institute at 301-951-3260.

How it works: Call 301-951-3260 to request information on Raynaud's disease or write:

National Institutes of Health, National Heart, Lung, and Blood Institute,
Bldg. 31, Room 4A-21
Rockville, MD 20292

REHABILITATION (See also DISABILITY, EQUIPMENT, and specific diseases such as SPINAL CORD INJURY or ARTHRITIS.)

Tip # 1: Contact the National Rehabilitation Information Center (NARIC) at 1-800-346-2742.

How it works: The staff at the National Rehabilitation Information Center will find an appropriate rehabilitation program in your area for your needs including physical therapy, speech therapy, and therapy for cancer, spinal cord injury, brain tumor and other problems. They will also advise you on how to find funding for treatment.

NARIC staff will also do searches from their ABLEDATA database.

Individual copies of fact sheets are available free on these subjects: van lifts, car seats, bath lifts, reclining bath seats, powered scooters, ramps, stair lifts, patient lifts, tilt in space wheelchairs, seat cushions, standing aids, modular seating components, assistive devices for arthritis, and funding for assistive technologies.

Single copies of NARIC resource guides on spinal cord injury, traumatic brain injury, and stroke are available free. NARIC will also send without charge a directory of National Institute on Disability and Rehabilitation Research (NIDRR) projects. A packet of all the NARIC resource guides, all the ABLEDATA fact sheets, and the NIDRR project listings are available as a package for $5. Most NARIC and ABLEDATA publications are available in large-print, braille, cassette, and computer diskette. Call between 8 a.m. and 6 p.m. Eastern time.

RETINITIS PIGMENTOSA (See also EYE CARE, BLINDNESS, and RARE DISEASES.)

Tip # 1: Contact the National Retinitis Pigmentosa Foundation at 1-800-683-5555 for information and referral.

REYE'S SYNDROME

Tip #1: Contact the National Reye's Syndrome Foundation at 1-800-233-7393.

How it works: The Foundation promotes community awareness about Reye's Syndrome and offers support to families of Reye's Syndrome patients.

RHEUMATIC FEVER

Tip # 1: Contact the National Institute of Allergy and Infectious Diseases of the National Institutes of Health at 1-301-496-5717.

How it works: the National Institute of Allergy and Infectious Diseases will send information on the disease, its treatment, and possible experimental studies for which patients are being sought

as subjects. If you qualify as a subject, treatment will be free. See
STUDIES.

ROCKY MOUNTAIN SPOTTED FEVER

Tip # 1: Call the Centers for Disease Control and Prevention (CDC)
at 404-332-4555 for current information on Rocky Mountain spotted fever.

How it works: The CDC has very detailed, recorded information on
Rocky Mountain spotted fever 24 hours a day including information on prevention, symptoms, diagnosis, treatment, and prevalence of the disease. To save money, call during low telephone rate
hours. To receive written information on Rocky Mountain spotted
fever and answers to other questions ONLY AFTER listening to the
recorded information, call the CDC public inquiry number 404-
639-3534 weekdays except federal holidays 8:30 a.m. to 5 p.m.
Eastern time.

RUNAWAYS

Tip #1: Call the National Runaway Switchboard at 1-800-621-4000.

How it works: The Switchboard provides counseling, travel assistance, and referrals to shelters nationwide to child and adolescent
runaways. It relays messages or sets up conference calls with
parents at the request of the child.

RUSSELL-SILVER SYNDROME (See RARE DISEASES.)

SARCOIDOSIS (See also RARE DISEASES.)

Tip #1: Contact the Sarcoidosis Family Aid and Research Foundation at 1-800-223-6429 or 201-676-7901.

How it works: The organization provides printed information to
those who call the 800 number at any hour; staff members answer
questions personally at the 201 number between 1 p.m. and 5 p.m.
Tuesday through Friday.

Tip # 2: Consider participating in an experimental study of treatment of sarcoidosis. (See STUDIES.)

How it works: Experimental treatment studies often offer free
treatment to patients who qualify as subjects. In particular, the
Clinical Center of the National Institutes of Health in Bethesda,

MD, has ongoing studies of sarcoidosis. For information about getting into a study at this or other institutions, see STUDIES.

SCLERODERMA

Tip # 1 : Contact United Scleroderma Foundation at 1-800-722-HOPE or 408-728-2202 in California.

How it works: The organization provides information, lists of publications on the disease, and chapters throughout the United States. Call between 8 a.m. and 5 p.m. Pacific time.

SEAT BELTS

Tip # 1: Wear seat belts.

How it works: Wearing seat belts is a major preventative measure you can take against injury for infants, children and adults.

SELF-HELP

Tip # 1: Contact the American Self-Help Clearinghouse at 201-625-7101 (TDD 201-625-9053 for the deaf) or the National Self-Help Clearinghouse at 212-642-2944.

How it works: Self-help is an important part of health care. What ever you can do for yourself you don't have to pay others for. Sometimes you just need information to get started. Both organizations above can refer you to state self-help clearinghouses or can refer you to any listing in their national directory.

SEX EDUCATION

Tip # 1: Contact the Sex Information and Education Council of the U.S. (SIECUS) at 212-819-9770.

How it works: SIECUS acts as a clearinghouse of information for sex education, human sexuality, and related issues. It also operates the Mary Calderone Library which covers all aspects of sexuality.

SEXUALLY TRANSMITTED DISEASES (STD) (See also AIDS, GONOR-RHEA.)

Tip # 1: Contact the National STD Hotline at 1-800-227-8922.

Tip # 2: Call the Centers for Disease Control and Prevention (CDC) at 404-332-4555 for current information on sexually transmitted diseases.

How it works: The CDC has very detailed, recorded information on sexually transmitted diseases 24 hours a day including information on prevention, symptoms, diagnosis, treatment, and prevalence of sexually transmitted diseases. To save money, call during low telephone rate hours. To receive written information on STD and answers to other questions ONLY AFTER listening to the recorded information, call the CDC public inquiry number 404-639-3534 weekdays except federal holidays 8:30 a.m. to 5 p.m. Eastern time.

SHOTS (See IMMUNIZATIONS.)

SICKLE CELL DISEASE

Tip # 1: Contact the National Association for Sickle Cell Disease at 1-800-421-8453.

How it works: The National Association for Sickle Cell Disease offers genetic counseling and an information packet and will refer you to local chapters which give counseling, education, and may have some programs of financial aid.

SIDS (See SUDDEN INFANT DEATH SYNDROME.)

SKIN CANCER (See also CANCER and DERMATOLOGY.)

Tip # 1: Get free screening exams for skin cancer often offered at health fairs.

How it works: Sometimes hospitals sponsor skin screenings which include a check of a particular spot of skin and whole body checks by dermatologists. You may free yourself of worry without spending $30 or more on an office visit. If suspected skin cancer is found, you should make an immediate appointment for verification and treatment.

Tip # 2: Avoid prolonged exposure to direct sun, use sun screen, and avoid indoor tanning.

How it works: Skin cancer is on the increase. It can be largely prevented by limiting exposure to direct sunlight. For free information on tanning and skin cancer risk, order the FDA publications # FDA90-8278 and FDA87-8272. Write FDA, 5600 Fisher's Lane, Mail Code HFE-88, Room 1663, Rockville MD 20857 or call 301-443-3170.

Tip # 2: Contact the Skin Cancer Foundation.

How it works: The SCF provides 13 brochures, videos, slides and information. Contact the SCF at 245 Fifth Avenue, Suite 2402, New York, NY 10016, or phone 212-725-5176.

SLEEP DISORDERS (See also NARCOLEPSY.)

Tip # 1: Contact the American Sleep Disorders Association at 507-287-6006 for information and referrals.

SMELL AND TASTE DISORDERS

Tip # 1: Contact a research center that studies smell and taste disorders.

How it works: For information and referral and, sometimes, treatment for smell and taste disorders, contact one or more of these research centers:

Smell and Taste Research Center
University of Pennsylvania
3400 Spruce St.
Philadelphia, PA 19104-4283
Phone: 215-662-6580

Taste and Smell Center
Connecticut Chemosensory Clinical Research Center
University of Connecticut Health Center
Farmington, CT 06032
Phone: 203-679-2459

Rocky Mountain Taste and Smell Center
Box 111
University of Colorado Health Sciences Center
420 East 9th Avenue
Denver, CO 80262
Phone 303-270-7464

Monell Chemical Senses Center
3500 Market St.
Philadelphia, PA 19104
Phone: 215-898-6666

Clinical Olfactory Research Center
SUNY Health Sciences Center at Syracuse

766 Irving Ave.
Syracuse, NY 13210
Phone: 315-464-5588

SMOKING

Tip # 1: Get help to give up smoking.

How it works: Smokers, the best thing you can do to improve your long term health and save money on health care is to give up smoking. There is no one method that works best for everybody. To help choose a method for your individual smoking habits and to address issues such as weight control and withdrawal symptoms, order the excellent free booklet "Out of the Ashes" from the U.S. Public Health Services Centers for Disease Control. Call 404-488-5705 or write Office on Smoking and Health, MS-K50, 4770 Buford Highway NE, Atlanta, GA 30341.

Tip # 2: Contact the Smoking Education Program of the National Heart, Lung, and Blood Institute at 301-496-1051.

How it works: The Heart, Lung, and Blood Institute of the National Institutes of Health can give you written information on smoking and quitting. It also helps people set up courses and workshops for people who want to stop smoking.

SPANISH-SPEAKING HEALTH CARE (See HISPANIC HEALTH.)

SPEECH DISORDERS (See also STUTTERING.)

Tip # 1: Contact a non-profit organization concerned with speech disorders for information and referral.

How it works: The following organizations will give information on diagnosis, treatment, and support.

American Speech-Language-Hearing Association
10801 Rockville Pike
Rockville, MD 20852
Phone: 1-800-638-TALK or TDD 301-897-5700 for the deaf or speech impaired

Rehabilitation Services Administration,
Deafness and Communication Disorders
330 C Street SW, Room 3218

Washington, DC 20202-2736
Phone: 202-727-0981 or TDD 202-732-2848 for the deaf or
speech impaired

Tip # 2: Consider participating in an experimental study of treatment of your speech disorder. (See STUDIES.)

How it works: Experimental treatment studies often offer free treatment to patients who qualify as subjects. In particular, the Clinical Center of the National Institutes of Health in Bethesda, MD, has ongoing studies of many speech disorders including stuttering, dysarthria, verbal apraxia, Tourette syndrome, dystonia, Parkinson's disease, Huntington's chorea, cerebellar disorders, essential tremors, spastic or spasmodic dysphonia, voice tremor, vocal cord paralysis, and laryngeal nodules or polyps. For information about getting into a study at this or other institutions, see STUDIES.

SPINA BIFIDA

Tip #1: Contact the Spina Bifida Association of America at 1-800-621-3141.

How it works: The Spina Bifida Association gives information about the disease and referral to state chapters which may have financial resources to help families. English and Spanish speaking staff are available.

SPINAL CORD INJURIES (See also REHABILITATION, EQUIPMENT, and DISABILITY)

Tip # 1: Contact the National Spinal Cord Injury Association at 1-800-962-9629 for information and referral.

How it works: The National Spinal Cord Injury Association (NSCIA) provides financial support for education, research and general assistance. They publish *Spinal Cord Injury Life*, a quarterly newsletter, the annual NSCIA directory, a National Resource Directory, *Options: Spinal Cord Injury and the Future*. They offer free reference services and operate a pharmacy service. Write NSCIA at 600 West Cummings Park, Suite 2000, Woburn MA 01801.

Tip # 2: Contact the American Paralysis Association Hot line at 1-800-526-3456 for information and referral.

How it works: The American Paralysis Association (APA) provides support for research. The APA Spinal Cord Injury Hotline is an information and referral resource for the spinal cord injured, their families, and professionals working in the field. The APA publishes *The APA Annual Review, Walking Tomorrow, Progress in Research* and the *APA Alert*.

Tip # 3: If you are a veteran, contact Paralyzed Veterans of America (PVA) at 202-872-1300.

How it works: PVA is a service organization for veterans paralyzed by spinal cord injury or disease. The organization provides sporting activities and free information to its approximately 14,000 members. It publishes *Paraplegia News* and *Sports 'n Spokes* and other publications. Contact PVA at 801 18th Street NW, Washington, DC 20006.

Tip # 4: Contact the Spinal Cord Society (SCS) at 218-739-5252.

How it works: SCS has about 9000 members including those with spinal cord injuries, their families, friends, and interested professionals. An affiliated medical center in Minneapolis incorporates recent spinal cord injury research in their treatment services. SCS offers computerized data and referral services, publishes a newsletter, and has an annual conference. Write SCS at 2410 Lakeview Drive, Fergus Falls, MN 56537.

Tip # 5: Contact the National Rehabilitation Center at 1-800-346-2742 for information on equipment, funding, and programs.

How it works: See REHABILITATION, Tip # 1.

SPORTS MEDICINE (See also FITNESS.)

Tip # 1: Contact the American College of Sports Medicine at 317-637-9200.

How it works: The American College of Sports Medicine provides consumer related publications and pamphlets on exercise.

Tip # 2: To choose a sports medicine doctor, ask for referrals from teams, athletes, sports and fitness associations, and doctors who engage in sports themselves.

How it works: Sports medicine is a broad term encompassing a variety of health professionals. It is not a board recognized specialty. The field includes health care professionals in orthopedics, cardiology, gynecology, podiatry, dentistry, and psychology, among others. Sports medicine practitioners include exercise physiologists, who deal with functional physical and chemical changes that occur during exercise; biomechanists, who apply physics to exercise and can be helpful in determining how injuries occur; sports psychologists, who deal with how the mind influences performance; motor control specialists, who are concerned with how the brain and spinal cord interact in movement; and sports nutritionists, who advise athletes on diet; and sports podiatrists who treat and advise on prevention of foot injuries. Athletic trainers help team physicians and individuals take care of and prevent injury.

Quality check: Choose a specialist in sports medicine that has experience and interest in the same sports area in which you are engaged. Membership in the American College of Sports Medicine (ACSM) may indicate a doctor has an interest in keeping up with the latest innovations and research.

Tip # 3: For information on safety in competitive sports, contact an organization concerned with the appropriate age group.

How it works: For school age children's sports, contact the National Youth Sports Foundation for the Prevention of Athletic Injuries at 10 Meredith Circle, Needham, MA 02192.

For college-age players, contact the NCAA Committee on Competitive Safeguards and Medical Aspects of Sports at 6201 College Blvd., Overland Park, KS 66211.

Specific sports often have their own organizations to promote health in sports. An example is the American Medical Soccer Association, in care of Dr. Robert Cosby, 3508 Cheshire Drive, Birmingham, AL 35242-3100.

All these organizations can give you statistics on the incidence of certain injuries, the effectiveness of preventive measures, and other information on keeping sports safe.

SSI (See SUPPLEMENTAL SECURITY INCOME.)

STREP

Tip #1: Take <u>all</u> of the supply of antibiotics prescribed by a doctor for strep.

How it works: Failure to finish the whole supply of prescribed antibiotic is a major reason for recurring streptococcus (strep) infections. This is costly in terms of money and health. Certain strep infection improperly treated can turn into rheumatic fever, a heart-damaging disorder that is on the rise in the U.S. after a long period of decline.

Quality check: If you should develop a side effect to the medication, call your doctor immediately.

STRESS

Tip # 1: For a bibliography on stress and stress management, contact the National Heart, Lung, and Blood Institute.

How it works: Stress indirectly contributes to disease and lowering stress is good preventive medicine. For a selected bibliography of publications available on stress and stress management call the National Heart, Lung, and Blood Institute at 301-951-3260 or write the NHLBI Education-Programs Information Center at 4733 Bethesda Avenue, Suite 530, Bethesda MD 20814.

Tip # 2: Exercise reduces stress. See FITNESS for more information on exercise.

STROKE (See also DISABILITY, HIGH BLOOD PRESSURE, PARALYSIS, PHYSICAL THERAPY.)

Tip # 1: To learn about atrial fibrillation, a heart ailment that indirectly causes stroke, call 1-800-423-1925.

How it works: Atrial fibrillation affects 16% of men and 12% of women over 70 and increases the risk of stroke by six times. Effective drug treatment is available but underused, according to the National Stroke Association which, along with the Alliance for Aging, sponsors the toll-free hotline number above.

Tip # 2: Contact the National Heart, Lung, and Blood Institute (NHLBI) of the National Institutes of Health.

How it works: For information on stroke, its prevention and treatment, call the National Heart, Lung, and Blood Institute at 301-951-3260 or write the NHLBI Education-Programs Information Center at 4733 Bethesda Avenue, Suite 530, Bethesda MD 20814.

Tip # 3: Consider participating in an experimental study of treatment of stroke.

How it works: Experimental treatment studies often offer free treatment to patients who qualify as subjects. For information about getting into a study see STUDIES.

STUDIES OF EXPERIMENTAL TREATMENT

Tip # 1: Consider becoming a subject in a medical research study at the Warren Grant Magnuson Clinical Center (CC) of the National Institutes of Health.

How it works: The Clinical Center currently has over 1000 active research protocols or studies on hundreds of different diseases at any given time. If you qualify for a study and are accepted as a subject, all your medical care, tests, and hospitalization is absolutely free. The only cost to you is transportation to the Center in Bethesda, MD, which could be less than the deductible on your insurance policy.

An annual listing of ongoing studies, clinical directors, and physicians is available from the National Institutes of Health, Bethesda, MD 20892. You must be referred to the Center by your doctor or dentist who can call the general patient referral number: 301-496-4891 or the specific numbers listed in the annual listing.

Quality Check: Treatment at the Clinical Center is cutting edge treatment by experts in the field. By law, experimental treatment used in clinical trials must have shown a high probability of safety and effectiveness in previous research. However, because it is experimental, it has not been tested as long as traditional treatment and is more likely to have possible side effects or unknown effectiveness.

Also, in some cases, a patient accepted to a study may be designated a control subject and receive traditional treatment with which the experimental treatment can be compared. This quality check applies to all the kinds of studies mentioned below.

Tip # 2: Consider participating as a subject in a National Institutes of Health research study by contacting the appropriate Institute directly.

How it works: The National Institutes of Health consist of 18 Institutes, each concerned with a different health area, although there is a great deal of overlap and some diseases are of interest to more than one Institute. Each Institute has its own procedure for finding and selecting patients for research studies. Not all studies require frequent visits to NIH by the patient.

Contact the Information Specialist at each Institute and ask about studies of a particular disorder or use the patient referral numbers listed below.

National Institute on Aging (NIA) 301-496-1752
Patient referral to social worker at 301-496-4754

National Institute on Alcohol Abuse and Alcoholism (NIAAA) 301-496-9705
Patient referral to studies at 301-496-1993

National Institute of Allergy and Infectious Diseases (NIAID) 301-496-5717
Patient Referral to AIDS studies at 1-800-243-7644

National Institute of Arthritis and Musculoskeletal and Skin Diseases (NIAMS) 301-496-8188
Patient referral to investigators listed by interest

National Cancer Institute (NCI) 301-496-5583
Patient referral to physicians listed by interest

National Institute of Child Health and Human Development (NICHD) 301-496-5133
Patient Referral to branch chiefs; for information call the clinical director at 301-496-1068

National Institute on Deafness and Other Communication Disorders (NIDCD) 301-496-7243
Patient referrals to studies, 301-496-7491 or TDD 301-496-0771 for the deaf or speech impaired

National Institute of Dental Research (NIDR) 301-496-4261
Patient referral to investigators

National Institute of Diabetes and Digestive and Kidney Diseases (NIDDK) 301-496-3583
Patient referral to physicians in each subject area

National Center for Human Genome Research 301-402-0911

National Eye Institute (NEI) 301-496-3123
Patient referral to clinical director at 301-496-3123.

National Heart, Lung, and Blood Institute (NHLBI) 301-496-4236
Patient referral to branch physicians

National Institute of General Medical Sciences (NIGMS) 301-496-7301

National Institute of Mental Health (NIMH)
Patient referrals to studies 301-496-1337

National Institute of Neurological Disorders and Stroke (NINDS) 301-496-5924
Patient referrals to branch physicians

National Center for Nursing Research
301-496-0207

Clinical Center (CC) 301-496-2563
Patient referral to 301-496-9320 or 1-800-AIDS-NIH for critical care medicine and to 301-496-1380 for medical genetics

Tip # 3: Consider becoming a subject in a medical research study at the National Institutes of Health (NIH) General Clinical Research Centers.

How it works: In 76 General Clinical Research Centers (See map of locations on next page) across the nation, NIH funded research is taking place on hundreds of diseases. Research areas are oncology, nutrition, cardiology, gastroenterology, immunology, infectious diseases, endocrinology, genetics, nephrology, neurology, sleep disorders, dermatology, and hematology. If you qualify as a subject and are accepted, your testing and treatment may be free or at a reduced cost.

The names and phone numbers of the General Clinical Research Centers are as follows:

Locations of the General Clinical Research Centers

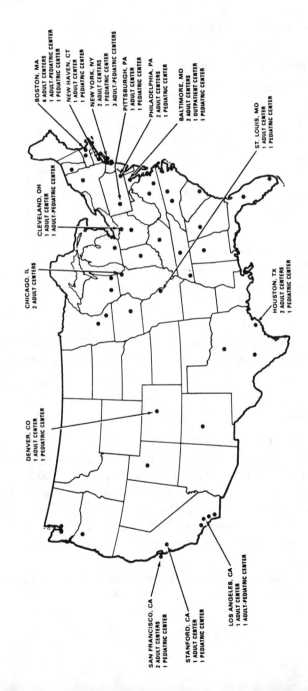

EACH DOT INDICATES THE LOCATION OF ONE OR MORE GCRC's

BOSTON, MA
4 ADULT CENTERS
1 ADULT-PEDIATRIC CENTER
1 PEDIATRIC CENTER

NEW HAVEN, CT
1 ADULT CENTER
1 PEDIATRIC CENTER

NEW YORK, NY
2 ADULT CENTERS
1 PEDIATRIC CENTER
3 ADULT-PEDIATRIC CENTERS

PITTSBURGH, PA
1 ADULT CENTER
1 PEDIATRIC CENTER

PHILADELPHIA, PA
2 ADULT CENTERS
1 PEDIATRIC CENTER

BALTIMORE, MD
2 ADULT CENTERS
1 OUTPATIENT CENTER
1 PEDIATRIC CENTER

ST. LOUIS, MO
1 ADULT CENTER
1 PEDIATRIC CENTER

CLEVELAND, OH
1 ADULT CENTER
1 ADULT-PEDIATRIC CENTER

CHICAGO, IL
2 ADULT CENTERS

HOUSTON, TX
2 ADULT CENTERS
1 PEDIATRIC CENTER

DENVER, CO
1 ADULT CENTER
1 PEDIATRIC CENTER

SAN FRANCISCO, CA
2 ADULT CENTERS
1 PEDIATRIC CENTER

STANFORD, CA
1 ADULT CENTER
1 PEDIATRIC CENTER

LOS ANGELES, CA
1 ADULT CENTER
1 ADULT-PEDIATRIC CENTER

ALABAMA
University of Alabama at Birmingham: 205-934-4852
CALIFORNIA
Harbor-University of California, Los Angeles Medical Center (Torrance): 213-533-2503
Scripps Clinic and Research Foundation (La Jolla): 619-554-8925
Stanford University—(1) adults, (2) premature infants: 415-723-7496
University of California, Los Angeles: 213-825-7117
University of California, San Diego: 619-543-6180
University of California, San Francisco (Moffitt Hospital) for adults: 415-476-9232
University of California, San Francisco (Moffitt Hospital) for children: 415-476-4009
University of California, San Francisco General Hospital: 415-826-3381
University of California (Los Angeles): 213-226-4632
COLORADO
University of Colorado (Denver) for adults: 303-270-8383
University of Colorado (Denver) for children: 303-837-2957
CONNECTICUT
Yale University (New Haven) for adults: 203-785-4424
Yale University (New Haven) for children: 203-785-5817
FLORIDA
University of Florida (Gainesville): 904-395-0032
University of Miami: 305-549-7044
GEORGIA
Emory University (Atlanta): 404-727-3536
ILLINOIS
Northwestern University (Chicago): 312-908-8186
University of Chicago: 312-702-6980
INDIANA
Indiana University (Indianapolis): 317-274-0949
IOWA
University of Iowa (Iowa City): 319-335-8651

KENTUCKY
University of Kentucky College of Medicine (Lexington): 606-233-6623

LOUISIANA
Tulane/Louisiana State Universities (New Orleans): 504-585-4000

MARYLAND
Francis Scott Key Medical Center (Baltimore): 301-550-1850
Johns Hopkins University (Baltimore) for adults: 301-955-5888
Johns Hopkins University (Baltimore) for children: 301-955-3859
Johns Hopkins University (Baltimore) for outpatients: 301-955-5888

MASSACHUSETTS
Beth Israel Hospital (Boston): 617-735-4269
Boston University: 617-638-4542
Brigham and Women's Hospital (Boston): 617-732-7793
Children's Hospital (Boston): 617-735-7541
Massachusetts General Hospital (Boston): 617-726-3288
Massachusetts Institute of Technology (Cambridge): 617-258-6430
New England Medical Center Hospitals (Boston): 617-956-6149

MICHIGAN
University of Michigan (Ann Arbor): 313-936-8083

MINNESOTA
Mayo Foundation (Rochester): 507-255-4056
University of Minnesota (Minneapolis): 612-624-9159

MISSOURI
Washington University (St. Louis) for adults: 314-362-7625
Washington University (St. Louis) for children: 314-454-2089

NEW MEXICO
University of New Mexico (Albuquerque): 505-843-2523

NEW YORK
Columbia University (New York City): 212-305-2071
Cornell University Medical College (New York City) for adults: 212-746-4742

Cornell University Medical College (New York City) for children: 212-746-3453

Mount Sinai School of Medicine (New York City): 212-241-6045

New York University (New York City): 212-263-6410

Rockefeller University (New York City): 212-570-8062

State University of New York (Brooklyn): 718-270-1542

University of Rochester: 716-275-6409

NORTH CAROLINA

Duke University (Durham) 919-684-3806

University of North Carolina (Chapel Hill) 919-966-4767

OHIO

Case Western Reserve University (Cleveland): 216-459-4691

Ohio State University (Columbus): 614-293-8749

University Hospitals of Cleveland: 216-844-1589

OREGON

Oregon Health Sciences University (Portland): 503-494-4324

PENNSYLVANIA

Children's Hospital of Philadelphia: 215-590-3169

Children's Hospital of Pittsburgh: 412-692-5573

Temple University (Philadelphia): 215-221-8987

University of Pennsylvania School of Medicine: 215-662-2641

University of Pittsburg: 412-647-6016

SOUTH CAROLINA

Medical University of South Carolina (Charleston): 803-792-3256

TENNESSEE

University of Tennessee (Memphis): 901-528-5308

Vanderbilt University (Nashville): 615-322-2390

TEXAS

Baylor College of Medicine (Houston) for adults: 713-790-4306

Baylor College of Medicine (Houston) for children: 713-798-1353

University of Texas Health Science Center (Houston): 713-797-4269

Universtiy of Texas Health Science Center (San Antonio): 512-567-4632

University of Texas Medical Branch at Galveston: 409-761-1950

University of Texas Southwestern Medical Center (Dallas): 214-590-7783

UTAH

University of Utah (Salt Lake City): 801-581-3670

VERMONT

University of Vermont (Burlington): 802-656-5033

VIRGINIA

University of Virginia (Charlottesville): 804-924-2073

Virginia Commonwealth University (Richmond): 804-786-9230

WASHINGTON

University of Washington (Seattle): 206-543-4365

WISCONSIN

Medical College of Wisconsin (Milwaukee): 414-259-3010

University of Wisconsin-Madison: 608-263-3271

Quality check: See Quality check, Tip # 1.

Tip # 4: Call the Dean's Office of a medical school or the head of specific department in a medical school near you and ask for referrals to experimental studies.

How it works: Doctors in almost every medical school are participating in research including clinical studies of investigational and experimental treatment. These may be funded by the National Institutes of Health, by other institutes and organizations, or by drug companies. They often need subjects for clinical studies and you may be referred to one simply by asking. Not all studies require patients to make frequent visits to the research center. Free testing or a physical exam, which determines if you qualify for a study, is often worthwhile in itself.

Tip # 5: Watch the newspaper for requests for volunteers for studies.

How it works: During one three-month a newspaper in one city advertised studies in the classified personals ads or in the health notes seeking subjects for experimental treatment as follows:

• The medical school of a local university was seeking women with osteoporosis who were otherwise healthy and not on estrogen therapy for a five-year study. Treatment would include injections of calcitonin, a drug known to slow down bone deterioration.

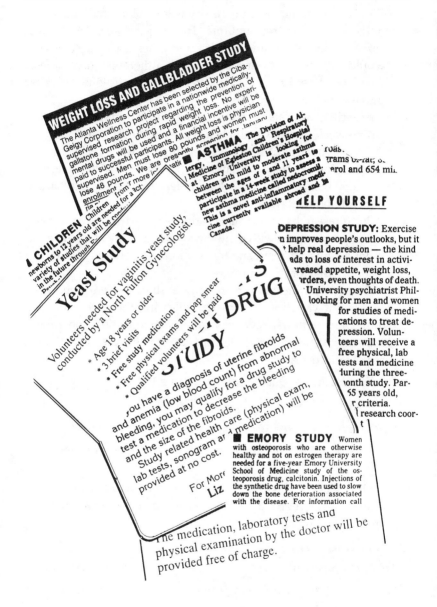

WEIGHT LOSS AND GALLBLADDER STUDY

The Atlanta Wellness Center has been selected by the Ciba-Geigy Corporation to participate in a nationwide medically-supervised research project regarding the prevention of gallstone formation during rapid weight loss. No experimental drugs will be used and a financial incentive will be paid to successful participants. All weight loss is physician supervised. Men must lose 80 pounds and women must lose 48 pounds. We are presently screening for January enrollment for more in-

CHILDREN newborns to 12 years old are needed for a variety of studies that will be con-
in the future through...

Yeast Study

Volunteers needed for vaginitis yeast study, conducted by a North Fulton Gynecologist.

* Age 18 years or older
* 3 brief visits
* Free study medication
* Free physical exams and pap smear
* Qualified volunteers will be paid

...R DRUG STUDY

...you have a diagnosis of uterine fibroids and anemia (low blood count) from abnormal bleeding, you may qualify for a drug study to test a medication to decrease the bleeding and the size of the fibroids.

Study related health care (physical exam, lab tests, sonogram and medication) will be provided at no cost.

For More
Liz

■ **ASTHMA** The Division of Allergy, Immunology and Respiratory Medicine of Egleston Children's Hospital at Emory University is looking for children with mild to moderate asthma between the ages of 6 and 11 years to participate in a 14-week study to assess a new asthma medicine called nedocromil. This is a novel anti-inflammatory medicine currently available abroad and in Canada.

roas.

...rams or rat; o.
...erol and 654 mi..

HELP YOURSELF

DEPRESSION STUDY: Exercise ..n improves people's outlooks, but it ...t help real depression — the kind ...ads to loss of interest in activi-...reased appetite, weight loss, ...rders, even thoughts of death. ...University psychiatrist Phil-...looking for men and women for studies of medications to treat depression. Volunteers will receive a free physical, lab tests and medicine during the three-...onth study. Par-...55 years old, ...r criteria. ...l research coor-...t

■ **EMORY STUDY** Women with osteoporosis who are otherwise healthy and not on estrogen therapy are needed for a five-year Emory University School of Medicine study of the osteoporosis drug, calcitonin. Injections of the synthetic drug have been used to slow down the bone deterioration associated with the disease. For information call

...e medication, laboratory tests and physical examination by the doctor will be provided free of charge.

- Researchers at the same university were looking for female volunteers suffering from bulimia. The subjects, ages 18-65, must currently binge, eat and vomit three times a week. Treatment would include one-hour sessions with a therapist three times a week for three weeks, then at intervals for up to one year after initial treatment.

- Researchers were also seeking people with extremely dry eyes for a nine-week study to evaluate a cyclosporin ointment.

- A blood cholesterol study was evaluating the effectiveness of various doses of the drug Questran (R). Subjects with cholesterol over 250 willing to follow a low cholesterol diet were to participate for about 20 weeks.

- A local research center collaborating with a drug company was seeking volunteers with genital warts for a study of a new treatment. Exams, lab tests, and medication were offered free as well as up to $100 for time and travel.

Throughout the year many more studies were conducted involving a variety of disorders. Following the notices of such studies in the newspaper may get you free testing and free or reduced-cost treatment and a connection with researchers in the area of your disease.

Quality check: See Quality check for Tip # 1.

Tip # 6: For AIDS studies see AIDS, Tip # 9.

STURGE-WEBER DISEASE (See RARE DISORDERS.)

Tip # 1: Contact the Sturge-Weber Disease Foundation at 1-800-627-5482.

How it works: The organization provides lists of publications, long distance support groups, and referrals. Call between 8 a.m. and 4 p.m. Mountain time.

STUTTERING (See also SPEECH DISORDERS.)

Tip # 1: Contact a non-profit organization concerned with stuttering.

How it works: The following organizations provide information, referral and support to stutterers.

Foundation for Fluency
9242 Gross Point Rd., # 305

Skokie, IL 60077
708-677-8280

National Council on Stuttering
P.O. BOx 344
Rochelle, IL 61068

National Stuttering Project
4601 Irving St.
San Francisco, CA 94122-1020
415-566-5324

Stuttering Foundation of America
123 Oxford Rd.
New Rochelle, NY 10804
1-800-232-4773

SUDDEN INFANT DEATH SYNDROME (SIDS)

Tip # 1: Contact the SIDS Alliance at 1-800-221-SIDS for support group information for people who have lost a baby.

Tip # 2: Contact Sudden Infant Death Syndrome Clearinghouse at 1-703-821-8955.

How it works: The SIDS Clearinghouse maintains a data base and bibliography on SIDS and its impact on the family. The Clearing- house will send you fact sheets and help you find additional information.

SUPPLEMENTAL SECURITY INCOME (SSI)

Tip # 1: Apply for Supplemental Security Income (SSI), if you are eligible.

How it works: Aged, blind, and disabled people, including children, who have low income and resources may be eligible for a monthly payment through a federal program called SSI. U.S. citizens, lawful permanent residents, or aliens with lawful claim to remain in the U.S. may apply. Income and resource limits may change each year; the 1993 income limit for an individual is $434 and for a couple is $652. Resource limits for 1993 are $2000 for an individual and $3000 for a couple but the value of your home and car (depending on its value), $1500 burial fund and $1500 of life insurance are excluded in the determination. Generally, those who qualify for SSI are also eligible for food stamps and to have Medicaid pay for the insurance premiums for Part B of Medicare, Medicare co-insurance payments, and Medicare deductibles under the QMB program. (See MEDICARE.)

SURGERY (See also ARTHROSCOPIC SURGERY and LASER SURGERY and names of particular surgeries.)

Tip # 1: Get an independent second opinion before agreeing to surgery.

How it works: Some surgeries are done unnecessarily. If you go to a surgeon, he/she may be more likely to recommend surgery than non-surgeons in the same specialty area. You may wish to get a second opinion from other surgeons in the specialty and/or from non-surgeons who specialize in your disease. For example, compare the opinions of a neurosurgeon with those of a neurologist or the opinions of a heart surgeon with those of a cardiologist.

Be sure your second opinion is an independent one, that is, do not seek your second opinion from a partner of the doctor who gave the first opinion.

If you need a second opinion referral, call the National Second Opinion Program at 1-800-638-8480 or 1-800-492-6603 in Maryland. For cancer treatment, multi-disciplinary second opinion panels of volunteer doctors can be arranged through the Cancer Information Service at 1-800-4-CANCER.

Quality control: Remember that the second opinion is not necessarily the correct one. If a second opinion disagrees with the first, seek a third. Ask each doctor why they disagree with the others.

Tip # 2: Consider outpatient surgery instead of hospitalization.

How it works: The list of surgeries which may be done on an outpatient basis is long. It includes bunion surgery, cataract removal, arthroscopic knee surgery, some biopsies, tonsillectomy, dilation and curettage (D & C), tubal ligations, some hernia repairs, some plastic surgery, and new procedures every year. Because it does not involve an overnight stay, outpatient surgery is usually much less expensive than inpatient surgery. Sometimes the presence of a friend or relative to stay by you during recovery in the outpatient facility is required. This also cuts down on costs by saving on nursing staff.

An insurance company survey of outpatient surgery in one state found that costs of 21 frequently performed surgeries at freestanding ambulatory facilities averaged 47% less overall than the same 21 performed in a hospital. For example, a tonsillectomy was $998 in a hospital, $464 at the outpatient facility. Ask your doctor if the procedure you need can be appropriately done in an outpatient surgery setting.

Quality check: In certain cases, your doctor may recommend you be hospitalized for a procedure often done on an out-patient basis because of complications such as other disorders you may have. Out-patient facilities are accredited by The Accreditation Association for Ambulatory Health Care, Inc., in Skokie IL, which can provide a list of approved centers. Phone 708-676-9610.

Tip # 3: Look at your insurance coverage to compare out-patient coverage with hospitalization coverage.

How it works: Some health insurance policies, particularly older ones, pay for in-patient procedures, that is, hospitalization, but do not pay for any out-patient services. If you have such a policy, even though out-patient treatment charges are less, hospitalization may save you money.

Tip # 4: Before your surgery, get prior approval or pre-certification from your insurance company.

How it works: Many insurance companies pre-approve or pre-certify treatment, especially surgery. This means they ask questions about your case and compare it with their guidelines based on research studies of the outcome of different procedures. They want to know if the treatment you are considering is the most appropriate, in their opinion. Often companies will not pay as much of the bill for a procedure that is not pre-approved; in fact, some will not pay at all.

Tip # 5: If your insurance company rules a surgical procedure is experimental and ineligible for coverage, consider challenging it.

How it works: Insurance companies often do not cover experimental treatment, especially surgery, because it has not been proven to their satisfaction to be helpful or appropriate. This ruling may be successfully challenged. Ask your doctor to demonstrate the potential of the surgery and a lawyer can provide additional pressure. If you have the surgery in spite of a negative ruling by the insurance company, a successful outcome could provide evidence to make the company change its mind.

SYPHILIS (See SEXUALLY TRANSMITTED DISEASES.)

TANNING (See SKIN CANCER.)

TARSAL TUNNEL SYNDROME (See RARE DISEASES.)

TASTE and SMELL DISORDERS (See SMELL and TASTE DISORDERS.)

TAY-SACHS DISEASE (See also RARE DISEASES.)

Tip # 1: Contact the National Institutes of Health, Child Health and Human Development at 301-496-5133 for free information on Tay-Sachs disease.

TB (See TUBERCULOSIS.)

TESTING, SCREENING and DIAGNOSTIC (See also CHECK-UPS, ROUTINE.)

Tip # 1: Consider having common screening tests done at health fairs.

How it works: Common screening tests like those for blood pressure; glucose, cholesterol, and triglyceride levels; blood profiles; dental, vision, and hearing screenings, mammograms and prostate tests are often offered free or at greatly reduced cost at health fairs and disease awareness events. Watch health notes in the newspaper and take advantage of low cost screenings once a year. Note date and results and keep any written results to show your doctor.

Quality check: Note who is sponsoring health fairs, whose equipment is being used and what kind of technician. Evaluate the qualifications of all involved just as you would evaluate any service. For example, ask if the mammography device, technician, and radiologist are from a certified mammography center. (See MAMMOGRAPHY.)

Tip # 2: Follow directions for preparing for tests exactly. For example, don't eat anything for the recommended time period before a fasting blood specimen is taken.

How it works: A common reason for doing tests more than one time is that patients don't comply with the directions, laboratory directors say. People who drink a glass of orange juice, for example, on the morning before a blood work-up that required fasting often get an unusual finding that necessitates a repeat of the test or another kind of test at additional cost.

Tip # 3: Before testing, tell a doctor about the medicines you are taking.

How it works: Some people fail to tell a doctor they are taking birth control pills or aspirin or other medication they consider too routine to mention. For example, both of these medications can throw off results of a blood clotting test that is commonly done before surgery. Failure to inform a doctor may be both costly and dangerous.

Tip # 4: Ask your doctor if the outcome of a test will change the treatment.

How it works: Ask your doctor, "Will the outcome of this test change the treatment?" If the answer is no, ask why it is necessary. As an illustration, a child had his fingers mashed in the door of a car. The mother thought one finger might be broken. The doctor was preparing to X-ray the hand when the mother asked what the doctor would do if the finger was broken. The doctor said the best thing to do was tape the broken finger together with the other fingers so that it would heal in the right position. And if it's not broken, only hurt? Tape the fingers together and give them a rest, the doctor said. The result of this conversation was that they skipped the X-ray and taped the fingers together since the results of the X-ray in this case were not going to change the treatment.

Tip # 5: Ask your doctor why certain tests are being ordered and question the cost consequences.

How it works: Many doctors do not themselves see the lab fees charged the patient. They may be more conscious of the cost to them of liability insurance and they may order tests to protect themselves from charges of insufficient testing. Doctors walk a fine line between too little and too much testing. Just alerting your doctor to the fact that cost is an important issue for you may cause him/her to limit testing unnecessary for your diagnosis. If the doctor explains the pros and cons of doing certain tests, you may decide together on whether to go ahead with testing. The discussion may limit your spending and the doctor's liability.

Tip # 6: Ask your doctor to consult resources available at major labs about how to diagnose with the least costly lab fees.

How it works: If you have certain symptoms, a doctor may order tests for all the possible disorders related to those symptoms. This will probably pinpoint the problem. However, it is usually much less expensive to do fewer tests ruling out certain more common causes of your symptoms and not move onto further testing until the results of the first indicate additional tests are necessary. One reason a doctor may order all the tests related to your symptoms rather than just the ones initially necessary may be that he/she does not know the most efficient sequence for progressive diagnosis of your problem which may be uncommon in his/her specialty. Your doctor can get a great deal of cost-saving information by asking the physician who directs the lab this simple question: How can I get at this diagnosis without spending a lot of money?

Tip # 7: Ask your insurance company if your policy will cover specific tests you are considering.

How it works: While your health insurance may cover lab testing for diagnostic purposes, it may not cover every test. Individual labs sometimes devise their own tests, which may be better, worse, or equally effective compared to more widely used tests. Insurance companies, however, may not cover some of these independently devised tests. Also, there are some tests which, while being accepted by the medical community as excellent (some cancer markers tests, for example), are not yet approved by the Food and Drug Administration (FDA) and are considered experimental. Your policy may not pay for these. If your policy does not cover an expensive test your doctor has ordered, ask your doctor if there is an equally effective (possibly more expensive) test that your insurance company does cover; or ask your doctor to demonstrate to the insurance company that the test not covered by your policy should be covered in your case.

Tip # 8: Question how you will be billed for lab testing.

How it works: In some cases, testing charges from the lab come through the doctor and he/she may mark the price of each test up. In other cases, patients get a bill directly from the lab. Direct billing might eliminate a mark-up on tests and savvy patients can check the tests on the bill. Remember, however, that compensation for drawing blood or taking tissue samples is still justifiably billed by the doctor. Sometimes doctors prefer not to draw blood themselves. Instead patients are sent to a sampling station. This may be a service provided free of additional charge by the laboratory. The least expensive lab arrangement may be one in which an independent lab draws samples and bills the patient directly. On the other hand, some tests can be run very inexpensively in a doctor's office.

Quality check: The independent lab does nothing but testing and may make fewer mistakes than personnel in a doctor's office. However, personnel in the doctors's office have closer access to your doctor if clinical questions arise.

Tip # 9: Ask your doctor what lab he/she uses and how its prices compare with others for the testing you need done.

How it works: Common lab tests (strep tests or vaginal smears, for example) done in a doctor's office lab tend to be less expensive than tests sent out of the office. For outside testing, hospital labs tend to be more expensive than independent labs called reference labs. Moreover, prices vary widely. Fees for an SMA 20 blood test in hospitals surveyed in one Louisiana city varied from $80 to $168 and urinalysis ranged from $19 to $56. In addition, large labs because of high volume and the economies of scale can offer lower prices than small labs. Smaller labs must often charge more to cover costs, and, also, when they do not have facilities for a certain test, they commonly send it out to a larger lab and then mark up the price for the service. However, some labs win a doctor's business in certain instances not by keeping prices low but by offering the physician extra services from which the patient may or may not directly benefit. Physicians establish relationships with labs just as all business people establish relationships with suppliers. Insisting on a test being done by a lab unfamiliar to your doctor is probably not a good idea, but asking your doctor to compare prices periodically or to choose the less expensive lab for your test when he/she deals with more than one is a good idea. Where samples are taken may also affect the price of a test. Some independent labs offer drawing stations in doctor's buildings where blood samples are drawn without additional charge, whereas there may be a charge for drawing blood if it is done by the doctor's office personnel. Factor in this variable when comparing costs of lab tests.

Quality check: If a lab your doctor uses is not a large, familiar company, call the lab and ask if it is licensed. Don't hesitate to ask for a copy of the license to be mailed to you. Additional certification by the College of American Pathologists is recommended. To see if a particular lab is accredited by this organization, call 1-800-323-4040 and press 2 for accreditation listings.

Tip # 10: *If you are healthy,* consider donating blood at the Red Cross as a good deed and as a means to having your hemoglobin level checked free of charge.

How it works: In a healthy person, low hemoglobin is fairly common and often correctable through iron supplements available at any drug store without prescription. Red Cross staff test the hemoglobin levels of all potential donors for their protection as well as the protection of recipients. If your blood level is low, the Red Cross will tell you so and will not take your blood. If you are rejected for low hemoglobin, call your doctor. Do not take iron supplements on your own as there are several causes of low hemoglobin that need to be ruled out.

Quality check: The Red Cross test for a low blood count is likely to be as reliable as one anywhere else. The donation of blood after a satisfactory test may result, however, in a temporary low blood count for a few days while your body replaces the blood you gave.

DO NOT DONATE BLOOD EVER WHEN YOU SUSPECT YOU HAVE ANY KIND OF ILLNESS.

Tip # 11: Consider using self-administered screening tests available in a drug store.

How it works: A test administered by you in your home is cheaper than an office visit for a similar test. The following self-administered tests available in drug stores are reasonably reliable: pregnancy tests, ovulation tests, and stool cards for detecting occult blood. Home glucose tests are helpful, although more crude than lab tests, for diabetics who are trained in their use. Such tests can be used for screening and monitoring.

Quality check: Tests sold for home use are good for screening but they (like all tests) sometimes result in a small number of both false positives and false negatives even when directions are followed carefully. If any test is positive for a disorder or pregnancy, consult a doctor for confirmation.

Tip # 12: Check your local health department for what tests are done at low or no cost.

How it works: Some health departments give tests for tuberculosis, sexually transmitted diseases, pregnancy, blood glucose levels. The cost usually ranges from nothing to an amount considerably less than at a doctor's office. A sliding scale often applies.

Tip # 13: If you are a college student or work at a college, see what tests the student health clinic gives.

How it works: Most colleges have student health facilities. Public universities may offer the most service for the least cost. One university for example charged students and employees $3 for a pregnancy test.

Tip # 14: Ask for copies of your test results and take them to other doctors you may consult.

How it works: You are entitled to a copy of the results of your tests, although one is rarely offered to patients. These results can be valuable information to bring along when you move, go to a specialist, or change doctors for any reason. Without the tests, new doctors may have to duplicate tests and charge you for them. If your tests are current, it can save time and money. In any case, a series of tests you may have had done, shows a progression over time that may help in diagnosis or monitoring a disorder.

THALASSEMIA, MAJOR and MINOR (See RARE DISEASES and COOLEY'S ANEMIA)

THYROID DISEASE

Tip # 1: For thyroid problems, call 301-496-3583 for information.

How it works: The National Institute of Diabetes, Digestive and Kidney Diseases of the National Institutes of Health will give you information and answer questions on thyroid disease.

Tip # 2: Consider participating in an experimental study of treatment of your thyroid disorder. (See STUDIES.)

How it works: Experimental treatment studies often offer free treatment to patients who qualify as subjects. In particular, the Clinical Center of the National Institutes of Health in Bethesda, MD, has on-going studies of many thyroid disorders including hyper- and hypothyroidism and inappropriate secretion of TSH. For information on getting into an experimental study, see STUDIES.

TINNITUS (ringing in the ears)

Tip # 1: Contact the American Tinnitus Association.

How it works: Almost 40,000,000 adults suffer from tinnitus, ringing or other noise in the ears. The causes are usually sensory-neural. The American Tinnitus Association in Portland, OR, will send you literature, refer you to tinnitus clinics, and put you in touch with local support groups.

TOURETTE DISEASE or SYNDROME (See also RARE DISORDERS)

Tip # 1: Contact the Tourette Syndrome Association at 1-800-237-0717 or in New York at 718-224-2999.

How it works: The organization provides an answering service to take requests for literature. To speak with a staff member, use the 718 number.

TORCH SYNDROME (See RARE DISEASES.)

TORSION DYSTONIA (See RARE DISEASES.)

TOXIC SHOCK SYNDROME

Tip # 1: Call the FDA at 301-443-3170 or order the FDA publication on toxic shock syndrome and tampon use.

How it works: The Food and Drug Administration (FDA) provides current information in booklet form on a wide range of subjects. Order FDA92-4251 for information on toxic shock syndrome and tampon use. (Add an S to number for Spanish version.) Write FDA, 5600 Fisher's Lane, Mail Code HFE-88, Room 1663, Rockville MD 20857 or call 301-443-3170.

TOXOPLASMOSIS (See RARE DISEASES.)

TRAVEL

Tip # 1: Contact your local health department for immunizations necessary for foreign travel.

How it works: Most health departments give immunizations at lower cost than you would pay at a doctor's office, and they should have the latest information on which immunizations you will need for your destination.

Tip # 2: Call the Centers for Disease Control and Prevention (CDC) at 404-332-4555 for current information on diseases, food and drinking water conditions, and other health hazards in specific foreign countries.

How it works: The CDC has very detailed, recorded information on travel precautions for foreign countries 24 hours a day including region-by-region information on prevention and prevalence of diseases, activities that put you more at risk, vaccination requirements, food and drinking water conditions, and ways to prevent diarrhea. To save money, call during low telephone rate hours. To receive written information on international travel precautions and answers to other questions ONLY AFTER listening to the recorded information, call the CDC public inquiry number 404-639-3534 weekdays except federal holidays 8:30 a.m. to 5 p.m. Eastern time.

Tip # 3: Pregnant women should avoid certain vaccines.

How it works: Certain vaccines are recommended for travel in some countries. If you are pregnant, however, or likely to be pregnant within three months, you should avoid attenuated-virus vaccines. This may mean you should postpone a trip. Ask your doctor to help assess the risks.

Tip # 4: Ask for a free list of English-speaking doctors in other countries, immunization guides, health risks, and climate charts.

How it works: Contact the International Association for Medical Assistance to Travelers, 417 Center St., Lewiston, NY 14092 or call 716-754-4883. Also, travel agents in foreign countries and American embassies or consulates usually have lists of physicians and medical services.

Tip # 5: Learn how to say, "Please get me to a doctor," and "I have——," in the native language of countries you plan to travel in.

How it works: Carry with you and learn to say phrases to help you get emergency help in a foreign country. Appropriate foreign phrases such as, "I have diabetes," "Or I am deaf," or "Do not give me aspirin," are phrases you should learn to say and carry in written form in your wallet or tape to a medical information bracelet.

Tip # 6: For travelers with medical problems and medications take special precautions.

How it works: Have a check-up before you leave. Buy extra amounts of your important medications at home and carry some of each in your luggage and some on your person to guard against loss of your whole supply. Carry a letter signed by your doctor stating your disease, a summary of treatment, and all the medicines you take and carry your medicines in the original bottle to prevent delays by drug inspectors at customs. Ask your doctor how to take timed medications when crossing time zones. Ask airlines in advance for special dietary meals you need.

Tip # 7: Take extra contacts, glasses, hearing aid batteries, etc.

How it works: Many products you may rely on are not available in foreign countries. Labeling may be different, prices may be unreasonable, quality may be unassured. Take all such necessities and extras with you.

Tip # 8: Avoid insect-carried diseases abroad.

How it works: Many diseases are spread by infected insects. Avoiding insects and using repellents can help keep you safe. Avoid being outside at twilight and dawn, dusk and evening, especially in rural areas or near bushes and water. Wear hats, long sleeve shirts, and pants tucked into shoes or boots. Avoid sandals. Tuck in bed clothes and sleep under mosquito nets where available. Spray clothing, shoes, hats, and bedding, including mosquito nets. Repellents containing Permethrin are recommended, and special shampoos containing permethrin may help. Repellents containing Deet should have concentrations of less than 30% because higher concentrations may be toxic. Avoid breathing or ingesting spray. Avoid repellents for pregnant or nursing women. Do not spray children's hands with repellant as they often put their hands in their mouth. Using repellant sparingly as a light cover is just as effective as saturation. One application lasts about 4 hours. Wash it off the skin when coming indoors to stay.

Tip # 9: Avoid disease from unsanitary water and food.

How it works: Travelers' diarrhea and other diseases are contracted from fecally-contaminated and untreated food and water. In areas where there is no water chlorination and/or poor hygiene, drink only boiled water beverages such as hot tea and coffee, canned or carbonated water, beer and wine. In some countries, some so-called bottled water in hotels and restaurants is actually unsafe tap water used to refill old water bottles. Be sure there is a manufacturer's seal on a bottle and an indication that the water is bottled and sealed in a developed nation. Drink directly from the can or bottle rather than a questionable container. Avoid ice because ice is no safer than the water it's made from. Boil water, if possible, rather than using expensive tablets for purification. Avoid swimming in fresh water. Washed fruits or vegetables may also be contaminated. Peel fresh fruit and vegetables before eating. Cook food thoroughly and reheat thoroughly if it has been left unrefrigerated.

Tip # 10: Do not handle or purchase goat skin articles in the Caribbean because of a risk of anthrax, a serious disease.

Tip # 11: Avoid blood transfusions in developing countries.

How it works: Blood screening for disease is not done in many developing countries. While blood transfusions must sometimes be done to save a life, in all but critical situations, consider refusing transfusion.

Tip # 12: Consider buying travel insurance when going to other countries

How it works: Medicare will not pay for medical care in foreign countries. There may also be limitations on international health care coverage by private insurance. In countries with national health care, non-citizens may not be eligible for free care. In England, for example, while you can receive free emergency care at National Health Services emergency rooms, if you are hospitalized, you will be billed. For these reasons, buying travel insurance for foreign travel may be prudent. Travel insurance may be good to have for domestic travel also as it covers money you lose if the trip has to be canceled because of a medical problem. Consider buying the insurance at the time you book the trip because claims based on last minute insurance purchases may be viewed skeptically by the insurance company. To buy travel insurance, see your travel agent or travel club.

TUBERCULIN SKIN TEST   (See TUBERCULOSIS.)

Tip # 1: Do not get an X-ray as a screening test for TB.

How it works: A tuberculin skin test identifies those who may have been exposed to tuberculosis. The skin tests are inexpensive and safe. Only those who have positive results should seek further testing. Unnecessary X-rays should be avoided because of their cost and the risks of exposure to radiation.

Tip # 2: Get a tuberculin skin test at a local health department at low or no cost.

How it works: Tuberculosis is on the rise after decades of decline. Early diagnosis saves you a lot of grief as well as prevents the spread of the disease. A tuberculin skin screening test which detects exposure to the tuberculin bacteria is often required for employment or enrollment in a school. Typically, a private clinic or doctor's office charges about $20 for the test without consultation with a doctor. A local health department typically does the test at no charge or for less than $10.

TUBERCULOSIS (TB) (See also TUBERCULIN SKIN TEST.)

Tip # 1: Consider going to a local health department for treatment. One health department offers TB treatment free or $1 for a month's medication.

Tip # 2: Keep taking medication as long as recommended by the doctor at the health department. The incidence of TB is on the rise and it is very important to continue the medicine until you are cured.

TUBEROUS SCLEROSIS (See also RARE DISORDERS)

Tip # 1: Contact the National Tuberous Sclerosis Association at 1-800-225-6872 or in Maryland at 301-459-9888.

How it works: The organization answers questions and provides literature about this genetic disorder involving uncontrolled seizures, autism, and tumors of major organs. The Association also makes parent to parent contract referrals.

TURNER SYNDROME (See also RARE DISEASES.)

Tip # 1: Read *Understanding Growth Hormone* by Neil Shulman M.D. and Letitia Sweitzer (Hippocrene, New York, 1993).

How it works: This book explains all aspects of growth hormone including growth hormone treatment for short stature, a common symptom of Turner Syndrome. Growth hormone treatment, in the case of the Turner Syndrome, although not yet approved by the FDA at this writing, is common and effective and frequently paid for by insurance and HMO benefits. See a pediatric endocrinologist for medical advice.

TWINS

Tip # 1: Contact the National Organization for Mothers of Twins Club at 505-275-0955.

How it works: Raising twins has its own set of issues that parents must deal with: how much to keep them together, how to encourage their individuality, what to do about the comparisons outsiders make, how to be two places at once, etc. The friendship and support of other parents of twins can be helpful. The National Organization on Mothers of Twins has local chapters and information.

Tip # 2: Contact the Turner's Syndrome Society at 612-475-9944 for information and referral to local groups.

ULCERS

Tip # 1: Contact the Digestive Disease Clearinghouse at 301-468-6344 for an informational packet on ulcers.

URTICARIA (See RARE DISEASES.)

URINARY TRACT INFECTION (See also BLADDER problems and CYSTITIS.)

Tip # 1: Ask your doctor if there are special money saving drug programs for your urinary tract infection.

How it works: Some pharmaceutical companies which sell medication for urinary tract infection guarantee the medication will work and offer free medicine if you have a re-occurrence of urinary infection within six months of using their drug. Also consider generic drugs. See also MEDICATION for money saving tips.

ULCERS (See IMMUNIZATIONS and specific diseases.)

VENEREAL DISEASES (VD) (See Sexually Transmitted Diseases.)

VENOUS DISORDERS (See LYMPHEDEMA.)

VITILIGO (See RARE DISEASES.)

VOCATIONAL REHABILITATION (See also DISABILITY and REHABILITATION.)

VOICE DISORDERS

Tip # 1: Contact organizations concerned with voice disorders for information and referral.

How it works: The following organizations offer information, referral, and support for people with voice disorders.

International Association of Laryngectomies
American Cancer Society

1599 Clifton Rd. NE
Atlanta, GA 30329
404-320-3333

American Speech-Language-Hearing Association
10801 Rockville Pike
Rockville, MD 20852
Phone: 1-800-638-TALK or 301-897-5700 TDD/ voice

American Academy of Otolaryngology
Head and Neck Surgery
One Prince St.
Alexandria, VA 22314
Phone 703-836-4444

Voice Foundation
1721 Pine St.
Philadelphia, PA 19103
Phone: 215-735-7999

VON GIERKE DISEASE (See RARE DISEASES.)

VON WILLEBRAND'S DISEASE (See RARE DISEASES.)

WALDMANN DISEASE (See RARE DISEASES.)

WALK-IN CLINICS (See also EMERGENCIES.)

Tip # 1: Choose a walk-in, minor emergency walk-in clinic now, before you need it. Ask if physicians there are paid a flat hourly fee or if they get a percentage of monthly charges.

How it works: A study from *The New England Journal of Medicine,* April 12, 1990, showed that fifteen physicians in one clinic changed their rate of ordering diagnostic tests when the clinic stopped paying them a flat rate and gave them a percentage of monthly charges. In the first three months after the change, physicians ordered 23% more laboratory tests per patient visit and 16% more X-rays. Choosing a clinic that pays a flat hourly rate may eliminate the incentive to order more or higher-priced tests.

WATER QUALITY

Tip # 1: Call the federal Environmental Protection Agency (EPA) Water Hotline at 1-800-426-4791 for information about water quality.

How it works: The EPA information specialists will answer individual questions about water quality, direct you to local sources of information about your local water quality, and send you printed information on such subjects as water filtering devices or lead in water.

WEGENER'S GRANULOMATOSIS (See RARE DISEASES.)

WIC (See also NUTRITION and FOOD STAMPS.)

Tip # 1: If you have young children or are pregnant and have a low income, contact the WIC (Women, Infants, and Children) program for free nutrition assessment and vouchers for free food.

How it works: WIC, funded by the federal government, provides vouchers weekly for free food for low-income pregnant women, infants, and children 5 and under, after a nutritional assessment is made by WIC staff. Mothers can exchange vouchers for foods such as milk, cheese, eggs, juice, and cereal for children and formula for infants. Vouchers are for certain quantities of products, for example, 8 ounces of cheese, and mothers can get any kind, even more expensive brands, in that quantity. Pregnant mothers also are eligible for food vouchers for themselves. To make appointments for a nutritional assessment and to apply for WIC assistance, call your local health department or Family and Children's Services. Take to the appointment recent employment check stubs, Medicaid card, or food stamps card, and other indication of income. WIC's dieticians will answer nutrition questions and help you plan your diet.

WILSON'S DISEASE (See RARE DISEASES.)

WISKOTT-ALDRICH SYNDROME (See RARE DISEASES.)

WOLF-HIRSCHORN SYNDROME (See RARE DISEASES.)

WOLFF-PARKINSON-WHITE SYNDROME (See RARE DISEASES.)

WOMEN'S HEALTH (See also BIRTH CONTROL, BREAST CANCER, BREAST FEEDING, BREAST IMPLANT, ENDOMETRIOSIS, FERTILITY, HYSTERECTOMY, MAMMOGRAM, OVARIAN CANCER, PAP, PMS, PREGNANCY, PREGNANCY UNWANTED, STDs.)

Tip # 1: Contact the National Women's Health Network.

How it works: The Network will send you for $5 a packet on health issues of concern to women. To order, call 202-347-1140.

WORKPLACE HEALTH (See OCCUPATIONAL HEALTH, VOCATIONAL REHABILITATION.)

WYBURN-MASON SYNDROME (See RARE DISEASES.)

X-LINKED JUVENILE RETINOSCHISIS (See RARE DISEASES.)

X-LINKED LYMPHOPROLIFERATIVE SYNDROME (See RARE DISEASES.)

XERODERMA PIGMENTOSUM (See RARE DISEASES.)

X-RAYS

Tip # 1: Take recent X-rays with you from one doctor to another so that you are not X-rayed twice for the same problem.

How it works: If you consult more than one doctor for the same problem, a primary physician and a specialist, for example, or two specialists for two opinions, each doctor will want X-rays. Have X-rays done only once, and carry them with you from doctor to doctor. It is better to ask for a duplicate of your X-rays so that if you lose them your doctor still has the originals.

Quality check: For this to work the X-rays must usually be recent and done for the same purpose as the current problem. Reducing the number of X-rays protects you from too much exposure to radiation.

Tip # 2: If your doctor owns X-ray equipment, question more closely the necessity for ordering X-rays for you.

How it works: Doctors who own their own X-ray equipment are more likely to order X-rays than doctors who do not own their own equipment, according to a study in the *New England Journal of Medicine* (December 1992). These doctors have paid for the equipment and they have an incentive to use it often and charge for it. The same study showed that these doctors also charged more for the tests than a radiologist does. An additional advantage of having X-rays ordered from a radiologist is that a specialist in radiology as well as your primary doctor will read them.

Quality check: The convenience of having an X-ray done in the doctor's office during your visit may outweigh possible savings. Also, some doctors may charge less for the office visit if they take X-rays themselves.

YAWS (See RARE DISEASES.)

YELLOW FEVER

Tip # 1: Call the Centers for Disease Control and Prevention (CDC) at 404-332-4555 for current information on yellow fever.

How it works: The CDC has very detailed, recorded information on malaria 24 hours a day including information on prevention, symptoms, diagnosis, treatment, and prevalence of yellow fever. To save money, call during low telephone rate hours. To receive written information on yellow fever and answers to other questions ONLY AFTER listening to the recorded information, call the CDC public inquiry number 404-639-3534 weekdays except federal holidays 8:30 a.m. to 5 p.m. Eastern time.

YELLOW NAIL SYNDROME (See RARE DISEASES.)

ZELLWEGER SYNDROME (See RARE DISEASES.)

ZOLLINGER-ELLISON SYNDROME (See RARE DISEASES.)

APPENDIX A

U. S. Senate Report on Aging

102d Congress }   **COMMITTEE PRINT**   { S. Prt.
2d Session   102–104

A STATUS REPORT:

ACCESSIBILITY AND AFFORDABILITY OF PRESCRIPTION DRUGS FOR OLDER AMERICANS (ANNOTATED)

(INCLUDES A DIRECTORY OF PHARMACEUTICAL MANUFACTURER INDIGENT PATIENT PROGRAMS)

A STAFF REPORT

OF THE

SPECIAL COMMITTEE ON AGING UNITED STATES SENATE

SEPTEMBER 1992

Serial No. 102–Q

This document has been printed for information purposes. It does not represent either findings or recommendations formally adopted by this committee.

U.S. GOVERNMENT PRINTING OFFICE

58–560   WASHINGTON : 1992

Drug	Manufacturer

A

Drug	Manufacturer
Activase	Genentech
Actimmune	Genentech
Adriamycin PFS	Adria
Adrucil	Adria
Aldactazide	Searle
Aldactone	Searle
Aldomet	Merck
Alupent	Boehringer
Anaprox	Syntex
Ansaid	Upjohn
Antivert	Pfizer #1
Anusol HC	Parke-Davis
Apresoline	Ciba-Geigy
Aralen	Sanofi-Winthrop
Atrovent	Boehringer
Axid	Eli Lilly
Augmentin	SmithKline #1
AZT (Retrovir)	Burroughs-Wellcome

B

Drug	Manufacturer
Bactrim	Hoffman-LaRoche
Bactrim DS	Hoffman-LaRoche
Bactroban	SmithKline #1
Beconase	Glaxo
Beconase AQ	Glaxo
BICNU	Bristol-Myers #3
Blenoxane	Bristol-Myers #3
Bucaldin-S	ICI/Stuart
BuSpar	Bristol-Myers #1

C

Drug	Manufacturer
Calan	Searle
Calan SR	Searle
Capoten	Bristol-Myers #2
Capozide	Bristol-Myers #2
Carafate	Marion Merrell Dow
Cardene	Syntex
Cardizem	Marion Merrell Dow
Cardizem CD	Marion Merrell Dow
Cardizem SR	Marion Merrell Dow
Cardura	Pfizer #1
Carnitor	Sigma Tau
Catapres	Boehringer
Ceclor	Eli Lilly

Drug	Manufacturer
CEENU	Bristol-Myers #3
Ceftin	Glaxo
Cefzil	Bristol-Myers #1
Clinoril	Merck
Clozaril	Sandoz
Cogentin	Merck
Compazine	SmithKline #1
Cordarone	Wyeth-Ayerst
Corgard	Bristol-Myers #2
Corzide	Bristol-Myers #3
Coumadin	Du Pont Merck
Cyclospasmol	Wyeth-Ayerst
Cytotec	Searle
Cytovene	Syntex
Cytoxan	Bristol-Myers #3

D

Drug	Manufacturer
Dalmane	Hoffman-LaRoche
Danocrine	Sanofi-Winthrop
Dantrium	Norwich-Eaton
Desyrel	Bristol-Myers #1
Diabinese	Pfizer #1
Dilantin	Parke-Davis
Diflucan	Pfizer #2
Diprolene	Schering-Plough
Diprosone	Schering-Plough
Dolobid	Merck
Duricef	Bristol-Myers #1
Dyazide	SmithKline #1
Dymelor	Eli Lilly

E

Drug	Manufacturer
E–Mycin	Upjohn
Efudex (Fluorouracil Injection)	Hoffman-LaRoche
Eldepryl	Sandoz
Eminase	SmithKline #2
Epogen	Amgen
Ergamisol	Johnson and Johnson
Estrace	Bristol-Myers #1
Eulexin	Schering-Plough

F

Drug	Manufacturer
Flexeril	Merck
FML	Allergan
Folex	Adria

Drug	Manufacturer
Fulvicin	Schering-Plough

G

Glucotrol	Pfizer #1

H

Halcion	Upjohn
HMS	Allergan

I

Idamycin	Adria
Ifex	Bristol-Myers #3
Imuran	Burroughs-Wellcome
Indocin	Merck
Insulin Products	Eli Lilly
Interferon-A Recombinant	Hoffman-LaRoche
Intron-A	Schering-Plough
Isordil	Wyeth-Ayerst

K

K-Lyte	Bristol-Myers #1
Keflex	Eli Lilly
Kerlone	Searle
Kinesed	ICI/Stuart
Klonopin	Hoffman-LaRoche
Klotrix	Bristol-Myers #1

L

Lanoxin	Burroughs-Wellcome
Leukine	Immunex
Librium	Hoffman-LaRoche
Limbritol	Hoffman-LaRoche
Lindane Lotion/Shampoo	Reed and Carnrick
Lioresal	Ciba-Geigy
Lithobid	Ciba-Geigy
Lo/Ovral	Wyeth-Ayerst
Lopressor	Ciba-Geigy
Lotrimin	Schering-Plough
Lotrisone	Schering-Plough
Lyophilized Cytoxan	Bristol-Myers #3
Lysodren	Bristol-Myers #3

M

Macrodantin	Norwich-Eaton
Medrol	Upjohn

Drug	Manufacturer
Megace	Bristol-Myers #3
Mesnex	Bristol-Myers #3
Micronase	Upjohn
Minipress	Pfizer #1
Minizide	Pfizer #1
Monopril	Bristol-Myers #3
Motrin	Upjohn
Mycostatin	Bristol-Myers #1

N

Naphcon-A	Allergan
Naprosyn	Syntex
Nasalide	Syntex
Natalins RX	Bristol-Myers #1
NebuPent	Fujisawa
Neosar	Adria
Neupogen	Amgen
Nicorette	Marion Merrell Dow
Nitrodisc	Searle
Nolvadex	ICI/Stuart
Nordette	Wyeth-Ayerst
Normodyne	Schering-Plough
Norpace	Searle
Norpace CR	Searle
Noroxin	Merck
Norplant System	Wyeth-Ayerst

O

Oculinium	Allergan
Optimine	Schering-Plough
Orinase	Upjohn
Orudis	Wyeth-Ayerst
Ovcon	Bristol-Myers #1

P

Paraplatin	Bristol-Myers #3
Parlodel	Sandoz
Pavabid	Marion Merrell Dow
Pepcid	Merck
Periactin	Merck
Persantine	Boehringer
Pilogan	Allergan
Platinol	Bristol-Myers #3
Plendil	Merck
Ponstel	Parke-Davis

Drug	Manufacturer
Pravochol	Bristol-Myers #2
Premarin	Wyeth-Ayerst
Prilosec	Merck
Prinivil	Merck
Procan	Parke-Davis
Procan SR	Parke-Davis
Procardia	Pfizer #1
Procardia XL	Pfizer #1
Procrit	Johnson and Johnson
Prokine	Hoechst-Roussel
Pronestyl SR	Bristol-Myers #2
Propine	Allergan
Protropin	Genentech
Proventil	Schering-Plough
Provera	Upjohn
Prozac	Eli Lilly
Pyridium	Parke-Davis

Q

Drug	Manufacturer
Questran Light	Bristol-Myers #2
Quinamm	Marion Merrell Dow

R

Drug	Manufacturer
Relafen	SmithKline #1
Rocaltrol	Hoffman-LaRoche
Rocephin	Hoffman-LaRoche

S

Drug	Manufacturer
Sandimmune	Sandoz
Sandoglobulin	Sandoz
Sandostatin	Sandoz
Sectral	Wyeth-Ayerst
Septra DS	Burroughs-Wellcome
Seldane	Marion Merrell Dow
Seldane D	Marion Merrell Dow
Sinemet	Du Pont Merck
Sinemet CR	Du Pont Merck
Sorbitrate	ICI/Stuart
Survanta	Abbott
Symmetrel	Du Pont Merck
Synalar	Syntex
Synemol	Syntex

T

Drug	Manufacturer
Tagamet	SmithKline #1

Drug	Manufacturer
Tarabine	Adria
Tenormin	ICI/Stuart
Tenoretic	ICI/Stuart
TheraCys	Connaught Labs
Timolol	Merck
Timoptic	Merck
Tofranil	Ciba-Geigy
Trandate	Glaxo
Triostat	SmithKline #2
Triphasil	Wyeth-Ayerst

V

Drug	Manufacturer
Vagistat	Bristol-Myers #1
Valium	Hoffman-LaRoche
Vasodilan	Bristol-Myers #2
Vasoretic	Merck
Vasotec	Merck
VePesid	Bristol-Myers #3
Videx	Bristol-Myers #4
Vincasar	Adria
Voltaren	Ciba-Geigy

W

Drug	Manufacturer
Wellcovorin	Burroughs-Wellcome
Winstrol	Sanofi-Winthrop
Wytensin	Wyeth-Ayerst

X

Drug	Manufacturer
Xanax	Upjohn

Z

Drug	Manufacturer
Zantac	Glaxo
Zarontin	Parke-Davis
Zestril	ICI/Stuart
Zestoretic	ICI/Stuart
Zithromax	Pfizer #1
Zoloft	Pfizer #1
Zovirax	Burroughs-Wellcome
Zyloprim	Burroughs-Wellcome

APPENDIX

Directory of Pharmaceutical Manufacturer Indigent Patient Programs

---

ABBOTT LABORATORIES/ROSS LABORATORIES

(Pharmaceutical Products Division)

CONTACT FOR THE PROGRAM:

Survanta Lifeline
Medical Technology Hotlines
555 13th Street NW Suite 7E
Washington, DC 20004–1109

202–637–6889
202–637–6690 (FAX)

PROGRAM CHARACTERISTICS

(a) The pharmaceutical products which are covered:

The product covered under this program is Survanta. Abbott has other pharmaceutical products, but did not indicate whether these are covered under an indigent patient program.

(b) The quantity of the product which can be obtained at any one time:

A complete course of therapy is covered (usually 1 to 4 vials), which depends on the patient's condition.

(c) The patient eligibility criteria that have to be met:

The patient cannot have public or private insurance coverage, or HMO coverage.

(d) To whom the products are sent for distribution to the patient:

The hospitals are reimbursed for product used for qualifying patients.

(e) The specific forms that have to be completed, if any, to be enrolled in the program, and from whom the forms are obtained:

Hospitals are sent the enrollment form after calling the Survanta Lifeline, 1–800–922–3255.

(f) How refills for the products are obtained:

The product is an acute-use hospital product; therefore, refills are extremely unlikely.

(g) Restrictions on the use of the program:

Must be used on qualifying patients, consistent with approved labeling.

(h) Any copayments or cost-sharing that the company requires from the patient:

None.

NUMBER OF PATIENTS SERVED BY THE PROGRAM

Immediately following FDA approval of the drug, 13 hospitals enrolled in the program. Abbott did not provide data concerning the number of patients that benefited from the program.

ADDITIONAL COMMENTS

The company indicated that it is in the process of developing an indigent patient program for Biaxin (Clarithromycin). However, at the time of publication of this directory, the program was not yet in effect. The company had established the Clarithromycin Information Line, 1–800–688–9118.

Under the proposed program, the drug would be available for an initial supply of 90 days of treatment. Additional quantities would be available upon completion by a physician of a case report form and financial requalification form. In order to qualify, the program would require that the patient have an annual income of less than $25,000, be a single person, have no dependents, have no insurance coverage, be ineligible for Medicaid, or have applied, but not yet enrolled in the State Medicaid program.

———

ADRIA LABORATORIES, INC.

CONTACT FOR THE PROGRAM:

Adria Laboratories Patient Assistance Program
P.O. Box 16529
Columbus, OH 43215–6529

614–764–8100
614–764–8102 (FAX)

PROGRAM CHARACTERISTICS

(a) The pharmaceutical products which are covered:

The company reported that the following products are covered by this program: Adriamycin PFS, Adrucil, Folex, Idamycin, Neosar, Tarabine, and Vincasar.

(b) The quantity of the product which can be obtained at any one time:

Two months' supply.

(c) The patient eligibility criteria that have to be met:

Physician must certify that patient is unable to afford the cost of the drug, and is unable to obtain assistance elsewhere.

(d) To whom the products are sent for distribution to the patient:

Physician.

(e) The specific forms that have to be completed, if any, to be enrolled in the program, and from whom the forms are obtained:

An initial request letter must be received from the treating physician containing the following information: patient's name, drug requested, intended dose and treatment schedule, primary diagnosis, and a statement that the patient cannot afford drug requested and cannot obtain reimbursement elsewhere. A serial-numbered one-page application form is sent to the physician.

(f) How refills for the products are obtained:

Submission of certificate form.

(g) Restrictions on the use of the program:

1. Program is available to patients of physicians who purchase Adria oncology products; 2. Intended use of the product must be within the scope of the package insert; 3. Drugs are to be used only within the United States.

(h) Any copayments or cost-sharing that the company requires from the patient:

None required of the patient. However, Adria requests that the treating physician provide his or her services for administration of the drug at no charge to the patient.

The company estimates that the program serves about 700 people each year, but could not provide any additional data.

ALLERGAN PRESCRIPTION PHARMACEUTICALS

CONTACT FOR THE PROGRAM:

Judy McGee

1–800–347–4500 Ext. 6219

PROGRAM CHARACTERISTICS

(a) The pharmaceutical products which are covered:

All Allergan prescription products are covered, which include Naphcon A, Propine, FML, HMS, and Pilogan.

(b) The quantity of the product which can be obtained at any one time:

Course of therapy, up to a maximum of 6 months' supply.

(c) The patient eligibility criteria that have to be met:

Eligibility criteria is at the physician's discretion.

(d) To whom the products are sent for distribution to the patient:

Products are distributed to prescribing physician via prescription request.

(e) The specific forms that have to be completed, if any, to be enrolled in the program, and from whom the forms are obtained:

No formal enrollment is required.

(f) How refills for the products are obtained:

Refills can be obtained from the prescribing physician's office.

(g) Restrictions on the use of the program:

Eligibility criteria is at the physician's request.

(h) Any copayments or cost-sharing that the company requires from the patient:

None.

The company does not require any formal enrollment, and could not supply any information about the number of patients enrolled in its program.

ADDITIONAL COMMENTS SUPPLIED BY THE PROGRAM

Allergan also has a program that supplies Oculinum (Botulinum Toxin Type A) free of charge to patients that meet certain eligibility criteria. Eligibility forms are to be completed by the physician and patient (1 page each) and are obtained by contacting Lloyd Glenn or Brian Visconti at the Allergan office in Irvine, CA (714–752–4500, FAX: 714–752–4214). To be eligible, the patient must have income of $12,000 or less for a one or two person household, $19,000 or less for three or more person household, and no insurance of any type. The product is sent to the physician for distribution to the patient.

———

AMGEN, INC.

CONTACT FOR THE PROGRAM:

Amgen Safety Net Programs

Medical Technology Hotlines

1–800–272–9376

(637–6688: Washington, DC)

PROGRAM CHARACTERISTICS

(a) The pharmaceutical products which are covered:

Both of the company's currently marketed products are covered under this program: Epogen and Neupogen.

(b) Amgen has two programs:

An Uninsured Patient Program and a Variable Cap Program.

Uninsured Patient Program

1. Covers anemic patients on dialysis receiving Epogen who:
   • Have an annual gross family income of less than $25,000; and

   • Have no, and are ineligible for, health insurance for dialysis or for Epogen (except for State kidney programs, county or charitable funds).

Amgen provides free replacement product.

2. Covers patients receiving Neupogen for a medically appropriate application who:

- Have an annual gross family income of less than $25,000; and

- Have no, and are ineligible for, medical insurance.

Amgen provides free replacement product.

Variable Cap Program

1. Covers anemic patients on dialysis receiving Epogen who:

- Have an annual gross family income of less than $50,000;

- May have medical insurance; and

- Incur significant financial liabilities for Epogen relative to income.

After the patient's documented financial liabilities for Epogen exceed a percentage of the patient's gross family income, Amgen provides free replacement product.

Patient's financial liabilities for Epogen are capped at a level which varies with patients' annual gross family income.

2. Covers patients receiving Neupogen for a medically appropriate application who:

- Have an annual gross family income of less than $50,000;

- May have medical insurance; and

- Incur significant financial liabilities for Neupogen relative to income.

After the patient's documented financial liabilities for Neupogen exceed a percentage of the patient's gross family income, Amgen provides free replacement product.

Patients' financial liabilities for Neupogen are capped at a level which varies with patients' annual gross family income.

Quantities Provided: Generally, 1 months' supply of Epogen and one treatment cycle of Neupogen are provided per shipment at the health care provider's request.

Additional Requirements of the Safety Net Program: Patients must receive Epogen or Neupogen from qualified health care providers who purchase Epogen or Neupogen and who enroll in the Safety Net Program by providing the required information. Eligibility is determined on a calendar-year basis, and patients must reapply each year if they require treatment in consecutive years. Special consideration may be given families facing extraordinary circumstances.

The company stated that since June 1989, the Epogen program has helped over 530 patients, and in the first 10 months since approval, the Neupogen program has helped over 100 patients.

ASTRA PHARMACEUTICALS, INC.

CONTACT FOR THE PROGRAM:

Linda Braun, Research Coordinator

FAIR Program (Foscavir Assistance and Information on Reimbursement)

State and Federal Associates

1–800–488–3247

703–683–2239 (FAX)

PROGRAM CHARACTERISTICS

(a) The pharmaceutical products which are covered:

The pharmaceutical product covered under this program is Foscavir (Foscarnet Sodium). The company did not indicate whether its other pharmaceutical products are covered under an indigent patient program.

(b) The quantity of the product which can be obtained at any one time:

One months' supply of Foscavir.

(c) The patient eligibility criteria that have to be met:

Patient's income must be below $27,500 if there are no dependents; income must be below $45,000 with dependents.

(d) To whom the products are sent for distribution to the patient:

The physician's office, hospital pharmacy, or home health agency.

(e) The specific forms that have to be completed, if any, to be enrolled in the program, and from whom the forms are obtained:

Forms (called the ''Foscavir Patient Assistance Program Qualification Form'') are obtained from the FAIR program analyst.

(f) How refills for the products are obtained:

Physician must contact FAIR program analyst at number above.

(g) Restrictions on the use of the program:

Contact FAIR analyst for any specifics at number listed above.

(h) Any copayments or cost-sharing that the company requires from the patient:

None.

The program began in October 1991. Through the end of the 1991, 17 patients were covered under the program.

BOEHRINGER INGLEHEIM PHARMACEUTICALS, INC.

CONTACT FOR THE PROGRAM:

Sam Quy

203–798–4131

PROGRAM CHARACTERISTICS

(a) The pharmaceutical products which are covered:

All Boehringer Ingleheim pharmaceutical products are covered, which include Persantine, Atrovent, Alupent, and Catapres. Prelu–2 is a controlled substance and not covered under an indigent patient program.

(b) The quantity of the product which can be obtained at any one time:

One or 2 months' supply.

(c) The patient eligibility criteria that have to be met:

Patient must be on a fixed income.

(d) To whom the products are sent for distribution to the patient:

Physician.

(e) The specific forms that have to be completed, if any, to be enrolled in the program, and from whom the forms are obtained:

A letter from the patient's physician, indicating the reason and attesting to the fact that they are indigent. (Must indicate that the patient has a fixed income and/or no insurance coverage.) The company indicated that it preferred to have a social services recommendation.

(f) How refills for the products are obtained:

A written prescription must be made for each request.

(g) Restrictions on the use of the program:

The company indicated that it will discontinue providing the service if the physician does not ask for each shipment, or if the patient's situation improves.

(h) Any copayments or cost-sharing that the company requires from the patient:

None.

NUMBER OF PATIENTS SERVED BY THE PROGRAM

The company was unable to provide data on the number of patients served by the program.

BRISTOL-MYERS SQUIBB #1

(General Indigent Patient Program)

CONTACT FOR THE PROGRAM:
Bristol-Myers Squibb
Indigent Patient Program
P.O. Box 9445
McLean, VA 22102–9998
1–800–736–0003
703–760–0049 (FAX)

PROGRAM CHARACTERISTICS

(a) The pharmaceutical products which are covered:

The company indicated that the following pharmaceutical products are covered under this program: Duricef, Cefzil, BuSpar, Desyrel, Estrace, Ovcon–35, Ovcon–50, Natalins, Natalins RX, Vagistat–1, Mycostatin.

(b) The quantity of the product which can be obtained at any one time:

Three months' supply.

(c) The patient eligibility criteria that have to be met:

Physician's request.

(d) To whom the products are sent for distribution to the patient:

Physician.

(e) The specific forms that have to be completed, if any, to be enrolled in the program, and from whom the forms are obtained:

Forms available from the company sales representative.

(f) How refills for the products are obtained:

By physician prescription every 3 months.

(g) Restrictions on the use of the program:

The program is not designed to reimburse hospitals for uncompensated inpatient care. However, any physician that is willing to follow a patient on an ongoing basis in the outpatient setting may enroll in the program.

(h) Any copayments or cost-sharing that the company requires from the patient:

None.

NUMBER OF PATIENTS SERVED BY THE PROGRAM

The company indicates that the program served about 1,440 patients in 1989, 1,760 patients in 1990, and 2,836 patients in 1991.

———

BRISTOL-MYERS SQUIBB #2

(Cardiovascular Access Program)

CONTACT FOR THE PROGRAM:

Cardiovascular Access Program
P.O. Box 9445
McLean, VA 22102–9998
1–800–736–0003
703–760–0049 (FAX)

PROGRAM CHARACTERISTICS

(a) The pharmaceutical products which are covered:

This program provides access to the company's cardiovascular products, which include Capoten, Capozide, Corgard, Klotrix, K–Lyte, Monopril, Naturetin, Pravochol, Pronestyl–SR, Questran Light, Rauzide, Saluron, Salutensin, Vasodilan, and Betapen–VK.

(b) The quantity of the product which can be obtained at any one time:

Three months' supply.

(c) The patient eligibility criteria that have to be met:

First, the patient must work through an enrolled physician. Second, the patient must not be eligible for other sources of drug coverage. Third, the patient must be deemed financially eligible, as determined by a "means" and "liquid assets" test.

(d) To whom the products are sent for distribution to the patient:

Product is shipped to enrolled physicians.

(e) The specific forms that have to be completed, if any, to be enrolled in the program, and from whom the forms are obtained:

Physician enrollment forms can be obtained from the company's sales representatives. An application form must be completed for each individual patient. This is sent to the physician after the patient calls 1–800–763–0003 and is screened for third-party coverage eligibility.

(f) How refills for the products are obtained:

When the 90-day supply of product is near an end, the program will send a letter to the physician asking the physician to sign a renewal card if the patient requires the drug for an additional 90 days. The physician must return the renewal card with a valid prescription. Upon receipt of a renewal prescription, the company sends the product refill to the physician. Patients must re-apply to the program every 6 months.

(g) Restrictions on the use of the program:

The program is not designed to reimburse hospitals for uncompensated inpatient care. However, any physician that is willing to follow a patient on an ongoing basis in the outpatient setting may enroll in the program.

(h) Any copayments or cost-sharing that the company requires from the patient:

None.

NUMBER OF PATIENTS SERVED BY THE PROGRAM

The company indicates that the program, which began in March 1992, has enrolled 6,600 physicians. The company did not provide any information on the number of patients that have been served.

BRISTOL-MYERS SQUIBB #3

(Cancer Patient Access Program)

CONTACT FOR THE PROGRAM:

Bristol-Myers Squibb
Cancer Patient Access Program
P.O. Box 9445
McLean, VA 22102–9998
1–800–736–0003
703–760–0049 (FAX)

PROGRAM CHARACTERISTICS

(a) The pharmaceutical products which are covered:

The company indicated that the following cancer drugs are covered under this program: BICNU, CEENU, Lysodren, Mutamycin, Mycostatin Pastilles, Paraplatin, Platinol, Platinol–AQ, VePesid, Blenoxance, Cytoxan, Lyophilized Cytoxan, Ifex, Mesnex, and Megace.

(b) The quantity of the product which can be obtained at any one time:

Three months' supply.

(c) The patient eligibility criteria that have to be met:

Physician's assessment of patient's financial need and confirmation by local sales representative.

(d) To whom the products are sent for distribution to the patient:

Physician.

(e) The specific forms that have to be completed, if any, to be enrolled in the program, and from whom the forms are obtained:

Form available from company sales representative.

(f) How refills for the products are obtained:

By physician prescription every 3 months.

(g) Restrictions on the use of the program:

The program is not designed to reimburse hospitals for uncompensated inpatient care. However, any physician that is willing to follow a patient on an ongoing basis in the outpatient setting may enroll in the program.

(h) Any copayments or cost-sharing that the company requires from the patient:

None.

The company indicated that the program served about 3,000 patients in 1989, 3,152 patients in 1990, and 3,432 patients in 1991.

_____

BRISTOL-MYERS SQUIBB #4

(Videx Assistance Program)

CONTACT FOR THE PROGRAM:

Videx Temporary Assistance Program

1–800–788–0123

703–760–0049 (FAX)

PROGRAM CHARACTERISTICS

(a) The pharmaceutical products which are covered:

Videx (Didanosine).

(b) The quantity of the product which can be obtained at any one time:

One months' supply.

(c) The patient eligibility criteria that have to be met:

The patient must not be eligible for other sources of drug coverage and deemed financially eligible, as determined by a "means" and "liquid assets" test.

(d) To whom the products are sent for distribution to the patient:

Physician.

(e) The specific forms that have to be completed, if any, to be enrolled in the program, and from whom the forms are obtained:

The physician must complete a patient/physician enrollment form, which is then sent to the physician after the physician or patient calls the toll-free number (1–800–788–1023) and is screened for third-party drug coverage eligibility.

(f) How refills for the products are obtained:

Each month after the initial shipment, renewal cards are mailed to the physician. In response, the physician must return a valid prescription. Upon receipt of the renewal prescription, the company sends the next month's supply of Videx to the physician. The patient and the physician must reapply to the program every 3 months.

(g) Restrictions on the use of the program:

The program is not designed to reimburse hospitals for uncompensated inpatient care. However, any physician that is willing to follow a patient on an ongoing basis in the outpatient setting may enroll in the program.

(h) Any copayments or cost-sharing that the company requires from the patient:

None.

NUMBER OF PATIENTS SERVED BY THE PROGRAM

Videx was approved by the FDA in October 1991, and through the end of 1991, the company indicated that 75 patients were served by this program.

BURROUGHS-WELLCOME

CONTACT FOR THE PROGRAM:

Jonas B. Daugherty

Manager, Professional Information Services

Burroughs-Wellcome Co.

3030 Cornwallis Road

Research Triangle Park, NC 27709

919–248–4418

919–248–0421 (FAX)

1–800–722–9294 (Program Enrollment)

or

Bernard Streed

Supervisor, Special Projects

Burroughs-Wellcome Co.

Patient Assistance Program

P.O. Box 52035

Phoenix, AZ 85072–9349

602–494–8725

602–996–7731, 7732 (FAX)

1–800–722–9294 (Program Enrollment)

(a) The pharmaceutical products which are covered:

All Burroughs-Wellcome products are covered by the program, which include Septra, Septra DS, Lanoxin, AZT (Retrovir), Zovirax, Zyloprim, Imuran, and Wellcovorin.

(b) The quantity of the product which can be obtained at any one time:

The products are available in a 30-day supply, with a maximum of 90 days therapy.

(c) The patient eligibility criteria that have to be met:

1. Gross monthly income must be less than 200 percent of Federal poverty guidelines.

2. All applications will be reviewed within established criteria and on a case-by-case basis.

3. Patients must be residents of the United States.

4. All alternative funding sources must be investigated.

5. All required information must be provided for consideration of eligibility.

6. Patients may be approved (occasionally) by exception if extreme extenuating circumstances exist.

(d) To whom the products are sent for distribution to the patient:

Products are provided to the patients by local pharmacist.

(e) The specific forms that have to be completed, if any, to be enrolled in the program, and from whom the forms are obtained:

No forms are necessary for the original prescription; however, physicians are required to provide a completed, signed application form from an enrollment package. Subsequent refills are not available until the completed package is received.

(f) How refills for the products are obtained:

Physician request.

(g) Restrictions on the use of the program:

The company has placed a $10 million annual cap on available benefits.

(h) Any copayments or cost-sharing that the company requires from the patient:

None.

According to the company, over 10,000 patients have received free drugs through a variety of programs, including Investigational New Drug (IND) programs. The company could not provide more specific data about the number of patients currently served by the program.

CIBA-GEIGY CORPORATION, PHARMACEUTICALS DIVISION

CONTACT FOR THE PROGRAM:

Jackie Laguardia
Senior Information Assistant
Ciba-Geigy Corporation
556 Morris Avenue
Summit, NJ 07901
908–277–5849

PROGRAM CHARACTERISTICS

(a) The pharmaceutical products which are covered:

According to the company, through its Patient Support Program, Ciba-Geigy's policy is that any patients who are unable to afford their products can receive a free supply of the drug. The company's products include Lopressor, Lioresal, Lithobid, Voltaren, Brethine, Tofranil, and Apresoline. Ritalin and Rimactane are controlled substances and not available under this program.

(b) The quantity of the product which can be obtained at any one time:

Up to 3 months' supply.

(c) The patient eligibility criteria that have to be met:

To become eligible for the Ciba-Geigy Patient Support Program, the company requires the following:

1. The physician must attest to the patient's lack of third-party reimbursement and the financial inability to purchase the product.

2. The physician must complete an application form and include a completed prescription.

3. The completed prescription must include the patient's name and an indication that the medication will be accepted without a safety closure.

4. The medication is sent to the physician's office.

5. To continue receiving the medication, the company requires a new prescription and application every 3 months. There are no automatic refills.

(d) To whom the products are sent for distribution to the patient:

Physician.

(e) The specific forms that have to be completed, if any, to be enrolled in the program, and from whom the forms are obtained:

The form can be obtained by contacting the person listed above or the company's sales representative.

(f) How refills for the products are obtained:

After completing an application form, the physician can obtain an initial 3 months' supply for the patient. Physician must reapply every 3 months by submitting a new application and prescription.

(g) Restrictions on the use of the program:

As indicated above.

(h) Any copayments or cost-sharing that the company requires from the patient:

None.

NUMBER OF PATIENTS SERVED BY THE PROGRAM

According to the company, between January 1991 and March 1992, it had provided 1,100 patients with approximately 2,300 prescriptions free of charge.

CONNAUGHT LABORATORIES, INC.

CONTACT FOR THE PROGRAM:

David Hunt
Product Manager
Connaught Laboratories, Inc.
Route 611, P.O. Box 187
Swiftwater, PA 18370–0187
717–839–4617

(a) The pharmaceutical products which are covered:

The company reports that the only product covered under an indigent patient program is TheraCys (BCG live intravesical for the treatment of carcinoma in situ of the urinary bladder).

(b) The quantity of the product which can be obtained at any one time:

At the physician's discretion, the company provides for a full course of therapy—the induction and maintenance doses—which may be as many as 11 doses (6 for induction and 5 for maintenance).

(c) The patient eligibility criteria that have to be met:

Patient cannot be insured, be ineligible for Medicare or Medicaid, and in the physician's best judgment, is unable to afford the treatment.

(d) To whom the products are sent for distribution to the patient:

Physician.

(e) The specific forms that have to be completed, if any, to be enrolled in the program, and from whom the forms are obtained:

The company must receive a note on physician's letterhead confirming that the patient is unable to afford treatment, is uninsured, and is ineligible for Medicare or Medicaid. The patient must also be diagnosed with CIS, the only approved indication for the drug.

(f) How refills for the products are obtained:

Not applicable.

(g) Restrictions on the use of the program:

In addition to the patient's meeting the above criteria, the physician must agree that the drug will not be sold, traded, or used for any other purpose than to treat the patient.

(h) Any copayments or cost-sharing that the company requires from the patient:

None.

NUMBER OF PATIENTS SERVED BY THE PROGRAM

Since January 1992, the company reports that 5 patients have received the drug under the program.

The company does not have an indigent patient program for its flu vaccine because it stated virtually all State and many county and city health departments offer the vaccine to high-risk patients free of charge.

DU PONT MERCK

CONTACT FOR THE PROGRAM:

Du Pont Merck Pharmaceuticals
Barley Mill Plaza
P.O. Box 80027
Wilmington, DE 19880–0027

PROGRAM CHARACTERISTICS

(a) The pharmaceutical products which are covered:

The company reports that all Du Pont Merck retail oral solid pharmaceutical products are covered under this program. These include Coumadin, Sinemet, Sinemet CR, and Symmetrel. The program does not cover the company's controlled substances, which includes Percodan and Percocet.

(b) The quantity of the product which can be obtained at any one time:

Thirty days' supply.

(c) The patient eligibility criteria that have to be met:

The patient must be indigent and cannot be eligible for a Federal or State Government pharmaceutical assistance program.

(d) To whom the products are sent for distribution to the patient:

Physician.

(e) The specific forms that have to be completed, if any, to be enrolled in the program, and from whom the forms are obtained:

Physicians can request free medications by written request accompanied by a signed and dated prescription and a letter stating the financial status and need of the patient. Form letters and multiple requests are not honored. Samples are given to the patient at the discretion of the physician.

(f) How refills for the products are obtained:

Does not provide for automatic refills, but will permit refills with appropriate documentation from the patient's physician.

(g) Restrictions on the use of the program:

As stated above.

(h) Any copayments or cost sharing that the company requires from the patient:

None indicated by the company.

NUMBER OF PATIENTS SERVED BY THE PROGRAM

The company just began its program in 1991, and was unable to determine the number of patients that had been served by the program.

FUJISAWA PHARMACEUTICAL COMPANY

CONTACT FOR THE PROGRAM:

Richard G. White
NebuPent Patient Assistance Program
Fujisawa Pharmaceutical Company
Parkway North Center
3 Parkway North
Deerfield, IL 60015
708–317–8638
708–317–5941 (FAX)
1–800–366–6323 (Reimbursement Hotline)

PROGRAM CHARACTERISTICS

(a) The pharmaceutical products which are covered:

NubuPent (pentamidine isethionate)

(b) The quantity of the product which can be obtained at any one time:

NebuPent is made available to nonprofit clinics who administer the drug, rather than directly to users. The quantity of NebuPent that is provided to eligible organizations is based upon the number of HIV-infected individuals that the organization cares for that require assistance.

(c) The patient eligibility criteria that have to be met:

The NebuPent Patient Assistance Program provides the drug based on organization-specific criteria, for administration to persons who are indigent. The health care organization, once it receives a donation, is responsible for determining which of its patients qualify for assistance. Fujisawa does not set income or asset criteria.

(d) To whom the products are sent for distribution to the patient:

All product is sent directly to the health care organization; no product is sent directly to the patient.

(e) The specific forms that have to be completed, if any, to be enrolled in the program, and from whom the forms are obtained:

A nonprofit organization interested in participating in the program should contact Richard G. White at the number and address provided above. Once the company receives a written letter of inquiry from an organization on the program, a questionnaire is sent to the organization. Upon receipt of the complete questionnaire, the company supplies a contract that:

1. Specifies the number of vials to be donated;

2. States that the product will be administered as per labeling;

3. States that the product will be stored appropriately; and

4. Contains other provisions.

Once the contract is returned, the drug is shipped.

(f) How refills for the products are obtained:

Users of the drug would deal directly with the participating clinics on the mechanisms of how subsequent administrations would be scheduled. Additional donations of NebuPent to organizations that have previously received product under the program are reviewed by Fujisawa on a case-by-case basis.

(g) Restrictions on the use of the program:

The agreement with the providing organizations contains various restrictions to assure that they are tax-exempt organizations and will utilize the drug properly. The program has no restrictions applicable to patients other than broad eligibility requirement of indigency.

(h) Any copayments or cost-sharing that the company requires from the patient:

None.

According to the company, because the program is not "patient-specific," the company does not know how many patients have used the 14,150 vials donated to the program to date.

ADDITIONAL COMMENTS PROVIDED BY THE COMPANY

Fujisawa operates a Reimbursement Hotline (1–800–366–6323) that informs third-party payers, physicians, patients, and other interested persons about current reimbursement policies related to NebuPent.

GENENTECH, INC.

CONTACT FOR THE PROGRAM:

Genentech Reimbursement Information Program
Mailstop #99
c/o Genentech, Inc.
460 Point San Bruno Blvd
S. San Francisco, CA 94080
1–800–879–4747

PROGRAM CHARACTERISTICS

(a) The pharmaceutical products which are covered:

The company reports that its three currently marketed products are covered under the program: Protropin (Human Growth Hormone), Activase (TPA, Tissue Plasminogen Activator), and Actimmune (Interferon Gamma–1b).

(b) The quantity of the product which can be obtained at any one time:

Company reports that quantity provided is variable.

(c) The patient eligibility criteria that have to be met:

The company reports that its eligibility criteria are variable. Generally, patients are asked to provide sufficiently detailed information to assure the company that they are uninsured and cannot afford the required payments. (For Activase: If an uninsured patient has gross family income of $25,000 or less, the company provides replacement product to the hospital.).

(d) To whom the products are sent for distribution to the patient:

The distribution point depends upon the product. The distribution of Activase is to hospital pharmacies. The other two products are sent directly to the patient.

(e) The specific forms that have to be completed, if any, to be enrolled in the program, and from whom the forms are obtained:

The company does have a form for its uninsured patient program, which can be obtained directly from Genentech. Initial contact should be made with the company by the treating physician.

(f) How refills for the products are obtained:

Refills are not applicable for Activase. The procedure for obtaining continued coverage for the company's other drugs varies with the nature of the patient's financial situation.

(g) Restrictions on the use of the program:

None.

(h) Any copayments or cost-sharing that the company requires from the patient:

Depends upon the individual patient situation.

NUMBER OF PATIENTS SERVED BY THE PROGRAM

From 1986 through 1991, the company reports that 3,257 patients participated in the Human Growth Hormone program and 2,505 patients participated in the TPA program.

GLAXO, INC.

CONTACT FOR THE PROGRAM:

Laura J. Newberry
Supervisor, Trade Communications
Glaxo, Inc.
P.O. Box 13438
Research Triangle Park, NC 27709
1–800–GLAXO77
919–248–7932 (FAX)

PROGRAM CHARACTERISTICS

(a) The pharmaceutical products which are covered:

According to the company, all Glaxo pharmaceutical products are covered, which include Zantac, Ceftin, Ventolin, Beconase, Beconase AQ, and Trandate.

(b) The quantity of the product which can be obtained at any one time:

Maximum 3 months' supply.

(c) The patient eligibility criteria that have to be met:

Patient must be a private outpatient who the physician considers medically indigent and is not eligible for any other third-party reimbursement. Physician must waive fees for the patient.

(d) To whom the products are sent for distribution to the patient:

Physician.

(e) The specific forms that have to be completed, if any, to be enrolled in the program, and from whom the forms are obtained:

Glaxo Indigent Patient Program applications can be obtained by contacting 1–800–GLAXO77.

(f) How refills for the products are obtained:

Repeat requests can be accommodated upon receipt of a signed note on the physician's letterhead or prescription blank specifying the patient's identification and the drug required.

(g) Restrictions on the use of the program:

As stated above.

(h) Any copayments or cost-sharing that the company requires from the patient:

None.

NUMBER OF PATIENTS SERVED BY THE PROGRAM

According to the company, approximately 2,000 new and refill prescription requests were filled in 1991. Approximately 500 new and refill requests were filled in the first quarter of 1992.

HOECHST-ROUSSEL PHARMACEUTICALS, INC.

CONTACT FOR THE PROGRAM:

Jannalee Smithey

Technology Assessment Group

1–800–PROKINE

PROGRAM CHARACTERISTICS

(a) The pharmaceutical products which are covered:

Prokine (sargramostim) is covered under the program described here.

The company indicated that it provides other products to indigent patients upon receipt of a prescription and a physician's letter certifying that the patient is indigent. Eligibility is on a case-by-case basis. This policy covers patients who are ineligible for a third-party payer or Medicaid. The company's other products include Lasix, Trental, and Diabeta.

(b) The quantity of the product which can be obtained at any one time:

One course of therapy (usually 2–3 weeks).

(c) The patient eligibility criteria that have to be met:

Lack of insurance or ability to pay.

(d) To whom the products are sent for distribution to the patient:

Usually the hospital.

(e) The specific forms that have to be completed, if any, to be enrolled in the program, and from whom the forms are obtained:

There are no forms to enroll in the program; the Reimbursement Service number must be contacted.

(f) How refills for the product are obtained:

Refills are not applicable to this product.

(g) Restrictions on the use of the program:

Only two patients per physician at a single time.

(h) Any copayments or cost-sharing that the company requires from the patient:

None.

NUMBER OF PATIENTS SERVED BY THE PROGRAM

The company reported that about 30 patients were enrolled in the Prokine program in 1991.

HOFFMAN-LaROCHE, INC.

CONTACT FOR THE PROGRAM:

Inge Shanahan
Medical Communications Associate
Roche Laboratories
340 Kingsland Street
Nutley, NJ 07110
1–800–526–6367 Teleprompter #2
201–235–5624 (FAX)

PROGRAM CHARACTERISTICS

(a) The pharmaceutical products which are covered:

All Roche pharmaceutical products are covered by this program, which include Valium, Librium, Limbritol, Dalmane, Bactrim, Bactrim DS, Klonopin, Efudex (Fluorouracil Injectable), Gantrisin, Gantanol, Interferon 2A Recombinant, Rocephin Injectable, and Rocaltrol.

(b) The quantity of the product which can be obtained at any one time:

Three months' supply.

(c) The patient eligibility criteria that have to be met:

Eligibility limited to private practice outpatients who are considered by the physician to be medically indigent and who are not eligible to receive Roche drugs through any other third-party reimbursement program. Inpatients and those that can obtain drug reimbursement from other sources are not eligible. The physician's signature and DEA number are required for all applications, whether or not the request is for a controlled substance.

(d) To whom the products are sent for distribution to the patient:

Physician.

(e) The specific forms that have to be completed, if any, to be enrolled in the program, and from whom the forms are obtained:

Roche Indigent Patient Program Forms are required, and are available from the Professional Services Department.

(f) How refills for the products are obtained:

Repeat requests require an additional application, but that application need only specify the patient identification by initials, or other identifier, the drug, and the amount required.

(g) Restrictions on the use of the program:

The program is only available to private patients, not covered by third-party insurance programs.

(h) Any copayments or cost-sharing that the company requires from the patient:

None.

The company reports that approximately 2,000 patients were enrolled in 1989, 3,000 patients in 1990, and 5,000 patients in 1991.

ICI/STUART PHARMACEUTICALS

CONTACT FOR THE PROGRAM:

Yvonne A. Graham

Manager, Professional Services

ICI Pharmaceuticals Group

P.O. Box 15197

Wilmington, DE 19850–5197

302–886–2231

PROGRAM CHARACTERISTICS

(a) The pharmaceutical products which are covered:

The company reported that the following pharmaceutical products are covered under this program: Nolvadex, Zestoretic, Bucladin–S, Kinesed, Sorbitrate, Tenormin, Tenoretic, and Zestril.

(b) The quantity of the product which can be obtained at any one time:

One to 3 months' supply.

(c) The patient eligibility criteria that have to be met:

None indicated on the survey.

(d) To whom the products are sent for distribution to the patient:

Physician.

(e) The specific forms that have to be completed, if any, to be enrolled in the program, and from whom the forms are obtained:

Forms are obtained from the ICI Pharmaceuticals Group Professional Services Representatives.

(f) How refills for the products are obtained:

Refills are automatically given for 1 year. Reapplication has to be made every 12 months.

(g) Restrictions on the use of the program:

Eligibility for all available alternative programs must first be considered.

(h) Any copayments or cost-sharing that the company requires from the patient:

None.

According to the company, about 5,000 patients were served in 1989, 6,000 in 1990, and 8,000 in 1991.

IMMUNEX CORPORATION

CONTACT FOR THE PROGRAM:

Michael L. Kleinberg

Director of Professional Services

Immunex Corporation

206–587–0430

206–343–8926 (FAX)

1–800–321–4669

PROGRAM CHARACTERISTICS

(a) The pharmaceutical products which are covered:

The pharmaceutical product covered under this program is Leukine 250 mcg. and Leukine 500 mcg.

(b) The quantity of the product which can be obtained at any one time:

One cycle.

(c) The patient eligibility criteria that have to be met:

Physician must attest that the patient requires the drug and that all the reimbursement options for the patient have been tried.

(d) To whom the products are sent for distribution to the patient:

Physician.

(e) The specific forms that have to be completed, if any, to be enrolled in the program, and from whom the forms are obtained:

A patient assistance program enrollment form is obtained by the physician from the company's medical service representative.

(f) How refills for the products are obtained:

Up to two refills may be requested by the physician with the initial request. Refills are sent based on cycle time. Further refills may be requested on an as needed basis.

(g) Restrictions on the use of the program:

The patient must not be entitled to any other governmental program or other reimbursement.

(h) Any copayments or cost-sharing that the company requires from the patient:

None.

NUMBER OF PATIENTS SERVED BY THE PROGRAM

The company reported that, since March 1991, 168 patients have been served by the program.

———

JOHNSON AND JOHNSON (ORTHO BIOTECHNOLOGY)

CONTACT FOR THE PROGRAM:

Carol Webb, Executive Director

Hematopoietic Products

908–704–5232

908–526–4997 (FAX)

The Ortho Financial Assistance Program

1800 Robert Fulton Drive

Reston, VA 22091

1–800–447–3437 (Financial Assistance)

1–800–441–1366 (Cost Sharing Program)

PROGRAM CHARACTERISTICS

(a) The pharmaceutical products which are covered:

The pharmaceutical product covered under this program is Procrit (Epoetin-alfa).

(b) The quantity of the product which can be obtained at any one time:

Determined by physician, normally 4–8 weeks.

(c) The patient eligibility criteria that have to be met:

1. Financial Assistance Program—Less than $35,000 annual total household income, and no other prescription drug coverage.

2. Cost-Sharing Program—The program is activated when Procrit expenditures for a patient exceed $8,500 for a calendar year, regardless of third-party coverage.

(d) To whom the products are sent for distribution to the patient:

Physician.

(e) The specific forms that have to be completed, if any, to be enrolled in the program, and from whom the forms are obtained:

A Financial Assistance Program form must be completed, which can be obtained from the company's sales representative or by contacting the company directly.

(f) How refills for the products are obtained:

Through the patient's physician, by requalifying every 60 days.

(g) Restrictions on the use of the program:

None indicated.

(h) Any copayments or cost-sharing that the company requires from the patient:

None, except for cost sharing program mentioned above.

NUMBER OF PATIENTS SERVED BY THE PROGRAM

The company reported that 200 patients were served by the program in 1991.

————

JOHNSON AND JOHNSON (JANSSEN PHARMACEUTICALS)

CONTACT FOR THE PROGRAM:
Ellen McDonald
Assistant Product Manager
Janssen Pharmaceuticals
40 Kingsbridge Rd
Piscataway, NJ 08854
908–524–9409
908–524–9118 (FAX)

PROGRAM CHARACTERISTICS

(a) The pharmaceutical products which are covered:

The pharmaceutical product covered under this program is Ergamisol (Levamisole HCL).

(b) The quantity of the product which can be obtained at any one time:

Two months' supply.

(c) The patient eligibility criteria that have to be met:

1. Less than $25,000 total annual household income.

2. Can have Medicare or private insurance, but cannot have prescription coverage.

(d) To whom the products are sent for distribution to the patient:

Physician.

(e) The specific forms that have to be completed, if any, to be enrolled in the program, and from whom the forms are obtained:

Physician may obtain forms from company sales representatives or by contacting the company's headquarters.

(f) How refills for the products are obtained:

Refills are obtained from the patient's physician every 2 months. The patient must be requalified for the program every 6 months.

(g) Restrictions on the use of the program:

Diagnosis must be for Duke C Colon Cancer.

(h) Any copayments or cost-sharing that the company requires from the patient:

None.

NUMBER OF PATIENTS SERVED BY THE PROGRAM

The company reported that the program served 140 patients in 1990 and 411 in 1991.

———

ELI LILLY AND COMPANY

CONTACT FOR THE PROGRAM:

Indigent Patient Program Administrator
Eli Lilly and Company
Lilly Corporate Center
Drop Code 1844
Indianapolis, IN 46285
317–276–2950
317–276–9288 (FAX)

(a) The pharmaceutical products which are covered:

The company reported that all Eli Lilly prescription products are covered, which include Ceclor, Keflex, Prozac, Dymelor, and Axid. The company also indicated that it makes its insulin products available through its indigent patient program. These insulin products include NPH insulin, Regular insulin, Lente insulin, and Humulin insulin. The program does not cover controlled substances, which include Darvon and Darvocet products.

(b) The quantity of the product which can be obtained at any one time:

Quantities are dependent upon the product, the diagnosis, and the physician's instructions. Generally, one course of therapy is supplied for acute care products. Quantities of chronic care products are determined on a case-by-case basis in consultation with the prescribing physician.

(c) The patient eligibility criteria that have to be met:

Patient eligibility is determined on a case-by-case basis in consultation with the prescribing physician. The intent is to provide products to individuals with limited resources and lacking third-party assistance.

(d) To whom the products are sent for distribution to the patient:

Physician.

(e) The specific forms that have to be completed, if any, to be enrolled in the program, and from whom the forms are obtained:

Access to this program is qualified through consultation with the prescribing physician. Patients are not required to complete enrollee forms.

(f) How refills for the products are obtained:

Requests for refills are evaluated in a manner similar to original requests.

(g) Restrictions on the use of the program:

Controlled substances are not provided. No product is provided for indications not approved by FDA.

(h) Any copayments or cost-sharing that the company requires from the patient:

None.

The company would not provide data on the number of patients that had been served by the program.

———

MARION MERRELL DOW, INC.

CONTACT FOR THE PROGRAM:

Bill Lawrence
Supervisor of Product Contributions
P.O. Box 8480
Kansas City, MO 64114
816–966–4250

PROGRAM CHARACTERISTICS

(a) The pharmaceutical products which are covered:

The company reported that all Marion Merrell Dow pharmaceutical products are covered under this program, which include Cardizem, Cardizem CD, Cardizem SR, Carafate, Pavabid, Seldane, Seldane D, Nicorette, Rifadin, Quinamm, and Lorelco.

(b) The quantity of the product which can be obtained at any one time:

Three months' supply.

(c) The patient eligibility criteria that have to be met:

The physician determines whether the patient is eligible for the program. The intent of the program is to assure access to drug products for patients that fall below the Federal poverty level and have no other means of health care coverage.

(d) To whom the products are sent for distribution to the patient:

Historically, the products have been sent to the physician; however, the company reports that a revised program will include the pharmacist.

(e) The specific forms that have to be completed, if any, to be enrolled in the program, and from whom the forms are obtained:

Physicians can obtain program certificates from the company.

(f) How refills for the products are obtained:

Physician request.

(g) Restrictions on the use of the program:

Indigent patients.

(h) Any copayments or cost-sharing that the company requires from the patient:

None.

The company reported that 15,000 requests were received and honored in 1989, 52,000 in 1990, and 105,000 in 1991.

MERCK SHARP AND DOHME (HUMAN HEALTH DIVISION, U.S.)

CONTACT FOR THE PROGRAM:

Professional Information Department
Merck Human Health Division, U.S.
West Point, PA 19486
215–540–8600

PROGRAM CHARACTERISTICS

(a) The pharmaceutical products which are covered:

According to the company, generally all Merck pharmaceutical products are covered by this program, with the exception of injectable medicines. Merck products include Mevacor, Plendil, Pepcid, Prilosec, Prinivil, Timoptic, Timolol, Clinoril, Flexeril, Periactin, Noroxin, Cogentin, Indocin, Aldomet, Dolobid, Vasoretic, and Vasotec.

(b) The quantity of the product which can be obtained at any one time:

Requests for 3 months' supply are generally honored.

(c) The patient eligibility criteria that have to be met:

The patient's physician must: provide a written statement of medical need; indicate the existence of financial hardship; indicate the lack of patient eligibility for prescription coverage from insurance or government assistance programs.

(d) To whom the products are sent for distribution to the patient:

Physician.

(e) The specific forms that have to be completed, if any, to be enrolled in the program, and from whom the forms are obtained:

No specific forms have to be completed; requests should be made to the contact listed above.

(f) How refills for the products are obtained:

The patient's physician can made subsequent requests for additional medications.

(g) Restrictions on the use of the program:

Multiple, simultaneous requests from one physician cannot be considered.

(h) Any copayments or cost-sharing that the company requires from the patient:

None.

NUMBER OF PATIENTS SERVED BY THE PROGRAM

The company reported that thousands of requests from physicians had been honored over the past decade. It could not provide specific data on the number of patients that had been served each year.

NORWICH-EATON PHARMACEUTICALS (PROCTOR AND GAMBLE)

CONTACT FOR THE PROGRAM:

R.M. Brandt, Manager
Coverage and Reimbursement
607–335–2079
607–335–2020 (FAX)
1–800–448–4878

PROGRAM CHARACTERISTICS

(a) The pharmaceutical products which are covered:

The company reported that all Norwich-Eaton pharmaceutical products are covered under this program, which include Macrodantin and Dantrium.

(b) The quantity of the product which can be obtained at any one time:

The quantity varies depending upon the situation, but at least a 1 months' supply can be obtained upon receipt of a physician's prescription.

(c) The patient eligibility criteria that have to be met:

The company relies on the physician's appraisal of the patient's need. The company also helps the patient identify other sources of financial help to pay for the patient's medications.

(d) To whom the products are sent for distribution to the patient:

Physician.

(e) The specific forms that have to be completed, if any, to be enrolled in the program, and from whom the forms are obtained:

None.

(f) How refills for the products are obtained:

The physician must send another prescription to the company.

(g) Restrictions on the use of the program:

Determination of patient eligibility is made on a case-by-case basis, based on the physician's assessment of the patient's need.

(h) Any copayments or cost-sharing that the company requires from the patient:

None.

NUMBER OF PATIENTS SERVED BY THE PROGRAM

The company indicated that it has not tracked requests, and could not provide specific information to respond to this question.

———

PARKE-DAVIS

CONTACT FOR THE PROGRAM:

Parke-Davis
201 Tabor Road
Morris Plains, NJ 07950
201–540–2000

PROGRAM CHARACTERISTICS

(a) The pharmaceutical products which are covered:

The company indicated that all pharmaceutical products except controlled substances (Centrax) are made available to patients on an informal, ad hoc basis through their physicians.

The company's pharmaceutical products include Dilantin, Mandelamine, Accupril, Pyridium, Nitrostat Sublingual, Tabron, Ponstel, Procan, Anusol HC, and Zarontin.

(b) The quantity of the product which can be obtained at any one time:

There are no formal limits. The quantity of the product to be distributed to indigent patients is governed by both relevant Federal, State, and local law and the physician's determination of the indigent patient's medical need.

(c) The patient eligibility criteria that have to be met:

The program is managed on an informal, ad hoc basis, and thus no formal criteria exist. The physician's good-faith determination of need is the chief restriction on the use of the program.

(d) To whom the products are sent for distribution to the patient:

Physician.

(e) The specific forms that have to be completed, if any, to be enrolled in the program, and from whom the forms are obtained:

None required.

(f) How refills for the products are obtained:

See (b) above.

(g) Restrictions on the use of the program:

See (c) above.

(h) Any copayments or cost-sharing that the company requires from the patient:

None.

NUMBER OF PATIENTS SERVED BY THE PROGRAM

The company indicated that it did not keep statistics on enrollment in the program, and did not respond in more detail to this question.

PFIZER PHARMACEUTICALS, INC. PROGRAM #1:

PFIZER LABS, ROERIG DIVISION, PRATT PHARMACEUTICALS

CONTACT FOR THE PROGRAM:

Richard Vastola

Manager, Professional and Consumer Programs

Pfizer, Inc.

235 East 42nd Street

New York, NY 10017

212–573–3954

PROGRAM CHARACTERISTICS

(a) The pharmaceutical products which are covered:

All Pfizer outpatient pharmaceutical products are covered by this program, which include Antivert, Marax, Diabinese, Cardura, Minizide, Navane, Sinequan, Zithromax, Feldene, Procardia, Procardia XL, Vibramycin, Vistaril, Zoloft, Minipress, Minizide, and Glucotrol. (Diflucan is covered by another program described separately.).

(b) The quantity of the product which can be obtained at any one time:

Up to 3 months' supply, as prescribed by the physician.

(c) The patient eligibility criteria that have to be met:

Any patient that a physician is treating as indigent is eligible. Patients must not be covered by third-party insurance or Medicaid.

(d) To whom the products are sent for distribution to the patient:

Physician receives products for distribution to patient.

(e) The specific forms that have to be completed, if any, to be enrolled in the program, and from whom the forms are obtained:

Forms are not necessary. The patient's physician must write a letter to Pfizer stating the need, and include the written prescription for the drug.

(f) How refills for the products are obtained:

Through the request of the physician.

(g) Restrictions on the use of the program:

The physician must be treating the patient as indigent, and in a letter must indicate financial need and inability to pay on part of the patient.

(h) Any copayments or cost-sharing that the company requires from the patient:

None.

NUMBER OF PATIENTS SERVED BY THE PROGRAM

According to the company, about 2,000 free courses of therapy were provided to indigent patients from 1989 through 1991. The company did not report on the number of patients that have been served.

ADDITIONAL COMMENTS

Pfizer also participates in the Arkansas Health Care Access Program and the Kentucky Health Care Access Program. These programs make all Pfizer prescription drugs available free of charge to patients that each respective State certifies as being below the Federal poverty level, without health insurance benefits, and ineligible for any government entitlement program. More information about the programs is available from:

Arkansas

Pat Keller

Program Director

Arkansas Health Care Access Foundation

P.O. Box 56248

Little Rock, AR 72215

501–221–3033

1–800–950–8233

Kentucky

Arch Manious, Jr.

Execitive Vice President

Kentucky Health Care Access Foundation

147 Market Street, Suite 200

Lexington, KY 40507

606–255–7442

606–254–5846 (FAX)

PFIZER INC. PROGRAM #2: ROERIG DIVISION

CONTACT FOR THE PROGRAM:

Diflucan Patient Assistance Program

1–800–869–9979

PROGRAM CHARACTERISTICS

(a) The pharmaceutical products which are covered:

Diflucan (Fluconazole).

(b) The quantity of the product which can be obtained at any one time:

Up to 3 months' supply.

(c) The patient eligibility criteria that have to be met:

Patient must not have insurance or other third-party coverage, including Medicaid.

Patient must not be eligible for a State AIDS drug assistance program.

Patient must have an income of less than $25,000 a year without. dependents; or less than $40,000 a year with dependents.

(d) To whom the products are sent for distribution to the patient:

Physician.

(e) The specific forms that have to be completed, if any, to be enrolled in the program, and from whom the forms are obtained:

A one-page qualification form completed and submitted by the physician is required for enrollment. The form can be obtained by contacting the 1–800 number listed above.

(f) How refills for the products are obtained:

Refills are obtained by the physician resubmitting a one-page qualification form.

(g) Restrictions on the use of the program:

None, beyond income and coverage limitations.

(h) Any copayments or cost-sharing that the company requires from the patient:

None.

Information provided by the company indicate that 1,217 patients were enrolled in the program in 1991. In 1990, the year for which records were most readily available, 440 courses of therapy were provided through the program. The number of patients served in 1990 was not reported by the company.

REED AND CARNRICK/BLOCK DRUG COMPANY

CONTACT FOR THE PROGRAM:

Conrad Erdt
Customer Service Associate
Reed and Carnrick Pharmaceutical Company
One New England Ave
Piscataway, NJ 08854
908–981–0070
908–981–1391 (FAX)

PROGRAM CHARACTERISTICS

(a) The pharmaceutical products which are covered:

The company indicated that all its prescription products are covered by the program (when accompanied by a prescription form signed by a physician), which include Lindane Shampoo and Lindane Lotion. The company's nonprescription products are also covered under the program.

(b) The quantity of the product which can be obtained at any one time:

One months' supply.

(c) The patient eligibility criteria that have to be met:

The company makes a determination of eligibility based on income information provided by the physician.

(d) To whom the products are sent for distribution to the patient:

Physician.

(e) The specific forms that have to be completed, if any, to be enrolled in the program, and from whom the forms are obtained:

Written request from physician to company representative or direct to company headquarters, accompanied by signed physician prescription form.

(f) How refills for the products are obtained:

Written request by the physician, accompanied by signed physician prescription form.

(g) Restrictions on the use of the program:

As above.

(h) Any copayments or cost-sharing that the company requires from the patient:

None.

NUMBER OF PATIENTS SERVED BY THE PROGRAM

According to the company, only one patient was enrolled in the program in 1991.

SANDOZ PHARMACEUTICALS

CONTACT FOR THE PROGRAM:

Gilbert Honigfeld, Ph.D.
Director of Scientific Affairs
59 Route 10
East Hanover, NJ 07936–1951
201–503–8341
201–503–7185 (FAX)

Maria Hardin, Director
Sandoz Drug Cost Sharing Program (DCSP)
P.O. Box 8923
New Fairfield, CT 06812
203–746–6518
1–800–447–6673
203–746–6481 (FAX)

Carol Lee-Kantor
Director, Clozaril Assistance Program
P.O. Box 8923
New Fairfield, CT 06812–1783
1–800–937–6673
203–746–6481 (FAX)

PROGRAM CHARACTERISTICS

The National Organization for Rare Diseases (NORD)/Sandoz Drug Cost Share Program (DCSP) is solely administered by NORD.

(a) The pharmaceutical products which are covered:

The company reported that Sandimmune, Sandoglobulin, Sandostatin, Parlodel, and Eldepryl are covered under one program. Clozaril is covered under a different program, as described below. The company did not indicate if it had a program for its other pharmaceutical products, which include Restoril and Mellaril.

(b) The quantity of the product which can be obtained at any one time:

Patient is awarded up to 1-year's worth of drug, which is shipped in 3-month supplies via the mail-order pharmacy utilized by the program.

Clozaril—Patient is eligible to receive up to 1-year's supply of the drug, dispensed only 1 week at a time, per dispensing requirements of package label.

(c) The patient eligibility criteria that have to be met:

NORD determines eligibility by medical and financial criteria, and applies a cost share formula. The patient/applicant must demonstrate financial need above and beyond the availability of Federal and State funds, private insurance or family resources. NORD also makes determination of patient eligibility for Clozaril program.

(d) To whom the products are sent for distribution to the patient:

Products are sent directly to the patient via a mail order pharmacy. For Clozaril, the drug is supplied by local pharmacists, and NORD reimburses the pharmacist for the drug plus a dispensing fee. NORD also may reimburse laboratories for weekly blood tests.

(e) The specific forms that have to be completed, if any, to be enrolled in the program, and from whom the forms are obtained:

An application packet which also includes a separate physician form is available from NORD for both the general program and the Clozaril program.

(f) How refills for the products are obtained:

Patient's physician must complete DCSP dosage quarterly updates. A new prescription must accompany physician's up-date when a dosage change has occurred.

Clozaril—dispensed 1 week at a time at local pharmacy, after laboratory check of patient's white blood cell (WBC) count, per physician's prescription.

(g) Restrictions on the use of the program:

All applicants must be citizens or permanent residents of the United States. There is no income ceiling. For Clozaril, patients must apply each year to requalify.

(h) Any copayments or cost-sharing that the company requires from the patient:

A percentage of the costs, up to 100 percent, of an eligible applicant's drug therapy, is subsidized according to financial need. Patient is responsible for shipping and handling costs of the drug. For Clozaril, patients must pay for the percentage of the medication costs that they can afford.

NUMBER OF PATIENTS SERVED BY THE PROGRAM

According to the company, the general Sandoz indigent patient program served 79 patients in 1989, 504 in 1990, and 1,005 in 1991. The Clozaril program served 1,249 patients in 1990 and the same number in 1991.

SANOFI WINTHROP PHARMACEUTICALS

CONTACT FOR THE PROGRAM:

Sanofi Winthrop
Product Information Department
90 Park Avenue
New York, NY 10016
212–907–2000

PROGRAM CHARACTERISTICS

(a) The pharmaceutical products which are covered:

The company indicated that all Sanofi Winthrop pharmaceutical products are available under this program, which include Aralen, Danocrine, and Winstrol.

(b) The quantity of the product which can be obtained at any one time:

One unit or 1 months' supply, as required.

(c) The patient eligibility criteria that have to be met:

Subject to acceptance by the company, patients can obtain medications by having their physician contact the company to request the product, provide a written order for the product, and confirm the patient's need.

(d) To whom the products are sent for distribution to the patient:

Physician.

(e) The specific forms that have to be completed, if any, to be enrolled in the program, and from whom the forms are obtained:

Pharmaceuticals can be obtained by contacting the local sales representative or calling the product information department, and providing a written prescription.

(f) How refills for the products are obtained:

Specific requests must be made for additional product.

(g) Restrictions on the use of the program:

Each request is handled on a case-by-case basis.

(h) Any copayments or cost-sharing that the company requires from the patient:

None.

NUMBER OF PATIENTS SERVED BY THE PROGRAM

According to the company, patients are handled on a case-by-case basis, and are not enrolled in a formal program. Therefore, the company did not provide any data on the number of patients that the program served.

SCHERING-PLOUGH

CONTACT FOR THE PROGRAM:

For Intron/Eulexin Products:
>Roger D. Graham, Jr.
>Marketing Manager, Oncology/Biotech
>Service Programs
>Schering Laboratories
>2000 Galloping Hill Road
>Building K–5–2 B2
>Kenilworth, NJ 07033

For Other Schering Products:

Drug Information Services
Indigent Program
Schering Laboratories/Key Pharmaceuticals
2000 Galloping Hill Road
Building K–5–1 C6
Kenilworth, NJ 07033
908–298–4000
1–800–822–7000

PROGRAM CHARACTERISTICS

(a) The pharmaceutical products which are covered:

Intron A—Initial supply is for 2 months; renewals available for 4 months at a time.

Eulexin—Initial supply is for 6 months; renewals available for 6 months at a time.

Other Schering products, which include Trinalin, Lotrimin, Lotrisone, Diprosone, Diprolene, Fulvicin, Proventil, Vancenase, Normodyne, and Optimine, are provided for an initial 3 months' supply, with renewals available for up to 3 months at a time.

(b) The quantity of the product which can be obtained at any one time:

As indicated above.

(c) The patient eligibility criteria that have to be met:

Patient eligibilty is determined on a case-by-case basis, based on the internal criteria (economic status) as well as through consultation with the prescribing physician. The consultation includes a review of the specific case as well as the availability of other means of health care assistance.

(d) To whom the products are sent for distribution to the patient:

Physician.

(e) The specific forms that have to be completed, if any, to be enrolled in the program, and from whom the forms are obtained:

The physician either completes a request form in the case if Intron A and Eulexin or submits a formal written request for assistance for other Schering drugs.

(f) How refills for the products are obtained:

Refills are sent directly to the physician.

(g) Restrictions on the use of the program:

According to the company, the program is designed to assist those patients who are indigent and ineligible for public or private insurance reimbursement, and cannot afford treatment.

(h) Any copayments or cost-sharing that the company requires from the patient:

None.

NUMBER OF PATIENTS SERVED BY THE PROGRAM

According to the company, 2,100 patients were enrolled in the program in 1991. Data were not provided for earlier years.

G.D. SEARLE AND CO.

CONTACT FOR THE PROGRAM:

For health care professionals:
Michael Isaacson
Vice President, "Patients in Need" Foundation
Searle Co.
5200 Old Orchard Rd.
Skokie, IL 60077
1–800–542–2526
708–470–3831
708–470–6633 (FAX)

For general information about the program:
Laura Leber
Associate Director, Public Affairs
708–470–6280
708–470–6719 (FAX)

PROGRAM CHARACTERISTICS

(a) The pharmaceutical products which are covered:

The company indicated that the following pharmaceutical products were covered under the program: Aldactazide, Aldactone, Calan, Calan SR, Cytotec, Kerlone, Nitrodisc, Norpace, Norpace CR.

(b) The quantity of the product which can be obtained at any one time:

Supply is based on the physician's assessment of the needs of the patient.

(c) The patient eligibility criteria that have to be met:

The program is conducted through the physician, who determines the patient's eligibility based on medical and economic need. Searle provides suggested guidelines to the physician to consider when determining patient eligibility.

(d) To whom the products are sent for distribution to the patient:

"Patients in Need" program certificates for new and refill prescriptions are made available to the physician. The physician gives the completed certificate to the patient, who takes it to the pharmacy with a prescription for the Searle product. The pharmacist submits the certificate to Searle, and the pharmacist is reimbursed by the company at the pharmacy's usual and customary charge.

(e) The specific forms that have to be completed, if any, to be enrolled in the program, and from whom the forms are obtained:

The physician enrolls the patient in the program through the "Patients in Need" certificate. The patient does not have to complete any forms. Certificates are available from Searle medical representatives or by calling the toll-free number.

(f) How refills for the products are obtained:

Refills can be obtained through the physician by utilizing "Patients in Need" program certificates. There is no limit to the number of refills under the program, so a patient could receive a lifetime supply of medication through the program.

(g) Restrictions on the use of the program:

There are no time or monetary limitations on patients using the program.

(h) Any copayments or cost-sharing that the company requires from the patient:

None.

NUMBER OF PATIENTS SERVED BY THE PROGRAM

Since 1987, the company reports that nearly 5 million certificates worth $150 million have been distributed to physicians around the country. However, the company did not provide data on the number of patients that have been served by the program.

———

SIGMA-TAU PHARMACEUTICALS

CONTACT FOR THE PROGRAM:

Michele McCourt
Carnitor Drug Assistance Program
Administrator
National Organization for Rare Diseases
P.O. Box 8923
New Fairfield, CT 06812–1783
1–800–999–6673
203–746–6518
203–746–6481 (FAX)

Barbara J. Bacon
Manager, Marketing Operations
Sigma-Tau Pharmaceuticals
200 Orchard Ridge Drive
Gaithersburg, MD 20878
1–800–447–0169
301–948–1041
301–948–1862 (FAX)

PROGRAM CHARACTERISTICS

(a) The pharmaceutical product which is covered:

Carnitor (Levocarnitine).

(b) The quantity of the product which can be obtained at any one time:

Three months' supply, up to 1 year.

(c) The patient eligibility criteria that have to be met:

The patient must have no other means for obtaining the drug through insurance or State or Federal assistance, or liquid assets, and cannot afford to purchase the drug. Must be a U.S. citizen or permanent resident.

(d) To whom the products are sent for distribution to the patient:

Product is sent directly to the patient.

(e) The specific forms that have to be completed, if any, to be enrolled in the program, and from whom the forms are obtained:

Applications are obtained through the NORD/Sigma-Tau Carnitor Drug Assistance program.

(f) How refills for the products are obtained:

Physician sends new quarterly prescription. Voucher for free drug is sent out quarterly.

(g) Restrictions on the use of the program:

Program limited to patients who cannot afford to purchase the prescribed drug and have no other means of obtaining it.

(h) Any copayments or cost-sharing that the company requires from the patient:

Patient must pay for the shipping and handling of the drug.

NUMBER OF PATIENTS SERVED BY THE PROGRAM

The company reported that the program served 10 patients in 1989, 13 patients in 1990, and 18 patients in 1991.

SMITHKLINE BEECHAM: PROGRAM #1

CONTACT FOR THE PROGRAM:
Jan Stilley
SmithKline Beecham
One Franklin Plaza FP1320
Philadelphia, PA 10101
215–751–5760

PROGRAM CHARACTERISTICS

(a) The pharmaceutical products which are covered:

All SmithKline Beecham pharmaceutical products are covered under this program, which include Tagamet, Augmentin, Relafen, Dyazide, Ridaura, Bactroban, and Compazine. Eminase and Triostat are covered under different programs, described in the next section.

(b) The quantity of the product which can be obtained at any one time:

Up to 3 months' supply.

(c) The patient eligibility criteria that have to be met:

Physicians determine which patients are eligible.

(d) To whom the products are sent for distribution to the patient:

The physician makes the request of the local company sales representative. The requesting physician signs a form acknowledging receipt of the product.

(e) The specific forms that have to be completed, if any, to be enrolled in the program, and from whom the forms are obtained:

Patients do not have to be enrolled in the program. Requesting physicians are asked to forward to a letter to the company confirming patient need and eligibility.

(f) How refills for the products are obtained:

Physicians can obtain refills from the local company sales representative, and, upon delivery, sign an acknowledgement of receipt for another 3 months' supply.

(g) Restrictions on the use of the program:

None indicated by the company.

(h) Any copayments or cost-sharing that the company requires from the patient:

None.

NUMBER OF PATIENTS SERVED BY THE PROGRAM

The company indicated that it could not report this because it does not collect aggregate data about the program.

_____

SMITHKLINE BEECHAM: PROGRAM #2

CONTACT FOR THE PROGRAM:

Eminase and Triostat Programs
Helene Kennedy
Program Specialist
555 13th Street NW Suite 700 East
Washington, DC 20004
202–508–6512
202–637–6690 (FAX)

PROGRAM CHARACTERISTICS

(a) The pharmaceutical products which are covered:

Eminase (Antistreplase) and Triostat (Liothyronine Sodium Injection) are covered under the programs described below.

(b) The quantity of the product which can be obtained at any one time:

All Eminase and Triostat vials that the hospital uses to treat patients who meet the program requirements will be replaced by the company free of charge.

(c) The patient eligibility criteria that have to be met:

To be eligible for this program, patients must (1) demonstrate that they do not have private or public insurance coverage; (2) meet the program income requirements (single patients with annual incomes of $18,000 or less and married patients or those with one dependent are eligible if their income is $25,000 or less).

(d) To whom the products are sent for distribution to the patient:

After a hospital submits a request, Eminase and Triostat replacement vials will be shipped directly to the hospital within 30 days after the application has been approved.

(e) The specific forms that have to be completed, if any, to be enrolled in the program, and from whom the forms are obtained:

For each eligible patient, hospitals must submit a Hospital Consent Form and an Application Form with any one of the following documents: a copy of the patient's medical record, a copy of the patient's pharmacy record, a copy of the patient's bill. Forms can be obtained from the company's sales representative or by contacting the following:

For Eminase:

Compassionate Care Program
c/o Medical Technology Hotlines
555 13th Street NW Suite 7E
Washington, DC 20004

1–800–866–6273
202–637–6695

For Triostat:

Medical Technology Hotlines
P.O. Box 7710
Washington, DC 20004–7710

1–800–866–6273
202–637–6695

(f) How refills for the products are obtained:

Given the method of administration and treatment for these drugs, refills are not applicable.

(g) Restrictions on the use of the program:

None.

(h) Any copayments or cost-sharing that the company requires from the patient:

None.

NUMBER OF PATIENTS SERVED BY THE PROGRAM

Since its development in 1990, 110 patients have been enrolled in the Eminase program. The Triostat program was just developed in 1992.

SYNTEX LABORATORIES, INC.

CONTACT FOR THE PROGRAM:

Cytovene Medical Information Line

1–800–444–4200 (Syntex Provisional Assistance Program for Cytovene)

General Telephone Number to Inquire About Indigent Patient Programs:

1–800–822–8255

PROGRAM CHARACTERISTICS

(a) The pharmaceutical products which are covered:

The only product covered under this program is Cytovene (ganciclovir sodium) 500mg sterile powder.

The company indicated that its makes its other products available to indigent patients on an ad hoc basis through their physicians. The company's other products include Naprosyn, Anaprox, Cardene, Synalar, Synemol, and Nasalide.

(b) The quantity of the product (Cytovene) which can be obtained at any one time:

25 vials (dose depends on maintenance-vs-induction therapy, adjusted for patient's weight).

(c) The patient eligibility criteria that have to be met:

Syntex provides Cytovene free of charge when it is prescribed for an immunocompromised patient who has been diagnosed as having cytomegalovirus (CMV) retinitis, if that patient does not have the means to purchase the drug and that patient is not eligible for any form of third-party reimbursement to otherwise pay for the drug.

Specifically, the eligibility criteria for the Syntex Provisional Assistance Program for Cytovene are as follows:

If the physician indicates that the patient has CMV retinitis and cannot afford the cost of treatment, the patient is considered prequalified and an initial 25 vials are shipped directly to the physician. In addition, a Patient Eligibility Form is sent, and the treating physician or social worker completes the necessary information to indicate that the patient has no known source of reimbursement for Cytovene, including private or government insurance, or eligibility for other charitable means of assistance. If the treating physician and social worker determine the patient is "indigent" and all requirements for eligibility are duly documented, the patient's forms are retained on file and the patient is allowed to continue to receive assistance. Patients, once enrolled, will continue to receive drug unless financial or medical conditions change.

(d) To whom are the products sent for distribution to the patient:

Physician.

(e) The specific forms that have to be completed, if any, to be enrolled in the program, and from whom the forms are obtained:

Program structure is as outlined:

(1) The physician contacts the Cytovene Information Line and identifies a patient who has CMV retinitis but cannot afford Cytovene; patient is prequalified, and Syntex Order Department is instructed to drop ship 25 vials of Cytovene immediately to the physician, along with Eligibility Form and Request for Additional Product Form.

(2) When forms are completed and returned, they are reviewed as detailed above. If the patient meets the criteria for financial eligibility, the patient is considered qualified and further drug may be shipped to the physician as requested. The frequency of requests for additional supply varies, depending on the dosage regimen, but usually it is on a monthly basis.

(f) How refills for the products are obtained:

Once patients are deemed eligible and are enrolled in the program, physicians complete a Request for Additional Product

Form. The physician's signature and DEA number are required on all forms.

(g) Restrictions on the use of the program:

Patients must have a diagnosis of cytomegalovirus (CMV) retinitis and have documentation by their physician or social worker indicating that the patient does not have the means to purchase the drug and is not eligible for any form of third-party reimbursement to otherwise pay for the drug.

(h) Any copayments or cost-sharing that the company requires from the patient:

None.

NUMBER OF PATIENTS SERVED BY THE PROGRAM

The company reports that 81 patients have enrolled in the Cytovene Provisional Assistance Program, and 10 patients are pending eligibility approval to date.

ADDITIONAL COMMENT PROVIDED BY THE COMPANY

The company indicated that it is in the process of developing an indigent patient program for Synarel, recently approved by the FDA for the treatment of Central Idiopathic Precocious Puberty.

———

UPJOHN COMPANY

CONTACT FOR THE PROGRAM:

Wendell Pierce
National Professional Services Manager
Upjohn Company
7000 Portage Rd
Kalamazoo, MI 49001
616–323–6004
616–323–6332 (FAX)

PROGRAM CHARACTERISTICS

(a) The pharmaceutical products which are covered:

The company reports that any Upjohn product may be considered for the patient, which includes Ansaid, Motrin, Provera, E–Mycin, Halcion, Xanax, Medrol, Cleocin, Lincocin, Loniten, Micronase, Orinase, and Tolinase.

(b) The quantity of the product which can be obtained at any one time:

Generally, a 3-months' supply is provided. However, a physician can request a supply for a longer period of time.

(c) The patient eligibility criteria that have to be met:

The physician determines the patient's needs, and if there are available insurance or other social programs to help provide medications.

(d) To whom the products are sent for distribution to the patient:

Physician.

(e) The specific forms that have to be completed, if any, to be enrolled in the program, and from whom the forms are obtained:

There are no forms involved in making the request.

(f) How refills for the products are obtained:

Through follow-up requests by the physician to the Upjohn sales representative.

(g) Restrictions on the use of the program:

None indicated.

(h) Any copayments or cost-sharing that the company requires from the patient:

None.

NUMBER OF PATIENTS SERVED BY THE PROGRAM

The company indicated that this data was not available.

WYETH-AYERST LABORATORIES

CONTACT FOR THE PROGRAM:

Roger Eurbin
Associate Director, Professional Services
Wyeth-Ayerst
P.O. Box 8299
Philadelphia, PA 19101
215–971–5604

(a) The pharmaceutical products which are covered:

The company indicated that various products are covered under its program. The company's products include Sectral, Cyclospasmol, Premarin, Isordil, Phenergan, Dimetapp, Orudis, Wytensin, and Cordarone. The company also makes three oral contraceptives: Triphasil, Lo/Ovral, and Nordette, which are primarily provided by family planning clinics. The program to provide the Norplant System is described in the "Comments" section.

(b) The quantity of the product which can be obtained at any one time:

In general, 1–2 months' supply or the closet trade package size available is provided. For Cordarone, 1 months' supply or up to two bottles of 60 tablets is provided.

The number of cycles of oral contraceptives given to the patient is determined by a health care provider or the family planning clinic.

(c) The patient eligibility criteria that have to be met:

The patient must be medically indigent, with no form of coverage for pharmaceutical products. The family planning clinic determines eligibility for new and refill oral contraceptive cycles.

(d) To whom the products are sent for distribution to the patient:

Physician.

(e) The specific forms that have to be completed, if any, to be enrolled in the program, and from whom the forms are obtained:

No specific forms are needed; just a signed and dated prescription that includes the physician's professional designation, the State license or Federal DEA number, and a brief statement affirming that the patient is medically indigent and has no form of coverage for pharmaceutical products.

(f) How refills for the products are obtained:

Same as request for original prescription.

(g) Restrictions on the use of the program:

Subject to case-by-case approval.

(h) Any copayments or cost-sharing that the company requires from the patient:

None.

NUMBER OF PATIENTS SERVED BY THE PROGRAM

The company indicates that data about the program is not captured by a single source and is therefore not available.

COMMENTS

The company established a foundation in 1991 to provide the Norplant contraceptive system. Up to 5 years of use can be provided. The Norplant Foundation determines whether the patient is eligible to receive the system free of charge. Contact: The Norplant Foundation, P.O. Box 25223, Alexandria, VA 22314, 703–706–5933.

APPENDIX B

NORD List of Diseases and Order Form

NORD LITERATURE ORDER FORM

RARE DISEASE DATABASE ARTICLES

MAIL TO: NORD Literature — 100 Rt. 37. PO Box 8923. New Fairfield, CT 06812-1783

Reprints of disease articles from NORD's **Rare Disease Database** are available for $3.25 per copy, which includes postage and handling. The disorders are written in understandable language for patients and families. Each entry lists the disease name, synonyms, a general description of the disorder, symptoms, causes, affected population, standard treatments, investigational treatments (when applicable) and a list of resources that can be contacted for further information about the illness. Some of the listed disorders are not rare, but are included because **NORD** receives substantial inquiries about them.

Please use the order form below by **circling** the proper entry number and inserting the **quantity** of copies you wish to receive. Please **print** your name and address on this form and enclose the form with a check or money order for the total amount due (U.S. funds please). Expect delivery within 4 to 6 weeks.

For people with personal computers who wish to access the database directly, you can reach the **NORD Services** section of **CompuServe** by typing "GO NORD" at any prompt on the CompuServe Information System.

Cost per print	$ 3.25
Number of prints	X
Subtotal	$ _____
Add'l Tax Deductible Donation	_____
GRAND TOTAL	$ _____
Today's Date	_____

Name: _____

Address: _____

City, State, Zip: _____

Telephone: ( ) _____

Card Exp. Date

Charge my ☐ (mc) ☐ VISA ☐

Minimum Charge is $5.00

Cardholder's Signature

To order by mail, you may photocopy this order form and the portions of the catalog in which the disease in which you are interested is listed. Fill out the forms, and send the appropriate fee to NORD.

Entry	Disease Name	Qty
641	11q Syndrome	
643	13q Syndrome	
639	18p- Syndrome	
793	4q Syndrome	
522	5-Oxoprolinuria	
483	ACTH Deficiency	
78	AIDS (Acquired Immune Deficiency Syndrome)	
519	AIDS Dysmorphic Syndrome	
835	APECED Syndrome	
615	Aarskog Syndrome	
106	Aase Syndrome	
114	Acanthocheilonemiasis	
445	Acanthocytosis	
115	Acanthosis Nigricans	
118	Achalasia	
107	Achard-Thiers Syndrome	
876	Achondrogenesis	
80	Achondroplasia	
504	Acidemia, Isovaleric	
427	Acidemia, Methylmalonic	
500	Acidemia, Propionic	
818	Acne	
527	Acne Rosacea	
45	Acoustic Neuroma	
511	Acrodermatitis Enteropathica	
613	Acrodysostosis	
51	Acromegaly	
894	Acute Posterior Multifocal Placoid Pigment Epitheliopathy (APMPPE)	
584	Adams-Oliver Syndrome	
46	Addison's Disease	
825	Adie Syndrome	
97	Adrenal Hyperplasia, Congenital	
43	Adrenoleukodystrophy	
73	Agammaglobulinemias, Primary	
355	Agenesis of Corpus Callosum	
209	Agranulocytosis, Acquired	
155	Ahumada-del Castillo Syndrome	

Entry	Disease Name	Qty
49	Aicardi Syndrome	
473	Alagille Syndrome	
42	Albinism	
56	Alexander's Disease	
23	Alkaptonuria	
443	Alopecia Areata	
610	Alpers Disease	
53	Alpha-1-Antitrypsin Deficiency	
592	Alport Syndrome	
431	Alveolitis, Extrinsic Allergic	
432	Alveolitis, Fibrosing	
29	Alzheimer's Disease	
908	Ameiblastoma	
501	Amelogenesis Imperfecta	
70	Amenorrhea, Primary	
711	Amniotic Bands	
22	Amyloidosis	
57	Amyotrophic Lateral Sclerosis (Lou Gehrig's Disease)	
707	Anaphylaxis	
394	Andersen Disease	
83	Anemia, Aplastic	
450	Anemia, Blackfan-Diamond	
723	Anemia, Cold Antibody Hemolytic	
84	Anemia, Fanconi's	
771	Anemia, Hemolytic, Acquired Autoimmune	
770	Anemia, Hemolytic, Warm Antibody	
82	Anemia, Hereditary Non-Spherocytic Hemolytic	
81	Anemia, Hereditary Spherocytic Hemolytic	
423	Anemia, Megaloblastic	
79	Anemia, Pernicious	
351	Anemia, Sideroblastic	
596	Anencephaly	
411	Angelman Syndrome	
98	Angioedema, Hereditary	
524	Aniridia	
143	Ankylosing Spondylitis	
510	Anodontia	
187	Anorexia Nervosa	

Entry	Disease Name	Qty
672	Antisocial Personality Disorder	
99	Antithrombin III Deficiency, Congenital	
204	Antley-Bixler Syndrome	
254	Apert Syndrome	
901	Aplasia Cutis Congenita	
190	Apnea, Infantile	
68	Apnea, Sleep	
766	Apraxia	
444	Arachnoiditis	
312	Arginase Deficiency	
311	Arginino Succinic Aciduria	
85	Arnold-Chiari Syndrome	
221	Arteriovenous Malformation	
201	Arteritis, Giant Cell	
86	Arteritis, Takayasu	
263	Arthritis, Infectious	
899	Arthritis, Juvenile	
247	Arthritis, Psoriatic	
211	Arthrogryposis Multiplex Congenita	
851	Asherman's Syndrome	
918	Aspartyglycosaminuria	
680	Asperger's Syndrome	
737	Aspergillosis	
775	Astrocytoma, Benign	
277	Astrocytoma, Malignant	
7	Ataxia, Friedreich's	
674	Ataxia, Hereditary	
403	Ataxia, Marie's	
406	Ataxia Telangiectasia	
138	Atrial Septal Defects	
593	Attention Deficit Hyperactivity Disorder	
5	Autism	
120	Babesiosis	
121	Balantidiasis	
909	Baller-Gerold Syndrome	
122	Balo Disease	
722	Banti's Syndrome	

NORD LITERATURE ORDER FORM

MAIL TO: NORD Literature — PO Box 8923, New Fairfield, CT 06812-1783

Entry	Disease Name	Qty
173	Barrett Syndrome	
123	Bartonellosis	
589	Bartter's Syndrome	
259	Batten Disease	
913	Beals Syndrome	
52	Beckwith-Wiedemann Syndrome	
100	Behcet's Syndrome	
124	Bejel	
48	Bell's Palsy	
140	Benign Essential Tremor Syndrome	
167	Bernard-Soulier Syndrome	
481	Berylliosis	
197	Biliary Atresia	
614	Binswanger's Disease	
166	Blastomycosis	
17	Blepharospasm, Benign Essential	
165	Bloom Syndrome	
164	Blue Diaper Syndrome	
605	Blue Rubber Bleb Nevus	
95	Botulism	
608	Bowen's Disease	
813	Brain Tumor	
714	Branchio-Oculo-Facial Syndrome	
871	Branchio-Oto-Renal Syndrome	
163	Broad Beta Disease	
845	Bronchopulmonary Dysplasia (BPD)	
174	Brown Syndrome	
206	Brucellosis	

NORD LITERATURE ORDER FORM

MAIL TO: NORD Literature — PO Box 8923,
New Fairfield, CT 06812-1783

Entry	Disease Name	Qty
428	Bubonic Plague	
583	Budd-Chiari Syndrome	
712	Buerger's Disease	
188	Bulimia	
54	Bullous Pemphigold	
234	Burning Mouth Syndrome	
917	C Syndrome	
550	CHARGE Association	
807	Cancer, Breast	
808	Cancer, Colon	
804	Cancer, Lung	
803	Cancer, Prostate	
786	Cancer, Skin, General	
352	Candidiasis	
307	Carbamyl Phosphate Synthetase Deficiency	
503	Carboxylase Deficiency, Multiple	
677	Carcinoid Syndrome	
815	Carcinoma, Renal Cell	
764	Carcinoma, Squamous Cell	
852	Cardio-Auditory Syndrome	
877	Cardio-Facio-Cutaneous Syndrome	
60	Carnitine Deficiency Syndromes, Hereditary	
915	Carnitine Palmityltransferase Deficiency	
162	Carnosinemia	
606	Caroli Syndrome	
391	Carpal Tunnel Syndrome	
612	Carpenter Syndrome	
532	Castleman's Disease	

NORD LITERATURE ORDER FORM

MAIL TO: NORD Literature — PO Box 8923,
New Fairfield, CT 06812-1783

Entry	Disease Name	Qty
202	Ciguatera Fish Poisoning	
602	Cirrhosis, Primary Biliary	
310	Citrullinemia	
32	Cleft Lip and Cleft Palate (Hare lip)	
265	Clubfoot	
837	Coats Disease	
176	Cockayne Syndrome	
425	Coffin-Lowry Syndrome	
177	Coffin-Siris Syndrome	
751	Cohen Syndrome	
630	Colitis, Collagenous	
87	Colitis, Ulcerative	
141	Colorado Tick Fever	
754	Condyloma	
847	Cone Dystrophy	
863	Conjunctivitis Ligneous	
628	Conn Syndrome	
365	Conradi-Hunermann Syndrome	
690	Conversion Disorder	
137	Cor Biloculare	
136	Cor Triatriatum	
455	Corneal Dystrophy	
30	Cornelia de Lange Syndrome	
172	Cowpox	
735	Craniometaphyseal Dysplasia	
33	Creutzfeldt-Jakob Disease	
19	Cri du Chat Syndrome	
58	Crohn's Disease	
154	Cronkhite-Canada Disease	

NORD LITERATURE ORDER FORM

MAIL TO: NORD Literature — PO Box 8923,
New Fairfield, CT 06812-1783

Entry	Disease Name	Qty
419	Crouzon Disease	
910	Cryoglobulinemia, Essential-Mixed	
384	Cryptococcosis	
126	Cushing Syndrome	
175	Cutis Laxa	
889	Cyclic Vomiting Syndrome	
24	Cystic Fibrosis	
631	Cystic Hygroma	
171	Cysticercosis	
59	Cystinosis	
61	Cystinuria	
189	Cytomegalovirus Infection	
275	Dandy-Walker Syndrome	
485	Darier Disease	
364	Dejerine-Sottas Disease	
514	Dengue Fever	
505	Dentin Dysplasia, Coronal	
521	Dentin Dysplasia, Radicular	
551	Dentinogenesis Imperfecta, Type III	
632	Depersonalization Disorder	
490	Dercum Disease	
801	Dermatitis, Atopic	
571	Dermatitis, Contact	
262	Dermatomyositis	
479	Devic Disease	
466	Dextrocardia with Situs Inversus	
74	DiGeorge Syndrome	

NORD LITERATURE ORDER FORM

MAIL TO: NORD Literature — PO Box 8923,
New Fairfield, CT 06812-1783

Entry	Disease Name	Qty
335	Diabetes, Insipidus	
220	Diabetes, Insulin-Dependent	
482	Diastrophic Dysplasia	
225	Dilatation of the Pulmonary Artery, Idiopathic	
471	Diverticulitis	
464	Diverticulosis	
34	Down Syndrome	
516	Dracunculosis	
224	Duane Syndrome	
731	Dubin-Johnson Syndrome	
198	Dubowitz Syndrome	
208	Duhring Disease	
667	Dupuytren's Contracture	
874	Dyggve-Melchior-Clausen Syndrome	
47	Dysautonomia, Familial	
888	Dyschondrosteosis	
207	Dyslexia	
325	Dysphonia, Chronic Spasmodic	
572	Dysplasia, Epiphysealis Hemimelica	
838	Dysplasia, Fibrous	
839	Dysplasia, Polyostatic Fibrous	
633	Dysplastic Nevus Syndrome	
760	Dysthymia	
31	Dystonia, Torsion	
576	Dystrophy, Asphyxiating Thoracic	
357	Dystrophy, Myotonic	
859	Eales Disease	
794	Eaton-Lambert, Syndrome	

NORD LITERATURE ORDER FORM

MAIL TO: NORD Literature — PO Box 8923, New Fairfield, CT 06812-1783

Entry	Disease Name	Qty
64	Ectodermal Dysplasias	
634	Edema, Idiopathic	
240	Ehlers-Danlos Syndrome	
426	Eisenmenger Syndrome	
689	Elephantiasis	
902	Ellis-Van Creveld Syndrome	
922	Emphysema, Congenital Lobar	
635	Empty Sella Syndrome	
376	Encephalitis, Herpetic	
435	Encephalitis, Japanese	
415	Encephalitis, Rasmussen's	
867	Encephalocele	
416	Encephalomyelitis, Myalgic	
724	Endocarditis, Infective	
788	Endometriosis	
232	Endomyocardial Fibrosis	
607	Englemann Disease	
747	Enterobiasis	
783	Eosinophilia Myalgia	
814	Eosinophilic Fasciitis	
862	Epidermal Nevus Syndrome	
1	Epidermolysis Bullosa	
477	Epidermolytic Hyperkeratosis	
759	Epididymis	
41	Epilepsy	
781	Epilepsy, Myoclonic Progressive Familial	
609	Epitheliopathy, Acute Posterior Multifocal Placoid Pigment	
738	Erb's Palsy	

NORD LITERATURE ORDER FORM

MAIL TO: NORD Literature — PO Box 8923,
New Fairfield, CT 06812-1783

Entry	Disease Name	Qty
757	Erysipelas	
280	Erythema Multiforme	
245	Erythromelalgia	
195	Exstrophy of the Bladder	
827	FG Syndrome	
200	Fabry Disease	
480	Factor IX Deficiency	
66	Factor XIII Deficiency	
597	Fahr's Disease	
359	Fairbank Disease	
535	Farber's Disease	
368	Fascioliasis	
342	Felty Syndrome	
341	Fetal Alcohol Syndrome	
713	Fiber Type Disproportion, Congenital	
219	Fibroelastosis, Endocardial	
753	Fibromatosis, Cogenital Generalized	
266	Fibromyalgia	
116	Filariasis	
396	Forbes Disease	
153	Forbes-Albright Syndrome	
826	Forestier's Disease	
678	Formaldehyde Poisoning	
586	Fragile X Syndrome	
739	Fraser Syndrome	
442	Freeman-Sheldon Syndrome	
101	Frey's Syndrome	
102	Froelich's Syndrome	

NORD LITERATURE ORDER FORM

MAIL TO: NORD Literature — PO Box 8923,
New Fairfield, CT 06812-1783

Entry	Disease Name	Qty
227	Fructose Intolerance, Hereditary	
573	Fructosuria	
373	Galactosemia	
305	Ganglioside Sialidase Deficiency	
152	Gardner Syndrome	
719	Gastritis, Chronic Erosive	
119	Gastritis, Giant Hypertrophic	
733	Gastroenteritis, Eosinophilic	
668	Gastroesophageal Reflux	
923	Gastroschisis	
12	Gaucher Disease	
660	Gianotti-Crosti Syndrome	
492	Giardiasis	
317	Gilbert Syndrome	
281	Glioblastoma Multiforme	
774	Gluco-6-Dehydrogenase Deficiency	
749	Glucose-Galactose Malabsorption	
383	Glutaricaciduria I	
378	Glutaricaciduria II	
400	Glycogen Storage Disease VIII	
346	Goldenhar Syndrome	
279	Goodpasture Syndrome	
507	Gordon Syndrome	
832	Gorham's Disease	
128	Gottron's Syndrome	
840	Graft vs Host Disease	
456	Granuloma Annulare	

NORD LITERATURE ORDER FORM

MAIL TO: NORD Literature — PO Box 8923,
New Fairfield, CT 06812-1783

Entry	Disease Name	Qty
717	Granulomatosis, Lymphomatoid	
270	Granulomatosis, Wegener's	
682	Granulomatous Disease, Chronic	
560	Graves' Disease	
697	Greig Cephalopolysyndactyly Syndrome	
897	Grover's Disease	
865	Growth Delay, Constitutional	
866	Growth Hormone Deficiency	
40	Guillain-Barre Syndrome	
499	Hageman Factor Deficiency	
331	Hairy Tongue	
882	Hajdu-Cheney Syndrome	
498	Hallermann-Streiff Syndrome	
179	Hallervorden-Spatz Disease	
743	Hand-Foot-Mouth Disease	
347	Hartnup Disease	
683	Hashimoto's Syndrome	
880	Hay-Wells Syndrome	
720	Headache, Cluster	
530	Heart Block, Congenital	
669	Heavy Metal Poisoning	
699	Hematuria, Benign Familial	
13	Hemochromatosis, Hereditary	
776	Hemoglobinuria, Paroxysmal Cold	
670	Hemoglobinuria, Paroxysmal Nocturnal	
745	Hemolytic Uremic Syndrome	
39	Hemophilia	
285	Hemorrhagic Telangiectasia, Hereditary	

NORD LITERATURE ORDER FORM

MAIL TO: NORD Literature — PO Box 8923,
New Fairfield, CT 06812-1783

Entry	Disease Name	Qty
860	Hepatic Fibrosis	
345	Hepatitis B	
344	Hepatitis, Non-A, Non-B (Hepatitis C)	
199	Hepatitis, Neonatal	
664	Hepatorenal Syndrome	
772	Hermaphroditism, True	
353	Herpes, Neonatal	
457	Herpes, Zoster	
401	Hers Disease (GSD VI)	
708	Hiccups, Chronic	
358	Hidradenitis Suppurativa	
727	Hirschsprung's Disease	
623	Histidinemia	
408	Histiocytosis-X	
662	Hodgkin's Disease	
791	Holoprosencephaly	
523	Holt-Oram Syndrome	
463	Homocystinuria	
864	Horner's Syndrome	
282	Hunter Syndrome	
18	Huntington's Disease	
284	Hurler Syndrome	
130	Hutchinson-Gilford Syndrome	
369	Hydranencephaly	
10	Hydrocephalus	
811	Hypercholesterolemia	
474	Hyperchylomicronemia	
816	Hyperekplexia	

NORD LITERATURE ORDER FORM

MAIL TO: NORD Literature — PO Box 8923,
New Fairfield, CT 06812-1783

Entry	Disease Name	Qty
216	Hyperhidrosis	
750	Hyperkalemia	
624	Hyperlipoproteinemia, Type IV	
470	Hyperoxaluria Type I, Primary	
581	Hyperprolinemia Type I	
580	Hyperprolinemia Type II	
869	Hyperstosis Frontalis Interna	
784	Hypertension	
728	Hyperthermia	
591	Hypochondroplasia	
574	Hypoglycemia	
748	Hypokalemia	
703	Hypoparathyroidism	
518	Hypophosphatasia	
178	Hypoplastic Left Heart Syndrome	
769	Hypotension, Orthostatic	
616	Hypothyroidism	
329	Hypotonia, Benign Congenital	
304	I-Cell disease	
587	IGA Nephropathy	
542	Ichthyosis	
548	Ichthyosis, Chanarin Dorfman Syndrome	
549	Ichthyosis, CHILD Syndrome	
241	Ichthyosis Congenita	
556	Ichthyosis, Erythrokeratodermia Progressiva Symmetrica	
559	Ichthyosis, Erythrokeratolysis Variabilis	
558	Ichthyosis, Erythrokeratolysis Hiemalis	
557	Ichthyosis, Giroux-Barbeau Syndrome	

NORD LITERATURE ORDER FORM

MAIL TO: NORD Literature — PO Box 8923,
New Fairfield, CT 06812-1783

Entry	Disease Name	Qty
546	Ichthyosis, Harlequin Type	
547	Ichthyosis Hystrix, Curth-Macklin Type	
540	Ichthyosis, Keratitis Follicularis Spinulosa Decalvans	
884	Ichthyosis, Keratitis Deafness Syndrome	
544	Ichthyosis, Lamellar Recessive	
552	Ichthyosis, Multiple Sulfatase Deficiency	
553	Ichthyosis, Netherton Syndrome	
575	Ichthyosis, Peeling Skin Syndrome	
555	Ichthyosis, Sjogren Larsson Syndrome	
554	Ichthyosis, Tay Syndrome	
543	Ichthyosis Vulgaris	
545	Ichthyosis, X-Linked	
629	Imperforate Anus	
409	Incontinentia Pigmenti	
103	Interstitial Cystitis	
452	Intestinal Pseudoobstruction	
88	Irritable Bowel Syndrome	
758	Isaacs Syndrome	
740	Ivemark Syndrome	
704	Jarcho-Levin Syndrome	
886	Jejunal Atresia	
856	Job Syndrome	
110	Joseph's Disease	
20	Joubert Syndrome	
380	Jumping Frenchmen of Maine	
920	Kabuki Make-Up Syndrome	

NORD LITERATURE ORDER FORM

MAIL TO: NORD Literature — PO Box 8923,
New Fairfield, CT 06812-1783

Entry	Disease Name	Qty
848	Kallman Syndrome	
526	Kartagener Syndrome	
186	Kawasaki Disease	
367	Kearns-Sayre Syndrome	
562	Keratoconjunctivitis, Vernal	
578	Keratoconus	
762	Keratomalacia	
437	Keratosis, Seborrheic	
233	Kernicterus	
604	Kienboeck Disease	
861	Kikuchi's Disease	
679	Kinsborne Syndrome	
96	Klinefelter Syndrome	
659	Klippel-Feil Syndrome	
453	Klippel-Trenaunay Syndrome	
872	Kluver-Bucy Syndrome	
755	Kniest Syndrome	
800	Kohler Disease	
168	Korsakoff's Syndrome	
349	Kufs Disease	
536	Kugelberg-Welander Syndrome	
885	Lacrima-Auriculo-Dento-Digital Syndrome	
	(LADD)	
117	Lactose Intolerance	
260	Landau-Kleffner Syndrome	
821	Laron Dwarfism	
497	Larsen Syndrome	
104	Laurence-Moon-Biedl Syndrome	

NORD LITERATURE ORDER FORM

MAIL TO: NORD Literature — PO Box 8923,
New Fairfield, CT 06812-1783

Entry	Disease Name	Qty
308	Leber's Congenital Amaurosis	
534	Leber's Optic Atrophy	
563	Legg-Calve-Perthes Syndrome	
193	Legionnaire's Disease	
392	Leigh's Disease	
362	Leiner Disease	
887	Lennox-Gastaut Syndrome	
718	Leopard Syndrome	
387	Leprechaunism	
67	Leprosy	
389	Leptospirosis	
255	Lesch-Nyhan Syndrome	
858	Leukemia, Chronic Lymphocytic	
695	Leukemia, Chronic Myelogenus	
269	Leukemia, Hairy Cell	
676	Leukodystrophy	
157	Leukodystrophy, Canavan	
379	Leukodystrophy, Krabbe's	
212	Leukodystrophy, Metachromatic	
229	Lichen Planus	
252	Lichen Sclerosus	
460	Lipodystrophy	
454	Lissencephaly	
601	Listeriosis	
472	Locked-In Syndrome	
109	Lowe's Syndrome	
38	Lupus	
414	Lyelles Syndrome	

NORD LITERATURE ORDER FORM

MAIL TO: NORD Literature — PO Box 8923,
New Fairfield, CT 06812-1783

Entry	Disease Name	Qty
238	Lyme Disease	
439	Lymphadenopathy, Angioimmunoblastic with Dysproteinemia	
646	Lymphangioma, Cavernous	
410	Lymphangiomyomatosis	
239	Lymphedema, Hereditary	
447	Lymphocytic Infiltrate of Jessner	
773	Lymphoma, Gastric	
333	Macroglossia	
314	Macular Degeneration	
315	Macular Degeneration, Polymorphic	
778	Madelung's Disease	
433	Maffucci Syndrome	
434	Malaria	
8	Malignant Hyperthermia	
734	Mallory-Weiss Syndrome	
449	Manic Depression, Bipolar	
420	Mannosidosis	
131	Maple Syrup Urine Disease	
833	Marcus Gunn Phenomenon	
895	Marden-Walker Syndrome	
27	Marfan Syndrome	
868	Marineaco-Sjogren Syndrome	
283	Maroteaux-Lamy Syndrome	
820	Marshall-Smith Syndrome	
879	Marshall Syndrome	
441	Mastocytosis	
906	Maxillofacial Dysostosis	
160	May-Hegglin Anomaly	

NORD LITERATURE ORDER FORM

MAIL TO: NORD Literature — PO Box 8923,
New Fairfield, CT 06812-1783

Entry	Disease Name	Qty
395	McArdle Disease	
183	McCune-Albright Syndrome	
336	Measles	
661	Meckel Syndrome	
127	Mediterranean Fever, Familial	
585	Medium-Chain Acyl CoA Dehydrogenase Deficiency	
226	Medullary Cystic Disease	
223	Medullary Sponge Kidney	
300	Medulloblastoma	
235	Meige Syndrome	
684	Melanoma, Malignant	
599	Melkersson-Rosenthal Syndrome	
650	Melnick-Needles Syndrome	
272	Meniere Disease	
301	Meningioma	
539	Meningitis	
819	Meningitis, Bacterial	
805	Meningitis, Meningincoccal	
806	Meningitis, Tuberculous	
916	Meningococcemia	
603	Menke's Disease	
459	Mesenteritis, Retractile	
636	Metaphyseal Chondrodysplasia, McKusick Type	
870	Metatropic Dysplasia	
709	Microvillus Inclusion Disease	
205	Mikulicz Syndrome	
891	Miller Syndrome	
875	Mitochondrial Phosphoenolpyruvate Carboxykinase Deficiency (PEPCK)	

NORD LITERATURE ORDER FORM

MAIL TO: NORD Literature — PO Box 8923,
New Fairfield, CT 06812-1783

Entry	Disease Name	Qty
564	Mitral Valve Prolapse Syndrome	
338	Mixed Connective Tissue Disease (MCTD)	
451	Moebius Syndrome	
299	Morquio Syndrome	
656	Motor Neuron Disease	
619	Mountain Sickness, Acute	
617	Moyamoya Disease	
752	Mucha-Haberman Disease	
688	Mucopolysacchridosis	
15	Multiple Sclerosis	
552	Multiple Sulfatase Deficiency	
741	Mumps	
139	Muscular Dystrophy, Batten Turner	
598	Muscular Dystrophy, Becker	
37	Muscular Dystrophy, Duchenne	
590	Muscular Dystrophy, Emery-Dreifuss	
921	Muscular Dystrophy, Fukuyama Type	
911	Muscular Dystrophy. Landouzy-DeJerine	
904	Muscular Dystrophy, Limb-Gridle	
905	Muscular Dystrophy, Oculo-Gastrointestinal	
654	Mutism, Elective	
50	Myasthenia Gravis	
458	Mycosis Fungoides	
462	Myelitis	
244	Myelofibrosis-Osteosclerosis	
566	Myeloma, Multiple	
62	Myoclonus	
436	Myopathy, Scapuloperoneal	

NORD LITERATURE ORDER FORM

MAIL TO: NORD Literature — PO Box 8923,
New Fairfield, CT 06812-1783

Entry	Disease Name	Qty
649	Myositis, Inclusion Body	
366	Myositis Ossificans	
313	N-Acetyl Glutamate Synthetase Deficiency	
892	Nager Syndrome	
567	Nail-Patella Syndrome	
55	Narcolepsy	
484	Nelson Syndrome	
151	Nemaline Myopathy	
831	Neurasthenia	
3	Neurofibromatosis	
763	Neuroleptic Malignant Syndrome	
822	Neuropathy Congenital Hypomyelination	
802	Neuropathy, Giant Axonal	
799	Neuropathy Hereditary Type 1	
798	Neuropathy Hereditary Type 2	
246	Neuropathy, Peripheral	
857	Neutropenia, Chronic	
663	Neutropenia, Cyclic	
681	Nevoid Basal Carcinoma Syndrome	
75	Nezelof's Syndrome	
93	Niemann-Pick Disease	
746	Nocardiosis	
520	Non-Ketotic Hyperglycinemia	
412	Noonan Syndrome	
568	Norrie Syndrome	
422	Nystagmus, Benign Paroxysmal Positional	

442

NORD LITERATURE ORDER FORM

MAIL TO: NORD Literature — PO Box 8923,
New Fairfield, CT 06812-1783

Entry	Disease Name	Qty
515	Obsessive Compulsive Disorder	
912	Oculo-Dento-Digital Dysplasia	
495	Olivopontocerebellar Atrophy	
337	Ollier Disease	
828	Opitz Syndrome	
113	Opportunistic Infections	
531	Oral-Facial-Digital Syndrome	
829	Organic Mood Syndrome	
782	Organic Personality Syndrome	
309	Ornithine Transcarbamylase Deficiency	
700	Osgood-Schlatter's Disease	
16	Osteogenesis Imperfecta	
742	Osteomyelitis	
756	Osteonecrosis	
354	Osteopetrosis	
878	Oto-Palato-Digital Syndrome, Types I & II	
11	Paget's Disease	
787	Paget's Disease of the Breast	
512	Pallister-Killian Mosiac Syndrome	
900	Pallister-W Syndrome	
716	Pancreatic Islet-Cell Tumors	
286	Panic-Anxiety Syndrome	
744	Papillitis	
159	Paracoccidioidomycosis	
907	Paramyotonia Congenita	
398	Paraplegia, Hereditary Spastic	
150	Parenchymatous Cortical Degeneration of the Cerebellum	
4	Parkinson's Disease	

NORD LITERATURE ORDER FORM

MAIL TO: NORD Literature — PO Box 8923,
New Fairfield, CT 06812-1783

Entry	Disease Name	Qty
489	Parry-Romberg Syndrome	
726	Parsonnage-Turner Syndrome	
467	Pars Planitis	
230	Patulous Eustachian Tube	
158	Pelizaeus-Merzbacher Brain Sclerosis	
652	Pemphigold, Benign Mucosal	
44	Pemphigus	
790	Penta X Syndrome	
736	Perniosis	
191	Pertussis	
149	Peutz-Jeghers Syndrome	
488	Peyronie Disease	
502	Pfeiffer Syndrome	
65	Phenylketonuria	
533	Pheochromocytoma	
780	Phocomelia Syndrome	
914	Phosphoglycerate Kinase Deficiency	
214	Pica	
673	Pick's Disease	
651	Pierre-Robin Syndrome	
133	Pinta	
475	Pityriasis Rubra Pilaris	
725	Pneumonia, Eosinophilic	
648	Pneumonia, Interstitial	
789	Poems Syndrome	
440	Poland Syndrome	
666	Polyarteritis Nodosa	
561	Polychondritis	

NORD LITERATURE ORDER FORM

MAIL TO: NORD Literature — PO Box 8923,
New Fairfield, CT 06812-1783

Entry	Disease Name	Qty
237	Polycystic Kidney Diseases	
665	Polycystic Liver Disease	
236	Polycythemia Vera	
256	Polymyalgia Rheumatica	
278	Polymyositis	
142	Polyposis, Familial	
404	Pompe Disease	
675	Porphyria	
318	Porphyria, Acute Intermittent	
320	Porphyria, ALA-D	
319	Porphyria, Congenital Erythropoietic	
321	Porphyria Cutanea Tarda	
322	Porphyria, Erythropoietic Protoporphyria	
323	Porphyria, Hereditary Coproporphyria	
324	Porphyria, Variegate	
476	Post-Polio Syndrome	
494	Posterior Uveitis	
14	Prader-Willi Syndrome	
528	Precocious Puberty	
645	Primary Lateral Sclerosis	
810	Proctitis	
287	Progressive Supranuclear Palsy	
767	Prostatitis	
579	Proteus Syndrome	
478	Prune Belly Syndrome	
830	Pseudocholinesterase Deficiency	
303	Pseudo-Hurler Polydystrophy	
257	Pseudogout	
625	Pseudohypoparathroidism	

NORD LITERATURE ORDER FORM

MAIL TO: NORD Literature — PO Box 8923,
New Fairfield, CT 06812-1783

Entry	Disease Name	Qty
640	Pseudotumor Cerebri	
253	Pseudoxanthoma Elasticum	
843	Pseudomyxoma Peritonei	
836	Psittacosis	
468	Psoriasis	
594	Pulmonary Alveolar Proteinosis	
706	Pulmonary Hypertension, Primary	
671	Pulmonary Hypertension, Secondary	
506	Pure Red Cell Aplasia	
258	Purpura, Idiopathic Thrombocytopenic	
405	Purpura, Schoenlein-Henoch	
653	Purpura, Thrombotic Thrombocytopenic	
569	Pyoderma Gangrenosum	
873	Pyruvate Carboxlase Deficiency	
413	Pyruvate Dehydrogenase Deficiency	
465	Pyruvate Kinase Deficiency	
621	Q Fever	
846	Rabies	
264	Radiation Syndromes	
715	Rapp-Hodgkins Syndrome	
92	Raynaud's Disease and Phenomenon	
184	Reflex Sympathetic Dystrophy Syndrome	
348	Refsum Syndrome	
844	Reifenstein Syndrome	
283	Maroteaux-Lamy Syndrome	
105	Reiter's Syndrome	

NORD LITERATURE ORDER FORM

MAIL TO: NORD Literature — PO Box 8923,
New Fairfield, CT 06812-1783

Entry	Disease Name	Qty
691	Renal Agenesis, Bilateral	
685	Renal Glycosuria	
611	Respiratory Distress Syndrome, Adult	
618	Respiratory Distress Syndrome, Infant	
288	Restless Legs Syndrome	
21	Retinitis Pigmentosa (RP)	
289	Retinoblastoma	
327	Retinopathy, Arteriosclerotic	
316	Retinopathy, Diabetic	
328	Retinopathy, Hypertensive	
517	Retinoschisis	
231	Retrolental Fibroplasia	
849	Retroperitoneal Fibrosis	
182	Rett Syndrome	
108	Reye Syndrome	
251	Rh Disease	
469	Rheumatic Fever	
417	Rickets, Hypophosphatemic	
883	Rickets, Vitamin D. Deficiency	
854	Rieger Syndrome	
692	Roberts Syndrome	
696	Robinow Syndrome	
600	Rocky Mountain Spotted Fever	
407	Romano-Ward Syndrome	
595	Roseola Infantum	
694	Rothmund-Thomson Syndrmne	
785	Roussy-Levy Dyndrome	
274	Rubella	
276	Rubella, Congenital	

NORD LITERATURE ORDER FORM

MAIL TO: NORD Literature — PO Box 8923,
New Fairfield, CT 06812-1783

Entry	Disease Name	Qty
461	Rubinstein-Taybi Syndrome	
377	Russell-Silver Syndrome	
330	Saethre-Chotzen Syndrome	
94	Sandhoff Disease	
290	Sanfilippo Syndrome	
215	Sarcoidosis	
765	Sarcoma, Ewing's	
855	Schmidt Syndrome	
371	Schwachman Syndrome	
69	Scleroderma	
491	Seckel Syndrome	
374	Seitelberger Disease	
496	Septo-Optic Dysplasia	
77	Severe Combined Immunodeficiency	
228	Sheehan Syndrome	
853	Shprintzen Syndrome	
242	Shy-Drager Syndrome	
356	Sialadenitis	
302	Sialidosis	
25	Sickle Cell Disease	
487	Simian B Virus Infection	
777	Sirenomelia Syndrome	
6	Sjogren Syndrome	
291	Sly Syndrome	
292	Smith-Lemli-Opitz Syndrome	
271	Sotos Syndrome	
213	Spasmodic Torticollis	

NORD LITERATURE ORDER FORM

MAIL TO: NORD Literature — PO Box 8923,
New Fairfield, CT 06812-1783

Entry	Disease Name	Qty
28	Spina Bifida	
693	Split-Hand Deformity	
293	Spondyloepiphyseal Dysplasia, Congenital	
294	Spondyloepiphyseal Dysplasia Tarda	
111	Stein-Leventhal Syndrome	
402	Stenosis, Spinal	
295	Stevens-Johnson Syndrome	
421	Stickler Syndrome	
326	Stiff Man Syndrome	
890	Streptococcus, Group B	
809	Stroke	
306	Sturge-Weber Syndrome	
185	Subacute Sclerosing Panencephalitis	
626	Sucrose-Isomaltose Malabsorption, Congenital	
194	Sudden Infant Death Syndrome	
203	Sutton's Disease II	
424	Sweet Syndrome	
842	Syphilis, Acquired	
841	Syphilis, Congenital	
382	Syringobulbia	
381	Syringomyelia	
350	TORCH Syndrome	
385	Tangier Disease	
493	Tardive Dyskinesia	

NORD LITERATURE ORDER FORM

MAIL TO: NORD Literature — PO Box 8923, New Fairfield, CT 06812-1783

Entry	Disease Name	Qty
370	Tarsal Tunnel Syndrome	
397	Tarui Disease (GSD VII)	
9	Tay-Sachs Disease	
582	Telecanthus	
296	Temporomandibular Joint Dysfunction (TMJ)	
779	Tethered Spinal Cord Syndrome	
438	Tetrahydrobiopterin Deficiencies	
170	Tetralogy of Fallot	
796	Thalamic Syndrome (Dejerine-Roussy Syndrome)	
71	Thalassemia Major	
72	Thalassemia Minor	
372	Thomsen Disease	
156	Thrombasthenia	
577	Thrombocythemia, Essential	
657	Thrombocytopenia Absent Radius Syndrome	
570	Thrombocytopenia, Essential	
637	Tietze Syndrome	
210	Tinnitus	
399	Tolosa-Hunt Syndrome	
340	Tongue Carcinoma	
334	Tongue, Fissured	
332	Tongue, Geographic	
537	Tooth and Nail Syndrome	
2	Tourette Syndrome	
823	Townes-Brock Syndrome	
134	Toxic Shock Syndrome	
538	Toxocariasis	
268	Toxoplasmosis	

NORD LITERATURE ORDER FORM

MAIL TO: NORD Literature — PO Box 8923,
New Fairfield, CT 06812-1783

Entry	Disease Name	Qty
647	Treacher Collins Syndrome, Familial	
386	Tricho-Dento-Osseous Syndrome	
732	Trichorhinophalangeal Syndrome	
768	Trichotillomania	
273	Trigeminal Neuralgia (Tic Douloureux)	
710	Triploid Syndrome	
429	Trisomy	
218	Trisomy 13 Syndrome	
217	Trisomy 18 Syndrome	
89	Tropical Sprue	
180	Truncus Arteriosus, Persistent	
361	Tuberculosis	
35	Tuberous Sclerosis	
112	Turner Syndrome	
730	Typhoid	
446	Tyrosinemia, Hereditary	
249	Urticaria, Cholinergic	
565	Urticaria, Cold	
248	Urticaria, Papular	
250	Urticaria, Physical	
192	Urticaria Pigmentosa	
529	Usher's Syndrome	
486	VACTERL Association	
627	Valinemia	

NORD LITERATURE ORDER FORM

MAIL TO: NORD Literature — PO Box 8923,
New Fairfield, CT 06812-1783

Entry	Disease Name	Qty
686	Varicella Zoster Virus	
642	Vascular Malformations of the Brain	
705	Vasculitis	
698	Vasculitis, Chronic Necrotizing	
169	Ventricular Septal Defects	
541	Vitamin B12 Deficiency	
658	Vitamin E Deficiency	
243	Vitiligo	
393	Von Gierke Disease (GSD I)	
181	Von Hippel-Lindau Disease	
375	Von Willebrand Disease	
761	Vulvovaginitis	
430	Waardenburg Syndrome	
513	Waldenstrom Macroglobulinemia	
91	Waldmann Disease	
817	Weaver Syndrome	
297	Weber-Christian Disease	
388	Well Syndrome	
893	Weill-Marchesani Syndrome	
36	Werdnig-Hoffmann Disease	
135	Werner Syndrome	
90	Whipple's Disease	
824	Wiecker Syndrome	
298	Williams Syndrome	
343	Wilms' Tumor	
26	Wilson's Disease	
76	Wiskott-Aldrich Syndrome	
622	Wolf-Hirschorn Syndrome	

NORD LITERATURE ORDER FORM

MAIL TO: NORD Literature — PO Box 8923,
New Fairfield, CT 06812-1783

Entry	Disease Name	Qty
644	Wolff-Parkinson-White Syndrome	
850	Wolfram Syndrome	
588	Wyburn-Mason Syndrome	
797	X-Linked Juvenile Retinoschisis	
729	X-Linked Lymphoproliferative Syndrome	
339	Xeroderma Pigmentosum	
812	XYY Syndrome	
132	Yaws	
721	Yellow Fever	
834	Yellow Nail Syndrome	
363	Zellweger Syndrome	
360	Zollinger-Ellison Syndrome	
3A	NORD Brochures—Free	
3B	NORD Literature Order Forms—Free	
3C	Physician's Guide to NORD Services —Free	

Genetics: Investigating the Mosaic of Life. A curriculum
for junior high school teachers to inform students about
genetic science, heredity of genetic diseases, and applying
science to our daily lives as well as career opportunities.
$6.00 per copy includes shipping & handling.

NORD is continually updating and adding to the Rare Disease
Database. If you do not see the disease you are interested
in on the publication list, please write the name of the
disorder in the space above. We will mail the available
information to you as soon as possible. However, it may be
written in medical terminology which might be difficult to
understand.

Index

Page 2 02
211